Microsoft® Windows® 2000 Security Design Special Edition

COURSE TECHNOLOGY

THOMSON LEARNING

Australia • Canada • Mexico • Singapore • Spain • United Kingdom • United States

**COURSE
TECHNOLOGY**

THOMSON LEARNING

Microsoft Windows 2000 Security Design Special Edition

Managing Editor:
Stephen Solomon

Production Manager:
Melissa Panagos

Cover Design:
Julie Malone

Marketing Manager:
Toby Shelton

Manufacturing Coordinator:
Denise Sandler

Contents

Chapter 4—Defining a Security Baseline   103

Introduction

BOOK PURPOSE

This book is a component of a comprehensive training program created to provide network administrators with the knowledge they need to design and implement an effective security strategy in a corporate network environment. This book meets all of the exam criteria for Microsoft's Exam 70-220, Designing Security for a Microsoft Windows 2000 Network.

To be successful in this book, you should be familiar with basic Windows 2000 networking concepts, including the structure and design of Active Directory. You should also have a background in concepts relating to remote network access, TCP/IP concepts, and overall network management.

In addition to meeting all certification requirements, this book provides you with the practical information you need to start designing, implementing, and supporting security features in Windows 2000. People who are involved in Windows NT to Windows 2000 migration planning and implementation will also benefit from the information provided in this manual.

This manual includes case studies that test your comprehension of the material presented. No special hardware requirements are necessary to complete the questions associated with the case studies.

As you use this self-study manual, keep in mind that Microsoft has designed Windows 2000 to fully integrate security features. This integration allows you to apply layers of security to your network as they are required. However, network security in Windows 2000 is best implemented after analyzing the entire network and designing a comprehensive security plan–which is exactly what the material in this manual is designed to help you do.

BOOK GOALS

This self-study book will provide you with the information you need to complete the following:

- Analyze the existing and planned business security needs.

- Design a security baseline for a Windows 2000 network that includes domain controllers, operations masters, application servers, file and print servers, RAS servers, desktop computers, portable computers, and kiosks.

- Design the placement and inheritance of security policies for sites, domains, and organizational units.

- Select authentication methods. Methods include certificate-based authentication, Kerberos authentication, clear-text passwords, digest authentication, smart cards, NTLM, RADIUS, and SSL.

- Design a security plan that takes advantage of the following:

  - Public Key Infrastructure (PKI)

  - Certificate Authority (CA) hierarchies

  - Windows 2000 network services security

  - Windows 2000 DNS security

  - Remote Installation Services (RIS) security

  - Windows 2000 SNMP security

  - Windows 2000 Terminal Services security

  - Windows 2000 security for remote access users

  - IPSec solutions

SCENARIO-BASED LEARNING

This self-study manual uses two case studies that are referenced by several scenario-based learning exercises. An introduction to each case study is provided in Chapter 1, with additional, detailed information added as necessary in subsequent chapters. Based on the information provided, you will be asked to determine the best solution for each of the associated scenario questions. Suggested solutions, as well as the case studies (in their entirety), are provided at the back of the manual.

It is important that you take the time to work through the scenario-based exercises. These are an important supplement to the training materials and are meant to reinforce the textual information in your manual.

In addition to the exercises included in each chapter of this book, the section labeled "Special Supplemental Exercises" features more in-depth exercises designed to increase your hands-on proficiency with Windows 2000 security design. This section includes Review Questions, Hands-On Projects, and Case Projects that can be used to reinforce the skills needed for MCSE certification.

SIMULATIONS

Throughout the book, you will see icons asking you to use NEXTSim to practice the concepts you have learned. NEXTSim is an interactive simulation product that provides you with scenario-based training and hands-on experience in a *safe* environment. This tool should be used strictly as a supplement to the book and not to replace the book content. NEXTSim is included on the CD-ROM at the back of the book.

ASSESSMENT

The CD-ROM accompanying this book also includes a limited version of CoursePrep, an exam prep product that replicates the actual MCSE exam environment. CoursePrep can be used to prepare you fully for the MCSE certification exam.

INSTRUCTOR'S MATERIALS

The following supplemental materials are available to Instructors who use this book in a classroom environment:

- **Electronic Instructor's Manual.** The Instructor's Manual which accompanies this book includes:
  - Additional instructional material to assist in class preparation, including suggestions for lecture topics, suggested lab activities, tips on setting up the lab for hands-on assignments, and alternative lab setup ideas in situations where lab resources are limited
  - Solutions to all extra materials, including the Review Questions, Hands-on Projects, and Case Projects found in the Special Supplemental Exercises section

- **Course Test Manager 1.3.** Accompanying this book is a pwerful assessment tool known as the Course Test Manager. Designed by Course Technology, this cutting-edge Windows-based testing software helps instructors design and administer tests and pre-tests. In addition to generating tests that can be printed and administered, this full-featured program also has an online testing component that allows students to take tests at the computer and have their tests automatically graded.

ABOUT THE CD-ROM

The CD-ROM accompanying this book includes the following software products:

- NEXTSim, an interactive simulation product that can be used to practice the concepts presented in the book

- CoursePrep, an exam-preparation program that replicates the actual MCSE exam environment

CHAPTER 1

Security in Windows 2000

OBJECTIVES

This chapter is introductory material and does not map directly to any objectives for this test.

PRE-TEST QUESTIONS

The answers to these questions are in Appendix A at the end of this manual.

1. What are three of the main concepts involved in Windows 2000 network security?

    ....

    ....

2. What is the default Windows 2000 authentication method?

    ....

    ....

3. What is an ACL?

    ....

    ....

4. What is the purpose of a digital certificate?

    ....

    ....

5. How is IPSec used?

    ....

    ....

INTRODUCTION

The basic concept behind controlling security in any computing environment is to ensure that the resources in that environment can be accessed only by the appropriate users. Windows 2000 provides a multilayered approach to security that, when applied conscientiously, can offer a very high level of assurance against successful attacks on your network resources.

This chapter provides an overview of the concepts involved in a good Windows 2000 security system. You'll first read about the major goals in controlling access to resources. Next, you'll study the various authentication technologies employed by Windows 2000, followed by the encryption methodologies it employs. The auditing features are discussed next, followed by an introduction to the case studies used throughout this book.

CONTROLLING ACCESS TO RESOURCES

Security is all about controlling access to resources. Your basic goal in any security system is to curtail all inappropriate access to resources while not inhibiting the proper use of those resources by legitimate persons. This applies equally to your Windows 2000 networking environment. The resources on your Windows 2000 network may include files, printers, software packages, databases, and other objects. These items exist on the network solely because they are a necessary part of someone's duties, and access for legitimate reasons should be as simple as possible. However, any other access to those resources must be restricted, thereby limiting the chances that any problems can arise.

Multilayer Approach

Windows 2000 implements a multilayer approach to security. Each layer provides another obstacle between your resources and any misuse of them. In order for someone to gain inappropriate access to any network resource, either accidentally or maliciously, that person must successfully traverse all layers of security–a very daunting task even for experienced hackers.

The main layers of Windows 2000 security are arranged as follows.

Layer	Purpose
Authentication	This verifies the identity of each person or service that accesses any resource on the network, and thereby provides the ability to match that identity against the list of approved users of any resource being accessed.
Credential Management	Once authenticated, the system keeps track of each user who is logged on and checks identifying information against the list of users approved for access to each requested resource.
Nonrepudiation	By authenticating each user and appropriately logging access to resources, it's impossible for users to deny their use of the network and its resources, thereby providing a clear trail to monitor any potential misuse with.
Security Groups	Users on the network can be organized into security groups for ease of management. In most cases, a user must be a member of a specific group in order to access individual resources on the network.
Access Control Lists	Each object or resource on the Windows 2000 network has an associated Access Control List (ACL), which defines precisely which users can access the resource and what level of access is allowed, including such access levels as read, modify, and delete.
Communications Encryption	Whenever sensitive information is passed over the Windows 2000 network, it can be encrypted so that only the intended receiver can read it, making inappropriate interception practically impossible.
File Encryption	Data on Windows 2000 drives can be encrypted so that only the owner of that file can access it.
Auditing	Windows 2000 allows you to keep thorough logs of many aspects of activity on the network, providing a clear trail to the culprit should any inappropriate access to resources actually occur.

While this chapter provides an introduction to each of these security layers, subsequent chapters include specifics regarding the layers.

AUTHENTICATION

The most obvious consideration of a security solution is authentication of users attempting to access resources on the network. In order for the network to be secure, all users requesting access must authenticate in some manner.

The ability to authenticate users is one of the cornerstones of a good security system. The goal, of course, is to keep all of the network's resources shielded from everyone except for those few people who need access for actual company tasks. This access should be provided as simply and conveniently as possible for such users in order to facilitate their job efficiency.

Windows 2000, with its tightly integrated methods of authentication and access control, can provide these benefits when a good security solution is wholeheartedly adopted. Such a solution can take full advantage of the latest technologies in authentication methods, security protocols, and single sign-on provided by the domain trust relationships that are inherent to Windows 2000.

The following topics will be covered in this section:

- Identify Verification
- Access Control Lists (ACLs)
- Security Groups
- User Security

Identity Verification

Windows 2000 offers several interfaces and several protocols to authenticate the users on the system with. This section provides an overview of those interfaces and protocols as well as describes how Windows 2000 tracks the credentials each user is logged on with.

Authentication Interfaces

Windows 2000 has built-in support for two methods of supplying credentials: Graphical User Interface (GUI) logon and smart cards. GUI logon is the standard method whereby the user types a memorized username and password for identity verification. Smart cards require additional hardware to verify that the user is in possession of the smart card, but provide a greater confidence level in the verification process. Windows 2000 can also be configured to use other authentication interfaces, such as biometrics, but these need to be provided separately, as they do not come preconfigured with the operating system.

GUI Logon

The ubiquitous "Press *CONTROL+ALT+DELETE* to begin" has been a part of Windows network administrators' lives since the mid 1980s, and Windows 2000 is no different. The simple username and password method of authenticating a user remains the most common and acceptable method of ensuring the identity of the person interacting with the computer. However, enforcing some rules on the use of network passwords greatly increases the security of this logon method. By simply requiring your users to choose long, complex passwords, you sharply increase the difficulty potential hackers will have in guessing their way into your system through use of dictionary and brute-force attacks. In the Domain Security Policy Microsoft Management Console (MMC) Snap-in, you can set restrictions on various aspects of the passwords in use on the network, including their length, complexity, and the number of changes tracked before duplication is allowed.

Smart Cards

A much more secure method of authenticating users involves using *two-factor authentication*. This term refers to the requirement of a user proving possession of some identifying object, such as an ID card, as well as knowing the password or PIN that corresponds with that object. The common business-oriented technology in use today is the smart card, which is a credit card-sized card containing a chip. The chip stores a digital certificate and the user's private key. A card reader verifies that the user is actually in possession of the card and reads the certificate and private key into the computer. Matching the card up with the password that the user types in ensures the identity of the user. Once authenticated, the user automatically has a personal digital certificate and private key installed for secure transactions with any secured network resources.

Impersonation of a smart card is practically impossible due to the complexity of the information stored on the chip. While actually stealing the smart card itself is a possibility, good user practices can certainly prevent both the smart card and its associated password from being obtained together. Of course, neither the card nor its associated password is of any use without the other, so this is a very secure method of authentication.

Using smart cards does, of course, have some drawbacks. The expense of installing the card readers and providing cards to all users who need access to the system could be considerable. Training on use and on good practices to avoid card theft may also incur some expense, as will maintenance on the extra hardware involved. However, the security benefits provided could easily outweigh the up-front costs in a large organization with sensitive resources on its network.

Authentication Protocols

The authentication interface doesn't necessarily define how the supplied user credentials are validated and presented to the resources being accessed. This is the function of the authentication protocol. Windows 2000 supports many authentication protocols, including the following:

- Kerberos v5 authentication
- NT LAN Manager (NTLM)
- Certificate-based authentication
- Clear-text passwords
- Digest authentication
- Smart cards
- Remote Authentication Dial-In User Service (RADIUS)
- Secure Socket Layer (SSL)/Transport Layer Security (TSL)

At this point, we'll discuss the basics of the two most common protocols used in Windows 2000: Kerberos v5 and NTLM. You'll find details on the other protocols later in the course.

Kerberos v5 Authentication

In Windows 2000, the primary tool for authentication is the Kerberos v5 protocol. Kerberos v5 is a single sign-on network authentication technology that provides mutual authentication between the user and the object being accessed, thereby ensuring that all transactions are secure and legitimate to the best ability of the current authentication interface.

Kerberos v5 employs a ticket scheme in which a Ticket-Granting Server (TGS) grants tickets that authorize access to the various resources on the network. The user only needs to authenticate once with the Authentication Server (AS); all future transactions in the current session pass through the TGS and reference the original ticket granted by the AS, thus providing a single-sign-on experience for the user.

In detail, a Kerberos v5 logon occurs as follows:

1. The user presents the client computer with logon credentials.

2. The logon client uses a One-Way Function (OWF) to convert the password to an encryption key.

    OWF encryption is generally considered undecryptable, so once this encryption occurs, the password is secure and cannot be surreptitiously discovered.

3. At that point, the logon credentials consist of a username, an encryption key based on the password, and the domain the logon will be verified against.

    If the domain is not specified, then the current domain is assumed.

4. The client generates a message containing the username, the domain name, and a time stamp encrypted with the OWF password and passes the package to the Kerberos Key Distribution Center (KDC).

5. The KDC looks up the user in the Active Directory and uses the OWF password stored there to decrypt the time stamp.

6. Assuming the decrypted time stamp is legible (it, of course, wouldn't be if it were encrypted with anything other than the user's valid OWF password), it checks to see that the time stamp was generated within a nominal time period (within 5 minutes by default) to ensure that someone hasn't intercepted this message and then sent it again at a later date. This is a strategy known as a replay attack.

7. If the time stamp passes muster, then the KDC is assured of the user's identity.

    Once identity has been established, the KDC passes a session key and a Ticket-Granting Ticket (TGT), both encrypted with the user's OWF password, back to the client.

Once in possession of a TGT, the client is prepared to access network resources. When the client needs access to a particular resource, it generates a message consisting of the name of the resource it intends to access, the TGT, and a time stamp encrypted with the session key passed to the client at original logon. It passes this message to the TGS, which decrypts the TGT with the master key, thus extracting the client's session key. The TGS uses the session key to decrypt the time stamp, thus ensuring that this is not a replay attack, and upon verification, the TGS generates a new session key that the client and the desired resource can use to communicate privately with each other. The TGS encrypts two copies of this new key: one with the client's session key and the other with the resource's session key. It then passes both encrypted copies back to the requesting client.

The client can open its own copy of the new session key, but it cannot open the resource's copy since the client doesn't have the resource's logon session key. Instead, the client encrypts its request for access to the resource with its copy of the new session key. The client then passes that encrypted request and the resource's copy of the new session key to the resource. The resource decrypts its copy of the new session key with its logon session key, then uses that new session key to decrypt the client's request. The client and resource can then communicate using that new session key until the transaction is complete.

The client can optionally request that the resource authenticate itself as well. In this case, a mutual authentication request flag is sent to the resource along with the original request for service and the new session key. After authenticating the client, the resource checks to see if the mutual authentication flag is set. If so, it encrypts a time stamp with the new session key and returns it to the client for authentication. If the client can decrypt and read the time stamp and the time stamp is within the acceptable limits, then the transaction between the client and the resource can proceed.

NT LAN Manager (NTLM)

NTLM authentication, also known as Challenge Response authentication, is the protocol used for user authentication on Windows NT systems. When a user attempts to log on using NTLM, the server passes the client a challenge code. The client then uses OWF to encrypt the clear-text password supplied by the user. The OWF password is then compared with the OWF password that is stored in the Active Directory. A match means the user is authenticated and can be allowed to access certain network resources based on the permissions granted to that account.

Windows 2000 Credential Management

Once the user is logged on to a domain, the appropriate authentication protocol controls access to the various resources based on that user's rights and permissions. This applies for all resources on the network, including resources that reside in the current domain, in other domains in the same tree, or in other trees in the same forest. It may also allow access to resources in different forests if explicit trusts are set up for that purpose. This section gives you a little background on these concepts.

Domains, Trees, and Forests

The basic concept behind a Windows 2000 network is the *domain*. A domain is a logical collection of computers and network resources that all have entries in a single Active Directory. The Active Directory is a directory services database of information about network users and resources. This database includes information about how to authenticate, find, access, and validate permissions for resources on the network. Each Windows 2000 server can contain a copy of the Active Directory for a particular domain.

Two or more domains can be logically connected together into what is known as a *tree*. A domain tree is formed by adding child domains to the root domain. These domains in a tree share a common namespace. For example, one of our case studies involves a company called Barney's Bank. Under this company's structure, several trees can be created, including Loan.BarneysBank.com and Support.BarneysBank.com. Loan and Support are two child trees of BarneysBank.com because they share the same parent domain name.

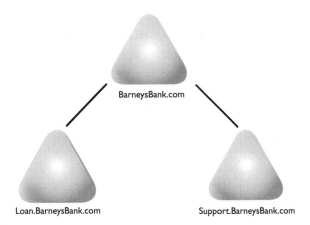

Two or more domain trees can also be logically joined into domain *forests*. A domain forest consists of trees that do not share the same namespace, but still belong to the same logical network. Computers in different forests still have access to each other's resources.

Trusts

The mechanism different computers within domains, trees, and forests can share resources by is known as a *trust*. If domain A trusts domain B, then when a user authenticates with domain B, that authentication is accepted as valid in domain A. This doesn't necessarily imply that the authenticated user has any rights to access any resources in domain A, just that the authentication is assumed to be legitimate and trustworthy. The authenticated user still needs to have permissions to access the resources in either domain before such access can occur. The difference is that a user who logs on to an untrusted domain *cannot* be granted permission to access any resources on that domain until either a trust relationship is established between the domains or the user authenticates in a trusted domain.

There are two main properties of domains that you need to be aware of. All trusts contain one aspect of both of the following properties:

- Transitive or nontransitive
- One way or two way

A transitive trust is one that passes credentials through from domain to domain. For example, if domain A trusts domain B, and domain B trusts domain C, and both of the trusts are transitive trusts, then domain A automatically trusts domain C. Nontransitive trusts, on the other hand, imply that the trust relationship is strictly between the two domains specified and goes no further.

For a trust to be one way means that domain A trusting domain B doesn't imply that domain B trusts domain A. In this situation, a user who logs on to domain B may be granted rights to access resources in domain A, but a user logged on to domain A may not access resources in domain B. Two-way trusts, conversely, allow users logged on to either domain to access resources in either domain.

Each domain in a Windows 2000 domain tree has a two-way transitive trust automatically defined with its parent domain and all of its child domains. The same holds true for domain forests. This means that any user or resource in any domain of a forest can potentially access any other user or resource in the entire forest. The only piece of this puzzle that may be missing is that the user must be granted permission to access that resource. The rest is automatically set up when the domain tree or forest is created.

In order for users to access resources in a domain from a different forest, an explicit trust needs to be defined. Trusts outside of the current forest are always nontransitive; that is, only the two domains directly involved in the trust will be affected by it, not any other domains that trust those two. You can create a one-way trust that allows users in one domain to access resources in the other or you can simulate a two-way trust by creating two one-way trusts in opposite directions, thereby allowing users in both domains to access resources in either.

Access Control Lists (ACLs)

Each object on the network has an ACL. These ACLs contain information describing the specific users and groups of users that have permission to access the object and precisely what permission is allowed. The granularity of this permission is extremely fine, allowing you to do such things as allow a specific user to use a particular font in a document even though no one, not even that user, can see the font name in the list. Files and folders have thirteen different permissions that can each be set individually for each specific user. You also have the ability to explicitly allow or deny permission to a resource, though denial of permission always takes precedence over allowed access.

Permissions set on the ACL of an object are inherited through the tree that the object is in. For example, if you grant rights for a certain group of users to have full control over a particular folder in the file system, then, by default, that group also has full control over all of the files and folders below that folder in the directory tree. This makes it easy for an administrator to make broad changes to the access rights of groups of users, but it also introduces the possibility of inadvertently granting inappropriate access to resources or restricting access that should be allowed. It is possible, however, to disable inheritance on any particular resource so that changes up the tree do not affect the rights on that object.

Security Groups

Security groups provide a convenient method of administering access of large groups of users to large pools of resources. By carefully designing your security groups, you can easily provide everyone in the organization with the appropriate level of access without having to manually assign each user specific rights to every resource.

Generally, you should not explicitly add users to the ACL of an object. Instead, you should group your users into security groups and then add the security groups to the ACL. This way, you can more efficiently manage access to your network's resources. In most cases, certain groups of users will all need access to the same set of resources. By placing those users into a specific security group, you can then assign that group access to the several resources they need. You can also add or remove members from the group in a single location without having to manage the ACL of each of the resources.

The following table describes the four types of security groups.

Security Group Type	Membership	Resource Access
Universal groups	Any user in the domain can be a member of Universal groups. You can also add Global groups or other Universal groups to Universal groups.	Universal groups can appear on ACLs anywhere in the forest.
Global groups	Only users in the Global group's domain can be members of a Global group. You can also nest Global groups.	Global groups can appear on ACLs anywhere in the forest.
Domain Local groups	Any users, Global groups, or Universal groups from the entire forest can be members of a Domain Local group. You can also nest Domain Local groups within a single domain.	Domain Local groups can appear on ACLs only within the domain the group exists in.
Local Computer groups	Any users, Global groups, or Universal groups from the entire forest can be members of a Local Computer group as well as Domain Local groups from the computer's domain.	Local Computer groups can appear on ACLs only on the computer the group exists on.

Universal groups can exist only in Windows 2000 native-mode domains, meaning that no Windows NT 4.0 domain controllers exist on the domain and that backward compatibility with Windows NT 4.0 has been disabled. Using Universal groups makes management of the domain much easier from the administrative point of view since they are accessible everywhere in the forest and can contain users from the entire forest. This power, however, comes at a price. In order to be able to accomplish this feat, Universal groups must be stored in the Global Catalog (GC), which is a catalog of all Active Directory information that replicates among all Global Catalog servers in the forest. With large and frequently changing membership in a Universal group, this can lead to an exceptional amount of bandwidth consumed for replication purposes, seriously degrading performance on your network. However, by populating the Universal group with Global groups from the various domains (which, in turn, don't need to replicate across domains), you can minimize replication traffic since membership in the Universal group will seldom change.

Local Computer groups are available only on Windows 2000 workstations and stand-alone servers, not on domain controllers. However, if these computers are members of a Windows 2000 domain, then their Local Computer groups can contain members and groups from any other domain in the forest, allowing simple management of access to resources on those computers.

Windows 2000 automatically creates several groups that define set privileges for their members, allowing them to handle common tasks. These groups are described in the following table.

Group	Description	Group Type
Account Operators	Handles account management tasks on the domain, exluding the ability to manage membership in administrative groups	Domain Local group
Administrators	Can access all resources on the computer	Domain Local group
Backup Operators	Allowed to perform backup and restore tasks	Domain Local group
Guests	An extremely limited account for logging on to computers other than Windows 2000 servers	Domain Local group
Print Operators	Allowed to manage all aspects of printing tasks	Domain Local group
Replicator	This is a special group that the replication service should belong to. No users should be members of this account.	Domain Local group
Server Operators	Similar to Administrators except that they can't manage security settings on servers	Domain Local group
Users	This is the standard account on workstations allowing users to log on and perform usual computing tasks such as using software and accessing files and printers. Members of this group do not have the right to log on interactively at servers.	Domain Local group
Cert Publishers	Certification and renewal agents for the forest belong to this group	Global group
Domain Admins	Members of this group have administrative privileges over all computers in the domain.	Global group
Domain Computers	All workstations and servers in the domain are in this group.	Global group
Domain Controllers	This group contains all of the domain controllers of the domain.	Global group
Domain Guests	Guests on the domain similar to the Guests account for the local computer	Global group
Domain Users	User account for the domain similar to the Users account for the local computer	Global group
Enterprise Admins	Administrators of the forest; this group is a member of the Administrators group of the local computer.	Universal group
Group Policy Creator Owners	Manage the group policies for the domain	Global group
Schema Admins	Manage the domain schema	Universal group
Anonymous Logon	All users who have not authenticated with a domain in this forest	Online users group
Authenticated Users	All users who are authenticated with a domain in the forest	Online users group

Group	Description	Group Type
Batch	All batch processes currently accessing resources on this computer	Online users group
Creator Owner	The creator or current owner of the resource being accessed	Online users group
Dialup	All users accessing resources on this computer via dial-up connection	Online users group
Everyone	All users accessing resources on this computer	Online users group
Interactive	All users logged on locally to the computer	Online users group
Network	All users accessing resources on this computer over the network	Online users group
Service	All services accessing resources on this computer	Online users group
System	The operating system of this computer	Online users group

You can't add or remove users from the Online users groups. Their membership is automatically managed as users log on to the computer or access its resources. For this reason, you won't find these groups in the Active Directory Users and Computers MMC Snap-in. They are, however, available on the ACLs of the various resources, and you can allow or deny permissions to their members as you would any other group.

User Security

All of these security measures are for nothing if the users of the system are careless in their use. If people use passwords that are easy to crack or write down their passwords and tape them to their monitor, none of the other security features will help. To have a secure network, you need to have the buy-in of the people using it, and they need to be properly educated on reasonable security precautions.

One of the critical facets of effective user security is keeping passwords secure. From this perspective, requiring users to use long and complex passwords may be a detriment to your network's security. Many people will feel unable to memorize such passwords, especially if they need to change passwords routinely. This means people will tend to write down their passwords, giving intruders an opportunity to find them. Another risk in this situation is people continually forgetting their passwords, adding a burden on the support staff to reset those passwords. If your security policy includes keeping track of previously used passwords before they can be reused, users will have an even harder time coming up with passwords they can remember.

Another common security hazard associated with user practices is users who leave their workstations logged on while unattended. In an office setting, this gives a variety of people ample opportunity to walk up to an unattended workstation, perform inappropriate tasks, and leave without being detected or without leaving a clear audit trail.

However, the situation is much worse if a workstation is left logged on and unattended in an off-site setting that is less controlled than the home office. For instance, a laptop user may travel to a client site and connect to the home network via dial-up or Virtual Private Network (VPN). Leaving such a connection unattended can pose serious security risks.

The most important solution to this type of problem involves user education. Teaching your users to be aware of potential security risks can go a long way toward keeping your network secure. Of course, user loyalty is a major factor in the lengths people are willing to go to for the sake of the organization and that must be taken into account when assigning network privileges.

You can impose another major control on this type of security threat by limiting users' access to only those resources absolutely necessary for their individual jobs. In this situation, the only damage that can be done is toward the resources specific to the job function of the potentially compromised user account. Of course, as the user's job function increases, the risk increases, but you can also expect a user with greater access to have a greater understanding of the need for security; however, this doesn't always translate to more responsible habits.

ENCRYPTION

In theory, authenticating every user on the network would allow us to completely control access to the resources on the network by explicitly allowing or denying access based on each user's identity. While this is a laudable goal, it's hardly realistic to believe that no one will ever gain unauthorized access to the network or that authorized users will always behave properly and according to the best interests of the organization.

In the event that someone manages to penetrate the authentication layers of the network security protocol, Windows 2000 still offers layers of security that will aid in the protection of sensitive network data. For this we rely on encryption. Windows 2000 provides methods of encrypting data while it's stored on disk and while it's in transit over the network. This means that the only time data needs to be unencrypted is when it's actually being accessed by a legitimate user.

Encryption is the encoding of data such that specific information must be possessed in order to decrypt and read the data. In Windows 2000, encryption generally uses certificates and public and private keys to handle the encryption and decryption tasks. You'll learn about these concepts in this section. The following topics will be covered in this section:

- Certificates and the Public Key Infrastructure (PKI)
- File Security
- Communications Security

Certificates and the Public Key Infrastructure (PKI)

Encryption in Windows 2000 is accomplished through the use of certificates. Certificates are basically public encryption keys that are digitally signed by a Certificate Authority (CA). This digital signature provides reasonable proof that the certificate was originally issued to the holder of the matching private key, which in turn can decrypt any message encrypted with the public key certificate. A CA, then, is an entity that is trusted to assign certificates to users, resources, and organizations. Trust is placed in the CA's ability to verify the identity of the recipient of the certificate before issuing it. CAs are also responsible for revoking certificates that, for whatever reason, are deemed to be no longer valid.

Public Key Encryption

The whole concept of certificates rests on the foundation of public key encryption. This concept basically works by having a pair of digital keys, one public and one private. Of course, being digital, these keys are simply a string of data, but used together with the proper algorithms, they can securely encrypt and decrypt data so that only the intended reader can access it.

Public key encryption works basically like this: Suppose person A wishes to have person B send a message that no one else should be able to read while it's in transit. Person A then obtains a public/private key pair and sends the public key to person B. Person B can then use the public key to encrypt the message. Once encrypted, only the holder of the private key can decrypt the message. Person B can send the message to person A via any available transport, including insecure networks such as the Internet, being certain that the message is undecypherable by anyone besides person A, who holds the public key. Once person A receives the message, the decryption algorithm can be used with the private key to decrypt the message, making it once again legible.

Using the public/private key method of encrypting and decrypting data means that only the encrypting key needs to be transmitted over the network. This allows anyone with possession of the public key to encrypt messages that only the holder of the matching private key can read.

Digital Signatures

A digital signature provides reasonable proof of the integrity and origin of a piece of data, whether it be a file on a disk, an e-mail message, or any other form of digital information. Digital signatures are normally used in cases where encryption is not necessarily required, but it may be important to know that the message actually came from the person listed, not from an imposter. In this situation, the digital signature operates much the same as a manual signature.

Digital signatures can also provide the added benefit of providing data integrity. While the message is not encrypted in the normal sense of the word, it is encoded with the digital signature. The idea here is that it would be extremely difficult to modify the original message without also damaging the digital signature. This means that if the signature arrives intact, then the message itself has very likely not been modified since the originator signed it.

Certificates

So how, then, does the person about to encrypt a message with a public key really know who holds the private key? Wouldn't it be possible, for instance, for a person with ill intent to mascarade as the person who rightfully should receive the data, send a public key and intend to intercept the message as it returns to the proper recipient, then decode it with the private key? That's where certificates come in. Digital certificates are simply digitally signed statements assuring that the identity of the person who originally obtained the public/private key pair has been verified. The certificate is attached to the public key when it's sent to the person expected to encrypt the message. Upon receipt of the certificate, the user has a certain level of verification that the person holding the matching private key is actually the person listed on the certificate as the owner.

In general, certificates are issued by CAs responsible for managing certificates. The authority who issued the certificate is known as the *issuer*. The person who requests the certificate is the *subject* of the certificate. The digital signature on the certificate is provided by the issuer, not the subject, since the issuer is certifying that the subject's identity has been verified. Basically this implies that we trust the issuer to be capable of verifying the subject's identity, and the issuer's signature is all the proof we need.

Digital certificates carry with them a certain amount of information about the parties involved. In general, you'll find the following information in a certificate:

- Issuer's identifying information
- Subject's identifying information
- Subject's public key
- Period that the cerificate is valid for (start and stop dates)
- Issuer's digital signature

With this information, the recipient of the certificate can decide whether to accept and use the enclosed public key.

Certificate Authorities (CAs)

CAs are responsible for issuing certificates and providing assurance that the associated public and private keys are valid and owned by the entity listed. Windows 2000 provides the ability to set up CAs on your network that can issue certificates to the various entities for internal use. You can also have your internal CAs validated with commercial CAs, thereby providing a level of trust that you can use with business partners or others outside your own network.

Public Key Infrastructure (PKI)

An organization's PKI is defined by its use of digital signatures, certificates, CAs, and other methods of verifying the integrity, origin, and security of data through the use of public key cryptography. In general, an organization's PKI includes one or more CAs on site; secure networking using technologies such as Internet Protocol Security (IPSec), Secure Socket Layer (SSL), or Transport Layer Security (TLS); secure e-mail; encrypted files on disks; and possibly secure logons using smart card technologies.

File Security

One of the new features of Windows 2000 is the Encrypting File System (EFS). This allows users to encrypt their files while they reside on the disk so that no one else can read them. Once a file is encrypted, it's virtually impossible for anyone to read it except the original owner.

EFS works by using the user's certificate to encrypt files. This means that only that user, holding the private key, can again access that file. While it's encrypted, virtually no one can access the file. Even if the computer is stolen and someone attempts to bypass the file system, the contents of the file are encrypted and cannot be recovered without the private key. To the user who owns the file, however, the encryption is transparent, and accessing encrypted files is no different from accessing any other file on the drive. EFS handles all of the encryption tasks in the background, so the user never needs to be concerned about it.

EFS only works on Windows 2000 NTFS volumes. Encrypted files cannot be stored on volumes using other file systems, including NTFS volumes from Windows NT 4.0. Copying an encrypted file to a non-Windows 2000 NTFS volume simply removes the encryption. This means that you need to protect files, encrypted or not, from read access by anyone besides the intended users.

You may wonder what the point of EFS is if someone can simply copy the file to a non-NTFS drive to gain access to its contents. If you need to have other security measures in place to keep the file from being read, why bother with encryption? The answer is that an encrypted file cannot be accessed by someone bypassing the file system. If someone were to manage to steal your hard drive, perhaps by stealing a laptop, but didn't know any of the passwords to access the files in the normal way, that person may attempt to read the data directly off the drive, bypassing the file system. While reading an NTFS volume without going through the file system is very difficult, it has been proven to be possible. With a file encrypted on the drive, however, there is no way to access the actual data in the file without possessing the certificate it was encrypted with. EFS, then, is another layer in an overall security system.

Also, files stored with EFS cannot be shared. EFS is not a means of securely transmitting sensitive files. Once removed from storage, the file is no longer encrypted and can be read by anyone who can access it. Therefore, attempting to e-mail an encrypted file will not result in a secure transmission of the data; it will simply be decrypted before being transferred.

Communications Security

Besides data stored on disks, you also need to protect data while it's in transit over network links. This is obvious when sending sensitive information over a public network like the Internet, but it should also be considered on internal networks and WANs. Whenever the information you're transferring could be compromised, and that compromise could be problematic for your organization, the transmissions should be secured.

Using a security solution based on IPSec solves the problem of unsecured data on network links. The concepts of IPSec require that the data be encrypted before it leaves the sending computer. None of the network links along the path of the data need to be aware that the data is encrypted, making this protocol completely network transparent. Only the receiving computer is capable of decrypting the data, so it is secure over the entire trip.

IPSec secures the data at the Internet layer (Layer 3 of the DoD Network Reference Model) of the network protocol stack, thereby providing an ease of implementation that security protocols such as SSL do not. SSL is implemented at the Application layer, meaning that all applications that intend to use SSL must have SSL code written into them. IPSec, on the other hand, is automatically enabled for all applications sending data over the network since it operates much deeper in the network stack.

IPSec can be configured to set security levels based on the IP address of the remote computer being communicated with. You can also set the level of security to be negotiated to one of three following levels:

Require security	This computer will only communicate with other computers running IPSec and only if the two can negotiate a secure channel. No unsecured communications are allowed.
Request security	This computer always requests a secure link, and if the other computer is capable of IPSec, then the two will communicate securely. However, if the other computer cannot or will not communicate via IPSec, this computer will negotiate an insecure link and communicate anyway.
Respond	This level is generally used on client computers that usually don't require secure communications. This computer doesn't request IPSec security, but will respond to a request from the remote computer by using it.

You can also specify the level of security that IPSec provides once enabled. By default, IPSec is set to use either the Encapsulating Security Payload (ESP) or Authentication Header (AH) as a security method. ESP performs encryption on the data of the IP packet, providing confidentiality, integrity, antireply protection, and authentication for the data. AH is considered medium security since it does not encrypt the information; it only provides a digital signature on it. This provides integrity, antireply protection, and authentication for the data but does not provide confidentiality. Someone may be able to read the data while it is in transit, but the intended recipient can still be confident that the data wasn't modified and that the specified source is valid.

By using a combination of IPSec filters to specify which remote computers should require secure communications and IPSec policies to specify the level of security required, you can institute a total communications security policy with IPSec.

AUDITING ACCESS TO RESOURCES

With all of the other security measures in place, you may think of auditing as being used after the damage has already been done and simply as a method of apprehending the culprit. This is not always the case. You'll find that Windows 2000 provides auditing features that can even help prevent attacks from succeeding in the first place if you manage the audits properly.

Audit Logs

Windows 2000 allows you to instigate auditing of a wide variety of events on your network. You can even differentiate between successful and failed attempts at the audited operation. By monitoring these events carefully, you can easily detect when unauthorized access has occurred, but more importantly, you can detect failed attempts at unauthorized access and handle them before they become successful.

The list of events that you've decided to audit will appear in the Security log, which you can access via the Event Viewer.

CASE STUDIES

You will be using the case studies presented in this section throughout the course. They will be referenced by several scenario-based learning exercises. This course will reference, at different times, the following two different case studies:

- Barney's Bank
- Fairco Manufacturing

In this chapter, you are going to be provided with a brief introduction to each of these case studies. More detailed information will be added, as necessary, in later chapters. A complete description of each case study company is provided in Appendix C at the end of the manual.

Sample answers to the questions asked at the end of each case study are provided in Appendix B at the end of the manual.

Barney's Bank

Barney's Bank is a full-service financial institution with branch offices in various locations across the United States. Barney's Bank also has several wholly owned subsidiaries with five different locations in Europe. The organization has grown traditionally through acquisition and plans to continue to use this as its primary growth model. Each of the remote offices has limited control over day-to-day decisions but all major decisions are made from the main office in Corpus Christi, Texas.

The overall network structure is a forest of Windows 2000 domains. Each of the U.S. locations controls its own domain, and these domains are organized into a single tree whose root represents the main office in Corpus Christi. The European subsidiaries each operate their own domains, which have different namespaces, and so are separate trees in the overall forest. The forest root is the Corpus Christi domain.

The bank network exhibits a variety of security issues that the security plan must address. The servers control a great deal of information that must be kept private in order for the bank to remain viable. Various groups of users on the network each have different access needs to that information, from the executive level down to the tellers. The bank has several kiosks that provide simple information about the bank as well as other kiosks and automated tellers that customers can access and manipulate account information by.

Barney's Bank management wants to overhaul the security on the network, and each of the noted issues must be properly handled by the security infrastructure being designed. The system needs to provide secure access to all users for their appropriate tasks while protecting all the resources from intruders.

Fairco Manufacturing

Fairco Manufacturing designs, manufactures, and distributes a wide variety of items for department stores in the United States. Sales are wholesale only to retail outlets. The organization employs a large number of outside salespeople who travel to the major customers on established routes.

Fairco Manufacturing has a large LAN configured as a single Windows 2000 domain. Access is provided to remote warehouses in strategic locations around the country via dial-in and VPN across the Internet. Field salespeople can post their orders on a private page on the company's Web site. Also, several of the retail outlets are participating in an early trial of Fairco's extranet, whereby they can directly order stock through automated inventory control software.

The organization wants to refine and revise its security systems. This includes securing the remote access as well as the extranet used by its customers.

SUMMARY

During this chapter, you were introduced to the following:

- Controlling resource access
- Authentication basics
- Encryption technologies
- Auditing systems
- Case studies to be used throughout this book

This chapter provides a good basis for the upcoming detailed look at each aspect of the security issue.

POST-TEST QUESTIONS

The answers to these questions are in Appendix A at the end of this manual.

1. What is Kerberos v5?

   ....

   ....

2. What is the difference between a transitive and a nontransitive trust relationship?

   ....

   ....

3. Who can be a member of a Global Security group?

   ....

   ....

4. What risk is involved in requiring long, complex passwords?

   ....

   ....

5. On what volume types can you use EFS?

   ....

   ....

CHAPTER 2

Analyzing the Company

MAJOR TOPICS

OBJECTIVES

At the completion of this chapter, you will be able to:

- Analyze the existing and planned business models.

- Analyze the company model and the geographical scope. Models include regional, national, international, subsidiary, and branch office.

- Analyze company processes. Processes include information flow, communication flow, service and product life cycles, and decision making.

- Analyze the existing and planned organizational structures. Considerations include management model; company organization; vendor, partner, and customer relationships; and acquisition plans.

- Analyze factors that influence company strategies.

- Identify company priorities.

- Identify projected growth and growth strategy.

- Identify relevant laws and regulations.

- Identify the company's tolerance for risk.

- Identify the Total Cost of Ownership (TCO).

- Evaluate the company's existing and planned technical environment.

- Analyze company size and user and resource distribution.

PRE-TEST QUESTIONS

The answers to these questions are in Appendix A at the end of this manual.

1. What is the distinguishing aspect of a regional organization?

    ....

    ....

2. What are the three common management models?

    ....

    ....

3. In the Matrix management model, people generally have more than one manager.

   A. True

   B. False

4. What is the basic concept behind TCO?

   ....

   ....

INTRODUCTION

Before you begin the actual design of your network security solution, you need to put a serious effort into understanding the operational and environmental aspects of your company's operations. This will allow you to build a security system that will be effective in all aspects of your company's business without interfering with the day-to-day activities of its employees. Consideration must be given to the business requirements of your organization, including such things as the business model your company operates under, its geographic scope, and its standard processes. You'll also want to evaluate the organizational structure of your company in order to effectively design a delegation strategy for your security solution.

In addition, you'll need to analyze the various strategies that your company utilizes in pursuit of its goals. You'll look at the priorities your company recognizes, its anticipated growth, and the laws and regulations that may affect it. You'll also need to consider the organization's tolerance for risk and the cost of implementing this new security system. Finally, you'll be analyzing the technical environment you'll be implementing this security solution into. This includes the size of your company and the distribution of the users and resources your network caters to.

OPERATIONAL ANALYSIS

The first step in analyzing your company's security needs is to look at the operational aspects of the organization. You need to determine how your company works, or how it does its business, in order to effectively implement your security solution. The following topics will be covered in this section:

- Analyzing Company Models
- Analyzing Company Processes
- Analyzing Organizational Structures

Analyzing Company Models

In designing your security model, you need to first consider the model that the company is built on with regards to its geographic scope. Obviously, a small regional company has different security needs than a giant multinational corporation. By taking into account the geographic distribution of your company, you can get a baseline of how to implement the security features.

A list of the five common geographic company models follows:

- Regional
- National
- International
- Subsidiary
- Branch Office

Each of these company models will follow a different security model. Your company will probably fit into one of these models, but in some cases you may find that you have a combination of two or more of these paradigms. Let's look at each of them as they relate to security.

Regional

For this discussion, a regional company is a relatively small organization with few locations, possibly only one. Each of the locations is within a short distance of the others, with reasonably wide bandwidth connecting them. In a case such as this, you should strive to build the network on a single-domain model, eliminating the need to build separate security models among different locations. This simplifies the security structure, providing fewer opportunities for potential weak spots in the system.

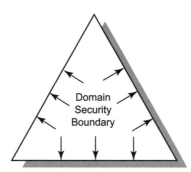

A domain acts as a security boundary. All security policies defined within a domain are effective for that domain only. With only one domain for the organization, you don't need to worry about synchronizing security policies across multiple domains or integrating the members of various domains in the different security groups.

With Windows 2000's method of organizing the domain into Organizational Units (OUs), you can still apply a fine-grained security model within a single domain. This allows you to delegate authority over specific groups of people and resources without having to grant domain administration privileges to those individual delegates.

National

In a national organization, you may have centers of operations in several widely dispersed locales across the country, presenting a more distributed management approach. In this case, a domain tree would likely be the appropriate scenario. This allows each local facility to have its own security policy while still allowing for easy sharing of resources. Since transitive, bidirectional trusts are automatically established and maintained in a domain tree, the management of interdomain communication doesn't add to the administrative burden.

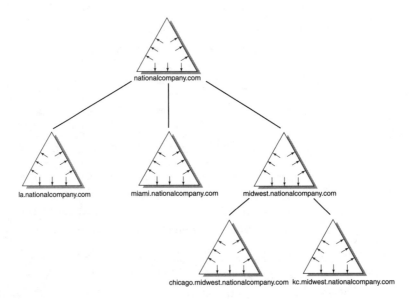

Structuring your network into a domain tree gives you a simple overall structure within a single contiguous namespace, yet provides the flexibility to allow the administrator of each domain to define security settings without necessarily affecting the entire network. Within each domain, you can still delegate administrative duties to people responsible for smaller groups of people or resources, retaining overall administrative powers for the actual administrators of the domains.

International

An international organization will generally be set up as a forest of domain trees. This allows each of the separate trees to have its own namespace but still provides for effective sharing of resources and single sign-on for people using the network.

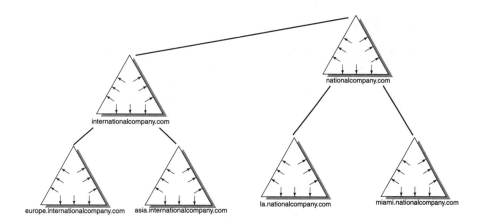

A forest may be somewhat less intuitive from a management perspective since it is simply organized by the order each domain tree is added in. This means that the root of the forest is the first tree defined; subsequent trees added to the forest are children of that root, though the discontiguous namespace does not necessarily reflect that fact. From a user's point of view, this shouldn't be a problem except when trying to do a forestwide search for people or resources, in which case the person searching will need to know where the root of the forest is. However, administrators will need to be aware of the structure of the forest to effectively manage it.

Subsidiary

A subsidiary of a larger company could implement a single Windows 2000 domain or an entire domain tree, making this a subtree of the larger corporate network. This provides local control over the security of the network while maintaining connectivity with the umbrella organization.

Branch Office

When designing the security structure for a branch office, you may decide to set it up as a domain connecting to the home office tree or as a remote connection to the home domain. The latter allows the overall security structure to be determined by the domain administrator at the home office, while local management chores can still be delegated to the manager of the branch office.

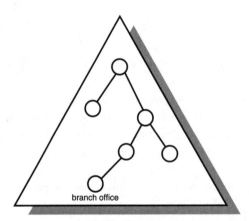

branch office

However, for this to be an effective setup, you'll need to be certain that sufficient bandwidth is available for routine intradomain network traffic such as logons, resource access, and domain controller replications. Generally, 512 Kbs or greater is considered wide bandwidth, though you may be able to get by with somewhat less depending on the amount of traffic that travels across the line.

Analyzing Company Processes

Having determined the proper security boundaries based on the geographic and organizational structure of the company, you are now ready to look at the processes normally used that may affect the security structure. At this point, the way that your company does business is the object of scrutiny, considering such topics as the following:

- Information Flow
- Communication Flow
- Service and Product Life Cycles
- Decision Making

Gaining a clear understanding of the methods used by your organization for each of these processes will help to shape the structure of your security plan.

Information Flow

The pathway that information takes as it travels through your company is an important part of the security process. You need to ensure that people who are distributing information have the ability to write it to the network and those receiving the information must be able to read it. Generally, you'll have an interconnected matrix of information-sharing pathways on your network that a variety of people need access to.

For instance, when a new client is signed, the sales staff will need to inform the production team that a more specific product or service will be required to meet the demand, whereas the development of a new or updated product requires the production team to inform the sales staff that it is available. Generally, you won't want an e-mail message from a developer to a salesperson to be the primary form of transmitting this information; in order for the information to be effectively distributed, you'll need a clear channel defined along with proper security permissions in place to allow the responsible parties to distribute that information. At the same time, you need to guard those information channels against unauthorized or inappropriate access to ensure that they are not corrupted either unintentionally or maliciously. Keeping proper security in place on the channels of information flow allows that information to flow smoothly without unexpected interruptions.

Communication Flow

Besides the flow of information, you also need to consider what types of communication technologies your organization utilizes. Intranetwork traffic can, in general, be deemed relatively secure for information that is not highly sensitive. However, even on an internal network, sensitive information should be secured before transmission. Of course, on public networks like the Internet, all company information must be secured to avoid interception by outsiders who may use the information inappropriately.

In both of these cases, a solution such as IPSec can solve the security issue. By applying the security at the network level, you are assured secure communications with practically no impact to the user.

Service and Product Life Cycles

Depending on the life-cycle stage of a service or product of your organization, its associated information may necessitate different security levels. During development of a new product, for instance, you need to keep all information about it internal to the company so that your competitors don't gain an upper hand on releasing a similar product. When the product is prepped for release, a marketing campaign must be built and that information needs to be spread appropriately to the various channels your product will be sold in. Finally, upon phasing out a product, you need to create secure storage for related information for use by members of your organization in reference situations.

In addition, different groups of people will need access to information about products during these varying stages. In the design phases of a product's life cycle, the developers will be the primary group accessing this information. On the other hand, once the product is on the market, the sales team will probably be much more likely to access that information. From an administrative point of view, you'll need to be able to easily manage the groups who are allowed access to the product or service information, making appropriate changes as the product moves through its normal life cycle.

Decision Making

What is the process involved in decision making at your company? The people responsible for making decisions must have access to the required information so they are properly informed about the topic at hand. This means creating security groups for decision makers so that they can access the information needed. In many cases you will also need to design the security structure so that the decision makers have authority to carry out their decisions when those decisions affect network resources.

Analyzing Organizational Structures

With the company processes thoroughly researched and analyzed, you need to turn your attention to your company's organizational structures. Again, building an appropriate security system for your organization depends on having a clear vision of how the organization functions, so being specific about the details of these organizational structures is an important part of your security system's design phase. Be sure to stay familiar with your company's external relationships and acquisition plans; both will affect how your company functions.

Management Model/Company Organization

Your company is probably organized into one of the three following common management models:

- Product Division Model
- Functional Division Model
- Matrix Model

Product Division Model

In the Product Division management model, the company is organized along product lines with relatively autonomous company divisions responsible for all stages of a particular product or group of products. The divisions generally share few resources but operate under the corporate umbrella of the parent organization. In this model, several resources may be duplicated in the different divisions, but the products offered by those divisions may be different enough to justify that duplication.

Management Umbrella		
Product Line A	**Product Line B**	**Product Line C**
Product Management	Product Management	Product Management
Production	Production	Production
Sales and Marketing	Sales and Marketing	Sales and Marketing

Functional Division Model

An organization utilizing the Functional Division model creates its divisions along functional lines. For example, an organization of this type may have a product development division, a production division, a sales and marketing division, and a human resources division. The sales and marketing division works with all products and services the company offers rather than having a separate sales department for each product as in the Product Division model.

Matrix Model

Other types of companies use the Matrix model, in which short-lived teams of people work on projects together, and each member of those teams reports to two or more managers. Organizations such as these often have responsibilities divided along product lines *and* along functional lines, so that a product manager and a sales manager will both have a certain amount of responsibility for the output of a particular group. This effectively cuts out many layers of the decision-making process often found in the other, more hierarchical models, but the multiple-managers situation can easily lead to conflicts in an employee's responsibilities.

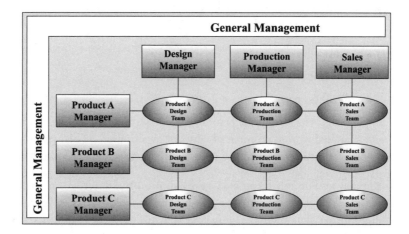

External Relationships

The external relationships of your company require serious consideration when designing your security model. You need to determine the extent to which you allow your vendors, customers, and business partners to access your network, if at all. Of course, the less access you grant external groups, the more secure your network will be, but with the advent of the Internet and online commerce, more and more companies prefer to do much of their business over the network. This necessitates certain information being available to groups outside your organization, which in turn requires a great deal of care in the design of the security systems to handle this type of access.

When analyzing the external relationships that your company is now or will be engaged in, you need to look at the following major points:

- Customer access
- Vendor access
- Business partners

In general, if you sell products to the general public, you will be able to set up an Internet site separated from your internal network by a firewall. This can provide a reasonable amount of security from access over the Internet through the public Web site.

You may also be able to provide a firewall-protected Internet site for access by your vendors. Of course, it's in your best interest to make access by legitimate vendors as simple as possible. Still, keeping your valuable network resources secure must be your first priority. In general, you will have a limited number of vendors and can create individual accounts for each of them, making access by them as secure as access by a remote employee.

The issue of business partners is handled a little differently. A business partner may not be accessing your network for the explicit purpose of buying or selling but may be doing so to share resources. Again, you will probably have a limited number of partners and can create individual accounts for them. In fact, you may be able to set up trust relationships between your networks, allowing you to assign users from the partners' networks to security groups and grant them specific access to the required resources.

Acquisition Plans

Is your company likely to be acquired by another soon, or do you routinely acquire other organizations? If so, then you need to consider this in your security strategy as well. If you expect the company to be acquired by a larger organization, then you should be prepared to reorganize the network security system to fit in with the anticipated parent corporation's network. Under ideal conditions, this could simply mean joining your domain tree to the forest of the acquiring organization. However, unless you already have an intimate knowledge of the network structure of the acquiring organization, you should be prepared to completely dismantle your current network structure and rebuild it from scratch.

On the other hand, if you expect to be acquiring one or more companies in the near future, then you should prepare to have a new domain tree merge into yours. In cases where you wholly acquire the other company and merge it completely into your network, you can simply add it as a subtree of your main domain tree. This will generally mean renaming its domain tree to fit into the namespace of yours. You may, however, choose to simply add the new network as a separate tree in your forest, in which case its network namespace does not need to be immediately changed. Over time, you might slowly integrate its resources into the parent domain tree, eventually phasing out its namespace completely.

Scenario 2-1: Determining Company Models and Organizational Structures

This scenario is based on the case studies introduced earlier in the course. Suggested answers are provided in Appendix B at the end of the manual.

Barney's Bank

Barney's Bank is a full-service bank offering a variety of features and services to its customers. Those customers range from individuals with simple savings accounts to large companies requiring complex credit lines and investment services.

The company has a layered approach to management. Upper management controls all major decisions but smaller decisions can be made at lower levels of the company tree. The company has at least partially merged the administrative functions of each of its acquisitions to streamline and normalize functionality as well as cut down on overhead. For example, each of the Accounting, Human Resources, and Marketing departments is centrally managed, with basic day-to-day functions being controlled by the personnel at each individual location.

1. Which model does the company follow?

   ....

   ....

2. Describe the organizational structure of the company.

   ....

   ....

Fairco Manufacturing

Fairco has only one location where all of their corporate operations take place, including management and manufacturing. The company has a central management that oversees the basic divisions but each division is responsible for its own product and controls the design, production, marketing, and sales of that product from start to end. The divisions tend to share information and ideas with each other but officially, they are separate entities that operate completely autonomously from one another.

1. Which model does the company follow?

   ....

   ....

2. Describe the organizational structure of Fairco Manufacturing.

   ....

   ....

ENVIRONMENTAL ANALYSIS

The other major factor that will influence the structure of your security system is the current and planned environment your organization operates in. Here you'll need to investigate such things as the company's priorities, growth, and costs as well as the applicable laws and the risks that your company faces. This also involves looking at the organization's technical environment, including the size of the company and the overall distribution of its users and resources. The following topics will be covered in this section:

- Analyzing Company Strategies
- Identifying Company Priorities
- Identifying Company Growth
- Identifying Relevant Laws and Regulations
- Identifying Tolerance for Risk
- Identifying Total Cost of Ownership (TCO)
- Evaluating the Technical Environment
- Analyzing Company Size
- Analyzing User and Resource Distribution

Analyzing Company Strategies

Your company may have several strategies it uses in hopes of reaching its overall goals. A good security design will protect the resources of the company while not hindering progress in following those strategies and reaching the goals. For example, if you have such tight security that people cannot access the information they need to do their jobs, your security system is interfering with the company operations. In order to design an effective security system, you need to know what the main strategies of your organization are so you can be sure not to interfere with them.

Identifying Company Priorities

The priorities and goals of your company determine how you go about doing business. Of course, the first priority of most commercial enterprises is to show a profit on the bottom line. The larger the profit, the more successful the organization. Not-for-profit groups, on the other hand, place various other goals ahead of generating financial income. In either case, though, the methods of achieving those goals must be closely analyzed to set up a security system that adequately protects the organization's resources without interfering with their realization.

For instance, in a good many organizations, one of the main priorities is to provide quality customer service so that current customers will be more likely to return. This means enabling the customers to access the information they need about your products or services. Customer service information provided on an Internet site can be a simple solution for that service. In some cases, you can require that the customer provide some proof of ownership of your product (a serial number or other product identifier delivered with the product itself) in order to gain access to the product information. You may also want to grant access to some more in-depth information to a group of customer service employees who deal directly with customers who didn't find the answers to their questions on the Internet site.

Identifying Company Growth

You need to assess the anticipated growth of your company as well as the methods that your company uses to grow. For example, do you anticipate massive growth spurts from the acquisition of other companies or is your organization more likely to grow slower as a result of a steady hiring of new employees? Either way, you need to have a plan as to how that growth will fit in with your network security system.

We covered the case of significant growth in short periods of time as the result of the acquisition of other companies in a previous section. Generally, such a change will bring its own network structure, which you can integrate into your existing network either as a new tree in your existing domain forest or by dismantling the other company's network structure and rebuilding it to fit with yours. The decision of which method to undertake will depend on the cost/benefit analysis of doing the complete changeover. Such a project could be quite expensive and time consuming. However, if it provides a truly homogeneous network in the end, the task could be worthwhile since the administrative chores of maintaining two separate network structures long term can be quite costly.

If, however, you expect that the company will grow more slowly, resulting from the addition of employees as a response to increased business on existing products or services, then the structure of your network can remain more stable. Major structural changes to your network, and therefore your security system, are much less likely. Of course you still must plan to add users and move existing users between departments and security groups, but these regular changes are a standard and expected part of managing a network.

Identifying Relevant Laws and Regulations

When analyzing your organization for the purpose of implementing a Windows 2000 security solution, you need to consider whether any laws or regulations will affect your deployment. For instance, is there any software that should not be exported to foreign countries? The federal regulations against exporting Windows 2000 security have been relaxed so that's no longer an issue, but you may run up against other laws depending on the software that you'll be deploying.

Identifying Tolerance for Risk

One of the major factors in your security plan must be the organization's tolerance for risk in different areas of its business. You may have some information that is so sensitive, such as merger plans, that it would be quite appropriate to make accessing that information rather difficult. On the other hand, typical e-mails between employees are probably not nearly as sensitive, so you generally would want to make it easy for employees to communicate with each other.

As you may have guessed, the basic idea here is to identify the level of risk intrinsic to the various areas of your network infrastructure and apply security precautions accordingly. This risk may be in forms other than outright theft of the information. You also need to protect information from loss due to disasters such as fire or flood, theft of the equipment the information resides on, and both negligent and malicious corruption. In the case of truly important information, any of these events could prove disastrous to your organization and appropriate security measures are in order.

Identifying Total Cost of Ownership (TCO)

When implementing any change in the organization, you need to evaluate the costs of that change. This includes not only the cost of the hardware and software (the materials) needed to affect the change, but also the labor required to implement the change and the labor and materials anticipated to support the system after the change is in place. This makes up the TCO of a particular project.

Some of the things to look at when evaluating the TCO of your security system are as follows:

- Hardware and software costs
- Labor anticipated in designing the new system
- Labor anticipated in rolling out the new system
- Down time anticipated in rolling out the new system

- Training for users of the new system
- Savings from ease of use of the new system after the learning curve levels out
- Savings from increased security resulting in less loss due to network attacks
- Savings in administrative workload

When implementing a large-scale change, such as an upgrade to Windows 2000 network security systems, a comparison with the TCO of staying with the old system is generally very helpful. Often you'll find that once it is in place, the decreased costs of operating the new system can quickly make up for the costs associated with rolling it out. With careful planning and attention to detail, implementation of a Windows 2000 security system can easily pay for itself through ease of use and the increased level of security it provides.

Evaluating the Technical Environment

Another major consideration when designing your Windows 2000 security system is the technical environment you'll be deploying it into. This includes the following three things:

- The hardware the systems will be run on
- Any legacy software that will continue to be used
- The technical expertise of the people who will use the system

As you might expect, Windows 2000 requires a more powerful hardware platform than many previous operating systems did. While it is common to include the price of new server hardware in the upgrade budget, you may not be able to upgrade many of the workstations right away. This means that you could be supporting a heterogeneous network environment for a time, with various operating systems comprising the security makeup of your network.

If your organization is currently using legacy software that doesn't participate in the Windows 2000 security structure or expects unrestricted access to sensitive information, you have two options: either upgrade the software to a more secure program with similar functionality or accept to the requirements of the legacy application. Either path presents a set of costs that must be analyzed before making a final decision. Retaining the older, less secure software presents potential security liabilities that could be quite harmful and expensive to the company. On the other hand, upgrading to a newer application requires an outlay of resources in order to purchase and deploy the new application, determine the functionality differences between the old and new software, and train the personnel on its use. The final decision ultimately rests on the balance of tolerance for risk versus TCO for the upgrade.

The third consideration in the organization's technical environment involves the people who will be using the software. In general, Windows 2000 security procedures should be easier to perform and, therefore, require less technical knowledge by those using the system than most previous operating systems. With the single sign-on Kerberos v5 authentication technology and the integration of nearly all of the security features with that system, the user experience should be fairly seamless. If your users can remember their passwords and don't lose their smart cards, then they should have no trouble working within the Windows 2000 security framework.

Analyzing Company Size

With the scalability of Windows 2000's security features, the size of the company in terms of numbers of employees is a factor only in the size of the deployment. With proper administrative delegation, no single person needs to be responsible for the management of the entire user base, so even the administrative chores are not outrageous for a network supporting thousands of people.

That's not to say, however, that you don't need to consider the size of your organization when designing your network security structure. The more people you have using the network, the greater the possibility that one of them will do something to inappropriately access information. A larger company generally means the analysis and design phase of your network security implementation will be more intricate, so careful planning is essential at this point.

In a small company of less than a hundred people, you can probably manage the entire user base by setting up a relatively small number of security groups and assigning them access to the various resources. With thousands of people to consider, the job of designing security groups becomes a serious task. You may have security groups dedicated to specific groups of resources, such as printers and file shares, that have a regularly changing membership. By delegating responsibility for membership in these groups to a local IT manager, you can effectively distribute the workload among enough people that it becomes manageable.

This is where proper design is essential. If you have set up your security system so that it breaks roughly along management or organizational lines of the company, then delegation of these tasks is a simple matter of assigning these chores to someone in the appropriate department. However, a security system that doesn't match the organization of the company on some basic level will remain very difficult to manage since the person responsible for a particular security boundary may not necessarily know the proper interaction or relationships between all of the people and resources being administered. This can cause a good deal of headache and frustration among both the IT personnel and the people trying to do their jobs with improper security settings.

Analyzing User and Resource Distribution

Not only is the sheer size of the company important, but the distribution of those resources across geographic and political boundaries can have an impact on the design of your network security system. You, of course, will want to have the person most directly responsible for administration of a group's security settings at the same location as that group, if this is at all possible. Also, if the company model allows it, the most efficient delegation of authority occurs when the delegate is within the same political boundary as the group being managed; this allows the group and the administrator to develop a working relationship in which they become familiar with each others' needs and manner of work.

Scenario 2-2: Technical Analysis

This scenario is based on the case studies introduced earlier in the course. Suggested answers are provided in Appendix B at the end of the manual.

Barney's Bank

While it's not yet implemented, the bank is currently planning an online banking feature, which would allow all of its customers to access and manipulate account information securely over the Internet. Currently, Barney's Bank offers dial-up access to a few of the larger accounts, but these transactions can't be made over the Internet yet. A couple of the larger accounts have expressed concern about the security of Internet banking, so Barney's Bank is still attempting to develop a detailed security structure prior to implementing this service.

Barney's Bank employs an educated group of people. Almost everyone working at the bank has achieved at least a high school education, while a good portion of them are college graduates.

The bank has a commitment to using hardware and software that will provide the greatest benefit to the bank's processes and to its customers. Whenever possible, the newest hardware is brought in to replace any failing systems. As soon as they can be thoroughly tested, new versions of the main software packages are deployed and the employees are trained in their use. However, due to the practice of acquiring other banks, the bank often has several legacy applications that need to be supported while the transitions are made. There typically is also a period following an acquisition when some legacy hardware needs to be supported while technical details and funding are managed in the replacement strategy.

1. What type of external network connectivity does Barney's Bank require?

    ....

    ....

2. Describe the growth plans of Barney's Bank in the case studies.

    ....

    ....

3. Evaluate the technical environment of each of the case study companies.

    ....

    ....

Fairco Manufacturing

While they have considered acquiring other companies in the past, Fairco currently believes that a slow, steady growth model based on sales is more appropriate for the company. Management at Fairco doesn't feel comfortable expanding into other facilities, nor do they believe it's necessary right now to add a large group of people or equipment.

Being a manufacturing company, much of Fairco's workforce is educated at the high school level or below. Even many of the team leaders have been promoted from the lines and are not very comfortable using complicated computer software. However, with only a few exceptions, members of the sales force have at least some college-level education with a fair background in standard computer usage.

While management believes in keeping the IT resources running smoothly, information is not really Fairco's main business, so when resources get tight, IT is one of the first to feel it. This translates to several workstations running Windows 95 as well as a couple of computers on the shop floor running DOS 5.0. Also, they haven't upgraded the accounting software in several years because the company that produces it hasn't released a version for Windows NT or Windows 2000.

1. What type of external network connectivity does Fairco Manufacturing require?

   ....

   ....

2. Describe the growth plans of Fairco Manufacturing in the case studies.

   ....

   ....

3. Evaluate the technical environment of Fairco Manufacturing.

   ....

   ....

SUMMARY

During this chapter, you were introduced to the following topics:

- Operational analysis of your company
    - Common business models
    - Processes affecting your company's security structure
    - Relationship between your company's organizational structure and security system design
    - Effects of external relationships and acquisitions on your company's security system
- Environmental analysis of your company
    - Analyzing your company's strategic plan
        - Priorities
        - Growth strategy
        - Tolerance for risk
        - Cost of ownership
        - Laws and regulations influencing your company

This chapter provides analysis suggestions that will help you gain a basic understanding of your company's structure. The next chapter provides information on analyzing the technical environment you'll be implementing a security system in.

POST-TEST QUESTIONS

The answers to these questions are in Appendix A at the end of this manual.

1. What would be a likely scenario for the security structure of a national company?

    ....

    ....

2. What are the five common geographic company models?

    ....

    ....

3. How is a Product Division model company organized?

    ....

    ....

4. What are the options when integrating an acquired company's network that follows a different security model than your own?

    ....

    ....

5. What is the bottom line when deciding whether to upgrade a legacy application that doesn't follow your Windows 20000 security structure?

    ....

    ....

Technical Analysis

OBJECTIVES

At the completion of this chapter, you will be able to:

- Analyze business and security requirements for the end user.

- Analyze the structure of IT management. Considerations include type of administration, such as centralized or decentralized; funding model; outsourcing; decision-making process; and change-management process.

- Analyze the current physical model and information security model.

- Analyze internal and external security risks.

- Evaluate the company's existing and planned technical environment.

- Assess the available connectivity between the geographic location of work sites and remote sites.

- Assess the net available bandwidth.

- Analyze performance requirements.

- Analyze the method of accessing data and systems.

- Analyze network roles and responsibilities. Roles include administrative, user, service, resource ownership, and application.

- Analyze the impact of the security design on the existing and planned technical environment.

- Assess existing systems and applications.

- Identify existing and planned upgrades and rollouts.

- Analyze technical support structure.

- Analyze existing and planned network and systems management.

PRE-TEST QUESTIONS

The answers to these questions are in Appendix A at the end of this manual.

1. What are some methods of determining the business requirements of your end users?

    ....

    ....

2. What are the two main types of IT administration?

    ....

    ....

3. Why would you want to implement your new security system prior to rolling out an application upgrade?

    ....

    ....

4. How might the implementation of the new security system affect bandwidth requirements?

    ....

    ....

INTRODUCTION

The next step in the planning phase of building your Windows 2000-based security structure is to analyze the technical environment you'll be implementing this system in. Here you'll need to take into account such things as the requirements of your end users, the structure of IT management, and the company's current security model, including any perceived security risks that may exist. You'll need to understand the various aspects of the company's technical landscape, including the distribution of resources, bandwidth and performance requirements, and network roles currently in effect. Finally, you'll need to take into account the impact of your new security design on the existing and planned technical environment.

SECURITY ANALYSIS

You are now at the stage where you need to determine the various security requirements for the people who will be using the network. In fact, this analysis will include not only people, but network services and applications that access resources over the network, for they, too, must have appropriate security settings in place before they can function properly. The following topics will be covered in this section:

- Analyzing Business and Security Requirements
- Analyzing the Structure of IT Management
- Analyzing Network Roles and Responsibilities

Analyzing Business and Security Requirements

To build a successful security system on your network, you need to have a clear idea of what the business and security requirements of your end users are. This means taking stock of the current practices of your network users. On a large network with many users, this could be a formidable task.

Determining the usage patterns of a large group of people could be a fairly long project. A survey is an effective way to gather such information, or you could perform an audit of sorts. If conducting a survey, you'll need the cooperation of the people being surveyed as well as their supervisors. Thus, you can gather the necessary information in one or more of the following ways:

- Individual Survey
- Departmental Survey
- Resource Monitoring

Often the best data will result from a combination of these different methods. We'll discuss each method in this section.

Individual Survey

While performing an individual survey of all network users is likely the most difficult and time-consuming method of gaining information about network usage patterns, it won't necessarily provide the most accurate data. You may find that the individual users are not necessarily aware of how they actually use network resources, especially if those users aren't particularly technically savvy. Still, with proper assistance from IT team leaders to help the users understand precisely what they're doing and reasonable interpretation of the results, this type of wide-scale information gathering could provide a very rich set of data to base a security model on.

To make this work properly, you'll need to clearly define the available network resources so that the users can understand them. For instance, if someone in the Accounts Receivable department uses a particular financial package to access client records but doesn't need access to vendor information, then a security line could be drawn there. However, it's possible that data for a particular vendor may be tied to the billings for a certain set of clients. In that case, the security line must include all pertinent information. If the financial package supports a granularity fine enough to allow setting permissions on specific accounts, then you may decide to do so; however, this may prove to be more of an administrative burden than is necessary. Once again, you'll have to weigh the needs against the risks involved in opening up the entire set of information to the person in that position.

Thus, in general, it's better to have the most detailed information possible in order to decide how to build the security system. You may not end up placing such tight controls on the data, but if you don't have the information, then you cannot properly make the decision whether to do so.

Departmental Survey

A departmental survey may be somewhat easier on the IT department since it only involves surveying department managers. Each department is then responsible for determining what resources it uses in whatever manner it deems most efficient. By spreading the responsibility to the departments, you may be able to get more accurate information. This is because a department manager should have a better idea of how his department's tasks relate to actual network resource usage. If he doesn't, he should have someone on staff that can gather that information.

Still, you'll probably end up with at least a few departments who will provide inaccurate information. In such situations, you should be prepared to employ one of the other methods to gather the required data.

Resource Monitoring

The other method of determining who is using the network's resources is to do intense audits of all available resources. Again, this method can be a formidable task for the IT group, but if done well, it can provide a fine level of information to build your security system on. This assumes that your current network operating system is capable of reporting such details as the specific user who accessed a particular resource at a certain time. Tracking such information for a minimum of a month would give you a very clear idea of how your network is being used.

There are two problems with this method. The first is that you really need to keep logs for an extended time period to catch all the necessary network activity. Certain tasks are performed only on a monthly basis, others annually. It's unlikely that you'll be able to keep such detailed logs for over a year, much less devote the resources to analyzing such logs. It's also doubtful that you can spend that much time in the discovery phase of this project before beginning its implementation.

The other major problem with this method is that on a large network, such detailed logs can become extremely large over the period of time required. This not only necessitates a huge amount of storage, but also entails a Herculean effort to decipher the logs. Such an undertaking requires a good deal of planning to be successful.

Combining Analysis Methods

With the problems inherent in each of the three methods of determining usage patterns of your network users, you should probably use some combination of the three to accurately determine the actual usage of your network resources. By starting with a departmental survey, you can gain a fairly good high-level view of the way the network is used. Following that with a brief and targeted monitoring of resources, based on some of the information gathered in the departmental survey, will help to determine the accuracy of the responses received in the survey. Finally, a brief and informal user survey can help clear up any discrepancies you find between the data from the departmental survey and the resource-monitoring effort.

Analyzing the Structure of IT Management

Another important factor in the structure of your security system is the related structure of IT management in your organization. By taking a detailed look at the different aspects of how your IT group operates, you can make informed decisions about how you can reasonably expect the security system to work as well as how much administration effort you can afford to build into that system.

Administration Type

For the purposes of this discussion, we'll look at IT management as being administered in one of the following two ways:

- Centralized
- Decentralized

A centralized IT group generally operates as a separate department of the company, much the way a human resources department might. It has its own management structure and internal organization and operates fairly independently of the other departments of the company. While this allows a good deal of discretion as to how the network, and hence the security system, will be structured, it also builds a certain barrier between IT and the rest of the organization, making it more difficult to really know how the other departments operate.

A decentralized IT group, on the other hand, actually has members within the other departments. IT may not actually have its own management structure, or if it does, it is only loosely responsible for the IT personnel in other departments. Many of the IT personnel report to the managers of other departments, meaning that they operate regularly as part of those groups. While this gives them unique insight into the day-to-day workings and style of other departments, it may result in a loss of network homogeneity as the different departments might operate slightly differently in their use of the IT personnel.

Funding Model

Often the funding for the IT department is intimately tied to the administration type. In a centralized administration model, the funding generally comes from the top as a function of the bottom line of the organization. In a decentralized IT group, the funding often comes from the departments the various IT personnel are working in. In many cases, you may have a combination of these two approaches, in which the IT budget is determined in part by the entire organization's budget and partly by the work done in each department. Either way, the funding for the set up of the security structure must be determined prior to commencement of the project to ensure that it can be completed without having to cut back the scope partway through. Building a complete security system from the ground up requires a predetermined amount of funding. Getting through the beginning design stages and then having to make changes to the overall plan is not only wasteful, it's likely to result in an inefficient and possibly unworkable security model.

Outsourcing

If much of your IT functionality is outsourced, then you will have yet another security issue to deal with. When defining the access rights for the IT group, you'll need to take into account that some of the members may not actually be employees of your company, but are contractors working for an outside agency. While such a situation should be addressed contractually with nondisclosure and privacy agreements, the potential for security risks rises with external access to your network being permitted.

Decision-Making Process

With all of the information you'll gather during this discovery phase of the security design project, you'll need a clear chain of decision making in order to sift out the relevant data to build your network security structure on. This decision making often depends on the administrative model that your IT department follows. However, it could also be a matter of decisions being handed down from above, as in a situation where upper management issues directives of how the security systems should function. While this may not be the most effective approach toward building a secure network system, this is a realistic scenario. In such cases, the necessity for building compelling arguments with clear, well-defined data backing them up becomes much more evident.

Change-Management Process

The next item to examine is the process that routine changes are made on your network by. For example, if a department grows to the point that upper management decides to split it into two peer departments, how does this affect your network security system? You need to have a clear understanding of the process that such a change is handled by so that you can build that type of functionality into your security design plan. Having such processes clearly mapped out makes life much easier when those changes actually start to occur, especially if you have new people in your department who weren't around for the design phase. You'll need to be able to give them a clear set of instructions that they can follow to appropriately handle these tasks without interfering with the overall structure of your security system.

Analyzing Network Roles and Responsibilities

When designing your security system, you need to determine who fills the various roles that play a part in your network system and how the responsibilities for various resources and tasks will be assigned. In general, you'll find that the following five roles will be occupied on your network:

- Administrators
- Users
- Resource Owners
- Services
- Applications

Each of these roles has a specific purpose on the network and is filled by a specific group of people or software that perform actions on the network. In fact, you'll find that these roles loosely match some of the security groups defined by default in Windows 2000. By putting some effort into discovering how these groups will be defined, you'll have a great advantage when actually building the groups, assigning permissions, and delegating responsibilities.

Administrators

With the Windows 2000 Active Directory security structure, you no longer have to give full administrative rights to everyone who needs to be able to manage security settings for small groups of people. This takes a great burden off the workload of the IT personnel without significantly increasing the security risk. By defining administrative roles specific to a particular OU, such as a department or group of resources, you can effectively spread out the responsibility for managing the network in the same way the organization distributes responsibility for managing noncomputer-related resources.

With this ability to delegate responsibilities, you'll need to determine how to organize the network resources for the most efficient administration. Once you have that specification laid out, you can decide who should control those resources in each group. Often you'll want to have an administrative group set up for specific tasks in each department, such as managing the user base, handling the network shares, and keeping track of the various resources used by those people. This would allow you to easily change the person or people in that group without having to manage the Access Control List (ACL) for each object being administered.

Users

The vast majority of people on your network will be users. Of course, the different users will have differing security needs based on their job functions, but to have them generally classed as users means that they're more likely to be using the network resources than managing them. This delineation allows you to set broad security guidelines that you can organize different groups of people into without having to individually manage each security group or OU.

Resource Owners

Resource owners have a certain amount of administrative control over the resources they are responsible for. They must ensure that the resources are available to those users who need access to them and must be sure that they are properly configured, updated, and deployed so that business is not impeded during attempts to work properly with them. However, the owner of a resource may or may not be responsible for managing security settings on that resource depending on the level of delegation you determine for your security structure. For example, the owner of a network printer would be responsible for ensuring that the printer functions properly, has adequate supplies of paper and toner, and may also handle problems with failed print jobs or other software issues. Depending on the structure of your security system, however, this person may not be able to specify which users can print to this printer. With Windows 2000 such granularity is possible, making it easier for you to assign tasks to people appropriate for each role and responsibility.

Services

Many of the network resources will take on the role of a service on your network. For instance, the Internet Information Service (IIS) is a set of resources that directly manages access to certain sets of other resources on your network. By viewing these services as having a specific role on the network, and therefore holding certain responsibilities, you can more effectively design the security system to work efficiently with that service. In this example, IIS has the responsibility of accessing files and other network resources and making them available to users of the intranet or Internet. Toward this purpose, IIS needs security permissions to access those files and resources, and it is responsible for making sure that those resources aren't accessed inappropriately. In much the same way that users must guard their access to the network, IIS must be designed and configured so that only appropriate access can be obtained through its interface.

Applications

Network applications have security settings much like those of network services. An accounting package needs to have permission to access the financial databases on the network, and it must take responsibility for making sure that only the appropriate access to that data is allowed. By deploying and using applications that are Kerberos v5- and Windows 2000-aware, you can generally build a network infrastructure that seamlessly handles all of your security needs.

Scenario 3-1: Security Requirements

Use the information presented in this section to assist in answering the questions. Suggested answers are provided in Appendix B at the end of the manual.

Barney's Bank

Barney's Bank consists of a variety of groups of people who are considered end users. A few of the more prominent divisions are as follows:

- Management

  Management personnel at Barney's Bank are responsible for overseeing day-to-day activities as well as medium- and long-range planning. Managers of the individual departments will typically create plans for their departments. These plans are expected to fit in with the plans and procedures of the other departments.

  Departmental plans are presented at biweekly management meetings and are then open for discussion with the other departments. Top management expects the departmental managers to present well thought-out plans that fit well with all other departments.

- IT staff

  Data integrity is a primary responsibility of the IT staff. Security planning is performed at the central office in Corpus Christi and implemented by small groups of professionals at the branch locations. All data backup is performed at the remote offices and is consolidated at the central office for archival on a daily basis.

  The IT staff in Corpus Christi expects that when a problem occurs in a remote office, the IT staff in that office will have the access and resources necessary to resolve the problem.

- Direct salespeople, including loan officers, banking representatives, and tellers

  People who have contact with the public have defined tasks and responsibilities. The bank has gone to great lengths to ensure that these representatives have the tools necessary to do their jobs. They expect, however, that these representatives do not have more access to the system than is necessary.

- The general public, who may use kiosks and ATMs

  In recent years, the bank has installed ATMs that allow customers access to their own account information by using a bank card and PIN. There is ongoing planning with the goal of providing Web-based banking for customers. The Web site would provide general information relating to bank products and programs. In addition, by using the ATM card number and PIN via the Web, a customer will be able to access personal account information. Several larger customers have expressed concerns about this level of customer access.

Each of these groups has specific needs in relation to network access and security.

Describe the security needs of the end users at Barney's Bank.

....

....

Fairco Manufacturing

Management at Fairco Manufacturing is very departmental. Each department is totally responsible for its own area of authority. Decision making is done on a departmental basis. For this reason, each manager expects access to as much information as possible.

The IT staff is centralized and is responsible for system integrity throughout the entire company. Backup of all data is performed centrally by the IT staff.

The end users at Fairco consist of the office personnel, who take care of business processes; the sales staff, who access the latest product information, inventory, and pricing data; and the production and warehouse crews, who utilize product design and team management software.

Describe the security needs of end users at Fairco Manufacturing.

....

....

ANALYZING GROWTH

In order to build a security system that will be useful over a period of time, you need to have an understanding of how your network is likely to grow. This means taking stock of the current state of your network and its available resources, then projecting the possible changes. The following topics will be covered in this section:

- Assessing Existing Systems
- Identifying Upgrades and Rollouts
- Analyzing Technical Support Structure
- Analyzing Network and Systems Management

Assessing Existing Systems

Before you can determine how your organization will grow, you need to have a clear idea of where it is now. This means taking a comprehensive inventory of all the resources available on the network. In this inventory, you'll need to include the following:

- Servers
- Workstations
- Routers
- Applications
- Network services
- File shares
- Printers
- Scanners
- COM objects

This list is by no means comprehensive, but it should serve as a starting point for building your network inventory.

Besides just listing the systems on your network, you also need to get some idea of how those systems are used. Of course, the analysis of the business and security requirements you made in the previous section should provide a good start on this task. However, this also involves determining such network needs as server capacity, connectivity, and bandwidth, which probably aren't directly identified in the inventory of network resources currently in use. Such concepts will require a certain amount of analysis by members of the IT team to provide useful statistics.

For example, you'll need to know if you have sufficient bandwidth to handle replication of the Global Catalog across your network, especially to remote sites that are contained within the domain forest. This means analyzing the amount of traffic currently flowing on that line and estimating the traffic that the Global Catalog replications will contribute. Comparing this to the available bandwidth will show you whether adding this security system will interfere with the daily activities of the current network users.

In some cases, you might find that the current network infrastructure will not support the planned security system. In these situations you'll need to weigh the pros and cons of upgrading the network systems or scaling back the security system. While upgrading systems can prove rather costly at times, the risks involved in a less secure network could easily outweigh the costs. Only detailed analysis of all factors involved can provide the information needed to make properly informed decisions.

Identifying Upgrades and Rollouts

Once you've determined what your existing systems are and whether they could adequately support the security system you're planning, you'll need to start looking at the upgrades and rollouts you have in mind for your network. Whether these changes are the result of the increased requirements of the new security system or are simply planned upgrades to accommodate the growth of your business, they need to be carefully analyzed to effectively merge them into your new security system. Since you are still in the planning stages of the security system, you have a choice of whether to roll out the new systems before or after implementing the security changes. In some cases, compatibility or technical issues will make the decision for you.

For example, you may want to upgrade your accounting package to one that integrates fully with Active Directory. In this case, you'll need to have Active Directory fully in place before you can deploy the new accounting package. On the other hand, if you need to upgrade a network server to support the increased computing requirements of the upgrade to Windows 2000, then that server must be in place before you can implement the security system.

Often, you will be able to determine which to roll out first based on other issues, such as budgeting or training needs. Either way, you will be wise to gain a clear knowledge of the security requirements of the planned system so that you can design your security structure to include that upgrade. Whether you first implement the security system or the other resource, having a plan for their integration will make both rollouts go much smoother and will ease the transition for your network users.

Analyzing Technical Support Structure

Another issue you need to contend with is the structure of technical support on your network. You probably have a multilevel technical support system in place, utilizing such resources as follows:

- Online documentation and Frequently Asked Questions (FAQs) documents
- E-mail access to support personnel
- Telephone access to support personnel
- Onsite support personnel

Each of these levels of support will need to be updated to reflect the changes introduced by the new security structure. In most cases, it should make support tasks easier since the single sign-on aspect of the Kerberos v5 authentication will eliminate some amount of the support costs of your network. However, you will need to allocate some resources to the training of support personnel so they will be able to effectively handle calls, which will inevitably rise resulting from any change of this scale made to the organization's network.

In addition to updating the support resources and training the personnel on the new issues, you will also need to make sure that those personnel have the necessary permissions to carry out their jobs. In many cases, support personnel have special security requirements that allow them to manage resources that others may not have access to. This allows them to fix problems caused by users and resolve issues that people discover during daily use of the network. Taking stock of the access methods that this special group is accustomed to will allow you to determine the proper security level that support personnel should have in the new environment.

Analyzing Network and Systems Management

The next aspect of network growth you need to be concerned with is the management of the network and associated systems. You'll need to take stock of how the network and its resources are currently managed and determine how this could change based on the upgrades to the security system as well as other unrelated changes that you may have pending, such as departmental restructuring or mergers and acquisitions.

Often in a Windows NT 4.0 domain you'll have a centralized IT management of the network, including all of the resources available on that network. Certain daily functions may have been handled by personnel more directly involved in the use of those systems, but basic management chores are nearly always handled by the centralized IT group. This is especially true of the security settings of the various network resources since only administrators have permissions to manage those settings in Windows NT 4.0. In fact, you may have domains set up specifically for management of network resources so that you can delegate control of the resource domain to someone who may not need administrative rights to the main domain of users (usually the master domain).

With Windows 2000 this is no longer necessary. You can fold the resources in separate domains into the common domain to simplify the network structure, then delegate administrative authority to those resources without having to grant Domain Admin privileges to people who only need access to the resources. This eases the administrative burden of the IT group and simultaneously tightens security by reducing the number of Domain Admin accounts without interfering with the functionality for the end users.

TECHNICAL ANALYSIS

You'll need a firm grasp on the technical aspects of your network to effectively implement an efficient security system that will protect your network resources without hampering user productivity. Taking inventory of the technical details of your network's current state provides you with a clear vision of where you're starting. You'll also need to anticipate the goals of your network so that you can plan your security solution to meet the anticipated needs of your users. The following topics will be covered in this section:

- Analyzing User and Resource Distribution
- Analyzing Connectivity
- Analyzing Bandwidth
- Analyzing Performance Requirements
- Analyzing Access Methods

Analyzing User and Resource Distribution

When preparing to analyze the technical state of your organization's network, you will probably want to start by examining the size of the network and paying attention to how the users and resources are distributed on it. On a small network with only a single location, this analysis will be simple. However, analyzing the distribution patterns of a large, multinational network with a forest of domains can be a major undertaking.

For this information to be useful, you need to prepare maps of both the physical and logical distribution of the users and resources. Often these two concepts do not correspond precisely. The logical distribution generally corresponds to divisions along political corporate lines, such as the sales department and the development department, whereas physical distribution depends on the actual location of the users or resources. For example, you may have several physical locations with their own sets of resources, including servers, file shares, printers, and so on. These locations are probably set up as distinct logical domains in a tree or at least as separate OUs in a Windows 2000 domain. However, a traveling or remote user may be working currently in Los Angeles but may actually belong logically to a domain that is physically established in New York. Hence, in this case, the physical and logical distributions don't correspond. Branch offices could also impose disparities between the physical and logical distribution of resources since the branch office will probably be included in a larger logical domain for ease of administration even though it is physically located in an entirely different place.

Getting a firm grasp on the distribution of these resources is imperative to building a proper security system. You need to plan for any resources that may need special communications security considerations to build the necessary infrastructure for that system. As you'll see in the upcoming sections, you'll also need this information to ensure that proper bandwidth and connectivity are available to facilitate secure operations without impeding users' work habits.

Analyzing Connectivity

Once you have a clear map of how the users and resources are distributed across your network, you need to make sure that proper connectivity is available between your main offices and any remote sites. At this point we're not concerned with the issue of bandwidth; we simply want to make sure that it's possible for remote users to connect to the resources they need to do their jobs.

There are several methods of connecting remote users to the main network. A few of the more common methods are as follows:

- Leased line between sites
- Direct dial-up to the home network
- Virtual Private Network (VPN) connection over a public network such as the Internet

A leased line between two sites is generally considered very secure since it doesn't travel across any public networks. However, it's only available for two physically stable sites. Traveling users don't have the option of having a leased line follow them around the world. Leased lines provide a high degree of up time since they can be permanently connected and the bandwidth is not shared by other parties. Of course, those benefits come at a relatively high price compared with the costs of using dial-up or Internet connections, but in many situations, the cost is easily justified by the benefits the leased line provides.

A direct dial-up line to the home network is also fairly secure since the data isn't traveling over an unsecured network like the Internet. Security is still an issue in such situations, however, since the public telephone network, in general, is not absolutely secure. A sophisticated criminal could still gain access to information transferred over a line directly dialed from a remote phone to the home network, so security measures such as IPSec should be implemented on transactions across such a connection.

Direct dial-up connections require administration of a bank of modems at the home network as well as modems for the remote users. This adds an administrative burden and a hardware expense to the connectivity. You may also need to include the costs of long-distance telephone charges if the remote users will be dialing in from outside the local calling area.

VPN over an unsecured network like the Internet absolutely requires some level of communications security since data will be traveling directly across public networks. Simple packet-sniffing software can easily pick out your data and read and/or modify it if the transmissions are not secured. In general, all Windows 2000 VPN connections are secured by IPSec, so it's simply a matter of configuring IPSec on these connections to provide the appropriate security level for your needs.

Setting up a VPN server on your home network means configuring a separate network connection to translate between the public Internet connection and the private intranet communications. On the remote side you'll need to provide your users with the hardware required to connect to the Internet, meaning either a modem for dial-up access or a network card if Ethernet is available. In the case of dial-up connections, you may need to include the price of an Internet Service Provider (ISP) in the cost of the connection as well as long-distance phone charges if the ISP doesn't have a point of presence in the remote user's local calling area.

Analyzing Bandwidth

Once you have established that your remote users will be able to connect to the resources necessary to do their jobs, you should start considering the available bandwidth on those connections. If you anticipate a large amount of network traffic over a remote connection, then you need to provide for some manner of high-speed access in order to facilitate the requirements of the users who will be working across it. If the Global Catalog for a domain will be replicating across a remote connection, then you should plan to provide a bandwidth of at least 512 Kbps. This amount should increase as you add other functionality that the connection must support, such as accessing remote applications or file shares.

In the case of dial-up or VPN users, be aware that dial-up speeds are generally limited to a maximum of 56 Kbps (or with multilink channel aggregation, up to 112 Kbps) due to the current state of modem technology. If your remote users have access to an Ethernet connection, then they can take advantage of the higher Internet speeds and use the full bandwidth available on the series of connections between the two sites. This means that VPN connections can often provide greater bandwidth than direct dial-up speeds unless the remote VPN user is accessing the Internet via dial-up connection.

Analyzing Performance Requirements

The next step in determining the technical aspects of your network is to analyze its performance requirements. You need to ensure that the addition of security systems does not degrade performance such that your users are unable to effectively discharge their duties. In general, you'll find that efficient organization of the network and careful implementation of the security systems will improve rather than degrade network performance. However, you need to ensure that proper network bandwidth is available for such situations as running network applications or replicating the Global Catalog.

You also need to ensure that both your servers and workstations are of sufficient caliber to handle the type of work your users are expected to perform. Keep in mind that Windows 2000 increases the baseline performance requirements of the underlying hardware, so machines that operated properly under Windows NT 4.0 may struggle to handle the same tasks with the new operating system.

Also, be aware of the possible upgrades that you will be bringing to your network when considering the performance requirements necessary. If you intend to roll out a new version of a software package currently in use, or perhaps a new application you haven't used before, note the technical requirements of that package while preparing your security system. For example, a network support system designed to run in a Web browser may have a smaller processing footprint on the client machine but require more horsepower at the server end. Such upgrades can change the necessary computing landscape dramatically and need to be taken into account when planning the new system.

Analyzing Access Methods

To effectively document the technical requirements of the methods employed by your users to access data and systems on your network, you need to consider both connectivity issues and the software involved. We covered connectivity and bandwidth issues in the previous two sections, so at this point you need to be concerned with the interfaces that people will use to access those network resources. The Windows 2000 computing environment provides a wide variety of access methods that you may need to implement on your network. Some of the more common methods are as follows:

- Client-Based Applications
- Network-Based Applications
- Web-Based Applications
- Thin-Client Applications
- Legacy Applications

You could very well have all of these application types running on your network, necessitating the implementation of a variety of security measures. We'll discuss each of the different access methods in this section.

Client-Based Applications

Standard client-based applications, such as Microsoft Office 2000, require very little network bandwidth in normal operation, except possibly when opening or saving files stored on a network share. Applications of this type typically require relatively powerful client workstations that a vast majority, if not all, of the processing is handled on. Such an application will normally only require that the user has read access to the appropriate application files on the local machine along with appropriate rights on the documents being accessed during standard operations.

Network-Based Applications

A standard format for many accounting packages is to have a portion of the program reside and execute on a network server, while a small client portion runs on the user's workstation. This presents a situation where the server requires a greater processing ability but relieves the workstation of some of that burden. It also creates a situation that generates a greater amount of network traffic in normal operation. Typically, an application of this type will access a database stored on the network. Since the portion of the application running on the server is actually responsible for accessing the database, it must manage the user permissions in order to guarantee that only the appropriate users are allowed access. Application designed to integrate with Windows 2000 and Active Directory can utilize the single sign-on capabilities of the Kerberos v5 authentication to handle this.

Web-Based Applications

Web-based applications operate in much the same manner as network-based applications, but rather than having clients designed to run natively on the remote client computer, they utilize the capabilities of a Web server, such as IIS, to interface with a Web browser on the client. In many cases, this allows an even lower processing requirement on the client since much of the interface functionality is handled by technologies such as XML and HTML. The security issues can be managed via the Web server security settings. This also permits a much greater freedom for the users, who can access these applications from any workstation with a browser and a network connection, without having to install the client portion of the software on the local machine. In cases where certain Java applets or ActiveX controls are required, these can be downloaded automatically without any user intervention, making these applications extremely user friendly.

Thin-Client Applications

The built-in Windows 2000 Terminal Services allow you to run Windows 2000 applications on any computer with connectivity to the Terminal Server. Extremely low-powered client computers can be used to provide your users with access to standard Windows 2000 applications. Here the security requirements are basically the same as for running the applications locally: the users require proper authorization to interact with the application and rights to work with the necessary documents required for their jobs.

Legacy Applications

Legacy applications will often be the most troublesome to administer from a security perspective. They generally will not integrate with Active Directory so they will not allow you to manage security settings based on the user's logon. Often these applications will have proprietary security solutions that will necessitate separate administrative tasks.

Scenario 3-2: Analyzing Connectivity

Use the information presented in this section to assist in answering the questions. Suggested answers are provided in Appendix B at the end of the manual.

Barney's Bank

Each of the U.S. locations of Barney's Bank is connected by a dedicated T1 line to the home office in Corpus Christi. The European offices, however, are all sharing bandwidth on a single T1 line back to the main office. The dial-up access that the bank provides to its major customers is serviced by a bank of 56K modems. The company intends to utilize a dedicated T1 line for its secure Internet banking service when that becomes available.

What are the shortcomings of the available connectivity for Barney's Bank?

....

....

Fairco Manufacturing

The company provides a bank of 56K modems for the warehouses and sales force to use. They also have a T1 connection to the Internet where they host their Web site and process orders placed by the traveling sales team. This connection is also being used for the current extranet trial. This T1 connection also provides the connectivity for the tunneling connections used by the VPN clients needing remote access to the network.

What are the shortcomings of the available connectivity for Fairco Manufacturing?

....

....

ADMINISTRATIVE SECURITY

Your next step is to determine how your new security design will fit into the existing corporate model. You need to determine how the old security systems will change and how that change will affect your users. The following topics will be covered in this section:

- Analyzing Administrative Structure
- Analyzing Physical Models
- Analyzing Information Security Models
- Analyzing Security Risks
- Analyzing the Impact of Security Design

Analyzing Administrative Structure

One of the basic goals when designing your security system is to provide a clear framework to build the system on so that its actual implementation goes smoothly. Toward this end, you need to understand how you will actually administer the system once it is in place. By planning the administrative structure that will work within your security framework, you can ease the transition to the new system.

In most cases, the goal should be to match your security system as closely as possible to the existing management structure. The model should follow your organization's natural patterns rather than change the organization to fit the network model. With the adaptability of the Windows 2000 Active Directory models, this becomes a fairly strong possibility—one that wasn't quite attainable with Microsoft's previous operating systems.

For this reason, you need to consider how your IT structure was shaped by the requirements of previous systems. You'll want to avoid unnecessarily carrying structures that were imposed on your organization by the lack of flexibility of your previous network systems into the new network system.

For example, if you had created resource domains to manage the number of domain admins of your main network domain, you probably have several people who are domain admins of that resource domain who do not need to have administrative powers over an entire domain. Perhaps each of these people should instead enjoy administrative control over a small group of network resources they work with on a regular basis. By organizing the resources from the Windows NT 4.0 resource domain into appropriate OUs in your organization's main domain, you can then assign administrative rights to precisely the people who deserve them. In this way, you can more closely model your network administrative structure after your organization's actual management structure.

Analyzing Physical Models

To understand your organization's physical models, you need to look at the organizational structures of the company as described in the previous chapter. Your company is probably designed loosely after one of the following three major categories or some combination of them:

- Product Division model
- Functional Division model
- Matrix model

The Product Division model organizes the company along product lines, as shown in the following figure.

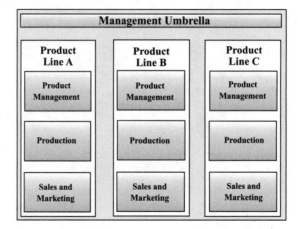

An organization built on the Functional Division model divides itself along lines of functionality, such as production, human resources, and accounting, as shown in the following figure.

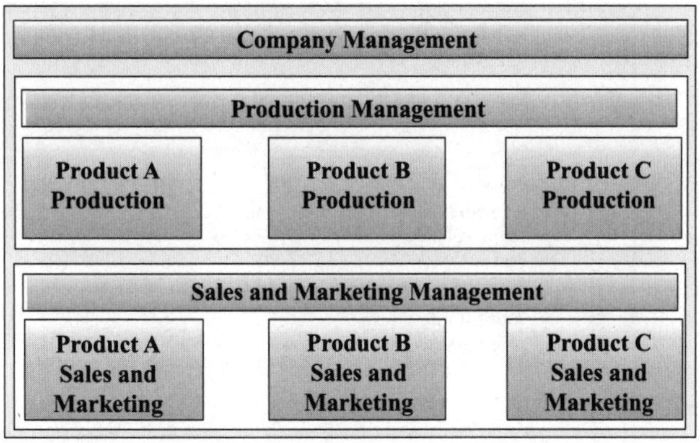

Company Management		
Production Management		
Product A Production	Product B Production	Product C Production
Sales and Marketing Management		
Product A Sales and Marketing	Product B Sales and Marketing	Product C Sales and Marketing

Finally, a Matrix model-based organization builds management structures both along product lines and functionality lines. The teams then report to more than one manager, as shown in the following figure.

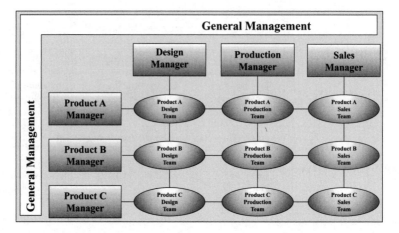

By determining how your organization fits into one or more of these basic models, you can decide how well your network and security structures match the physical model.

Analyzing Information Security Models

If your current information security model is based on an operating system such as Windows NT 4.0, then you probably do not have a close match between your organization's physical model and the current security model. In order to more appropriately build your new security structure following the company's organizational lines, you should first determine how that security system is designed now. This will provide you with a clear road map to plan the transition between the old and the new systems on.

First, you need to determine how many administrators you have in your current information security model and what those people are using their administrative abilities for. You'll need to map, as closely as possible, the current domain structure to the physical structure, attempting to understand how the two relate to each other and how they function in a practical way. Most likely, people have become used to the current state of things and have developed habits which, though possibly somewhat inefficient, may be rather hard to break. In order to properly align your network security system with the actual physical model of the company, you'll need to be able to coax people out of their old habits and into the new, more rational model or the resistance may prove difficult to overcome.

Analyzing Security Risks

Your next step is to determine what security risks your organization realistically faces. There are risks both from inside and outside the company; to plan an appropriate system, you need to be prepared for both.

Internal Risks

In most cases, you'll find that there is a small percentage of people in your organization who will go out of their way to avoid causing any damage to the company through negligence or outright destructive acts. Likewise, you'll also find a very small group who will purposefully steal information and perform other malicious acts simply out of spite or a general bad nature. However, the vast majority of the people in your company probably have no intention of causing any harm but either don't know or don't care enough to prevent small mistakes, such as accidentally overwriting an important file or occasionally leaving a logged-on workstation unattended.

Your security system needs to reflect these facts. Depending on the potential for harm to the company if a particular piece of information was inappropriately disclosed or damaged, you need to apply levels of security that will protect against both malicious attacks and simple negligence from users. Since these people may have legitimate access to certain network resources, you'll find great benefits in building a security system as tight as your budget, both in terms of finances and administrative capacity, will permit. By locking down security so that each individual only has access to resources that pertain directly to the job at hand, you can often avoid problems that could otherwise prove costly and disruptive.

External Risks

Though often more publicized, external risks are actually less likely to occur than internal risks. This does not mean, however, that you should take them lightly. Any time you open your network to anyone from outside your organization you are assuming a certain amount of risk. This includes allowing your users to access a public network such as the Internet, but it also means external access by people such as business partners, vendors, and clients. If you've established trust relationships between your domain and a business partner's domain, then you have suddenly opened up your network to all of the users on that partner's network. While this doesn't automatically impose a risk to your network resources, you need to be aware that those users may have access to your network and institute appropriate security measures to avoid unnecessary risk to your data.

Analyzing the Impact of Security Design

Finally, you need to determine how the new security structure will affect your organization's business practices. You need to ensure that employees receive appropriate training on how to work with the new security features. You also need to make sure that no one's job functions are hindered by the security measures you've implemented.

While in most cases the security features of Windows 2000 should provide users with an easier interface to the tools they use on a daily basis, you need to make sure that users understand the changes. Generally, the single sign-on technology will remove layers of password verification that your users have grown accustomed to; most often, people won't complain about having to remember fewer passwords and having to type them less often. Applying IPSec to network communications should invoke no noticeable change to the user experience but should provide a good deal more security to the communications system. Similarly, enabling the encrypting file system should not introduce any noticeable change to legitimate access to any information on the network.

You will likely find people complaining about not being able to access information that they shouldn't have had rights to in the first place but which they have grown accustomed to due to holes in the previous system. If it turns out that they actually don't need those resources to perform their jobs, then tightening security will likely eliminate some previous risks, which is the very goal of increased security. However, you will also run into situations where someone has been inadvertently cut off from information needed to perform a specific job. After determining that such access really is legitimate, you'll simply need to enable such access by placing that user in a security group that can reach the intended resource. Often these matters are capable of resolution at the departmental level since administrative control can be delegated to those people who more intimately know the workings of the local group of users and its associated resources.

Scenario 3-3: Upgrade Requirements

Use the information presented in this section to assist in answering the questions. Suggested answers are provided in Appendix B at the end of the manual.

Barney's Bank

The bank routinely tests and upgrades new software as it becomes available as well as deploys the currently used software at each newly acquired location. Their upgrade and training plan is very aggressive, including keeping up with all the latest security and functionality updates offered by the software makers.

How will the planned upgrades for Barney's Bank affect the security design?

....

....

Fairco Manufacturing

The IT group has been petitioning to buy an accounting package from a different vendor so they can upgrade the systems and shut down the legacy support required for the other package. The Accounting group, however, is resisting the change, and management is reluctant to spend money on something the Accounting group doesn't want. As computers become damaged or no longer fulfill the task they are assigned to, they are replaced by newer machines capable of running Windows 2000 Workstation and the standard upgraded software in use by the company, but no regular upgrade schedule is planned.

How will the planned upgrades for Fairco Manufacturing affect the security design?

....

....

SUMMARY

During this chapter, you were introduced to the following topics:

- End-user business, security, and performance requirements
- IT management structure
- Roles and responsibilities of network users
- Technical support structure
- Physical organization model and information security model
- Potential internal and external security risks
- Technical environment
- Connectivity and bandwidth between locations and network resource access methods
- Existing and anticipated systems and applications
- Impact of your security design

This information about the technical aspects of your network provide a solid basis that you can use when learning about building a security baseline in the next chapter.

POST-TEST QUESTIONS

The answers to these questions are in Appendix A at the end of this manual.

1. What are some of the drawbacks of performing an individual survey to determine the requirements of the end user?

    ....

    ....

2. How could outsourcing of your IT responsibilities affect your security system?

    ....

    ....

3. What are some common levels of technical support?

    ....

    ....

4. List the following in increasing order of typical bandwidth provided: leased line, direct dial-up, and VPN.

    ....

    ....

5. What are some likely problems with using legacy applications on your network?

    ....

    ....

CHAPTER 4

Defining a Security Baseline

OBJECTIVES

At the completion of this chapter, you will be able to:

- Identify the company's tolerance for risk.

- Analyze business and security requirements for the end user.

- Analyze the current physical model and information security model.

- Analyze internal and external security risks.

- Design a security baseline for a Windows 2000 network that includes domain controllers, operations masters, application servers, file and print servers, RAS servers, desktop computers, portable computers, and kiosks.

- Provide secure access to public networks from a private network.

- Provide external users with secure access to private network resources.

- Provide secure access between private networks.

- Provide secure access across a public network.

PRE-TEST QUESTIONS

The answers to these questions are in Appendix A at the end of this manual.

1. List three benefits of keeping server equipment physically behind locked doors.

    ....

    ....

2. Who should have direct local logon rights to your domain controllers?

    ....

    ....

3. What is the best security precaution for a public-access kiosk?

    ....

    ....

4. What is a brute-force logon attack?

....

....

5. What is the best practice in secure use of Web browsers?

....

....

INTRODUCTION

Having gathered a good deal of information about your network, it's now time to start designing its security structure. This involves setting up a security baseline for the various computers on the network. You'll also need to examine and assess the risks that your particular implementation faces, both internal and external to your network. Finally, you'll take a look at the ramifications of connecting your network to the Internet, which is practically a requirement for any operational business in today's technical climate.

AUDITING SECURITY

Your security baseline needs to include all aspects of your network. This means applying appropriate settings to each computer that belongs to the network as well as requiring stringent security on all points whereby external computers may gain access. You need to manage the Access Control List (ACL) of each network resource to ensure that only appropriate and authenticated users can access it and only in appropriate ways. This section will introduce you to appropriate security settings on the following systems:

- Servers
- Desktop Computers
- Portable Computers
- Kiosks

Servers

Your network servers require special settings to ensure that the sensitive information they're managing is secure. To this end, you should allow only a very limited group of trusted people to have direct access to them. The servers are, of course, on the network to provide services to your organization's users, so you need to ensure that your security policies don't hamper access to them for their intended use. Still, without tight enough security policies, your data could be compromised, stolen, or even destroyed, any of which could have disastrous effects on your organization's primary function.

One of the main and common points to consider regarding the security of your servers is their physical isolation. All servers should be safely locked in a secure facility where only trusted administrators can physically access them. This simple measure reduces quite a few risks, including the following:

- Outright theft of the equipment, which could also result in compromise of the data contained therein
- Physical destruction of the equipment by possibly disgruntled employees
- Direct access to the user interface by inappropriate people, which could result in a variety of problems, including data loss, data theft, and installation of software intended for spoofing
- Malicious installation of hardware intended to compromise network security
- Modification of audit logs

Any of these attacks could result not only in loss of data but network downtime, which can be equally expensive to your organization.

Another item of importance to all network servers is the training of all people trusted as full administrators. Allowing inexperienced or poorly trained people to administer the servers on your network can result in problems such as loss of data or opening of major security holes. In order to properly protect your network, you must have people running it who are competent and capable of performing the tasks required.

All of the servers on your network need to have special care taken to limit access via remote logon. While their purpose generally is to provide services to users via the network, you need to ensure that only those prescribed services are available and that they are properly secured. For instance, in most cases you don't need the File Transfer Protocol (FTP) service running on a domain controller. FTP bypasses the default Kerberos v5 authentication process, opting instead to transfer passwords over the network in clear text, which presents a serious security risk. By simply removing this service and any others that are not necessary for the server's defined operations, you minimize risks of this sort. In fact, disabling unnecessary services should be common practice on all of the computers on your network, but due to the sensitive nature of servers and the data they hold, you need to take particular care with them.

In addition, you may want to disable or remove any hardware in your servers that is not required for their normal operations. This includes serial ports, parallel ports, infrared ports, network cards, and any other physical connections an intruder could connect by extraneous devices without physically opening the case. Certainly the risk of this is minimized if the computers are secured in a locked facility, but the more difficult you make an attack, the less likely it is to succeed. From this standpoint, the removal of extraneous hardware becomes a simple procedure that provides yet another real layer in your security structure.

The following sections delve into details of your security baseline specific to the individual types of servers you may have on your network.

Domain Controllers

Due to their central and primary functions on the network, your domain controllers need to be particularly well secured. In most cases, only full administrators should be allowed to locally log on to these computers, and even administrators should not be logged on to a domain controller except when performing tasks with that computer that cannot be executed in any other way. Domain controllers should never double as workstations.

Being the repository of the Active Directory or your network's basic map, domain controllers are particularly important with regards to security. All information about users and resources in the domain is contained in the Active Directory, so inappropriate access could result in serious disruption of your network's functionality.

Operations Masters

Operations masters are special domain controllers on a Windows 2000 network that handle functions that must be carried out by a single server. The Active Directory domain model works on a multimaster scheme whereby all domain controllers share equally the burden of authentication and directory management. However, certain functions must be handled by an individual server in order to be properly managed without the possibility of data corruption during replication. Windows 2000 assigns these tasks to specific domain controllers as Flexible Single-Master Operations (FSMOs). The domain controller responsible for a FSMO is known as the operations master.

The following list describes the five different FSMO types possible on a Windows 2000 network:

Schema operations master
> Only one domain controller at a time can be responsible for the structure of the Active Directory schema. Before the schema can be modified on any domain controller, that controller must either already be the schema operations master or must request transfer of that role from the current schema operations master.

Domain naming master
> This operations master keeps track of changes to the domain structure of the current forest. It manages which domains are part of the forest as well as links to other directory services outside the current forest.

Infrastructure master

> Management of references to resources in other domains is the task of the infrastructure master, ensuring, for example, that changes to a username from a different domain are propagated to all groups that include that user.

RID operations master

> The Resource Identifier (RID) operations master manages the RID pool, by which domain controllers create security principals for resources on the network. Each resource requires a unique RID and in order to ensure that all RIDs are unique, a single server must be in charge of their assignment.

PDC emulator

> Since Windows NT 4.0 networks only recognized one Primary Domain Controller (PDC), only one Windows 2000 domain controller can emulate that function for downlevel clients and Backup Domain Controllers (BDCs). Under FSMO, however, responsibility for this functionality can move between domain controllers as necessary so long as only one PDC emulator exists in a particular domain at any one time.

The operations masters on your network should be treated with at least as much care as any other domain controller on your network. Since they manage very primary functions, their integrity is vital. Only full administrators should be allowed direct, local interaction with them and all unnecessary access points, such as extraneous hardware and network services, should be disabled. Only authenticated users and resources whose operative mission requires access to the operations masters should be allowed access to them and then only in such capacity as dictated by that mission.

Application Servers

Your application servers will be routinely accessed by the users of your network in performing their daily tasks. This means that the ACLs of the resources on these servers must be tightly monitored so that inappropriate access doesn't unexpectedly become available for resources other than those desired. Security groups should be defined that allow their members to run certain applications and membership in these groups should also be monitored regularly.

You'll also want to set up the permissions on these applications so that normal users can run, but not modify, the applications. This means setting up an application managers security group whose membership includes people responsible for installing, maintaining, and removing the network applications. In this way, you can have confidence in the trustworthiness of the applications themselves corresponding to the trust you place in the members of the application managers group. Inappropriate modification of network applications can lead to spoofing, completely subverting network security. Spoofing is described in detail in the section on internal risks.

File and Print Servers

Similar to application servers, file and print servers should be configured to allow specific groups of users access to the resources that they need in the proper execution of their duties. In this case, you'll generally have some users who are allowed full control over certain files and other resources, while others may be granted more limited rights, perhaps read only. Depending on the sensitivity of the data, you need to design a review schedule you can ensure that the users have the appropriate rights by and that only those users whose job functions prescribe it have access at all.

RAS Servers

A RAS server's function is to provide access to remote users via external connections, such as dial-up or tunneling, over a public network like the Internet. With this comes a certain amount of risk of external attack on your network, so RAS servers need to have strong security measures. By default, the RAS authentication methods, using the Kerberos v5 protocol, are equally as strong as standard Windows 2000 logons, so you do not need to make changes there. You will need to ensure, however, that only accounts that legitimately need remote access are allowed permissions to connect to your network via the RAS server, thereby minimizing the number of passwords that can make this connection.

Also, you need to implement a cryptographic security solution for any communications that travel across a public network. Windows 2000 implements IPSec for RAS connections by default, so again you should not have to modify this setting.

In general, it's wise to avoid publicizing the phone number or Internet address of your RAS server, thereby somewhat concealing the connection methods. However, a determined attacker will be able to discover this information, so in itself this is not a valid security measure. For example, port scanners can continually search the Internet for open VPN servers, and upon finding one, automatically begin a brute-force attack against it in an attempt to gain access. Such random attacks are occurring right now, so you need to be sure that your RAS connections are secured from unauthorized access.

Desktop Computers

Desktop computers will have slightly different security settings than will servers. For instance, you generally can limit the logon rights of a desktop computer so that only one person or possibly a small group of people can access it either locally or from the network. However, this could limit the ability of the users of this computer to create network shares that others on your network can access. This is simply a security/functionality trade-off that you'll need to evaluate with respect to the needs of your organization. In many cases, you can simply require that people use the public shared drive space for this purpose, which provides administrators with a greater level of control over the process.

However, in many respects, desktop computers need basically the same type of security as servers do. Keeping in mind that if someone gains access to any computer on the network, security is already compromised, and from that computer, the intruder can then surreptitiously access other network resources, you should attempt to make each computer on your network as secure as possible.

Since you cannot lock workstations into a closet and expect people to be able to get their jobs done, physical security takes on a different aspect with desktop computers. In some situations, it may be impossible to protect your workstations from access, even by the general public, such as in the case of an office salesperson who sits at a desk with a workstation. A variety of people may pass by that computer on a regular basis, many being complete outsiders and perhaps even competitors or rivals to your organization. In such cases, a policy of locking access to the computer whenever it's unattended is mandatory to ensure security. This can be accomplished automatically with a locking screen saver or you can rely on the users to lock the workstation upon leaving it.

In addition, you should probably limit the right to install software on the computer. Untrusted programs can do massive damage, especially if they are set to run automatically when someone with full administrative privileges logs on. Windows 2000 provides Remote Installation Services (RIS), which allows administrators to completely control the installation of software on all Windows 2000 workstations on the network. In most cases, there is no realistic need for users to be installing software on their machines.

In general, though, desktop computers need to be secured as much as possible without restricting access to the tasks assigned to those people using them. Only provide access to necessary information and only allow logons by people who are expected to be working there.

Portable Computers

Portable or laptop computers, as well as other remote computers that log on to the network via RAS, are a special class of workstations that require special security considerations. These computers have a high risk of theft, making them particularly vulnerable to inappropriate data access. After stealing a computer, an attacker has free reign to use all available resources to break the security of the machine. This means that in many cases, security takes precedence over functionality.

With portable computers, a user should be expected to secure the machine with longer, more complex passwords than would be required in a more controlled environment. Locking screen savers should be mandatory and should be set to come on after a relatively short interval of inactivity. No passwords should ever be saved on the system, particularly passwords used to access resources on the home network. And whenever possible, the machine should be physically secured with a locking cable to deter theft of the entire system.

In addition to these measures, the normal security features of other workstations should be applied. Access to resources should be permitted only on an as-needed basis and then only the minimum access necessary for proper dispensation of duties should be allowed. Users that are not normally expected to be working there should not be allowed to log on to the machine. Also, the right to install software should be strictly curtailed.

Kiosks

Kiosks, or workstations dedicated to use by the general public or other untrusted individuals, need a completely different security structure. If possible at all, these machines should be physically isolated from the network and should only contain information that is suitable for release to the general public. However, in cases where business reasons dictate that the kiosk be connected to the network, special considerations need to be adhered to.

On the kiosk, an account should be logged on that is specifically granted access only to the information directly related to that kiosk's functionality. The kiosk should be running software that cannot be terminated by any normal user under any circumstances, and this software should be set to load automatically along with the operating system. The prescribed software should be capable of performing the duties relegated to the kiosk and no others.

If these policies are strictly adhered to, then the kiosk should be safe for use in a public setting. Even if the kiosk is not intended to be accessed by the general public, it still should be treated as an unattended workstation and the same security policies should apply. The fact that no authenticated user is responsible for use of the kiosk means that it is basically an untrusted computer on your network and should be treated as though it were in use by the general public or even a professional rival. Access from this machine must be sharply curtailed for its presence to be tolerated.

EXTERNAL RISKS

Even if your network is not physically connected to a public network like the Internet, it faces external risks. Risks of theft, hardware modification, and even an intruder sitting down at an unattended workstation are all realistic threats to your network. Of course, adding a connection to a public network certainly increases the number of methods your network can be attacked by, but the recent business climate almost necessitates an Internet connection in order to remain competitive. In most cases, then, you'll need to weigh the business requirements against the risks when establishing such a connection.

The following topics are covered in this section:

- Hardware Theft and Modification
- Public Network Attacks
- Network Taps
- Business Partners and Trusts
- Brute-Force Logon Attacks
- Spoofing

Hardware Theft and Modification

Network attacks do not need to be sophisticated to be effective. An intruder with physical access to your computing hardware and ill intent can do immense damage simply by tipping over a couple of server racks. Just pulling the plug on a server or causing a hard shutdown can cause a certain amount of data loss. The gross theft or destruction of your computer equipment can have disastrous effects on your organization's productivity. Protecting your systems from physical access by outsiders should be a primary concern. Your computers face the risk of physical damage any time someone from outside has access to them.

Not only do you need to physically secure your computer hardware but your data as well. This includes any backup media that may be available. If a thief steals backups of your critical data, that information may be compromised since the thief could apply potentially unlimited computing resources toward accessing that data. Loss of backup media also puts your network at risk of actual data loss should the primary data source fail at the same time.

The other aspect of security covered by physically protecting your computer equipment is preventing the modification of its hardware. If an intruder were allowed an opportunity to install malicious hardware onto your network, it could be programmed to possibly siphon data and send it to the penetrator over the network or even via radio transmission. Malicious hardware could also be programmed to perform practically any other function without your knowledge.

One other item to consider in this area is the security of your data if a computer is stolen. If the thief does not have access to the computer through a legitimate or forged account, direct access to the data on the disk may be attempted. In such a situation, Encrypting File System (EFS) security measures will provide yet another layer of protection for your data. Even if the attacker manages to bypass the NTFS file system controls and the ACLs of the system, the encrypted data will still be inaccessible.

Public Network Attacks

Access to your network via public networks must be tightly secured or penetrators *will* find a way in. Hackers are out there every day attempting to break the security of each network port they can find. If your network is connected to the Internet, you absolutely must have a firewall in place, and that firewall must be configured to allow only traffic that is absolutely necessary to your organization's mission to pass through. All access to network resources must be authenticated by Windows 2000, and an appropriately authenticated account should only be allowed to access those resources legitimately associated with its needs.

Network Taps

Network taps are unauthorized methods of network access that can secretly access data as it's passed across the network. These taps can be either active or passive. A passive tap simply collects data that's passed on the network by other users. A simple policy of encryption, such as that provided with IPSec, will generally eliminate the risk associated with this type of attack.

An active network tap is one that not only listens to data on the network, but also introduces its own network traffic. This traffic could take the form of a replay attack, a modification of legitimate network transactions, or some other type of traffic. Again, IPSec encryption along with digital signatures and Kerberos v5 authentication should be sufficient to guard against these attacks.

Business Partners and Trusts

Whenever you open your domain structure to external users through trusts to other domains, you are introducing the possiblity of security risks. Again, the trade-off between the benefits your organization gains by establishing these trusts and the risk involved in having external access to your network must be thoroughly considered when planning such a connection. In most cases, reasonable security precautions can make such an arrangement very useful without any inordinate risk.

By careful management of the ACLs of resources on your network you can easily control access, allowing the external users to reach the intended resources without exposing any of the others to undue risk. By allowing certain specially created security groups to access those resources intended for the trusted business partner, you can even allow an administrator on the external network to manage the list of users included in that group. All you need to do is keep control of the ACLs on the resources in question. Delegation of that task can, in fact, be more secure than someone on your network managing group membership since the remote administrator is more likely to know who should be trusted in a particular group and who shouldn't.

Brute-Force Logon Attacks

Brute-force logon attacks are still a very common method of illegitimate access to private networks. This term refers to the repetitious and orderly attempting of all possible passwords in an attempt to happen across the correct one. You can apply quite a few protections against this type of attack with your Windows 2000 security policy.

The most obvious security against a brute-force attack is the enforcement of a complex password policy. By increasing the *space* (the total number of possible combinations a password of a given length and character makeup can consist of) of your users' passwords, you are effectively increasing the security of your network. In general, longer passwords are more secure than shorter ones. However, the character makeup of passwords contributes greatly to their space. A password consisting of all upper-case letters is easier to crack than one consisting of both upper-case and lower-case letters. Introducing numbers into the password increases its space again as does the addition of symbols and punctuation.

Some aspects of the increase in a password's space can have drawbacks, though. If an attacker is aware that all of your passwords have upper-case and lower-case letters, then the brute-force attack can exclude all combinations of just upper-case letters and just lower-case letters, which greatly reduces the number of attempts necessary to find the correct match. Simply allowing your users to choose passwords with both cases, but not requiring that complexity, increases the number of trials that a brute-force attack must go through to search each possible combination.

Also, enforcing a password policy that requires too much complexity may prompt users to write down their passwords, which further compromises the purpose of the password policy. However, you'll find that there are few methods you can force a lax user by to properly select and use passwords. Enforcing too strict of a policy encourages this user to write down passwords, while allowing too much leniency lets such users choose passwords that are easy to guess. Your policy here needs to reflect the demographic of users that will be involved, and accounts that you suspect of lax password usage should be allowed lesser permissions and undergo stricter monitoring.

Spoofing

Spoofing is the practice of accessing resources under the guise of an account with more power than your own. Often this is accomplished through the running of software under a more powerful account without the knowledge of the owner of that account. Spoofing requires that the malicious user has the ability to install or modify software as well as dupe the owner of a more powerful account to execute that software. This can happen in a variety of ways.

One of the most common methods of spoofing is for a user to install an application onto a system and instruct the operating system to run that application upon user logon. Then, each time someone logs on to the workstation, the application can load and check the permissions level. If the permissions do not allow the type of access the spoofing program is intended for, then the application quietly shuts down to avoid alerting the user of its presence. However, when an administrator or some other user with sufficient rights logs on to the machine, the program can perform its intended task with the rights of that user. By the time the access is discovered, the damage is usually already done.

Such attacks are a common scheme attempted by viruses. In order for the virus to do its damage, it relies on the expanded rights of the currently logged-on user, since the author of the virus is generally an outsider with no rights on the system being attacked.

Another common spoofing strategy is to modify the functionality of a legitimately installed program to carry out some other task. When the application is executed by some other user, the malicious code can carry out its functions under the account of the currently active and legitimate user.

Spoofing can be avoided by several methods. The first and most obvious is to disallow the installation or modification of applications by anyone other than trusted application installers. Also, only tested and trusted applications should be installed on your network. In addition, you should preclude access to the Registry keys that instruct Windows 2000 to load software upon user logon so that only trusted applications can start without being expressly executed by the user. This prevents untrusted software from ever being installed, much less executed, on your network.

Another important measure is to disallow full administrators and other powerful accounts permission to run applications in general. This way, even if a malicious program were to be installed, the powerful account would not be allowed to execute it without that person actually modifying the ACL of the program. While this doesn't remove the risk of trusted software being modified, it does keep new programs from being introduced and spoofed with an administrative account.

Scenario 4-1: Describing the External Risks

You have already seen all of the information you need in order to answer these scenario questions. However, you may find it helpful to review the case studies in Appendix C at the end of the manual. Suggested answers are provided in Appendix B at the end of the manual.

1. Describe the external risks for Barney's Bank.

   ....

   ....

2. Describe the external risks for Fairco Manufacturing.

   ....

   ....

INTERNAL RISKS

Not all security risks originate from outside your organization. Many of the risks your network faces are legitimately connected to your network right now. Either users maliciously taking inappropriate actions or people simply making mistakes that cause data loss can be highly detrimental to your network. The following topics are discussed in this section:

- Unqualified Personnel
- Hardware Security Issues
- Failure to Apply Recommended Security Patches
- Inappropriate Assumption of Rights
- Accidental Data Deletion or Corruption
- User Practices

Unqualified Personnel

One of the most serious threats to network security is the assignment of unqualified or untrained personnel to jobs instrumental to the proper implementation of security features. By allowing someone without the proper background to manage critical resources on your network, you are asking for trouble. At the very least you need to provide sufficient training to people expected to be in critical IT positions on your network, then you should also thoroughly test their knowledge before allowing the job to commence. Continue to monitor the new employee's effectiveness until you are certain that the appropriate tasks are being successfully executed.

Unfortunately, many organizations don't have the resources available to hire qualified personnel, nor are they in a position to provide such training or follow up on their employees' effectiveness. However, without taking these steps, practically every security measure on the network is compromised. A few simple mistakes by an unqualified individual can open security holes wide enough to allow an intruder full access to the network, thereby completely bypassing all other security measures.

For example, if a newly hired network administrator somehow allows a user to install a spoofing application on a machine, then when any other administrator logs on to that machine, the application will have newfound administrative rights, allowing it to access the security settings of the network and advance its author's status to include full administrative capabilities. At this point, the network security is completely compromised.

Hardware Security Issues

The hardware security issues mentioned in the External Risks section are not strictly limited to outsiders. You need to maintain strict controls on who can access your critical networking hardware at all times, allowing only trusted and well-trained personnel to enter the locked facility it's kept in. A disgruntled employee with a screwdriver can do as much damage as any sophisticated online attacker.

Failure to Apply Recommended Security Patches

Whenever security vulnerabilities become known and patches are made available, you need to ensure that those patches are applied to your network. Allowing known security holes to go unfixed provides attackers with easy access to documented means around your security systems. Keeping up with the security news and conscientiously taking action on publicized security issues is the only way to keep your network secure.

Inappropriate Assumption of Rights

Any time a network user secretly gains rights on the network, your network security is at risk. You may be aware of users who feel that they need expanded rights to properly do their jobs. If these users actually succeed in expanding their network security permissions, then your network is at risk not only from the person who has gained the expanded rights, but also from other vulnerabilities that this untrained and untrusted individual may inadvertently or malitiously create.

For example, many Windows 2000 services run under the all-powerful System account. By allowing users or even application installers to install services, you are giving them the power to execute software well beyond their intended security level. Under most circumstances, only full administrators should be allowed to modify the list of services running on any Windows 2000 or Windows NT 4.0 computers on your network.

Accidental Data Deletion or Corruption

Whenever anyone on your network has access to any of your organization's sensitive data, it is at risk of corruption or outright deletion. In most cases, your network users probably have good intentions and want to handle the organization's data in responsible ways, but there is no way to prevent accidents from happening. The inadvertent deletion of huge blocks of data can be disastrous to your company. Data corruption can also occur accidentally.

Probably the most effective countermeasure to accidental data corruption is proper training for those people who have access to your network. Making sure that people are aware of how to correctly use systems and can perform the tasks required by their jobs without struggling to understand them goes a long way toward ensuring data integrity.

However, even a well-trained workforce still makes mistakes. To cover these situations, two countermeasures are in order. First, be vigilant about ensuring that no one has rights that exceed those necessary for the proper execution of the job assigned. This limits the amount of damage that can be done by any mishaps that may occur.

Second, there is no substitute for a thorough backup policy. While not strictly a security measure, keeping good backups of all of your organization's data is vital to the continued well-being of the company. This means having regular backups onsite and offsite, which will allow you to recover from any data disaster with minimal loss and network downtime.

User Practices

Another major issue concerning internal security risks is the general practices of your user base. Again, this relates to their level of training and their capacity to implement that training, but it also reflects their loyalty to the company and willingness to perform their duties with security issues in mind. Your security system is only as strong as its weakest link and that link is often lax user practices.

Users who routinely select weak or easily guessed passwords provide potential attackers with easy access to the network. Also, users who write down their passwords compromise security in the same way. The password policy needs to be widely understood and strictly enforced for it to be effective. It also needs to be easy enough to use that your users can remember their passwords or you will have no way of keeping them from writing them down. You also need to keep close tabs on the password practices of your users. When you feel that a user is regularly lax about the password policy, you should strictly curtail that person's rights on the network to minimize risks should that account be compromised.

Another major area of concern regarding user practices is the handling of unattended workstations. Your network users must adhere to a policy of never leaving a workstation unattended without first locking it. This locking can be in the form of logging out of the network account; using the **Lock Workstation** button from the Windows Security dialog box, which is accessed by pressing *CONTROL+ALT+DELETE* from a running workstation; or by installing a locking screen saver. If screen savers are relied on, they need to begin after a short period of inactivity. This assures that no one can gain access to the workstation between the time the intended user leaves and the screen saver begins.

Scenario 4-2: Describing the Internal Risks

You have already seen all of the information you need in order to answer these scenario questions. However, you may find it helpful to review the case studies in Appendix C at the end of the manual. Suggested answers are provided in Appendix B at the end of the manual.

1. Describe the internal risks for Barney's Bank.

    ....

    ....

2. Describe the internal risks for Fairco Manufacturing.

    ....

    ....

SECURITY AND THE INTERNET

The Internet is a breeding ground for security compromises. Its widespread use has made it the ideal platform attackers can attempt to breech security from at a wide variety of networks, including government agencies, private enterprises, and not-for-profit organizations. Any network with a connection to the Internet faces a certain amount of risk.

However, in many ways the Internet has drawn attention to security awareness. A great many security vulnerabilities have been discovered due to the widespread use of the Internet and many of those discoveries have been made without the motive of directly taking advantage of them. In this way, overall security of many network resources has improved greatly since the Internet has become a popular medium for data communications. Windows 2000 in particular has benefited immensely from the security discoveries made on the Internet.

This by no means implies that your network is automatically safe from attack via the Internet. Quite the contrary, you need to keep a highly vigilant eye on any connection your network has with any public networks. Many of the hackers on the Internet have malicious intent, and new security risks are being developed all the time. This section attempts to lay out several of the more common issues to consider in relation to securing your network on the Internet. The following key topics are discussed in this section:

- Firewalls
- Web Browsers
- Internet E-Mail
- Denial of Service Attacks
- Inappropriate Services Installed

Firewalls

Any connection of your network to the Internet absolutely must be protected by a firewall of some sort. A firewall limits the network traffic that can pass from the Internet to the local network through a variety of methods, each of which helps to keep your network secure. The basic methods employed by firewalls for network protection are as follows:

- Packet filtering
- Proxy server
- Network Address Translation (NAT)
- Stateful inspection

Packet filtering involves the inspection of each packet that reaches the firewall. If a packet meets certain conditions based on source and destination IP address and port number, then it is allowed through; otherwise, it is discarded. In many cases, firewalls are configured to allow only traffic to and from Web browsers and mail clients, which greatly reduces the risks presented on the Internet.

Proxy servers act as a cache for Web documents. When a Web browser on the protected side of the proxy server requests a Web page from a server on the Internet, the request doesn't actually come from the originating computer. Instead, the proxy server requests the page, caches it, then delivers it to the computer that requested it. If another computer inside the protected network then requests the same page, the proxy server can deliver it without having to request it from the remote Web server again. Most proxy servers can be configured to allow Web requests only from certain servers on the Internet or to specifically disallow traffic from specific servers. This provides a certain degree of control over Web access, thereby increasing the safety of allowing users on the network to surf the Web.

NAT, on the other hand, actually allows the internal network computers to make requests directly to the remote Web servers. However, the network addresses of the internal computers are translated so that each computer on your network does not need to have a valid Internet IP address. This means that you can have an internal network built with the addresses defined as internal only, and NAT will handle the translation of addresses in order for those computers to access Internet resources. Web servers on the Internet will see a valid Internet address and won't be aware that the address translation is taking place. The router is then responsible for keeping track of the address translations and routing the appropriate data to the appropriate internal computers.

Stateful inspection checks the destination of each inbound data packet to ensure that it matches a previous outbound request. This prevents external systems from injecting unexpected packets into your network, which could have undesirable consequences. Only Web data that was directly requested by an internal Web browser can pass a stateful inspection firewall.

Web Browsers

Recent Web browsers, such as Microsoft Internet Explorer and Netscape Navigator, have become extraordinarily powerful applications. They are capable of running amazingly powerful applications that they download from the Internet on the fly. They also include fully functional scripting languages that can perform a wide variety of tasks on the client computer as directed by the Web server.

All this functionality leads to massive opportunities for security breaches. In fact, the modern Web browser has become one of the most popular methods of attacking the security of remote networks. As evidenced by the publicity surrounding Web browser security issues and their manufacturers' equally publicized efforts to counter each new compromise, Web browser security is a very intense battlefield.

You can hardly operate a business these days without providing at least some access to the Web for your network users. The resources available on the Web for practically every job function are immense. Thus, only under the most extreme security requirements could complete isolation from the Web be justified. The issue, then, becomes how to provide Web access with a reasonable expectation of security.

One of the most obvious and useful measures to take in this arena is the consistent use of the most current Web browser available and diligent application of all issued security patches. You may also find that standardizing on a particular Web browser for all computers on your network will reduce the administrative workload required to keep the browsers up to date.

Another issue to consider is the security settings of the browser you install. All modern browsers allow you to configure the level of access and functionality that you wish to permit for their use. In general, the default settings of common browsers like Internet Explorer and Navigator are strong enough to protect the average site, as long as the latest security patches are consistently applied. However, in certain situations, you may want to increase the security level of your browsers to disallow certain upper-level functionality, such as downloading or processing ActiveX controls, Java applets, or client-side scripting, any of which could, under certain conditions, constitute a breach of security. Just keep in mind the trade-off between functionality and security in these decisions and make the appropriate determination that protects your organization's resources while still allowing your users to properly do their jobs.

Internet E-Mail

Recent innovations in the capabilities of Internet e-mail clients have greatly increased the risk associated with using them. Computer viruses have increasingly been propagated via e-mail, both through executable attachments and in scripts that run directly in the e-mail client itself. The problem of e-mailed executable attachments can be handled by simple attachment filters enabled on the e-mail server that strip all .exe files from e-mail messages. This completely precludes the possibility of someone sending a legitimate program via e-mail, but in most cases, e-mail is simply the wrong medium for such a transaction. However, a strong policy of user education is probably much more useful here. E-mail users should be aware that no executable programs sent via e-mail are ever safe. Programs received in that manner should always be considered security threats and deleted without ever being run.

As for e-mail scripting viruses, the only truly effective security measure is diligent application of patches and review of current threats. Since recent viruses have been capable of executing upon receipt of the e-mail without the user even opening the message or taking any other action, there really is no other way to control such attacks short of stopping e-mail altogether. This would be a rather drastic and probably unworkable solution. However, user education remains an integral part of any Internet security measure and e-mail is no exception. Keeping your users informed on the latest security warnings and reasonable practices to avoid falling victim to an attack is an important line of defense in this ongoing struggle for security.

Denial of Service Attacks

Recently, public attention has been drawn to a form of network attack known as denial of service. Attacks of this form don't actually access data inappropriately but instead simply prevent legitimate users from carrying out their prescribed duties. Such attacks often interfere with server operations by flooding them with meaningless requests, each of which must be processed, thereby diverting all of the server's resources to this malicious flood of transactions. Since such attacks do not actually access any data, they are not correctly classed as security threats, but an Internet connection is the most likely source of such situations so they are discussed briefly here.

The most reasonable insurance against such an attack is the application of all current service patches for your network request processing services. You also need to be diligent about literature describing appropriate settings and configurations to properly handle denial of service attacks and be aware of what to do should your organization become the target of one.

Inappropriate Services Installed

One of the most common problems when connecting your network to the Internet is having unnecessary and inappropriate services installed. For example, if you have a File Transfer Protocol (FTP) server running on a client machine, an attacker could attempt to gain access to your network resources through that service. Since FTP does not integrate with the Windows 2000 single sign-on, clear-text passwords are passed over the network when accessing resources via this method. While a penetrator who manages to enter the system via FTP will still need appropriate rights to access any particular network resources protected by ACLs, allowing any access at all is a risk for your network. Still, once a penetrator finds any security hole into the system, means are available for dangerously expanding the rights, so keeping all unnecessary access locked down remains a high priority.

With this in mind, you should routinely survey the services installed on your network to ensure that no unnecessary services are running. On workstations or servers, you should disable any services that are not required for proper dispensation of the duties of that machine. If you are unsure whether a particular service should be removed, try running the computer without the service. If the necessary functions cannot be properly performed, reload the service; otherwise, leave it disabled.

Scenario 4-3: Designing an Internet Policy

You have already seen all of the information you need in order to answer these scenario questions. However, you may find it helpful to review the case studies in Appendix C at the end of the manual. Suggested answers are provided in Appendix B at the end of the manual.

1. Design an Internet policy for Barney's Bank.

    ....

    ....

2. Design an Internet policy for Fairco Manufacturing.

    ....

    ....

Scenario 4-4: Designing a Security Baseline

You have already seen all of the information you need in order to answer these scenario questions. However, you may find it helpful to review the case studies in Appendix C at the end of the manual. Suggested answers are provided in Appendix B at the end of the manual.

1. Design a security baseline for Barney's Bank.

    ....

    ....

2. Design a security baseline for Fairco Manufacturing.

    ....

    ....

SUMMARY

During this chapter, you were introduced to the following topics:

- Building a security baseline
  - Defining security settings for your network's servers, desktop computers, laptops, and kiosks
- FSMO types
- External risks to your network
  - Hardware damage
  - Network taps
  - Users from trusted domains
  - Brute-force logon attacks
  - Spoofing
- Internal risks to your network
  - Unqualified administration personnel
  - Hardware damage and theft
  - Lax application of relevant security patches
  - Users inappropriately gaining permissions
  - Accidental data deletion or corruption
  - Poor user practices

- Internet connection security
    - Firewalls
    - Web browsers
    - E-mail clients
    - Denial of service attacks
    - Installed Internet services

With this information, you can now procede to the building of your Windows 2000 security system.

POST-TEST QUESTIONS

The answers to these questions are in Appendix A at the end of this manual.

1. What are the five operations masters on a standard Windows 2000 network?

    ....

    ....

2. Who should be allowed to install software on computers on your network?

    ....

    ....

3. What is the difference between passive and active network taps?

    ....

    ....

4. Requiring extremely long and complex passwords always increases security on your network.

    A. True

    B. False

5. What is the stateful inspection method of firewall security?

    ....

    ....

Building Security for Windows 2000

OBJECTIVES

At the completion of this chapter, you will be able to:

- Analyze existing and planned network and systems management.

- Design a security baseline for a Windows 2000 network that includes domain controllers, operations masters, application servers, file and print servers, RAS servers, desktop computers, portable computers, and kiosks.

- Identify the required level of security for each resource. Resources include printers, files, shares, Internet access, and dial-in access.

- Design an audit policy.

- Design a delegation of authority strategy.

- Design the placement and inheritance of security policies for sites, domains, and Organizational Units (OUs).

- Design an Encrypting File System (EFS) strategy.

- Select authentication methods. Methods include certificate-based authentication, Kerberos authentication, clear-text passwords, digest authentication, smart cards, NTLM, RADIUS, and SSL.

- Design an authentication strategy for integration with other systems.

- Design a security group strategy.

- Design Windows 2000 network services security.

- Design Windows 2000 DNS security.

- Design Windows 2000 Remote Installation Services (RIS) security.

- Design Windows 2000 SNMP security.

- Design Windows 2000 Terminal Services security.

PRE-TEST QUESTIONS

The answers to these questions are in Appendix A at the end of this manual.

1. What is auditing?

   ....

   ....

2. ACLs should normally list security groups rather than user accounts to ease administration.

   A. True

   B. False

3. Describe the inheritance of permissions.

   ....

   ....

4. What is the main purpose of the Encrypting File System (EFS)?

   ....

   ....

5. What is the primary authentication protocol in Windows 2000?

   ....

   ....

6. Many Windows 2000 services run under the System account. What is a major risk of this situation?

....

....

7. What is the main concern with DNS security?

....

....

INTRODUCTION

With your security baseline defined and the risks to your network understood, you are now ready to begin building your security structure. In this chapter, we will discuss how to put your auditing system into place and you'll be introduced to the various aspects of security for your file system. You'll create and secure shared folders on your network and design an EFS strategy. The focus then turns to the various authentication services available in Windows 2000, and we will discuss how each is used and what its strengths and drawbacks are. Finally, you'll configure security settings for the network services running on your domain.

AUDITING POLICY

Auditing is a very important part of any security policy. Often people see auditing as being useful only after the damage is done, but that's not always the case. When properly managed, auditing can provide warning signs that someone is attempting a brute-force password attack. Of course, the data collected in audits can also help to mitigate the damage if a security attack actually penetrates your network defenses. Auditing, therefore, needs to be taken seriously and managed diligently.

The following topics are covered in this section:

- Auditing Basics
- Implementing Auditing
- Managing Audit Logs

Auditing Basics

In Windows 2000, auditing is the recording (in a log file) of events that occur on the network. This log file can later be examined to determine when certain events occurred and who performed them. This information, when properly used, can provide early warnings about password attacks currently occurring. It can also be used as a record to determine the culprit in a successful network attack and can be used as legal evidence should such an attack be brought to court.

Windows 2000 offers an incredible granularity of information that can be logged. You can specify precise actions on specific resources that should be recorded in the log. For example, files and folders have thirteen different events associated with them that audit entries can be recorded for, and for each of these events, you can choose to record successful and/or failed attempts to perform that action. The events available for a file or folder are as follows:

- Traverse Folder / Execute File
- List Folder / Read Data
- Read Attributes
- Read Extended Attributes
- Create Files / Write Data
- Create Folders / Append Data
- Write Attributes
- Write Extended Attributes
- Delete Subfolders and Files
- Delete
- Read Permissions
- Change Permissions
- Take Ownership

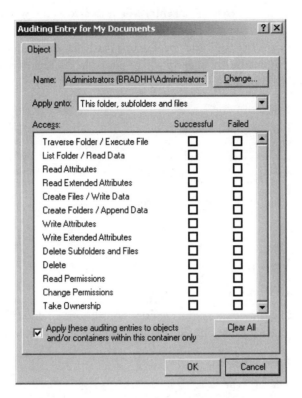

As you can see, this is exactly the same list of attributes you can modify for a file or folder's ACL. Such fine-grained control allows you to audit specifically those events that could contribute to a breach of security on your network.

Once auditing is enabled, an entry will be created in the Windows 2000 Security log each time an event that you have requested an audit for occurs. For example, if you specify that you want to audit the opening of a particular document, then each time someone opens that document an entry will be placed in the Security log. That entry contains the following information about the event:

- Date
- Time
- Type (success or failure)
- User who performed the event
- Computer the event occurred on
- Source
- Category
- Event ID
- Description

For each event category, the Description will contain different information. In an event describing the access of a file, the following details are recorded:

- Object Server
- Object Type
- Object Name
- New Handle ID
- Operation ID
- Process ID
- Primary User Name
- Primary Domain
- Primary Logon ID
- Client User Name
- Client Domain
- Client Logon ID
- Accesses
- Privileges

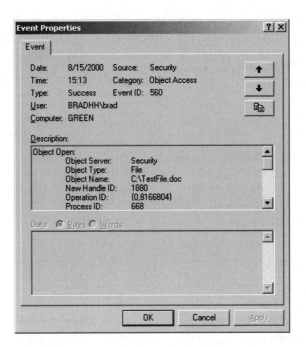

You can find the event listing in the Event Viewer, which is available in the Computer Management MMC. By expanding the Event Viewer and selecting Security, you can see the listing of all events that occurred on your systems.

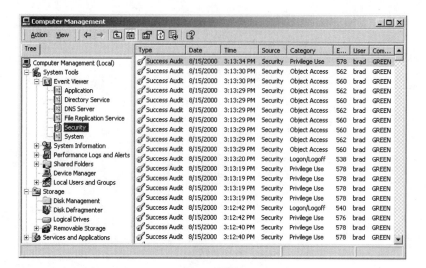

Auditing must be properly managed in order for it to be useful, however. Simply enabling auditing for every event on your system will not help to prevent or detect security breaches. You need to have a strict policy of examining the audit logs and that examination must take note of entries that could be related to security problems. For this reason, logging too many events could be counter productive since it will be harder to find important entries in a log filled with descriptions of routine and normal events.

The fact is that manual inspection of the audit logs is rarely sufficient in attempting to find anomalies. Some automated filtering of the logs is almost certainly required if you want to get any meaningful information from them. While Windows 2000 doesn't ship with any log-filtering tools, the section of this chapter on managing audit logs points out a couple of tools you may consider investing in.

Implementing Auditing

To implement auditing on your network you need to go through the following four steps:

- Configure your domain controller policy to enable auditing on your domain controllers.

- Configure your domain policy to enable auditing on other resources in the domain.

- Enable auditing on the computer managing the resources you want to audit.

- Specify which events should be audited for each resource.

These steps need to be taken in each domain that you wish to enable auditing for. In this section, we will discuss how to perform each of these tasks.

Enabling Auditing Policies

There are three MMC snap-ins that you need to enable auditing in for auditing to take effect on your domain. They are as follows:

- Domain Controller Security policy

- Domain Security policy

- Local Security policy

On domain controllers, the Domain Controller Security policy takes precedence over all other settings. If auditing is not defined for a particular type of event in the Domain Controller Security Policy MMC Snap-in, then the setting in the Domain Security MMC Snap-in takes effect. Likewise, if the setting in the Domain Security Policy MMC Snap-in is not defined, then the auditing policy is determined by the setting in the Local Security Policy MMC Snap-in. On computers other than domain controllers, the Domain Controller Security policy settings are ignored, so only the Domain and Local Security policies are valid.

The steps to enabling auditing are the same for each snap-in. The only difference is in which snap-in you open. All three of them are available in the Administrative Tools folder, which you can find by clicking on **Start | Programs | Administrative Tools**. The following instructions describe how to set the security policies in the Domain Security Policy MMC Snap-in.

1. Open the Domain Security Policy MMC by clicking on **Start | Programs | Administrative Tools | Domain Security Policy**.

2. In the Domain Security Policy console tree, expand Windows | Security Settings | Local Policies | Audit Policy.

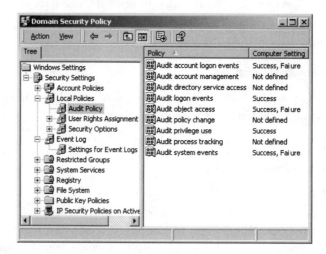

The Domain Security Policy Snap-in allows you to control the following nine broad groups of events that can be audited:

o   Account logon events

o   Account management

o   Directory service access

o   Logon events

o   Object access

o   Policy change

o   Privilege use

o   Process tracking

o   System events

3. Double-click on the item in the Details pane that you wish to audit to open the
    Security Policy Setting dialog box.

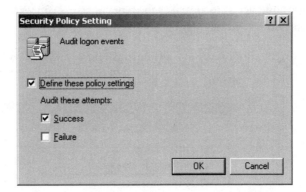

4. Enable the **Define these policy settings** checkbox to allow or disallow auditing to
    occur for these events in your domain, then select either **Success, Failure**, or both,
    depending on whether you want to record successful completion of these events,
    failed attempts, or all attempts.

Setting Auditing Options for Resources

Once you have enabled auditing for object access events, you can specify the objects you want to audit access to as well as the types of access you want to keep records of. For example, to set auditing options follow these steps:

1. Right-click on the My Documents folder in Windows Explorer and choose **Properties** from the shortcut menu to open the Properties dialog box.

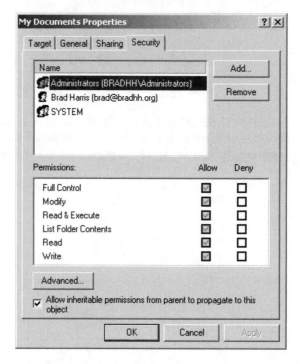

2. Switch to the **Security** tab of the Properties dialog box and click on the **Advanced** button to open the Access Control Settings dialog box.

3. Switch to the **Auditing** tab.

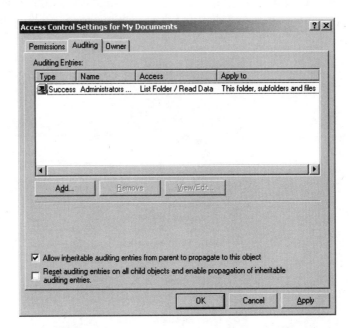

4. To add an auditing entry to the list, click on the **Add** button, which opens the Select User, Computer, or Group dialog box.

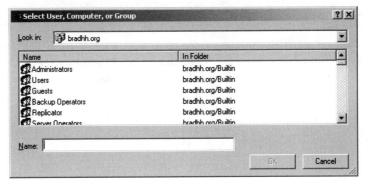

----

5. Select the appropriate entry or entries that you want to collect auditing data for from the list and click on **OK** to continue to the Auditing Entry for My Documents dialog box.

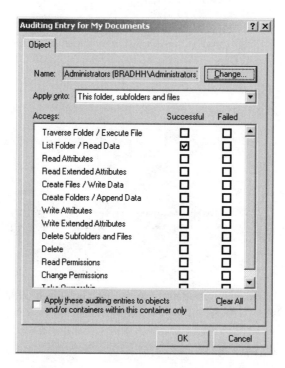

6. Enable the checkboxes corresponding to the types of events you want audited. For this example, enable **Successful** for the List Folder / Read Data access item column, then click on **OK** in all open dialog boxes to close them.

Managing Audit Logs

Collecting the audit information is the easy part of this task. Once you've done that, you need to have a way of sifting through the data to find meaningful entries that could alert you to security problems. You also need to find ways of avoiding problems that could arise when collecting this information as well as keeping the logs safe from deliberate modification by the intruders themselves. In this section, we will discuss:

- Strategies for managing audit logs.
- How to handle potential auditing problems.

Managing Audit Logs

In nearly every case, manually reviewing the audit logs will not be sufficient examination to consistently reveal the security issues that they're recording. Normally, some form of event log analysis tool is required to properly filter the logs and alert an administrator when important events occur. An example of such a product is the Event Log Monitor distributed by SystemTools LLP (http://www.systemtools.com). Without tools of this nature, though, you're likely to miss important events due to the massive number of other events that have little relevance to your site's security.

Windows 2000 provides rudimentary filtering tools in the Event log. By right-clicking on Security in the Event Log console tree and choosing **Properties** from the shortcut menu, you can open the Security Properties dialog box. Clicking on the **Filter** tab displays a group of options that can help you sort through the entries in your audit logs.

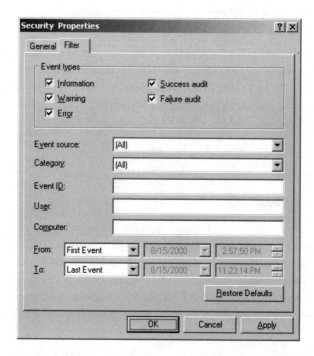

From this dialog box, you can instruct the Event log to display events only of a certain type, from a particular source, or in a specific category. You can also define an Event ID, User, or Computer that the log entry must match as well as a date and time range of events to be displayed. This can help significantly in finding specific events if you know what you're looking for but will do little to alert you of anomalies or notable unexpected security events. For that you'll still need a third-party Event log analyzer.

On the **General** tab of the Security Properties dialog box, you'll find several more settings that will assist in managing your audit trail. Here you can set the maximum size you'll allow for your audit log and how Windows 2000 should react if the log exceeds that size.

In most cases, you should set the Audit log to overwrite events as needed, under the assumption that you'll regularly monitor the size of this file, backing it up and clearing it before it reaches its maximum size. The theory here is that if you are regularly monitoring the events recorded in the log, you'll already know about significant past events before they are overwritten; but if new events are not stored because the log is full, you could miss important information. Overwriting after a certain number of days basically results in the same effect as the **Do not overwrite events** option since you have no way of knowing how long it will take the log to fill up, as explained in the Problems with Audit Logs section.

Problems with Audit Logs

Several problems can arise with auditing that can render the Audit log useless. These problems normally take the form of making it impossible to write events to the log or destroying the events that are already there. With a little planning, you can avoid these pitfalls.

One problem scenario involves the hard drive where the Security log is saved to running out of space. In this case, no more security audit information can be written to the log no matter what setting you selected from the Security log Properties dialog. To avoid this situation, you can place the Security log on a separate logical disk drive, either alone or with files of fixed size. By securing the ACLs of this logical drive so that no new files can be created on that drive, you can be assured that the Security log will always have enough room to grow to its maximum size.

The only way to specify a different location for the Security log is by directly editing the Windows 2000 Registry. Under the following Registry key:

```
HKEY_LOCAL_MACHINE\SYSTEM\CurrentControlSet\Services\EventLog\
    Security
```

the value named File contains the path to the Security log file. You can modify this entry in order to store the file in a location convenient to your network purposes.

Another problem may occur if you have the Security log set to overwrite events as needed. In this case, an intruder could perform some malicious action then deliberately cause a flood of other security events that will fill up the Security log, eventually overwriting the events that describe the original malicious action. Similarly, with the Security log set to stop writing events after it fills, the intruder could flood the log with meaningless security events then perform the malicious act without it being recorded at all.

A somewhat drastic solution to this type of problem is to cause the computer to crash when the Security log fills. By placing a REG_DWORD value named CrashOnAuditFail with a value of 1 in the following Registry key, you can force the system to shut down when the Security log exceeds its maximum size and **Do not overwrite events** is enabled in the Security Properties dialog box:

```
HKEY_LOCAL_MACHINE\SYSTEM\CurrentControlSet\Control\Lsa
```

However, this creates the possibility of an intruder mounting a denial of service attack on the server. You must determine what the appropriate needs are for your network when making the decision about how to configure your security logs.

Scenario 5-1: Auditing

This scenario is based on the case studies introduced earlier in the course. You may find it helpful to review the case studies in Appendix C at the end of the manual. Suggested answers are provided in Appendix B at the end of the manual.

Barney's Bank

What is an appropriate auditing policy for Barney's Bank?

....

....

Fairco Manufacturing

What is an appropriate auditing policy for Fairco Manufacturing?

....

....

FILE SYSTEM SECURITY

Keeping your files secure from inappropriate access is one of the main goals of your security policy. Nearly all data on your network is stored in the Windows 2000 file system; once an intruder gains full access to the file system, all secrets are lost and security is effectively broken. Windows 2000, therefore, provides network administrators with a great deal of control over how the file system is secured.

The following topics are covered in this section:

- NTFS Permissions
- Shared Folder Security
- Encrypting File System Security

NTFS Permissions

The primary focus of file system security is the Access Control List (ACL) provided by Windows 2000 NTFS. Every file and folder in an NTFS file system has an ACL, and each ACL has a variety of permissions that can be granted individually to different users and groups.

User Groups

Before you can work with ACLs, you need to define your security groups. This is the logical grouping of users for management purposes, allowing you to assign security groups to the ACLs of individual objects, then simply manage the membership of those groups. In most cases, this is the simpler approach since members of a security group will likely all have the same set of permissions for a wide variety of resources. Managing the ACL of each resource is an immense task. Normally there are considerably fewer security groups than resources, so managing the groups is much easier.

Available Permissions

Files and folders have basically the same set of permissions. When viewing the ACL from the **Security** tab of the Properties dialog box, you'll notice that folders have a List Folder Contents permission whereas files don't.

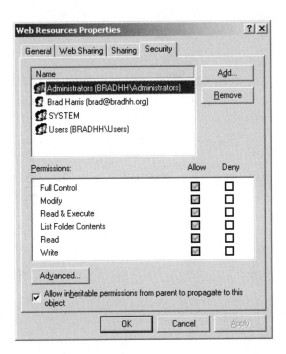

However, by clicking on the **Advanced** button to open the Access Control Settings dialog box, then clicking on **View/Edit** to edit the advanced security settings for any user, you'll see that files and folders have precisely the same permissions available.

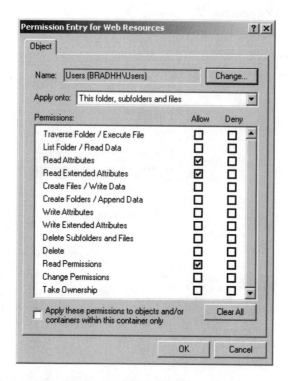

The meaning of some of the permissions differs slightly depending on whether they apply to a file or folder but basically, they have the same function. The available permissions for folders and files are as follows:

Traverse Folder / Execute File

For folders, this setting specifies whether the user is permitted to access files or subfolders of this folder even if that user has no rights to access this folder. For files, it specifies whether the user can execute this file, assuming it is an executable file.

List Folder / Read Data

For folders, this setting specifies whether the user can list the contents of the folder. For files, it specifies whether the user can read the file.

Read Attributes   This specifies whether the user can read the NTFS attributes of the file or folder, including such attributes as Hidden or Read-Only.

Read Extended Attributes

> This specifies whether the user can read the extended attributes of the file or folder. Extended attributes are created and written by programs other than the operating system. For example, Microsoft Word creates an extended attribute of Title on documents users create.

Create Files / Write Data

> For folders, this setting specifies whether the user can create files within this folder. For files, it specifies whether the user is allowed to modify data in the file, overwriting existing data.

Create Folders / Append Data

> For folders, this setting specifies whether the user can create subfolders within this folder. For files, it specifies whether the user is allowed to append data to the end of the file without modifying existing data.

Write Attributes

> This specifies whether the user can write the NTFS attributes of the file or folder, including such attributes as Hidden or Read-Only.

Write Extended Attributes

> This specifies whether the user can write the extended attributes of the file or folder. Extended attributes are created and written by programs other than the operating system. For example, Microsoft Word creates an extended attribute of Title on documents users create.

Delete Subfolders and Files

> For folders, this setting specifies whether the user is allowed to delete subfolders and files within this folder, regardless of whether the user has specific deletion permissions on those subfolders or files. This setting has no effect on files.

Delete	This specifies whether the user is permitted to delete this folder or file.
Read Permissions	This specifies whether the user is allowed to read the security permissions for this folder or file.
Change Permissions	This specifies whether the user is allowed to modify the security permissions for this folder or file.
Take Ownership	This specifies whether the user is permitted to take ownership of this folder or file. Having taken ownership, the user can then change permissions on the file, thereby taking full control of that file.

You can specify whether to allow or deny these permissions from each individual user or security group listed in the ACL. Deny settings always take precedence over allowed permissions, so if a file inherits permissions from a folder that allow the Users security group to read it, but the owner of that file has specifically denied that right for the file itself, then members of the Users security group will not be able to read that file.

Inheritance of Permissions

This brings up the point of inheritance of permissions. Each file and folder has a checkbox near the bottom of the Security page of its Properties dialog box called **Allow inheritable permissions from parent to propagate to this object**. If this checkbox is enabled, any permissions set on the parent that apply to this object will be automatically set on this object. Since, by default, this checkbox is enabled on all files and folders, it provides a simple method to make sweeping permission changes to an entire directory structure.

Keep in mind that the Deny setting always overrides the Allow setting in file and folder permissions whether or not the setting is inherited. Also, if you want to prevent inheritance of permissions for a particular directory tree, you can disable this checkbox for the root folder of that tree. This prevents settings made in folders above that folder from propagating into that tree but still allows changes made to that folder to propagate down to the rest of that tree.

For example, suppose you have a directory tree as shown in the following figure:

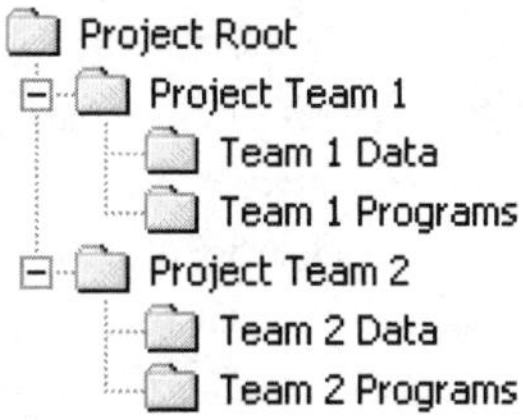

```
📁 Project Root
  └─📁 Project Team 1
       ├─📁 Team 1 Data
       └─📁 Team 1 Programs
  └─📁 Project Team 2
       ├─📁 Team 2 Data
       └─📁 Team 2 Programs
```

Suppose the **Allow inheritable permissions from parent to propagate to this object** checkbox is disabled for the Project Team 1 folder but enabled on all others. Any permissions changes applied to the Project Root folder will propagate to files in the Project Root folder as well as the Project Team 2 folder and all files and subfolders it contains but will not be applied to any objects in the Project Team 1 folder. However, any permissions changes made directly on the Project Team 1 folder will propagate to all of its files and subfolders.

Implementing NTFS Permissions

Setting permissions on NTFS files and folders is a very simple process. Right-clicking on a file or folder and choosing **Properties** from the shortcut menu opens the Properties dialog box for that object. After clicking on the **Security** tab (shown in the Available Permissions section of this chapter), you can work with the most common permissions for that object, or you can click on the **Advanced** button to open the Access Control Settings dialog box, whose **Permissions** tab is selected by default (see following figure). Here you can specify users or security groups that permissions should be set for by clicking on the **Add** button, or you can modify the advanced permissions for a particular user or security group by clicking on the **View/Edit** button to open the Permission Entry dialog box (also shown in the Available Permissions section of this chapter).

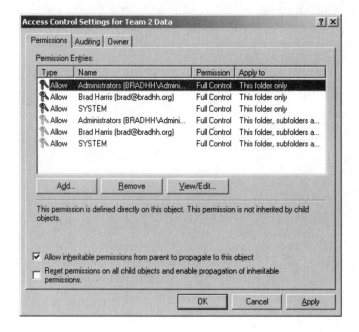

Shared Folder Security

NTFS permissions protect the files and folders on your computer from access by anyone who logs on to the computer either locally or over the network. For network access, however, you can specify another level of security. For the file system of a computer to be available to users across the network, one or more shared folders must be created. Each shared folder has its own ACL, and any user attempting to access files on that computer must have the right to access the shared folder before attempting to access any files or folders on the file system. This provides a convenient method that you can protect your computer from network attacks by: simply permit only the absolutely necessary users and security groups to have access to any shared folders on the system.

You can also limit the files being shared, thus limiting the computer's exposure to the network. If you only share a folder containing documents that you want others to access over the network, then only files and subfolders in that shared folder can be accessed via that share. This protects files and folders in other parts of the directory structure from attack over the network.

To set the permissions for a shared folder, right-click on the folder being shared and choose **Properties** from the shortcut menu to open the Properties dialog box, then select the **Sharing** tab. Click on the **Permissions** button to open the Permissions dialog box, where you can specify the permissions that you want each group to have on this share. By default, new shared folders give the Full Control permission to the Everyone security group, which, in general, is probably much too lenient. To tighten security, first add the groups that should have access to this shared folder, then remove the Everyone group from the list.

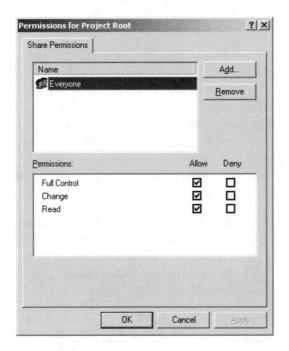

To add a new user or security group to the shared folder's ACL, click on the **Add** button to open the Select User, Computer, or Group dialog box and make your selection. Once you click on **OK**, the groups you selected will appear in the Name field of the Permissions dialog box. One at a time, select the users and security groups you added and set the appropriate permissions for those users or groups. Finally, remove the Everyone group by selecting it and clicking on the **Remove** button.

Encrypting File System Security

Windows 2000 offers the Encrypting File System (EFS), which provides data encryption for files stored on NTFS version 5 volumes. This provides yet another layer of security for your sensitive information. Even if an intruder attempts to bypass the Windows 2000 file system and its ACL protection, if your data is encrypted, it will still be secure and inaccessible to unauthorized people.

EFS is not a replacement for proper ACL protection on your files, but provides an added layer of security that protects your files in the event that the file system and its ACLs are bypassed. Keep in mind that if the ACLs for a file permit a user to copy the file to another location, that user can copy the file to a storage location that doesn't support EFS, such as a FAT drive, and the file will automatically be decrypted during the copy process. This makes the file accessible to the user in its new location.

Implementing EFS

Encrypting a file is a simple matter of enabling a checkbox in the file's Property dialog box. You can find this checkbox for any file by right-clicking on the file and choosing **Properties** from the shortcut menu. In the resulting Properties dialog box, click on the **Advanced** button in the Attributes section of the General page to open the Advanced Attributes dialog box. Enable the **Encrypt contents to secure data** checkbox to encrypt this file. Be aware that you cannot simultaneously encrypt and compress a file. Only one of these two options is available at a time.

Recovering Encrypted Files

If the user who originally encrypted a file is no longer available to decrypt it or the X.509 version 3 certificate that was used is lost, then the file can be recovered by a designated EFS recovery agent. An EFS recovery agent is a person responsible for a Windows 2000 account that holds an EFS recovery key. At least one EFS recovery agent must exist in the domain for users to encrypt files with EFS. Windows 2000 automatically defines the administrator of a domain as the default recovery agent for all computers in the domain. For Windows 2000 computers not connected to a domain, the administrator of the local computer is the default EFS recovery agent.

An EFS recovery agent must possess an X.509 version 3 EFS Recovery Agent certificate before being assigned to the task. To add a recovery agent to a domain, you add a user's X.509 version 3 certificate to the list of recovery agents as follows:

1. Open Active Directory Users and Computers and select the domain you want to add a recovery agent to. Right-click on the domain and choose **Properties** to open the Properties dialog box, then switch to the **Group Policy** tab.

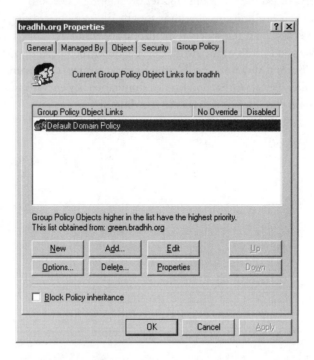

2. Select the policy you want to add the recovery agent in, then click on the **Edit** button to open the Group Policy Snap-In in the MMC.

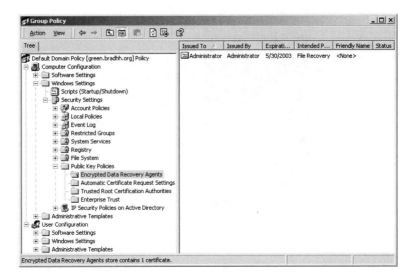

3. Expand the tree and select the following path:

```
Computer Configuration\Windows Settings\Security Settings\Public
    Key Policies\Encrypted Data Recovery Agents
```

4. Right-click in the Details pane and choose **Add** from the shortcut menu to start the Add Recovery Agent Wizard.

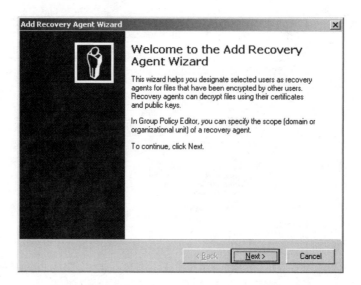

Click on **Next** and follow the instructions in the wizard to select an appropriate recovery agent.

How EFS Works

EFS works through a certificate system. Each user who wishes to encrypt files in your domain must have a valid X.509 version 3 certificate, which will be used in the encryption process. This certificate will be issued automatically if a user attempts to apply file encryption to a file and does not already have one. For more information about certificates, see the chapter on security tools, which covers the Public Key Infrastructure (PKI).

When a user applies EFS to a file, that file is encrypted with its own private encryption key. The file's encryption key is then encrypted, both with the user's public key and the recovery agent's public key. When the original person who encrypted the file opens it again, it is automatically decrypted with no action required by the user. The file's encryption key is automatically decrypted by the user's private key, then that key is used to decrypt the file. This decryption process is completely transparent to the original user.

Good EFS Practices

In most circumstances you should encrypt files at the folder level. Applying the encryption to a folder does not encrypt the folder itself but it does automatically apply EFS to all files created or copied into that folder. This is important if you use a program, such as Microsoft Word, to edit encrypted documents in that folder. Microsoft Word automatically creates copies of open documents in the original folder to facilitate editing and backup. If the original document is encrypted but the folder is not, then the copy of the document created by Microsoft Word will not be encrypted. However, applying EFS to the folder causes all files, including temporary files created by applications, to be encrypted in that directory.

Scenario 5-2: Securing the File System

This scenario is based on the case studies introduced earlier in the course. You may find it helpful to review the case studies in Appendix C at the end of the manual. Suggested answers are provided in Appendix B at the end of the manual.

Barney's Bank

1. How should Barney's Bank manage network file system security?

    ....

    ....

2. What is an appropriate EFS policy for Barney's Bank?

    ....

    ....

Fairco Manufacturing

1. How should Fairco Manufacturing manage network file system security?

   ....

   ....

2. What is an appropriate EFS policy for Fairco Manufacturing?

   ....

   ....

AUTHENTICATION SERVICES

Windows 2000 supports numerous methods of authenticating users attempting to gain access to your network. Several of these methods are holdovers from previous technologies available to support legacy applications, while others sport the newest technologies available. In most cases, you should attempt to utilize the newer authentication services whenever possible to increase the security of your network.

The following topics are covered in this section:

- Kerberos Authentication
- Certificate-Based Authentication
- Digest Authentication
- NT LAN Manager (NTLM)
- Clear-Text Passwords
- Remote Authentication Dial-In User Service (RADIUS)
- Secure Socket Layer (SSL)
- Integrating with Other Systems

Kerberos Authentication

Kerberos v5 is the primary authentication protocol of Windows 2000. Developed by MIT, it is widely regarded as a highly secure and easy-to-use authentication method. Many UNIX implementations also use Kerberos as their standard authentication protocol, which provides a built-in interoperability between the two systems.

Kerberos v5 offers high security features in its authentication methods. It never sends passwords over the network, so password security is never compromised during a Kerberos v5 logon. Once authenticated to a Windows 2000 server, the client can use that authentication for any other service on the network without having to re-enter a password.

The details of Kerberos v5 authentication were described previously. In general, though, the authentication process follows these steps:

1. A user presents a username and password to the logon client.

2. The client uses a hashing algorithm to generate an undecipherable hash of the password, then passes it, along with the username and some other information, to the Kerberos Key Distribution Center (KDC).

3. The KDC verifies the hashed password it received against the hashed password it has stored in the Active Directory. If they match, the KDC passes a Ticket-Granting Ticket (TGT) to the client.

4. The client uses the TGT to request session keys from a Ticket-Granting Server (TGS). It can use the session keys to communicate securely with resources on the network.

For the remainder of the user's logon session, the credentials established at logon will be used to validate this user's access to any resources on the network.

Certificate-Based Authentication

Certificate-based authentication allows users in possession of a trusted certificate to use that information to log on to the network. This form of authentication is commonly used in situations where the user may have logged on to a domain outside your forest and requires access to resources in your domain. A certificate stored on the client computer can be used to provide verification of the identity of the user. Certificate-based authentication is also used with smart cards. A smart card stores a certificate that corresponds to a PIN or password that only the holder of the smart card knows. By matching the PIN or password to the certificate, Windows 2000 can verify the identity of the user.

Use of certificate-based authentication has two prerequisites to proper operation:

- The user must have a certificate issued by a Certificate Authority (CA) listed in the certificate trust list of the domain.

- The certificate must be mapped to a user account in the domain.

For more information about certificates, including a description of mapping certificates to user accounts, see the next chapter.

Smart Cards

Smart cards are a form of certificate-based authentication in which the certificate is stored on the smart card. To allow users to authenticate via smart cards, you need a smart card reader at each point of logon. The user swipes the smart card through the reader, which extracts the certificate. The user must then enter the PIN or password that corresponds to that certificate. The matching certificate and password can then be used to complete a Kerberos v5 authentication, providing single sign-on service to the network.

Digest Authentication

Digest authentication is commonly used in remote access situations in which the client needs to authenticate across an unsecured network such as the Internet or the phone system. The server must have a reversible, or decryptable, copy of the password for any user who will be authenticating with digest authentication. This is because the protocol requires that the password be digested (hashed) on both the client and the server each time the user authenticates.

Digest authentication is very secure in that it does not transfer passwords over the network. However, since the passwords on the server are stored in a reversible form, extra precautions are required to secure the server's password database.

A standard digest authentication works as follows:

1. The server transmits a challenge to the client in clear text.

2. The client receives the credentials from the user and combines them with the challenge offered by the server, along with some information identifying the client computer, the domain, and the time of the logon. The client then performs a hash on the combined information.

3. The client transmits the hash along with the clear-text version of all of the other information (except the user's password) back to the server.

4. The server decrypts the password corresponding to the username passed by the client, then reconstructs the string that the client hashed and performs the same hash. If the two hashes match, then the user is authenticated.

In order for digest authentication to function properly, you need to enable storage of reversibly encrypted passwords on the Active Directory server. You can do this for the entire user database or for specific users one at a time. To do this for the entire user database, follow these steps:

1. Open the Domain Security Policy MMC Snap-in and select the following path:

    ```
    Computer Configuration\Windows Settings\Security Settings\Account
        Policies\Password Policy
    ```

2. In the Details pane, double-click on the Store password using reversible encryption for all users in the domain item to open the Security Policy Setting dialog box.

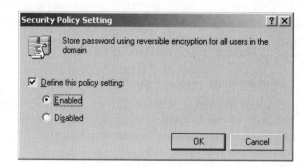

3. Enable the **Define this policy setting** checkbox and select **Enabled**, then click on **OK**.

To save only a particular user's password in a reversible format, do the following:

1. In the Active Directory Users and Computers MMC Snap-in, select Users from the console tree.

2. Right-click on the account you want to store the password in a reversible format. Choose **Properties** from the shortcut menu to open the Properties dialog box. Select the **Account** tab.

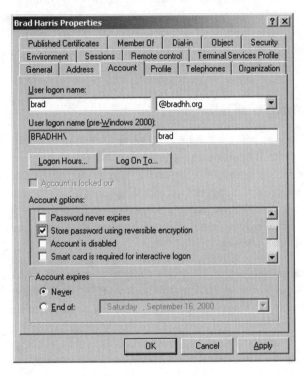

3. In the Account options area, enable the **Store password using reversible encryption** checkbox, then click on **OK**.

CHAP and MS-CHAP

Challenge Handshake Authentication Protocol (CHAP) and Microsoft Challenge Handshake Authentication Protocol (MS-CHAP) are very similar to digest authentication. CHAP, in fact, is a form of digest authentication, operating in basically the same manner. MS-CHAP, on the other hand, performs the same basic functionality but in such a manner that the server does not need to store a reversibly encryptable copy of the password, thereby allowing for greater security on the server. These two protocols are used primarily for logons across an unsecured network such as the Internet. In heterogeneous Microsoft environments, MS-CHAP will provide somewhat greater flexibility and security, but if you expect to service non-Microsoft clients, then you'll need to enable CHAP as well.

NT LAN Manager (NTLM)

In Windows NT 4.0 and previous versions of Windows NT and Windows 9x, NTLM was the default authentication protocol. Much like Kerberos and MS-CHAP, it securely authenticates users by passing only a hash of the password across the network, removing the possibility of network taps secretly gaining access to passwords. On Windows NT 4.0, the account passwords were stored in a flat file called the Security Accounts Manager (SAM), but in Windows 2000, the account information is stored in the Active Directory.

Windows 2000 retains backward compatibility with NTLM for situations in which you have both Windows 2000 and previous versions of Windows NT and Windows 9x on your network. This is called *mixed mode* and is the default mode for Windows 2000 when it is installed. If you are running a heterogeneous Windows 2000 environment, you can switch to *native mode*, which disables NTLM compatibility in favor of a strictly Kerberos v5 authentication environment.

Clear-Text Passwords

Clear-text passwords are the least secure but most compatible form of network authentication. Their security level is extremely low since anyone with a network tap can easily gain access to the password as it passes over the network. However, many applications, including such common ones as FTP and Telnet, only support clear-text authentication, so in certain situations it is the only option. However, if possible you should avoid allowing the same password to be used for clear-text-only authentications and your default Kerberos v5 logons. That separates the risk of exposure between the two systems so that if someone gains access to a password that accesses a clear-text-only application, it does not compromise the security of your domain.

Remote Authentication Dial-In User Service (RADIUS)

RADIUS provides a centralized method of authenticating remote access users on your domain. RADIUS is an IETF standard protocol published in RFC 2138 and RFC 2139 and is commonly used on UNIX networks to match dial-up users with their corresponding domain accounts. The Windows 2000 Remote Access Server (RAS) can act as a RADIUS client, passing logon credentials to the network RADIUS server for authentication. The RADIUS server checks the credentials against the Active Directory account credentials and responds to RAS by either authorizing or denying the remote logon.

Windows 2000 provides a RADIUS server called Internet Authentication Service (IAS). If you need centralized authentication services for remote access servers running operating systems other than Windows 2000, then you can install IAS, which is included on the Windows 2000 Server CD. It implements a full RADIUS server as defined by the IETF, so any RADIUS clients will function properly with it.

Secure Socket Layer (SSL)

SSL is a form of certificate-based authentication used primarily on the Web. You can use it to authenticate either Web servers or Web clients. For Web server authentication, you install a certificate on the server that allows clients to verify the identity of the server and securely submit information to the server via forms. Web clients can also install a certificate they can use to authenticate themselves to servers. This provides a seamless method for users to access secure areas of your Web site. As described in the Certificate-Based Authentication section, you can map client certificates to user accounts so that someone accessing your Web site with a certificate will enjoy all of the rights granted to the associated user account on the network.

Integrating with Other Systems

Windows 2000 closely follows many of the standard authentication methods defined by outside standards bodies. This allows for easy integration of other operating systems and clients into Windows 2000 domains as well as enabling Windows 2000 to fit into other standard networking environments. Kerberos, digest authentication, certificates, and RADIUS are all standards defined outside of Microsoft and supported by a variety of other vendors. Any clients or operating systems that properly implement these protocols will interoperate well with Windows 2000.

In particular, Windows 2000 meshes easily with Kerberos realms as implemented in popular versions of UNIX. You can set up trust relationships with an MIT-based Kerberos realm running on any operating system in the same manner that you create interdomain trusts in Windows 2000, thereby allowing users authenticated in the foreign realm to access resources in your domain under the standard ACL paradigm. UNIX servers or clients can also be members of a Windows 2000 domain, authenticating to the Active Directory under Kerberos v5 and providing resources to the network just as a Windows 2000 computer would.

You can also authenticate Windows 2000 clients in a UNIX realm under the Kerberos protocol just as though it were a Windows 2000 domain. As expected, this provides single sign-on to the realm and the local computer. Finally, client applications written to utilize Kerberos session tickets will operate equally well on a Windows 2000 domain or a UNIX realm.

Scenario 5-3: Authentication

This scenario is based on the case studies introduced earlier in the course. You may find it helpful to review the case studies in Appendix C at the end of the manual. Suggested answers are provided in Appendix B at the end of the manual.

Barney's Bank

Does Barney's Bank have a need for certificate-based authentication?

....

....

Fairco Manufacturing

Describe a reasonable policy that Fairco Manufacturing can authenticate users by on their extranet.

....

....

SECURITY FOR SERVICES

Windows 2000 services run when the computer boots and continues to operate in the background during operation of the computer. They typically service requests by applications and other services, both locally and across the network. Since Windows 2000 services normally run under the System account, they have far-reaching permissions on the system and the network and need to be carefully managed to avoid security problems.

The following topics are covered in this section:

- Common Services Security Issues
- Domain Name System (DNS) Security
- Remote Installation Services (RIS) Security
- Simple Network Management Protocol (SNMP) Security
- Terminal Services Security

Common Services Security Issues

Probably the best security for services is to disable any that are not essential to the operation of your network. For example, if you don't intend for people to access your computers via FTP, disable that service from all computers on the network. This completely removes a potential security threat.

Some services are essential to the proper operation of your network, though. These need to be properly managed to avoid security problems. Some points are common to all services running on your network computers:

- Run each service under an account with the minimum necessary permissions for its mission to be properly carried out. In most cases, the service requires the powerful System account to function correctly, but other services, such as backup tools, can be run under less powerful accounts without hindering their operations.
- Set the ACL of the local machine by going to the **Security** menu in Regedit32.exe and selecting **Permissions**. The permissions for HKEY_LOCAL_MACHINE Properties dialog displays. On the Security page, modify permissions so that only full administrators can install services.

  This prevents other, less-privileged users from installing services that run with administrative privileges, providing a prime opportunity for spoofing.

- Set the ACL of each service so that only appropriate accounts can modify its operations. In most cases, only full administrators should be permitted to manage services on your network, but some situations may prescribe assigning service management duties to members of the Server Operators group.

- Ensure that the ACLs on each service's executable and DLL files are set so that only administrators and application installers can modify them. This prevents malicious modification of these files, which would allow dangerous spoofing opportunities due to the wide capabilities of the System account.

- Unless it's absolutely necessary, disable each service's ability to interact with the desktop. This setting can be made for each service individually by enabling or disabling the **Allow service to interact with desktop** checkbox on the Log On page of the service's Properties dialog box. This ability provides the opportunity for an illegitimate service to present an interface to an unknowing user who could be persuaded to reveal sensitive information such as passwords.

Domain Name System (DNS) Security

By design, the information contained in the DNS is publicly accessible, so privacy is not the main concern of DNS security. However, you must be able to ensure that only legitimate changes can be made to DNS; otherwise, requests for a particular computer name could be maliciously redirected to a different machine, providing the attacker a variety of opportunities for spoofing and information theft.

The most important step toward protecting your Windows DNS servers is to set the ACL for the service to permit only appropriate people to administer it. You can do this by following these steps:

1. Open the Computer Management MMC and expand Computer Management | Services and Applications | DNS.

2. Right-click on the server you want to set the permissions for, choose **Properties** from the shortcut menu to open its Properties dialog box, and switch to the **Security** tab.

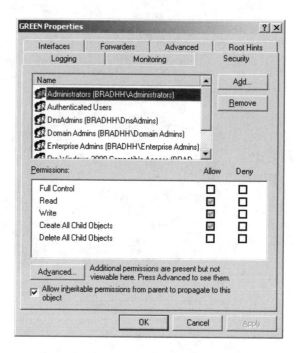

3. Set the permissions so that only trusted accounts are allowed to modify the DNS settings.

Remote Installation Services (RIS) Security

Client computer setup and configuration is typically considered a task best assigned to low-paid technicians. However, opportunities for security violations abound in this job. Installation of unauthorized software and improper configuration of approved software can do immense damage to your network. Windows 2000 RIS provides a solution to this problem by allowing a trusted administrator to design the installation configuration. The task of carrying out the installation procedure can then be delegated to a technician without compromising the integrity of the original installation plan.

The basic process of RIS is as follows:

1. An administrator installs the Windows 2000 Professional operating system on a computer and configures it with all of the appropriate applications and desired settings.

2. An administrator runs the Remote Installation Preparation Wizard, which creates an installation image on a network server.

3. The assigned client setup technician runs the Client Installation Wizard, which formats the client computer's hard drive and installs the prepared installation image.

The technician running the Client Installation Wizard doesn't need any more rights than the person who will be using the computer.

Another aspect of RIS security that you must consider is the authorization of RIS servers. To avoid the possibility of bogus RIS servers being used to create client computers with inappropriate installations, you need to authorize each RIS server before it can operate on your network. RIS servers are treated as DHCP servers on the network and are authorized by the same tools. Follow these steps to authorize your RIS server:

1. Open the DHCP MMC.

2. Right-click on the DHCP console tree root and choose **Manage authorized servers** from the shortcut menu. This opens the Manage Authorized Servers dialog box.

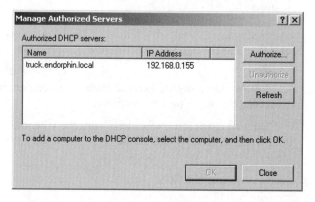

3. Click on **Authorize** to open the Authorize DHCP Server dialog box.

4. Enter the name or IP address of the RIS server you want to authorize and click on **OK**.

Simple Network Management Protocol (SNMP) Security

SNMP provides the ability to remotely monitor and manage many of the settings of your network. Using SNMP, you can configure computers on your network to send alert messages to the SNMP management system when significant events occur. This can provide you with an early warning if a system is the subject of a security attack.

The primary security concern with the SNMP service is ensuring that management messages are originating from a valid source. You can configure your SNMP agents to send an alert message if they receive messages from an unexpected source by following these steps:

1. Open the Computer Management MMC and expand Computer Management | Services and Applications | Services.

2. Double-click on the SNMP Service item in the Details pane to open its Properties dialog box, then switch to the **Security** tab.

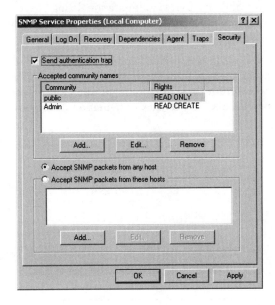

3. Enable the **Send authentication trap** checkbox.

4. Click on the **Add** button in the Accepted community names section to add a valid SNMP community this computer should participate in.

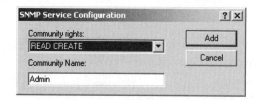

5. In the SNMP Service Configuration dialog box, enter the name of the community and specify the rights this computer should recognize for this community, then click on **Add**.

6. If all hosts in the specified communities should be trusted, then select the **Accept SNMP packets from any host** radio button; otherwise, select the **Accept SNMP packets from these hosts** radio button and click on the **Add** button beneath it to open the SNMP Service Configuration dialog box.

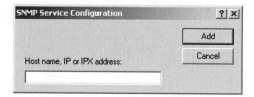

7. Enter the name or network address of a trusted host and click on **Add**.

8. Click on **OK** to close the Properties dialog box.

Terminal Services Security

Windows 2000 Terminal Services enable you to run Windows 2000 applications on virtually any computer on your network, including PCs, Macintosh computers, UNIX computers, or thin clients. Typically you'll need additional client software to process the client end of the transaction, but the Terminal Server is part of Windows 2000 Server.

Security for Terminal Services is similar to security considerations on any other network client. You need to provide secure communications over the network and control the accounts that are permitted to log on to the service.

These settings are configured in the Terminal Services Configuration MMC as follows:

1. Select Connections from the console tree, then double-click on the connection whose settings you want to modify to open its Properties dialog box.

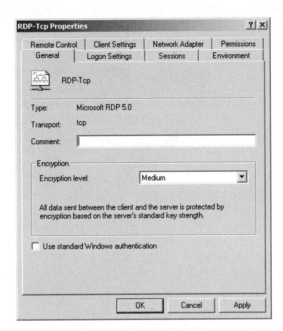

2. On the **General** tab, you can set the Encryption level to Low, Medium, or High. The settings differ from each other as follows:

   ○ Low

   Only data transferred from the client to the server is encrypted, protecting transmitted passwords and other typed information. The encryption level is 56 bits when using a Windows 2000 client and 40 bits for any other client.

   ○ Medium

   All data transferred to and from the client is encrypted. The encryption level is 56 bits when using a Windows 2000 client and 40 bits for any other client.

    o   High

All data transferred to and from the client is encrypted. The encryption level is 128 bits.

3. On the Sessions page, you can specify several parameters concerning timeout and reconnection of sessions. To do so, enable the **Override user settings** checkboxes; otherwise, these settings will be determined by the clients.

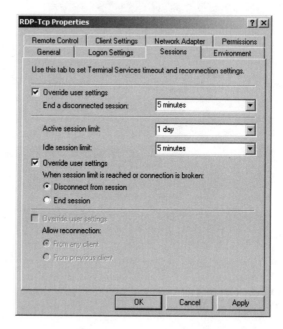

4. Click on **OK** when you have properly configured your Terminal Services settings.

Scenario 5-4: Securing Network Services

This scenario is based on the case studies introduced earlier in the course. You may find it helpful to review the case studies in Appendix C at the end of the manual. Suggested answers are provided in Appendix B at the end of the manual.

Barney's Bank

Describe the steps that Barney's Bank should take to securely install the operating system and application software.

....

....

Fairco Manufacturing

What problems might arise in implementing security for Fairco Manufacturing's network services?

....

....

SUMMARY

During this chapter, you were introduced to the following topics:

- Designing an audit policy
  - The basics of auditing
  - Implementation of auditing
  - Management of your audit logs
  - Security problems with audit logs
- File system security
  - NTFS security administration
  - Shared-folder management
  - Encrypting File System (EFS)
- Windows 2000 authentication services
  - Kerberos authentication
  - Certificate-based authentication
  - Digest authentication
  - NTLM
  - Clear-text passwords
  - RADIUS
  - SSL
  - Integrating with other systems
- Security for Windows 2000 services
  - Common security issues with Windows 2000 services
  - DNS security issues
  - RIS security issues
  - SNMP security issues
  - Terminal Services security issues

Stop now and complete the following NEXTSim exercises on the Interactive Learning CD-ROM:

Windows 2000 Network Security Design

Building Security for Windows 2000

Implement a Distributed Management Plan for an OU

POST-TEST QUESTIONS

The answers to these questions are in Appendix A at the end of this manual.

1. What is the danger of overauditing on your network?

   ....

   ....

2. Which security policy setting must be defined in order to be able to audit access to files and folders?

   ....

   ....

3. What security permission can allow you to delete a file even though its ACL denies you delete permissions?

   ....

   ....

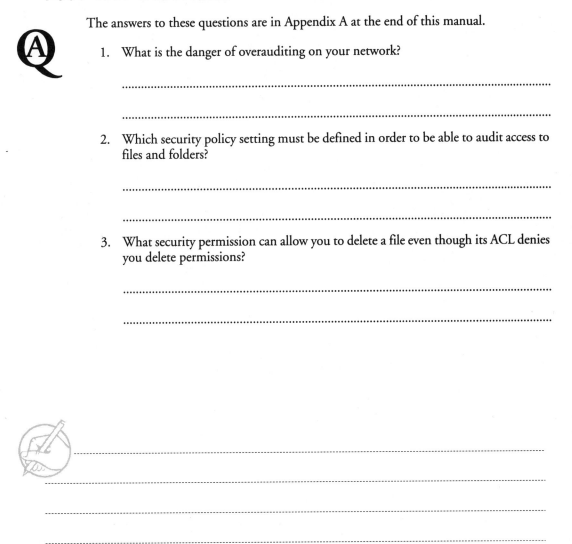

4. Describe digest authentication.

....

....

5. How can RIS aid in network security?

....

....

CHAPTER 6

Security Tools

OBJECTIVES

At the completion of this chapter, you will be able to:

- Design a Public Key Infrastructure (PKI).
- Design Certificate Authority (CA) hierarchies.
- Identify Certificate Server roles.
- Manage certificates.
- Integrate with third-party CAs.
- Map certificates.
- Provide secure access to public networks from a private network.
- Provide external users with secure access to private network resources.

PRE-TEST QUESTIONS

The answers to these questions are in Appendix A at the end of this manual.

1. What is a CA?

   ....

   ....

2. What are the common certification hierarchy organizations?

   ....

   ....

3. How does a CA notify users that a certificate is no longer valid?

   ....

   ....

4. How is delegation of authority more secure in Windows 2000 than it was in previous versions of Windows NT?

....

....

5. Name five of the nine main sections of the Domain Security Policy MMC Snap-in.

....

....

INTRODUCTION

Having built the basics of your security structure, you're now ready to set up some of the more far-reaching aspects of your network security design. This chapter will introduce you to the details of preparing a PKI on your network. We'll discuss certificates and CAs and how they interact with the resources on your network. We'll also discuss how to manage the overall rights and permissions that users and computers have on your network. You'll be introduced to delegation of authority and discover how broad security policies can be globally applied to all of the computers in your domain.

PUBLIC KEY INFRASTRUCTURE (PKI)

One of the most important aspects of your network security structure is the PKI. This is the basis of the certification of all of your users, computers, and network resources, providing a structure allowing each of these to trust one another. PKI provides encryption, secure communications, data integrity, and nonrepudiation for all aspects of your network. Your PKI can even assist in securing communications with external users and resources, integrating your network into a globally secure structure. The following topics are covered in this section:

- Understanding PKI
- Designing CA Hierarchies
- Managing Certificates
- Integrating with Third-Party CAs
- Mapping Certificates

Understanding PKI

A PKI consists of one or more CAs trusted to issue certificates to people, accounts, and resources on your network, along with the general guidelines that certificates are used by for authentication, verification, and nonrepudiation on your network. Basically, your PKI involves setting up a CA hierarchy on your network, which issues certificates to users, accounts, and resources. Those certificates can then be used for a variety of purposes, including the following:

- Authentication
- Digital signatures
- Secure communications using Internet Protocol Security (IPSec)
- Secure storage using the Encrypting File System (EFS)
- Secure e-mail
- Code signing

The two main concepts in PKI are certificates and CAs. A certificate is basically a string of digits that verifies that a particular person holds the private key corresponding to the public key in that certificate. Certificates are issued and signed by a CA, which is an entity created to validate the identity of users and resources, then issue certificates verifying that identity. For a certificate to have any meaning on your network, the issuing CA must be trusted, meaning that you must have faith in its ability to authenticate users and resources before issuing certificates to them. The CA also takes responsibility for revoking certificates that, for whatever reason, are no longer valid.

A standard certificate holds the following pieces of information:

- Issuer's identifying information
- Subject's identifying information
- Subject's public key
- Period that the certificate is valid for (start and stop dates)
- Issuer's digital signature

The certificate issuer is the CA that generated and issued the certificate. The subject is the person, account, resource, or organization the certificate was issued to. Trust must be placed in the issuer for a certificate to have any validity. If you trust the issuer of the certificate to properly verify the subject's identity prior to issuing certificates and to promptly revoke certificates that are no longer valid, then you can have faith that a certificate contains a public key corresponding to a private key held by the subject of the certificate.

To understand PKI you also need to have a handle on public key encryption. The idea is that a pair of keys, one public and one private, is issued to a particular person, organization, resource, or account. These keys are capable of encrypting and decrypting information for use in various situations on the network, including IPSec communications or EFS. The holder of the pair of keys distributes the public key to those people and resources who may need to securely communicate with the key holder. Those people or resources use the public key to encrypt a message. Only the corresponding private key can decrypt messages encrypted by the public key, so as long as the private key remains a secret possessed only by the original holder, only that person can decrypt messages encrypted with the corresponding public key, ensuring privacy of communications.

The key pair can also be used to digitally sign a message. Use this application in situations that don't require the message to be secure, but in which the integrity and nonrepudiation of the message are essential. A user digitally signs a message with a private key, then transmits the message (in clear text), the digital signature, and the certificate to the intended recipient. That recipient can then use the public key in the certificate to verify that the message was sent by the subject of that certificate.

Designing CA Hierarchies

Often a large organization will need more than one CA to function efficiently, much the way the organization requires multiple domain controllers. In order to properly manage the various CAs in your organization, you should organize them into a hierarchy, much like the domain structure is organized. In this manner, trust in the CAs is maintained by trust in the root of the hierarchy, known as the root CA.

In a CA hierarchy, a CA issues certificates to its child CAs. As with all other certificates, trust in the issuer translates to trust in the subject of the certificate, so if you trust the first CA then you can trust all of its child CAs. This transference of trust propagates all the way back to the root CA, which is the top CA in the hierarchy. You need to install the certificate for this CA in the trusted certificate store for each entity that is to trust any of the certificates issued by any of the CAs in the hierarchy. This one certificate validates the certificates issued by the rest of the CAs.

Each CA must take responsibility for maintaining a CRL for each certificate it issues, including certificates for child CAs. In this way, you can be sure that any CA not listed on its parent's CRL is a valid and trusted CA and that certificates it issues accurately bind public keys to the stated holders of the corresponding private keys.

There are many reasons to set up a CA hierarchy and just as many methods to follow in setting one up. Probably the most common use of a CA hierarchy is to provide better response to Certificate Services by increasing the number of CAs available on the network. Your choice of organization for your CA hierarchy determines the roles that the various CAs will take on. Some of the more common CA hierarchy designs are as follows:

- Certificate purpose organization
- Geographic organization
- Political organization

Certificate purpose organization bases your CA hierarchy on the purpose of the certificates being issued. For example, one CA or group of CAs could be responsible for issuing authentication certificates, another CA could issue EFS certificates, and yet a third could issue certificates for IPSec. You can specify the child CA's role in the certificate issued by its parent. This certificate validates the child CA's authority to grant certificates. For instance, if you assign a particular CA the right to issue only authentication certificates, then any other certificates from this CA will be ignored. This provides a clear division of authority on your network.

Another method of distributing the certification roles is to have CAs in each physical location of your organization. This allows you to minimize traffic over the slow network links between locations, providing local certificate services at each facility. Each CA's role is to provide Certificate Services to users and resources physically near it.

Another common CA hierarchy is organized along political boundaries in the company. Individual CAs can take on the role of servicing one of the departments of the company. For instance, the development team, and the accounting, sales, and human resources departments may each have its own CA. These individual CAs can operate independently of each other, effectively distributing the certification burden.

Another benefit of building a CA hierarchy is that if one of the subordinate CAs becomes unavailable due to its certificate being revoked or any other reason, it doesn't interfere with Certificate Services on the other CAs. If necessary, you can assign the tasks of the failed CA to other CAs on the network while restoring service to the failed CA.

To set up a CA hierarchy, you first need to define a root CA for your organization. This is simply a matter of choosing the Windows 2000 server that you wish to be the root CA and installing Certificate Services on it. In the process of installing Certificate Services, you can specify that this should be the root CA for your organization. You can do this by following these steps:

1. In the Windows 2000 Control Panel, double-click on Add/Remove Programs to open the Add Remove Programs dialog box. Click on the Add/Remove Windows Components icon on the left-hand side. This opens the Windows Components Wizard.

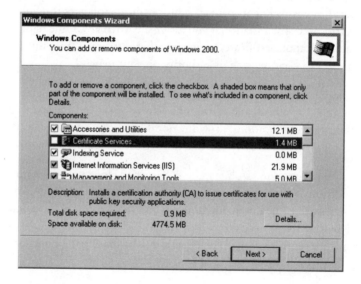

2. Double-click on Certificate Services to open the Certificate Services dialog box.

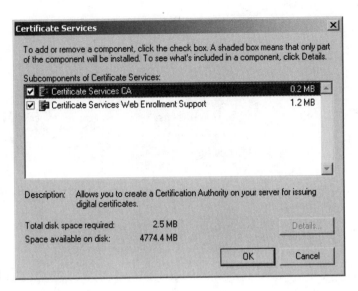

3. Enable the **Certificate Services CA** and **Certificate Services Web Enrollment Support** checkboxes. When enabling the **Certificate Services CA** checkbox, a dialog box will appear warning you that once Certificate Services are installed, you will no longer be able to rename the computer and it won't be able to join or leave a domain. Click on **Yes** to acknowledge the warning, then click on **OK** to close the Certificate Services dialog box.

4. Click on **Next** to configure Certificate Services.

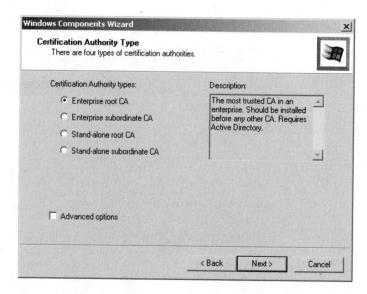

5. Here you'll need to select the type of CA you want this computer to be. The choices are as follows:

Enterprise root CA

Root CA in an Active Directory environment

Enterprise subordinate CA

A subordinate CA in an Active Directory environment. An enterprise root CA must be installed on your network prior to installing an enterprise subordinate CA.

Stand-alone root CA

Root CA on a network without Active Directory

Stand-alone subordinate CA

A subordinate CA on a network without Active Directory. A root CA must be installed on your network prior to installing a stand-alone subordinate CA.

To install your root CA on an Active Directory network, select **Enterprise root CA** and click on **Next** to continue.

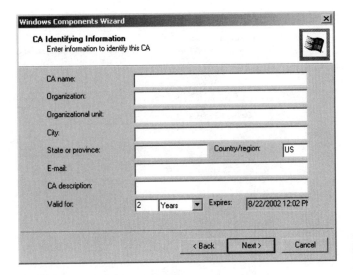

6. Enter the information identifying your CA. This information specifies details about the CA that will be included in each certificate it issues. Once installation is complete, none of this information can be changed.

7. Specify the time period this root CA is valid for. This relates to the time period you can have confidence for that the private key for this CA has not been compromised. For a 4,096-bit RSA key, and considering the current state of computing technology, a brute-force attack could take up to 20 years or more to compromise the key.

   You also need to consider the propagation of validity periods in certificates issued by this CA. By design, no CA can issue a certificate that expires after its own certificate expires. For example, if this CA's certificate expires in 9 months, the longest period it can only issue certificates that are valid for is 9 months, thus ensuring that no certificates it issues will still be in force after this CA's certificate expires. Since CAs typically issue certificates that should be valid for up to 2 years, you should probably set the Valid for field to 5 years and plan to reissue the root CA's certificate within the next 3 years.

   Click on **Next** to continue.

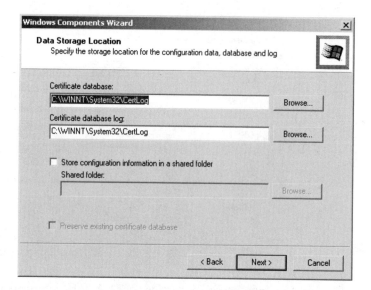

8. Next, you need to specify where you'll store the certificate database for this CA. In most cases, the default location is fine, but if you want to specify another location, click on the **Browse** button and select the desired location. For enterprise CAs, you don't need to store configuration information in a shared folder since the information is available in the Active Directory. Click on **Next** to complete the installation.

9. The installation will stop all IIS services running on this computer during installation of Certificate Services.

Installing subordinate CAs follows the same set of steps except that a step is added whereby you have to select the parent CA for the CA you are installing. Therefore, you end up building the CA hierarchy from the root down, and as each CA is installed, it is automatically trusted as a subordinate of its parent CA.

Managing Certificates

Once you have your CA hierarchy in place, you can begin the task of managing the certificates on your network. This involves several basic tasks, including the following:

- Defining Certificate Templates
- Managing CRLs

Defining Certificate Templates

The Windows 2000 PKI architecture allows you to set up certificate templates that users can select from when requesting certificates. This simplifies the request process from the user's end and helps to ensure that proper certificates are issued in proper situations, thereby easing the administrative burden.

A certificate template specifies a type of certificate that is available from a particular CA. For each CA on your network, you can select which certificate templates it can provide to users and resources. The possible certificate templates and their intended purposes are as follows:

EFS Recovery Agent	Recovers EFS files encrypted by other users in the domain
Basic EFS	Encrypts and recovers personal files via EFS
Domain Controller	Client and server authentication
Web Server	Server authentication
Computer	Client and server authentication
User	Basic EFS, secure e-mail, and client authentication
Subordinate Certification Authority	All Certificate Services

Administrator	Code signing, signing a list of trusted CAs, basic EFS, secure e-mail, and client authentication
User Signature Only	Secure e-mail and client authentication
Smartcard User	Secure e-mail, client authentication, and smart card logon
Authenticated Session	Client authentication
Smartcard Logon	Client authentication and smart card logon
Code Signing	Code signing
Trust List Signing	Signs a list of trusted root CAs
Enrollment Agent	Certificate request agent
Exchange Enrollment Agent (Offline request)	Offline certificate request agent
Enrollment Agent (Computer)	Certificate request agent for computers
IPSec	Internet Protocol Security
IPSec (Offline request)	Offline Internet Protocol Security
Router (Offline request)	Client authentication
CEP Encryption	Certificate request agent
Exchange User	Secure e-mail and client authentication
Exchange Signature Only	Secure e-mail and client authentication

You can specify which templates are available on a particular server by following these steps:

1. Open the Certification Authority MMC Snap-in by choosing **Start | Programs | Administrative Tools | Certification Authority,** then select Policy Settings.

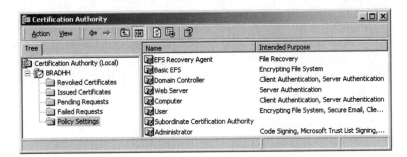

2. To add a certificate template, select **Action | New | Certificate to Issue.** The Select Certificate Template dialog box opens.

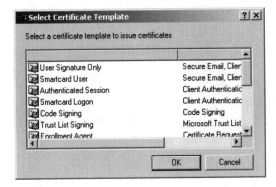

3. Select one or more templates you want this CA to provide and click on **OK.**

4. To remove a template from the CA, highlight it and click on **Delete.**

Managing CRLs

One of the main functions of a CA is to keep track of revoked certificates and maintain an up-to-date CRL. Whenever a certificate should no longer be trusted, it needs to be revoked, and notice of that revocation needs to be published in a place that will be checked by anyone attempting to validate a certificate.

For example, if a user's private key is stolen, the certificate can no longer be trusted. That certificate needs to be revoked but simply revoking the certificate doesn't prevent the thief from attempting to use it. Therefore, each time a certificate is used, the entity validating the certificate must check the published CRL for the CA that issued the certificate. If that certificate is on the CRL, use of the certificate will be denied.

Administrators can manually revoke a certificate whenever necessary, for instance, if an employee leaves the organization. To do so, follow these steps:

1. In the Certification Authority MMC Snap-in, select Issued Certificates.

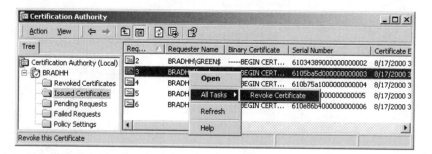

2. Right-click on the certificate you want to revoke and select **All Tasks | Revoke Certificate** from the shortcut menu to open the Certificate Revocation dialog box.

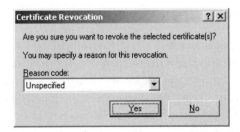

3. Select the reason that this certificate is being revoked from the Reason code drop-down list and click on **OK**. Possible reasons for revoking a certificate are as follows:

Unspecified

No reason is specified for revoking the certificate.

Key Compromise

The private key for this certificate was compromised.

CA Compromise

This CA was compromised. Normally this would require revoking all certificates issued by this CA.

Affiliation Changed

The user this certificate was issued to is no longer affiliated with this organization or OU.

Superseded

The certificate was superseded by another certificate.

Cessation of Operation

The resource this certificate was issued to is no longer operating.

Integrating with Third-Party CAs

If you are operating a Web site or have other interactions with people outside your own organization, you may want to integrate your certification hierarchy with a commercial CA. Many commercial CAs are available but the most common one currently operating is VeriSign, Inc. (http://www.verisign.com). Basically, a commercial CA sells a service of verification of the identity of the person, organization, or computer and issues certificates that reflect that verified identity. Of course, for the certificate to be valid, the resource the certificate is presented to must trust the commercial CA.

To establish trust in an external CA, you need to add that CA to the Trusted Root Certification Authorities policy for your domain. To do so, follow these steps:

1. Request a certificate from the external CA that you want to trust on your domain and save that certificate as a file accessible from the domain controller.

2. In the Domain Security Policy MMC Snap-in, select Trusted Root Certification Authorities by expanding Windows Settings | Security Settings | Public Key Policies.

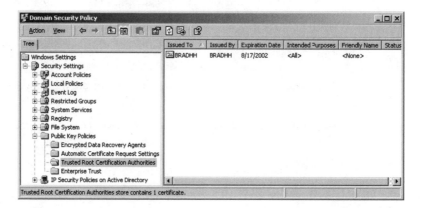

3. Select **Action | All Tasks | Import** to start the Certificate Import Wizard. Read the introductory text and click on **Next** to begin.

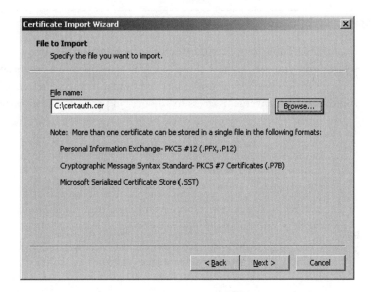

4. Click on **Browse** to find the certificate file received from the external CA, then click on **Next**.

5. Click on **Next** again to place the certificate in the Trusted Root Certification Authorities store, then click on **Finish** to complete the process.

Mapping Certificates

In order to be able to use certificates for authentication purposes, such as logging on with smart cards, you need to have those certificates mapped to a user account on the domain. Windows 2000 provides a simple method of mapping certificates to accounts, allowing you to provide convenient access to any user in possession of a trusted certificate.

To map a certificate to a user account, follow these steps:

1. In the Active Directory Users and Computers MMC Snap-in, select Users for the domain this user is in.

2. In the Details pane, right-click on the user account that the certificate should be mapped to and choose **Name Mappings** from the shortcut menu to open the Security Identity Mapping dialog box.

3. Click on the **Add** button to open the Add Certificate dialog box, which allows you to find the certificate you want mapped to this account.

4. Select the appropriate certificate and click on **Open**.

The Add Certificate dialog box opens automatically.

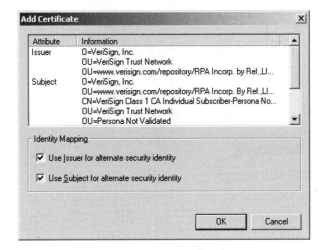

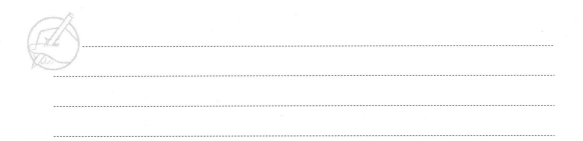

5. To ensure that this is a one-to-one mapping between the certificate and the user account, enable both the **Use Issuer for alternate security identity** and **Use Subject for alternate security identity** checkboxes. If you disable the first checkbox, then all certificates with the same subject will automatically apply to this user account and vice versa.

Scenario 6-1: Managing the Public Key Infrastructure

This scenario is based on the case studies introduced earlier in the course. You may find it helpful to review the case studies in Appendix C at the end of the manual. Suggested answers are provided in Appendix B at the end of the manual.

Barney's Bank

1. What is an appropriate certification hierarchy for Barney's Bank?

   ....

   ....

2. Should Barney's Bank consider integrating with an external CA?

   ....

   ....

Fairco Manufacturing

1. What is an appropriate certification hierarchy for Fairco Manufacturing?

   ....

   ....

2. Should Fairco Manufacturing consider integrating with an external CA?

   ....

   ....

MANAGING RIGHTS AND PERMISSIONS

Windows 2000 provides several tools to ease the management of rights and permissions for your network users and computers. Because Windows 2000 allows you to delegate authority for certain well-defined tasks, you can securely spread the management chores among several people on your network. You can also define policies that are enforced across the entire domain, giving you a consistent network platform your organization can carry out its tasks on. Central management of domainwide security policies also eases the administration burden, leaving you with more time to handle the larger issues on your network. The following topics are covered in this section:

- Delegation of Authority
- Security Policies

Delegation of Authority

One of the most useful features of Windows 2000 is the ability to delegate authority for various tasks to people more appropriately responsible for the tasks than full administrators. In previous versions of Windows NT, only administrators could do such things as manage user rights and design security groups. Now you can specify other accounts that have rights to manage such tasks within their own area of control without giving out complete control of the network to a large group of people.

Delegation of control is basically handled by the Delegation of Control Wizard. It allows you to:

- Select the users or groups who will have control.
- Specify which resources will be controlled.
- Set specific tasks that will be delegated.

This gives you a great deal of granularity in specifying exactly what tasks you will delegate on which objects. You manage this entirely from the Active Directory Users and Computers MMC Snap-in, conveniently placing management of your delegation strategy in a single interface.

For example, if you were to delegate the ability to manage user accounts in the Technical Production department to Joe Freeman, a member of that department, you would follow these steps:

1. In the Active Directory Users and Computers MMC Snap-in, right-click on the OU corresponding to the Technical Production department and select **Delegate Control** from the shortcut menu.

2. Read the introductory text for the Delegation of Control Wizard and click on **Next** to continue.

3. Click on **Add** to open the User, Computer, or Group dialog box, from which you can select users from your domain that you want to delegate control to. Click on **OK** to close the User, Computer, or Group dialog box and return to the Delegation of Control Wizard dialog box. Click on **Next** to continue.

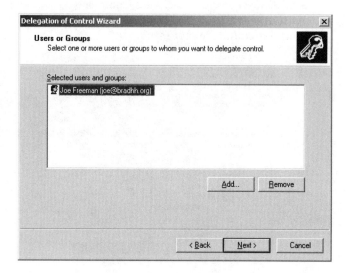

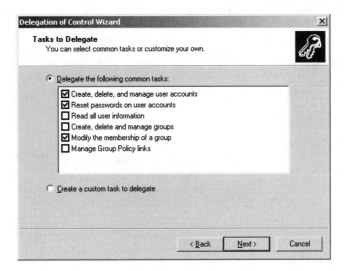

4. Select the tasks that you want to delegate to this user. A list of commonly delegated tasks is available here, but if you prefer to be specific about which objects and which rights the delegate should control, you can select **Create a custom task to delegate** before clicking on **Next**. For this example, however, Joe Freeman only needs to be able to manage user accounts through the three tasks selected in the figure.

5. Review the settings you selected, then click on **Finish** to apply the delegation.

With the delegation in place, Joe Freeman now has the right to manage the user accounts in the Technical Production department. In order to facilitate Joe's task, however, you can also create an MMC snap-in directly related to the job. To create a console based on the tasks defined in the previous example, follow these steps:

1. Start the MMC by choosing **Start | Run**, then typing "MMC" in the Run dialog box before clicking on **OK**. This opens a blank MMC console that you can customize.

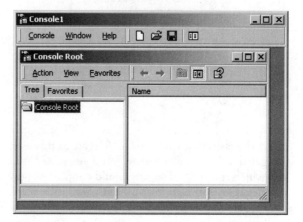

2. Choose **Console | Add/Remove Snap-in** to open the Add/Remove Snap-in dialog box.

3. Click on **Add** to open the Add Standalone Snap-in dialog box.

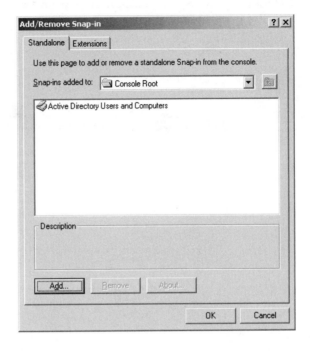

4. Select the Active Directory Users and Computers Snap-in. Click on **Add** to
    add it to the console, then on **Close** to close the dialog box and return to the
    Add/Remove Snap-in dialog.

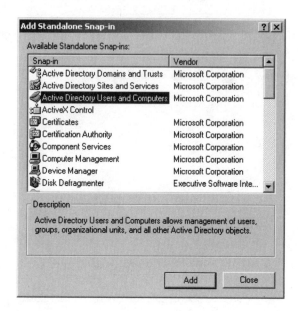

5. Close the Add/Remove Snap-in dialog box by clicking on **OK**.

6. Expand the console tree to find the OU that relates to the Technical Production department. Right-click on that OU and choose **New Window from Here** to open a new window with that OU as the console root.

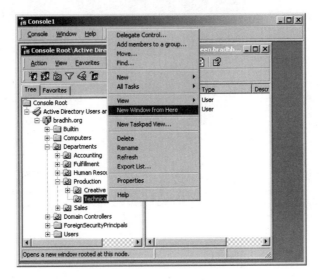

7. Close the window displaying the entire domain tree, then choose
    Console | Options to open the Options dialog box.

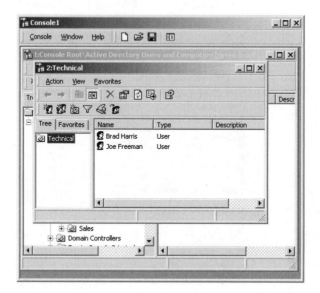

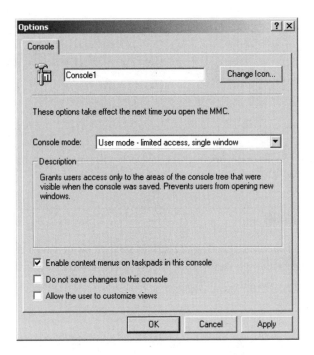

8. In the Console mode drop-down list, select User mode - limited access, single window. Select the **Enable context menus on taskpads in this console** checkbox and disable the other two checkboxes, then click on **OK** to save these changes.

9. Select **Console | Save As**, choose a suitable location for this console, give it a descriptive name, and click on **Save** to save it.

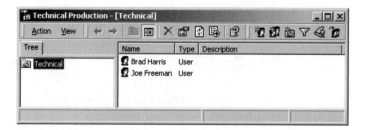

When Joe Freeman opens this console it will have only those controls necessary for the tasks assigned to him.

Security Policies

Another method of easing the administrative burden is to create broad security policies that affect all users in the domain. With the Domain Security Policy MMC Snap-in, you can set a wide variety of rights and permissions that affect virtually every aspect of your domain.

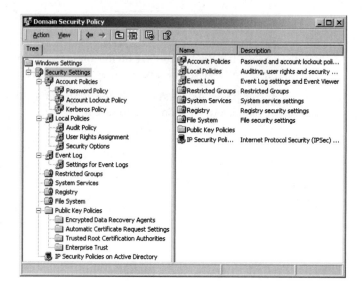

A detailed description of each setting in the Domain Security Policy MMC Snap-in is beyond the scope of this manual. However, the major groups contain the following types of settings:

- Account Policies

  Policies affecting user accounts

  o Password Policy

     Password length, complexity, and other settings

  o Account Lockout Policy

     Policies concerning account lockouts

  o Kerberos Policy

     Policies concerning Kerberos tickets and details of authentication

- Local Policies

  Policies affecting local computers and users

  o Audit Policy

     Policies determining which events can be audited

  o User Rights Assignment

     Policies specifying which users and groups have which specific rights

  o Security Options

     Various policies relating to system and network security

- Event Log

  o Policies concerning the Event logs

  o Settings for Event logs

- Restricted Groups

  Restrictions on access to and membership in security groups

- System Services

  Restrictions on startup mode and access to system services
- Registry

  Restrictions on access to Windows 2000 Registry settings
- File System

  Restrictions on access to the file system
- Public Key Policies

  Policies concerning PKI

  - Encrypted Data Recovery Agents

    Tools for management of EFS recovery agents
  - Automatic Certificate Request Settings

    Tools for management of automatic certificate requests by computers in the domain
  - Trusted Root Certification Authorities

    Tools for management of the trusted root CAs
  - Enterprise Trust

    Tools for management of enterprise-level Certificate Trust Lists (CTLs)
- IP Security Policies on Active Directory

  Policies concerning IPSec communications

Each of the settings made in the Domain Security Policy MMC Snap-in propagates to each resource in the domain, making this a very powerful tool. You can broadly apply settings to all users and computers from a central location. Also, the settings specified in the Domain Security Policy MMC Snap-in supersede any settings applied at the local computer level. The only exception to this rule is that settings made in the Domain Controller Security Policy MMC Snap-in take precedence over those made in the Domain Security Policy MMC Snap-in for domain controllers in your domain.

Scenario 6-2: Rights Management

This scenario is based on the case studies introduced earlier in the course. You may find it helpful to review the case studies in Appendix C at the end of the manual. Suggested answers are provided in Appendix B at the end of the manual.

Barney's Bank

1. What would be an appropriate delegation of authority for Barney's Bank?

    ....

    ....

2. Describe an aspect of the Domain Security policy appropriate for Barney's Bank.

    ....

    ....

Fairco Manufacturing

1. What would be an appropriate delegation of authority for Fairco Manufacturing?

    ....

    ....

2. Describe an aspect of the Domain Security policy appropriate for Fairco Manufacturing.

    ....

    ....

SUMMARY

During this chapter, you were introduced to the following topics:

- Public Key Infrastructure (PKI)
    - o   CA hierarchies
    - o   Certificate management
    - o   Integration with external CA
    - o   Mapping certificates to user accounts
- Delegation of authority
    - o   Defining authority of users
    - o   Designing custom MMC snap-ins
- Domain Security policies

You can now put this information to use in the design of a remote access security structure.

Stop now and complete the following NEXTSim exercises on the Interactive Learning CD-ROM:

Windows 2000 Network Security Design

Security Tools

Manage Certificates of Authority

POST-TEST QUESTIONS

The answers to these questions are in Appendix A at the end of this manual.

1. What information is stored in a certificate?

   ....

   ....

2. How does a certification hierarchy work?

   ....

   ....

3. What is the basic process involved in trusting an external CA?

   ....

   ....

4. At what level of the Active Directory is authority normally delegated?

   ....

   ....

5. Of the three MMC snap-ins dealing with policies, what is the order of precedence of the rights they assign?

   ....

   ....

CHAPTER 7

Remote Access Security

OBJECTIVES

At the completion of this chapter, you will be able to:

- Analyze internal and external security risks.
- Analyze the method of accessing data and systems.
- Analyze existing and planned network and systems management.
- Provide secure access to public networks from a private network.
- Provide external users with secure access to private network resources.
- Provide secure access between private networks.
- Provide secure access within a LAN.
- Provide secure access within a WAN.
- Provide secure access across a public network.
- Design Windows 2000 security for remote access users.

PRE-TEST QUESTIONS

The answers to these questions are in Appendix A at the end of this manual.

1. What is a Virtual Private Network (VPN)?

    ....

    ....

2. What security risks do you face when allowing dial-up access to your network?

    ....

    ....

3. The CHAP and MS-CHAP authentication protocols allow a reversibly encrypted password in order to function properly.

    A. True

    B. False

4. What is the purpose of a router?

....

....

INTRODUCTION

Remote access to LANs has become a very important and common part of the corporate environment. With increasing numbers of people working from home and traveling employees needing more access to network resources, the ability to provide remote connectivity is becoming a priority. This chapter describes the basics of remote access for a Windows 2000 network and defines the security needs and settings that you'll encounter in such situations.

THE RISKS OF REMOTE ACCESS

Setting up remote access on your network is much like inviting outsiders to attempt to break in. By defining methods allowing people to access your network from places other than your facilities, you are creating opportunities for intruders to attack from a relatively comfortable position. Remote access allows your users to access network resources by connecting across public networks such as the phone system or the Internet. Traffic on these networks is inherently less secure than on a private LAN, so a variety of risks appear. The following topics are covered in this section:

- Analyzing Access Methods
- Analyzing Remote Access Security Risks

Analyzing Access Methods

To determine your remote access security needs, you need to determine the amount and type of remote access connectivity that your organization needs. This could range from the most secure situation of allowing no remote access whatsoever, to the least secure situation of having all of your users connect by way of VPN across the Internet. You can also include connections between private LANs that utilize public networks such as router-to-router VPN connections over the Internet. For each of these situations, you need to apply security measures to protect your network resources from outsiders.

For networking environments in which security is a much greater priority than any other issue, disallow any connections outside the LAN. If you can physically control all computers that can connect to your network, you have much greater control over how those connections are used. Intruders first must gain physical access to your facilities before they can attempt to access your network resources. In many cases, this difficulty in accessing the network is enough of a deterrent to protect your resources from inappropriate access.

However, in today's computing environment, the benefits of allowing users to connect to the network remotely often reasonably outweigh the security concerns presented by remote access. If you decide to allow remote access to your network, you need to determine which access methods you will enable, then determine the risks associated with each.

One of the most common and traditional methods of remote access to a network is the dial-up connection. In this situation, people use modems to call the remote access server on your network. The remote access server maintains connections to a bank of modems, answering them when a remote user dials in. Upon authenticating the user, the remote access server grants appropriate network rights to the user, passing network data through the modem connection as though it were a local network connection. In this manner, the remote user has precisely the same access to network resources that would be available from a machine physically connected to the network.

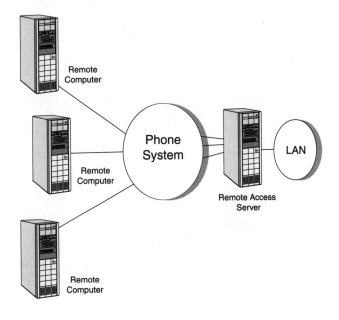

Another type of remote access becoming increasingly common is VPN. This allows the remote users to connect to the Internet, then establishes a virtual connection to your organization's LAN through a process called *tunneling*. A tunneled connection allows the remote user to interact with your network in the same method as a dial-up connection, only the information is passed over the Internet rather than the phone system. The clients can connect to the Internet in any of the following ways—whatever manner is feasible:

- Dial-up to an Internet Service Provider (ISP)
- High-speed cable or DSL connection
- Direct connection via a different network
- Direct connection via Frame Relay, T1, etc.

On the server side, a connection to the Internet replaces the modem bank; the number of connections possible depend on the bandwidth of the Internet connection rather than the number of modems connected to the server.

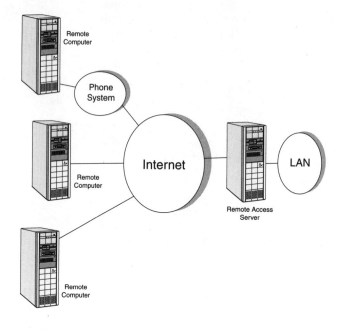

You need to determine which access methods best suit your users' needs. Direct dial-up connections are becoming less common as local Internet access increases in popularity. It's often more efficient to provide Internet accounts with a national ISP than to pay for the long-distance phone calls necessary for direct dial-up connections. The Internet accounts are typically accessed by a local call from anywhere in the country, and once connected, the users can initiate the VPN connection with no additional costs.

The server side of VPN administration is often simpler than managing a bank of modems. The remote access server only needs to manage two network connections: one to the Internet and one to your LAN. The server then translates information from the various VPN tunnels instantiated by the remote clients into requests on the LAN and returns data from the LAN to the remote clients through the same tunnels.

Analyzing Remote Access Security Risks

The different methods of remote access, of course, have different types of risks associated with them. Windows 2000 provides the same basic interface to remote access no matter what type of connection is being made. The only real differences, then, are inherent in the actual connection types.

With a dial-up connection, you have the possibility of an attacker discovering the phone number of your dial-up server. With that, the attacker can repeatedly call the server to attempt a brute-force logon attack. Similarly, with VPN, an outsider could discover the Internet address of your VPN server and repeatedly attempt logons over the Internet. Either way, the solution to this problem is going to lie in the strength of your Password policy combined with your Account Lockout policy.

Another risk that you face with both dial-up and VPN connections is eavesdropping. Both the phone system and the Internet are subject to taps (phone taps and network taps, respectively) by which intruders can attempt to eavesdrop on logon sessions or other network transactions, which allows them to scavenge passwords and sensitive information from your network. The solution to this problem involves an encryption policy for all information transferred over any public network, including all logon attempts and all network transactions.

Physical security of the remote computers is also of concern. Whenever possible you should take steps to ensure that only authorized personnel have any access to computers that might be used for remote access to your network. In many cases these computers are laptops being carried by traveling users, providing opportunities for theft of the computers. Training on proper handling of laptops while traveling can decrease this risk. Training should include teaching your users to never let go of a laptop in a public place and to always secure it via a locking cable when the computer is left in a hotel room or elsewhere.

Physical security of client computers also involves ensuring that inappropriate remote access connections cannot be made automatically from the laptop computer if an intruder gains access to it. This involves several levels of security, including the following:

- Strong passwords to access the remote computer itself
- Consistently locking the workstation when it's unattended
- Locking screen savers that start after a very short period of inactivity
- Never storing passwords to the remote access server on the client computer

The other main risk is that an unauthorized user will somehow gain access to a password and use it to illegitimately gain access to the network. While this problem exists even without involving remote access, the fact that the intruder can use this password from a remote and unknown location makes the attack even more threatening. As noted previously, without remote access being enabled an attacker must physically gain access to a computer on your LAN in order to take advantage of a stolen password. This adds considerably to the difficulty of carrying out the attack as well as increasing the likelihood that you'll be able to catch the intruder while the attack is in progress.

If an attacker can carry out this attack from a remote location, your chances of apprehending him are drastically reduced. Luckily, a couple of policies and controls can be enacted to help limit the possibility of such an impersonation attack from succeeding, including the following:

- Only enable remote access for accounts that are known to need it.
- For dial-up connections, enable callback to a preset phone number to limit the locations your users can connect from.

In addition, you should regularly review the state of your remote access system. Ensure that only the necessary accounts have remote access rights, require callback to a preset phone number for all dial-in accounts if possible, and take whatever steps are reasonable to protect the physical security of the remote computers.

Scenario 7-1: Risks of Remote Access

This scenario is based on the case studies introduced earlier in the course. You may find it helpful to review the case studies in Appnedix C at the end of the manual. Suggested answers are provided in Appendix B at the end of the manual.

Barney's Bank

What are the remote access risks that Barney's Bank faces?

....

....

Fairco Manufacturing

What are the remote access risks that Fairco Manufacturing faces?

....

....

SECURING REMOTE ACCESS

With the risks of remote access identified, you now need to begin preparing the remote access server and applying the appropriate security measures. This involves enabling and configuring the Routing and Remote Access Service (RRAS), defining the policies that control remote access, preparing the authentication measures you'll rely on, and configuring the user account that will access the network remotely. The following topics are covered in this section:

- Setting Up Remote Access
- Configuring Remote Access Policies
- Remote Access Authentication
- Enabling Remote Access for User Accounts

Setting Up Remote Access

The first step to setting up remote access is to enable RRAS on a server on your network. To do this, follow these steps:

1. Open the Active Directory Users and Computers MMC Snap-in. Expand the domain you wish to add a remote access server to, then expand Users. Right-click on the RAS and IAS servers security group and choose **Properties** from the shortcut menu. The Properties dialog box for that security group opens.

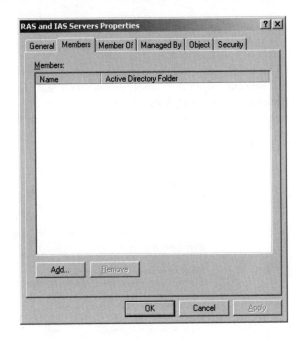

2. Select the **Members** tab and then click on **Add** to open the Select Users, Contacts, Computers, or Groups dialog box. Select the computer that will function as the remote access server and click on **OK** to close that dialog box. Click on **OK** to close the Properties dialog box.

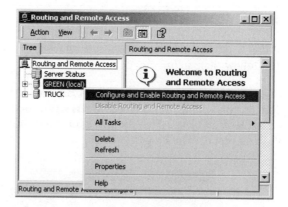

3. Open the Routing and Remote Access MMC Snap-in. Right-click on the server you want to enable as a remote access server and choose **Configure and Enable Routing and Remote Access** from the shortcut menu to open the Routing and Remote Access Server Setup Wizard. Read the introductory message, then click on **Next** to continue.

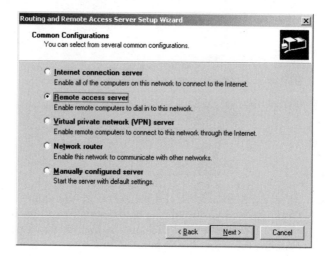

4. Select either **Remote access server** or **Virtual private network (VPN) server**, depending on the type of remote access you want to provide with this server, then click on **Next**.

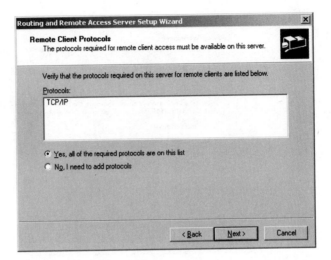

5. Ensure that the appropriate network protocols are listed. In most cases, you'll only require TCP/IP on a Windows 2000 network, but if your network uses other protocols as well, select **No, I need to add protocols** before clicking on **Next**.

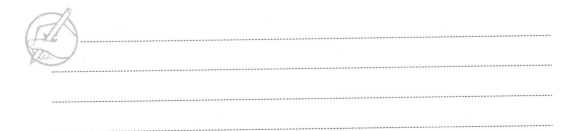

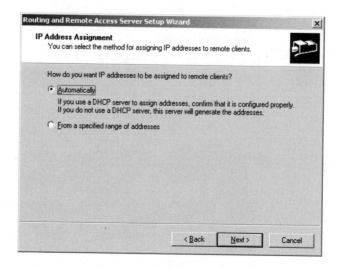

6. Select the method that you want to use to assign network addresses to client computers. In most cases, automatic assignment works well. If you have a DHCP server on your network, it can assign IP addresses to your remote clients; otherwise, the remote access server will assign the addresses itself. However, if you need to specify a certain range of addresses, you can select the second option and the wizard will allow you to do so. Click on **Next** when you are ready to continue.

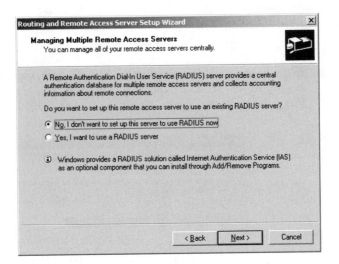

7. If you have a Remote Authentication Dial-In User Service (RADIUS) server on your network, you can select the second option here to configure this remote access server to use that RADIUS server for authentication. RADIUS is explained in detail in the Remote Access Authentication section of this chapter. If you are not using RADIUS or want to configure it later, select **No, I don't want to set up this server to use RADIUS now** before clicking on **Next**.

8. Click on **Finish** to set up and enable the remote access server.

A detailed discussion of the configuration of RRAS is well beyond the scope of this manual. However, once you have remote access configured to function properly, you can apply security settings by following these steps:

1. In the Routing and Remote Access MMC Snap-in, right-click on the server enabled for remote access and choose **Properties** from the shortcut menu. The Properties dialog box opens. Select the **Security** tab.

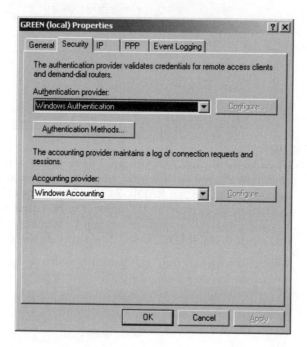

2. In the Authentication provider drop-down list, select either Windows Authentication or RADIUS Authentication. If you choose RADIUS authentication, you'll need to configure the remote access server to use the proper RADIUS server on your network by clicking on **Configure**. This opens the RADIUS Authentication dialog box.

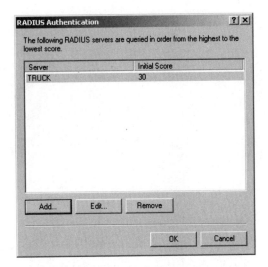

3. Click on **Add** to open the Add RADIUS Server dialog box.

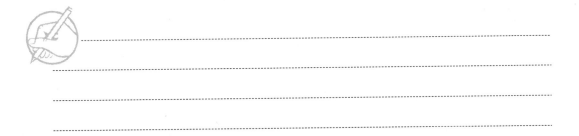

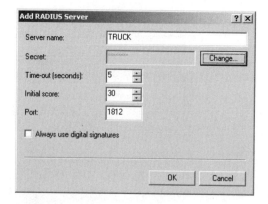

4. Configure the following settings in this dialog box:

   o Enter the name of your network's RADIUS server in the Server name field.

   o Specify the shared secret password that the RADIUS server will use to ensure secure communications with the remote access server.

   o In the Time-out (seconds) field, set how long the remote access server will wait for a response from the RADIUS server before trying another RADIUS server for authentication of a remote user.

   o In the Initial score field, set the initial responsiveness score for this RADIUS server. This value is dynamically adjusted as authentication requests are processed.

   o In the Port field, specify the TCP port to access this RADIUS server on.

   o Specify whether this remote access server should always use digital signatures based on the shared secret when communicating with the RADIUS server. In order for this to work, you also need to configure your RADIUS server to use digital signatures.

   Click on **OK** to close this dialog box when you are finished, then click on **OK** to close the RADIUS Authentication dialog box.

5. From the Properties dialog box, click on **Authentication Methods** to open the Authentication Methods dialog box.

6. Select the authentication protocols that you want to enable for this connection. The choices are as follows:

    o   EAP

        The Extensible Authentication Protocol allows you to add authentication methods to the authentication infrastructure, providing a mechanism to support smart cards and other strong security systems.

    o   MS-CHAP v2

        Microsoft Challenge-Handshake Authentication Protocol version 2 provides several security enhancements over version 1 but is less widely supported by clients and authentication servers.

    o   MS-CHAP

        Microsoft Challenge-Handshake Authentication Protocol is a challenge-handshake authentication protocol that does not require reversibly encrypted passwords on the authentication server.

○ CHAP

Challenge-Handshake Authentication Protocol authenticates the remote user without transmitting passwords across the network. However, CHAP requires that the authentication server store the passwords in a reversibly encrypted form so that it can generate the hash to compare to the client's transmitted hash to authenticate the user.

○ SPAP

The Shiva Password Authentication Protocol is a proprietary authentication method employed by the Shiva LANRover. Passwords are encrypted when transmitted over the network, but on each authentication, the same password encrypts to the same string, so this protocol is subject to replay attacks.

○ PAP

Password Authentication Protocol exchanges passwords over the network in plaintext form so anyone capturing the logon session can read and steal the passwords. In general, you should disable PAP.

○ Unauthenticated access

No usernames or passwords are sent. If this is enabled, the client can access the remote access server via the Guest account if that account is enabled and has any rights on the network.

For more information about these authentication protocols, see the chapter on authentication services elsewhere in this manual. After making your selection, click on **OK** to return to the Properties dialog box.

7. From the Accounting provider drop-down list, select the accounting provider that will store the Connection Request log for this remote access server. If you choose to store the Connection Request log on a RADIUS server, click on **Configure** to specify the settings for that server.

8. Select the **Event Logging** tab to specify what information will be logged for this remote access server.

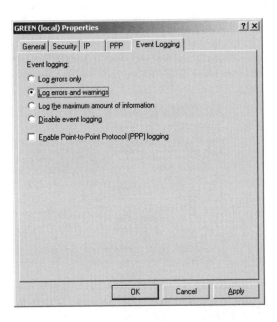

9. Select the option appropriate to the type of information you want to log for this remote access server, then click on **OK** to close this dialog box.

Configuring Remote Access Policies

With the remote access server set up and security configured, you now need to specify the policies that you will apply to your remote access connections. These settings determine whether connections are authorized, and if so, which policies will be applied to the connection.

To configure remote access policies, follow these steps:

1. In the Routing and Remote Access MMC Snap-in, expand the remote access server you want to configure policies for and select Remote Access Policies.

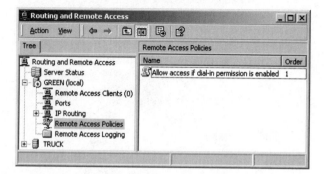

2. The only policy defined, by default, is Allow access if dial-in permission is enabled. This allows users to dial in to this server if their accounts are configured to permit dial-up access.

3. To create a new remote access policy, select **New Remote Access Policy** from the **Action** menu to open the Add Remote Access Policy Wizard.

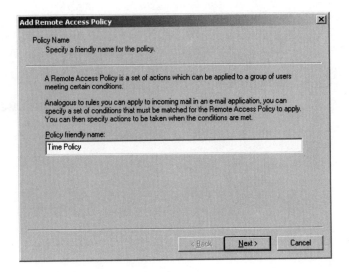

4. Type a name for your new policy and click on **Next**.

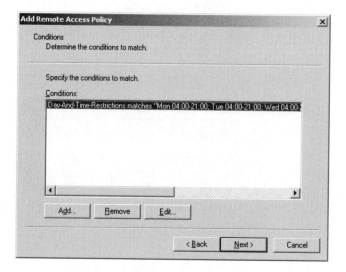

5. Click on **Add** to open the Select Attribute dialog box. You can specify the conditions that, if met, will trigger this policy.

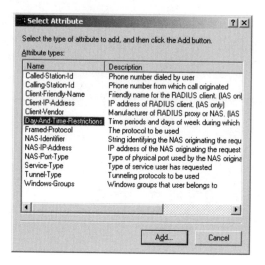

6. Select the condition you want this policy to check and click on **Add** to configure it.

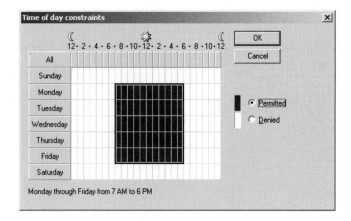

7. Specify the parameters appropriate for this policy, then click on **OK** to add this condition to the policy and return to the Add Remote Access Policy dialog box. Click on **Next** to move to the next step of the wizard.

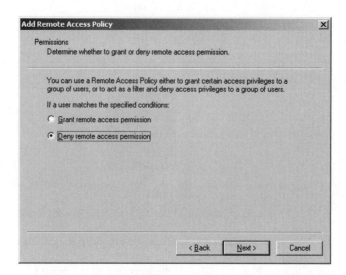

8. Specify whether this policy should grant or deny access to users who match the specified conditions, then click on **Next**.

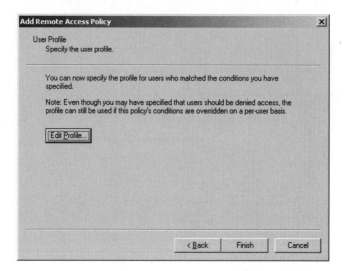

9. Click on **Edit Profile** to open the Edit Dial-in Profile dialog box. Here you can configure a variety of settings that apply to the account that dials in.

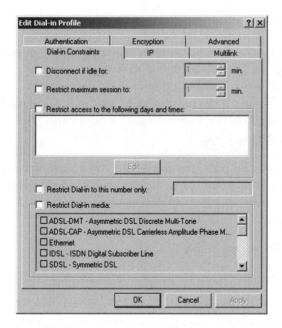

10. From this dialog box, you can specify a variety of settings restricting the rights and capabilities of the dial-in connection. These settings have to do with the duration and time constraints, DHCP server settings, multilink settings, authentication methods allowed, permitted levels of encryption, and other connection attributes. Click on **OK** to return to the wizard, then click on **Finish** to add this policy to the list.

Remote Access Authentication

Authentication for RAS can be accomplished either by the remote access server itself, through the Windows 2000 Kerberos v5 authentication process, or by using an external RADIUS server. Since the Kerberos v5 authentication is built into Windows 2000, that is the easier of the two to set up and configure. All you need to do is create a user account and select Windows Authentication on the Security page of the remote access server's Properties dialog box.

Setting up a RADIUS server has some advantages, though. By centralizing the authentication of remote users, you can control how many sessions they have at once and keep accurate records about their connection patterns. This also centralizes the administration tasks for the remote users' accounts.

RADIUS works like this:

1. A remote access client attempts a connection to a remote access server.

2. The remote access server receives logon credentials from the remote access client.

3. The remote access server passes the credentials to the RADIUS server.

4. The RADIUS server passes a message back to the remote access server stating the results of the authentication (allowed or denied).

5. The remote access server either allows or denies the remote access client access to the network based on the response from the RADIUS server.

Windows 2000 provides a RADIUS server that you can set up on your network called Internet Authentication Service (IAS). You can set up IAS by following these steps:

1. In the Windows 2000 Control Panel, double-click on Add/Remove Programs. In the Add/Remove Programs dialog box, click on Add/Remove Windows Components to open the Windows Components Wizard.

2. Select **Networking Services,** then click on **Details** to open the Networking Services dialog box.

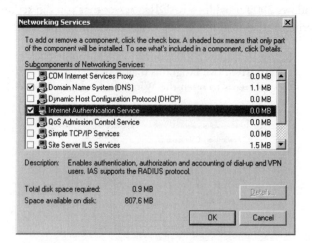

3. Enable the **Internet Authentication Service** checkbox and click on **OK** to close the Networking Services dialog box, then click on **Next** to continue.

4. After the wizard installs the IAS components, click on **Finish** to close the final dialog box.

You can now access the IAS MMC Snap-in by choosing **Start | Programs | Administrative Tools | Internet Authentication Service**. The first thing you need to do is register IAS in the Active Directory by right-clicking on Internet Authentication Service and choosing **Register Service in Active Directory** from the shortcut menu. This allows IAS to access usernames from the Active Directory, which is where IAS gets its database of user information for use in remote access authentication.

By right-clicking on Internet Authentication Service and choosing **Properties** from the shortcut menu, you can configure a few items concerning the operation of IAS. First, on the Service page, you can specify which items you want to appear in the Event log by enabling the appropriate checkboxes.

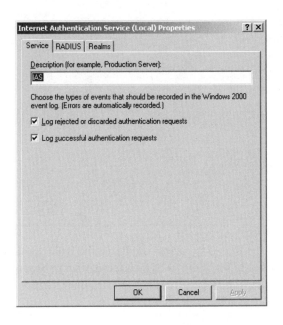

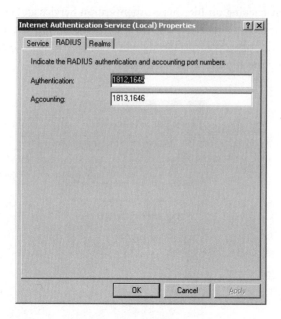

Next, on the RADIUS page of the Properties dialog box, you can set the TCP port number that IAS will use to communicate with remote access servers. The numbers on this sheet must match the numbers in the remote access setup in order for authentication to work successfully.

With IAS configured properly, you're ready to register the remote access servers that will be clients of IAS. To do so, follow these steps:

1. In the Internet Authentication Service MMC Snap-in, right-click on Clients and choose **New Client** from the shortcut menu.

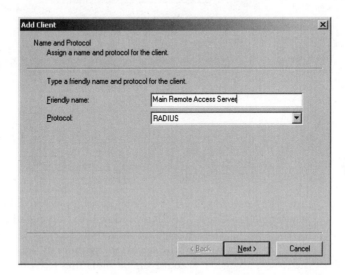

2. Give your client a name, choose RADIUS as the protocol, and click on **Next** to continue.

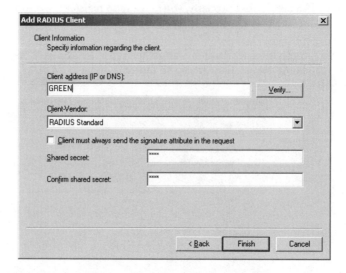

3. Enter the network address of the remote access server and specify RADIUS
    Standard in the Client-Vendor drop-down list. Enter and confirm the same shared
    secret password as you entered for the remote access server. You can also enable the
    Client must always send the signature attribute in the request checkbox to force
    the remote access server to use digital signatures in its authentication requests.
    Click on **Finish** to add this IAS client.

Enabling Remote Access for User Accounts

The only other task involved in setting up remote access security is to enable remote access for the individual accounts that actually need to access the network remotely. By minimizing the number of accounts that have this permission, you can lower the risk to your network. Enabling remote access for a particular user account can be done by following these steps:

1. In Active Directory Users and Computers, right-click on the user account that should be permitted to access the network remotely and choose **Properties** from the shortcut menu. The Properties dialog box opens.

2. For this user, make the following settings:

   o   Determine whether to allow or deny access or whether to control access through the Remote Access Policy.

   o   Specify a caller ID number, effectively limiting the user to calling from a single phone by checking the number the user calls from.

   o   Specify a callback number, again limiting the user to calling from a single phone by forcing the client computer to answer that phone in order to complete the connection.

   o   Assign a static IP address whenever this user logs on.

   o   Define static routes for router-to-router connections created under this user account.

3. Click on **OK** to apply the settings to this user account.

The next time this user attempts to make the remote connection, the changes you made will be applied.

Scenario 7-2: Remote Access Security

This scenario is based on the case studies introduced earlier in the course. You may find it helpful to review the case studies in Appendix C at the end of the manual. Suggested answers are provided in Appendix B at the end of the manual.

Barney's Bank

Would Barney's Bank benefit from using a RADIUS server?

....

....

Fairco Manufacturing

Would Fairco Manufacturing benefit from using a RADIUS server?

....

....

SECURITY BETWEEN LOCAL NETWORKS

The other aspect of routing and remote access is the connectivity between separate LANs. This can take the form of connecting a LAN to another remote LAN or it can be a connection between a LAN and a public network like the Internet. Either of these connections can be made either permanently or on an as-needed basis. Security in this situation involves protecting the connectivity methods and securing information as it travels from one network to another.

The following topics are covered in this section:

- Connecting a LAN to a Remote LAN
- Connecting a LAN to the Internet
- Securing Demand-Dial Router Connections

Connecting a LAN to a Remote LAN

The most basic purpose of a router is to connect two separate networks together and pass information between them. In this situation, you could have two physically separated LANs, perhaps a central office and a branch office. If you wanted all of the computers to be able to access each other as though they were all on the same network, you could set up a router between them. The router knows which network each computer is on, so if it sees a network request on one network for a computer on the other, it passes that request through.

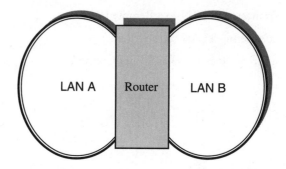

A Windows 2000 server can act as a router, keeping track of which computers are on each of the two different networks. This is managed in the Routing and Remote Access MMC Snap-in. In this situation, the only security settings necessary are those required to allow the users on one network to appropriately access resources on the other network. If the domain trusts, security groups, and Access Control Lists (ACLs) of the resources are set up properly, the network connections should be reasonably secure.

Connecting a LAN to the Internet

Technically, connecting your LAN to the Internet using a hard-wired connection, such as a T1 or Frame Relay solution, is basically the same as connecting two LANs together. However, once you connect your LAN to a public network such as the Internet, you're asking for trouble. Being a largely unauthenticated network, users on the Internet have little accountability. For that reason, you need to ensure that you have a secure firewall in place between your LAN and the public network. You also need to tightly control access to your user account information and provide ACLs on your resources that allow only absolutely necessary access by legitimate accounts.

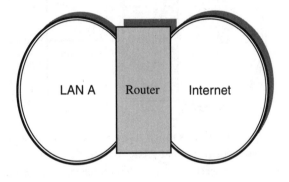

Securing Demand-Dial Router Connections

Demand-dial router connections do involve a level of security. A demand-dial router connection is basically a router connection between two networks that only exists as needed. When a router on one of the networks receives a network packet for delivery on the other network, it checks to see if the connection between the routers exists. If the connection doesn't exist, the router initiates the connection by dialing the other router.

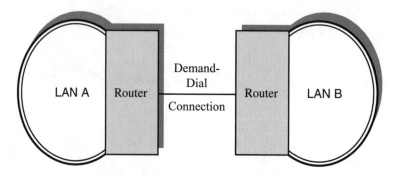

This dial-up connection is much like any other remote access dial-up connection. The calling router needs to present credentials to the answering router that correspond to an account on the answering domain, which has dial-up permissions enabled. This is the layer of security that must be managed carefully with demand-dial router connections. If the password to your demand-dial router connection falls into malicious hands, an entire network can be connected to your LAN, and each of the computers on the remote network can mount a separate attack on resources on your network.

For this reason, it is recommended that you configure the routers on both ends of the demand-dial connection with the appropriate account information, including a 14-character random password including upper-case and lower-case letters, numbers, and symbols. Once the password is installed on both routers, destroy all written copies of it. Then change the password on a regular basis, each time destroying all written copies of it. There is no reason that any person will ever have to use this account, so the password can remain secret from all people; only the routers need to know it.

SECURING DATA BETWEEN NETWORKS

One very common method of remotely connecting to a LAN is through Virtual Private Network (VPN). This involves securely passing information from one part of a network to another part of the network or another network. When you are sending information to another network, the connection can come in two forms. The data can pass from one router to another router across a private network or across the Internet. VPNs are used to securely and privately deliver data from one computer to another computer. The following topics are covered in this section:

- The Function of a VPN
- Tunneling Protocols
- VPN Management
- Setting Up Tunneling in Windows 2000

The Function of a VPN

When you are transferring sensitive information across a network, the possibility exists that someone other than the intended recipient will intercept that information. Once this occurs, the unwanted third party can possibly do two things with your transmission:

- Read the information
- Modify the transmission

Gaining the ability to read your private communications allows the intruder to inappropriately use that information. For instance, consider the case of transferring a credit card number to a merchant in order to make a purchase. If a third party can read your transmission, that person could then use your credit card information to make other purchases, possibly running up massive charges on your card.

Being able to modify the original transmission can be equally destructive. Suppose you were instructing a stock broker to sell shares of stock at a particular price. An intruder could modify your message, lowering the price, then immediately turn around and purchase those shares at the lower price.

Another possibility with network communications is that someone will send a message using another person's name. Referring back to the stock broker example, a third party could claim to be you and send a message to your stock broker with instructions to sell at a low price. Comprehensive communications security must provide a way of verifying the origin of a message. By establishing a VPN to connect users, we can secure communication within and outside the local network.

A VPN must include the following four basic elements:

- Data must be encapsulated.
- Encapsulated data must be encrypted.
- The VPN connection must have some way to authenticate the sender and receiver of the data.
- There must be some way to deliver the data to the proper computer after it reaches the receiving VPN connection.

We have already spent considerable time discussing authentication protocols and data encryption. We will now spend some time talking about how a VPN will use encapsulation and address translation to secure data and deliver it to the proper computer.

A VPN must satisfy the following three goals to ensure communications security:

1. Prevent unauthorized persons from reading messages in transit.
2. Ensure that the message arrives unmodified.
3. Verify the origin of the message.

Tunneling handles all three of these communications security goals. Tunneling allows you to connect two physically separate networks with a link consisting of a network of a different type. For instance, if you have two offices and want to be able to share information between them as though they were one network, you could physically run a wire between them and pass information over that wire just as you would over any other network cable. However, if one of the offices is in New York and the other is in San Francisco, running that wire could be very expensive.

However, these days there are already wires—either a private network or a public network, also known as the Internet—run between those two offices. Information travels between those two cities constantly. The problem is that data must be passed securely from the New York office to the San Francisco office.

That's where tunneling comes in. Tunneling allows you to take network data in the form of packets from one protocol and *encapsulate* them in packets of another protocol. This means that you can stuff a packet from the New York office inside a TCP/IP packet—the native protocol of the Internet—and pass that TCP/IP packet to the San Francisco office. The local packet can then be extracted from the TCP/IP packet and sent to the appropriate recipient on the San Francisco network.

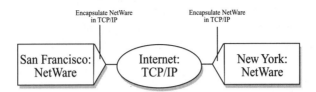

To do this, the tunneling protocol in use must be able to do the following:

- Encapsulation
- Address translation

Encapsulation, as you just saw, involves wrapping a packet of one protocol in a packet of another protocol.

Address translation is the process of keeping track of different ways of referring to a particular computer. Looking back to the previous example, when a computer in the New York office wants to send a message to a computer in the San Francisco office, it needs to know the address of the remote computer. Both of the computers involved in the transaction have addresses for their own LAN. These computers simply refer to each other by their local addresses.

The tunneling protocol needs to have a different way of referring to these computers, though, since the packets need to travel from one network to another. Computers and routers on the Internet will have no way of knowing how to find a local computer on a LAN in a San Francisco office. This means that the tunneling protocol will need to keep track of which specific computers are involved, but it must abstract that information so that routers on the Internet will be capable of properly forwarding the packets to the correct private network.

Normally, this means that when a local packet is being encapsulated for transmission outside the LAN, it will be addressed to the router on the remote network. The address of the specific computer on that private network is not important while the packet is in transit over the Internet. Once the remote router receives the packet, however, it must be able to find the address of the intended recipient on its local network to deliver the encapsulated packet. Different tunneling protocols handle this address translation differently. The details will be described later in this section.

Tunneling Protocols

There are two major tunneling protocols available in Windows 2000:

- Point-to-Point Tunneling Protocol (PPTP)
- Layer 2 Tunneling Protocol (L2TP)

Each has its own methods of handling the various tasks required of a tunneling protocol. In this section, we will discuss the specifics of each one.

Point-to-Point Tunneling Protocol (PPTP)

PPTP is Microsoft's proprietary tunneling solution. It's been available since Windows NT 4.0, and as such, has an installed base that requires that it be included in Windows 2000.

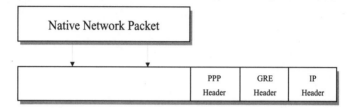

PPTP is an extension of the Point-to-Point Protocol (PPP) commonly used with dial-up access. It encapsulates each native network packet in three levels of network headers to ensure its secure arrival at the intended remote computer. Those network headers are as follows:

PPP header	The standard PPP header, providing the encryption and authentication for the PPTP protocol.
GRE header	The Generic Routing Encapsulation (GRE) header provides the address translation and native network routing information for the encapsulated packet.
IP header	The Internet Protocol (IP) header contains the routing information to get the encapsulated packet across the Internet to the appropriate remote private network.

PPTP leaves the authentication and encryption tasks of tunneling to PPP, which uses the proprietary Microsoft Point-to-Point Encryption (MPPE) methods. MPPE can employ either the standard Microsoft Challenge-Handshake Authentication Protocol (MS-CHAP) or the Extensible Authentication Protocol - Transport Layer Security (EAP-TLS) for authentication and encryption. Each of these is described in detail in previous chapters of this manual. In general, though, these methods use the keys provided by the underlying Kerberos v5 protocol to accomplish the necessary authentication and encryption tasks.

Each native network packet is encapsulated in a PPP packet. The resulting packet is then encapsulated in a GRE packet to provide the necessary routing information for the address translation, including the native network addresses of the source and destination computers.

Windows 2000 incorporates a process known as Network Address Translation (NAT) where the VPN server does all of the address translation, allowing the computers on either side of the connection to completely ignore the fact that they are on a network with private addresses. NAT has the ability to monitor the creation of a PPTP VPN tunnel and build a table of the appropriate GRE information. The GRE information is then used by NAT to route packets to the proper local computer.

Finally, the entire packet is encapsulated in an IP packet with the appropriate addressing information, including the source IP address of the router sending the packet and the destination IP address of the router intended to receive the packet.

Layer 2 Tunneling Protocol (L2TP)

In contrast to the proprietary nature of PPTP, L2TP is a standards-based tunneling protocol defined in RFC 2661. It integrates with the IPSec standard provided with Windows 2000 to enable security and authentication.

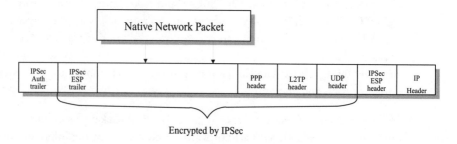

L2TP utilizes five layers of encapsulation for each native network packet. These layers are as follows:

PPP header	This is the standard PPP header.
L2TP header	The L2TP header, providing the address translation to route the packet between the appropriate computers on the remotely connected networks.
UDP header	The User Datagram Protocol (UDP) header specifies UDP port number 1701 for the tunneled information to pass through.

IPSec ESP header	The Internet Protocol Security (IPSec) Encapsulating Security Payload (ESP) header provides the encryption, authentication, and integrity for the native network packet. The IPSec encapsulation also includes the IPSec authentication trailer, which provides the authentication and integrity for the packet.
IP header	The IP header works for L2TP just as it did in PPTP, containing the routing information to get the encapsulated packet across the Internet to the appropriate remote private network.

Encryption and authentication is provided by the IPSec protocol, which is tightly integrated with the Windows 2000 Kerberos v5 authentication system, as described previously in this chapter.

VPN Management

Most of the VPN management procedures are the same as those discussed for RAS servers. The following are a few key points:

- Connection management

  As with other types of connections, the Internet connection properties are set through Network and Dial-up Connections. This is where you will enter and manage information, such as your local IP address and subnet mask, username and password for connecting to the Internet, and so forth.

- Policies and profiles

  Policies and profiles are used in the same manner as they are with routers and remote access servers. The same policy and profile options are available.

- Authentication

  As was mentioned before, you have the same authentication types available. You will have to configure your VPN server to support either Windows authentication or Remote Authentication Dial-In User Service (RADIUS) authentication.

- User management

  If at all possible, avoid managing users individually on each server, especially if you are supporting multiple servers. You should manage user information for a central location, either by using Active Directory Users and Groups or by setting up a RADIUS (IAS) server.

User access can be managed either by user or by group. As with RAS clients, by-user access can be managed through user properties. As you saw previously, you can allow access, deny access, or manage access through policy.

You can also manage VPN access by group through the use of policy. You can create a Security group to contain all users who need to be allowed VPN access and create a policy to allow that group access.

Since VPN is used as a way of protecting data from unauthorized interception, your security requirements are also going to have a significant impact on server placement.

One option is placing the VPN server in a screened subnet. This solution works especially well when you want to use VPN to support traffic such as replication updates. You can often place the server you are supporting in the same screened subnet as the VPN server. If you have sufficient server resources, you may even be able to have them both running on the same machine.

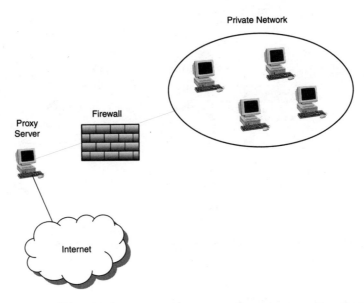

It is common to use a VPN server in combination with a firewall to provide additional security. You can place the VPN server outside the firewall if exposing the server to the Internet won't compromise your network security. Typically, you will want to install VPN on a stand-alone Windows 2000 server in this configuration. The firewall isolates your private network from the Internet and you can configure your network so that the VPN server is the only way through the firewall.

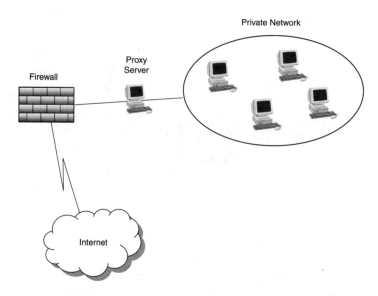

If exposing your VPN server to the Internet can compromise security, you have the option of placing it inside the firewall. This does make setting up filtering more complicated at the firewall since you must allow PPTP- and L2TP-based traffic for the VPN IP address range.

In practice, you will need to set packet filtering on the firewall's Internet interface. Depending on the tunneling protocol you are using, you will need to configure the input and output filters properly.

For PPTP, you will need to filter all traffic–except traffic to ports 1723 and 47. PPTP uses port 1723 for PPTP tunnel maintenance traffic. Port 47 is used for PPTP-tunneled data.

All traffic for L2TP, except traffic to and from ports 500 and 50, should be filtered. L2TP uses port 500 for Internet Key Exchange (IKE) traffic. Port 50 is used by IPSec for ESP-tunneled payloads. The IPSec ESP payload portion of an L2TP packet includes encrypted data and tunnel maintenance information.

Setting Up Tunneling in Windows 2000

Windows 2000 makes setting up tunneling a fairly easy process. You first need to set up the tunneling server, then set up the tunneling client to match the server's configuration.

In the situation of setting up a tunneling server for a Windows 2000 network to tunnel packets across the Internet, you are actually tunneling IP packets across an IP network. At first glance this may seem unnecessary, but it is actually a very useful tool. The Windows 2000 LAN does not need to have permanent public IP addresses for each computer on the LAN. Instead, you can set up an internal network using a set of predefined local network addresses such as 192.168.x.x. These IP addresses are not allowed on the public Internet. The VPN server, though, can pass packets between computers on the two private networks, using tunneling technologies to move the packets across the public Internet.

For this to be possible, the VPN server needs to have two network interface cards with separate IP addresses: one for use on the private network and one for use on the public Internet. This allows computers both on the Internet and on the private network to access the VPN server natively. The VPN server, then, has the task of translating the addresses between the two networks.

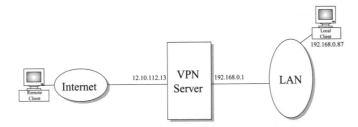

To install the VPN server on a Windows 2000 server, follow the steps for installing a remote access server described elsewhere in this chapter. The only difference is that you'll need to select the connection that VPN clients will use to access this server. This will be the network interface connected to the Internet.

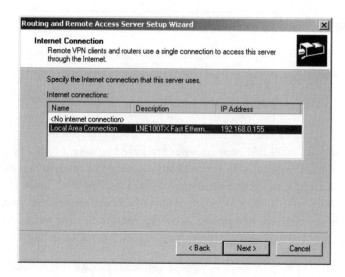

The rest of the steps are identical to that procedure.

Once your server is set up, you simply need to set up your VPN clients. To set up a remote computer as a VPN client, follow these steps:

1. Click on **Start | Settings | Network and Dial-up Connections | Make New Connection**.

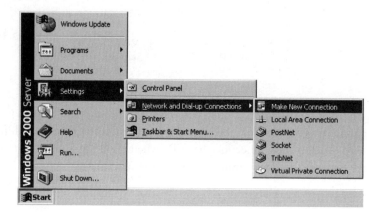

2. Click on **Next** to pass the Welcome screen of the Network Connection Wizard, select **Connect to a private network through the Internet,** then click on **Next** to continue.

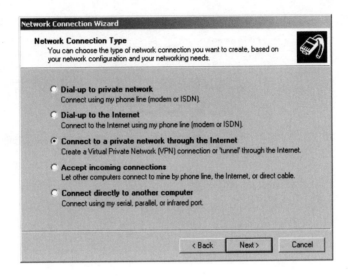

3. If you have a permanent connection to the Internet from this client, select **Do not dial the initial connection**; otherwise, select a dial-up connection to open prior to attempting the VPN connection.

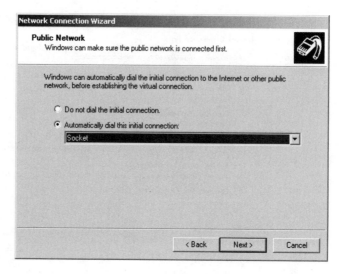

4. Type either the name or the IP address of the VPN server, then click on **Next** to continue.

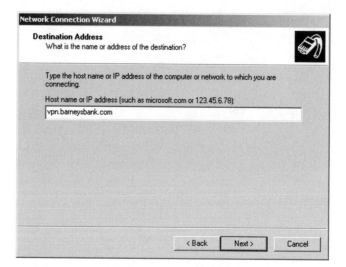

5. If you want everyone who logs on to this computer to be able to access this VPN connection, then select **For all users**; otherwise, select **Only for myself**. Keep in mind that even if the connection is available, each person using it will need to know the username and password to complete the connection.

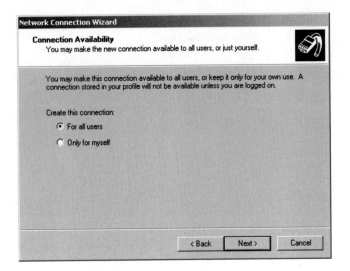

6. If you want to share this connection with all computers on your local network, then check the **Enable Internet Connection Sharing for this connection** checkbox. This effectively creates a small-scale demand-dial router-to-router VPN connection between the two networks. Click on **Next** to continue.

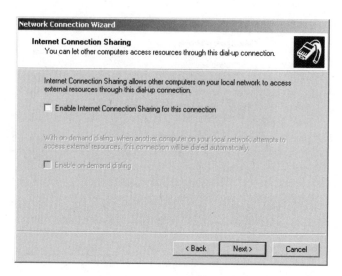

7. Give this connection a name, then click on **Finish** to create the connection.

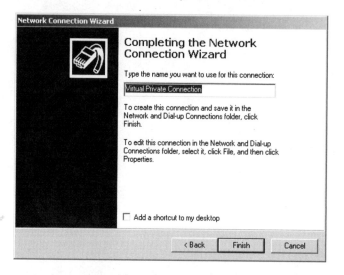

Once the connection is created, you can connect to the VPN server at any time by double-clicking on the connection icon and supplying the correct logon information.

Scenario 7-3: WAN Security

This scenario is based on the case studies introduced earlier in the course. You may find it helpful to review the case studies in Appendix C at the end of the manual. Suggested answers are provided in Appendix B at the end of the manual.

Barney's Bank

How could Barney's Bank make use of a VPN router connection?

....

....

Fairco Manufacturing

How could Fairco Manufacturing make use of a demand-dial router connection?

....

....

SUMMARY

During this chapter, you were introduced to the following topics:

- Analysis of remote access methods
- Analysis of remote access security risks
- Setup and configuration of remote access, including the following:
    - Remote access policies
    - Remote access authentication
    - Remote access user accounts

- Securing router connections, including the following:
  - o   LAN-to-LAN connections
  - o   LAN-to-Internet connections
  - o   Demand-dial router connections
  - o   VPN router connections

In the next chapter, we will discuss the details underlying communications security with the IPSec protocol and Server Message Block (SMB) signing.

Stop now and complete the following NEXTSim exercises on the Interactive Learning CD-ROM:

Windows 2000 Network Security Design

Remote Access Security

Secure the File System
Secure the Wide-Area Links
Manage a Remote Access Server

POST-TEST QUESTIONS

The answers to these questions are in Appendix A at the end of this manual.

1. What is the most secure policy regarding remote access?

    ....

    ....

2. How can the EAP authentication protocol provide increased security?

    ....

    ....

3. Describe the purpose of a RADIUS server.

    ....

    ....

4. When defining the dial-up properties for a particular user, how does caller ID differ from the callback number?

....

....

5. What is the best password policy for a demand-dial router-to-router connection?

....

....

Communications Security

OBJECTIVES

At the completion of this chapter, you will be able to:

- Design an Server Message Block (SMB) signing solution.
- Design an IPSec solution.
- Design an IPSec encryption scheme.
- Design an IPSec management strategy.
- Design negotiation policies.
- Design security policies.
- Design IP filters.
- Define security levels.

PRE-TEST QUESTIONS

The answers to these questions are in Appendix A at the end of this manual.

1. Describe SMB signing.

....

....

2. Describe IPSec.

....

....

3. How does an IP filter work in IPSec?

....

....

INTRODUCTION

Your network security scheme is only as strong as its weakest link. In order to fully protect your data, you need to ensure that it is safe while being transmitted over the network. This includes not just unsecured networks like the Internet and the public phone network, but also your LAN and WAN links. Through proper application of IPSec and SMB signing, you'll be able to provide all-around security for your information while it is being transmitted across the wires.

SMB SIGNING

When Microsoft released Service Pack 3 for Windows NT 4.0, they included a technology called SMB signing. This allowed administrators to enable digital signatures for all network transactions to and from any particular computer, thereby providing a method of ensuring data integrity for all network transactions. However, SMB signing did not provide any cryptography, so the data was not secured from being secretly observed by a third party while in transit.

For this reason, Windows 2000 has substituted the SMB signing technology with IPSec, which performs both data integrity verification *and* cryptography. In order to provide backward compatibility with Windows NT 4.0, though, you can still enable SMB signing on your Windows 2000 computers. This allows you to retain the proof of data integrity when communicating with computers that have not yet been upgraded to Windows 2000 and IPSec.

SMB signing is managed by directly manipulating values in the Windows 2000 Registry. To enable SMB signing on a Windows 2000 Server system, find the following Registry key:

```
HKEY_LOCAL_MACHINE\SYSTEM\CurrentControlSet\Services\lanmanserver\
  parameters
```

There you will have the following two REG_DWORD values:

- Enablesecuritysignature
- Requiresecuritysignature

Setting these values to one enables them; setting them to zero disables them.

In Windows 2000 Professional, you'll find the same REG_DWORD values in the following key:

```
HKEY_LOCAL_MACHINE\SYSTEM\CurrentControlSet\Services\
    lanmanworkstation\parameters
```

Again, setting these values to one enables them and setting them to zero disables them.

Keep in mind when working with SMB signing that it does slightly degrade network performance due to the fact that each network packet must be digitally signed and the signature must be read at the receiving end. However, this does not significantly affect network bandwidth since the digital signature adds only an inconsequential amount of data to each packet.

SECURITY AND TCP/IP

IPSec is an up-and-coming communication security protocol that is currently being defined by the Internet Engineering Task Force (IETF). While not yet completely specified, the concepts are already being widely used to protect data on the network because of the urgent need for such protection and the ease and effectiveness of their implementation. Windows 2000 includes a fairly standard implementation of IPSec. The following topics are covered in this section:

- Understanding IPSec
- Designing an IPSec Encryption Scheme
- Negotiating Security
- Designing IPSec Policies
- IPSec Management

Understanding IPSec

Internet Protocol Security (IPSec) is a convenient yet powerful set of tools that protect information while it's in transit over network connections. IPSec can utilize a variety of technologies to secure network communications, and for each connection with another computer, the details of the security methods employed can be negotiated.

IPSec uses a concept called a Security Association (SA) in each secured connection. An SA is basically a contract between two computers specifying the encryption algorithm, integrity algorithm, authentication method, and Diffie-Hellman group (explained later in this section) used in their communication. IPSec can implement the following encryption technologies:

- Data Encryption Standard (DES)

  A 56-bit DES using secret-key cryptography. DES provides very fast decryption, but the secret key must be generated on both sides using information passed via private key encryption.

- 3DES

  An enhancement to DES that encrypts the information three times using three separate keys, providing a very high level of encryption.

- 40-bit DES

  A weaker version of DES, using only a 40-bit key instead of a 56-bit key.

The integrity algorithms available for IPSec are as follows:

- Message Digest 5 (MD5)

  This one-way hash function generates a hash of the information that cannot be reversed. The sending computer generates the hash and transmits it along with the message. The receiving computer then performs the same function on the message, and if the resulting hash is the same as the one sent along with the message, you can be certain that the message was not modified in transit.

- Secure Hash Algorithm (SHA)

  This is considered a more secure hashing function than MD5 but it is slower. The basic concept behind its functionality is the same as that for MD5, though.

IPSec can use any of these authentication protocols:

- Certificate-based authentication

  Each party in the transaction uses public key certificates to authenticate the transaction.

- Preshared key authentication

  Both sides have already agreed on a secret key that will be used to protect the data.

- Kerberos v5 authentication

  The default Windows 2000 authentication method integrates the Kerberos session tickets to authenticate the IPSec communications.

Diffie-Hellman is a method of generating the same secret key in two separate places without actually passing that secret key over the network. The process will not be discussed in detail here, but basically both parties in the IPSec transaction publicly agree on a pair of numbers and each secretly generates a third number. They then perform a specific calculation using the shared numbers and the secret number, then pass the results of that calculation to each other. Each party then performs the same calculation using the passed number in place of one of the original agreed-upon numbers. The result of this calculation is the shared secret key used to encrypt and decrypt the remainder of the information during the IPSec transaction.

When defining your IPSec policies for your network, you can choose the size of the secret key generated based on the values the two computers agreed on when beginning the secret key generation process. In Windows 2000, you can choose to generate either a 96-bit key or a 128-bit key, corresponding to low (Diffie-Hellman Group 1) or medium (Diffie-Hellman Group 2) security.

By using shared secret key encryption, IPSec is much faster than if it utilized public key cryptography. This means that the overhead is very low for using IPSec. However, you may still find that you don't need such secure communications in all of your network transactions. For this reason, IPSec allows you to choose whether you want to enable data encryption or simply digitally sign your transactions as well as the level of encryption and integrity you want to provide. It is a very flexible protocol that scales well, from common transactions that require little security to the most sensitive messages you send on your network.

Designing an IPSec Encryption Scheme

When designing an encryption scheme for your network, you need to consider the various types of information that will be transmitted and where that information is located. Data on domain controllers, file servers, and database servers may be sensitive enough that it requires encryption, whereas information on the standard user's workstation probably isn't nearly as sensitive and may only need to be digitally signed. In many cases, the security needs lie somewhere in between. IPSec allows you to define security policies that a server will request encrypted communications from clients in but will allow unencrypted sessions if the client doesn't support IPSec. Similarly, you can specify that your clients will use IPSec whenever a server requests it but that your clients will not initiate it themselves.

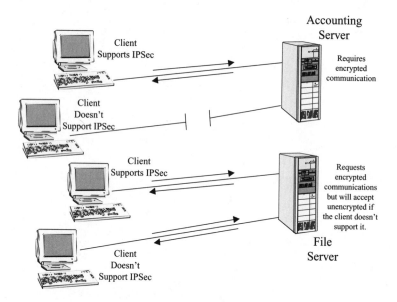

In order to design an effective IPSec encryption scheme, you need to take into account all of the data you gathered during the planning phases of the security implementation. Determine which computers require strong security, which should request security but can downgrade if necessary, and which should respond to the IPSec requests of other computers. This encryption scheme can then be applied as explained in the Designing IPSec Policies section.

Negotiating Security

IPSec is a powerful tool that can enhance the security of communication across the Internet. The encryption and authentication tools can secure a communication channel between two properly configured computers. However, what happens when one of the two computers is not configured to communicate using IPSec policies? The answer is found in the ability of IPSec to adjust to the communication situation. When an IPSec-configured computer is confronted with a situation where it is asked to establish a session with a non-IPSec-aware computer, the IPSec computer will attempt to negotiate a level of security for the session.

You can configure IPSec security policy using the Local Computer Policy MMC Snap-in. Expand Computer Configuration | Windows Settings | Security Settings and highlight the IP Security Policy on Local Machine. In the right-hand panel of the Local Computer Policy Snap-in, you will notice three predefined policies for IPSec negotiation.

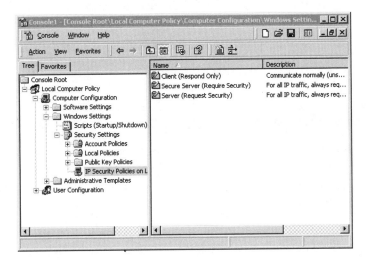

The standard policy templates are as follows:

- Client (Respond Only)

  When this policy template is applied, the client computer will respond to IPSec requests from another computer but will not attempt to establish an IPSec session.

- Secure Server (Require Security)

  This policy is the highest level of security. It ensures that only IPSec secure communication will take place. When a computer uses this policy, it will not negotiate a lower level of security with a non-IPSec computer. This assures that no communication will be unsecured.

- Server (Request Security)

  A computer using this negotiation policy will first attempt to establish an IPSec session. If the remote computer is able to communicate using IPSec rules, the IPSec rules will be used. If, however, the remote computer is not capable of using IPSec security, the local computer will communicate using standard data transmission techniques. This policy is used to ensure that communication will be established regardless of the security state of the two computers.

These security templates are here for convenient configuration of IPSec security policy. You should consider custom configuring an IPSec negotiation policy that is best for your situation.

Designing IPSec Policies

Before you can design IPSec policies, you must first establish what level of security must be used. These levels are best set on a department-by-department basis. You will once again use your interviewing skills to determine what level of security is needed by the department.

You should be aware that in most cases, the people in a department will not have a clear picture of the ramifications that IPSec implementation will have. It is your duty to make the need for security clear as well as describing what can happen when security levels are improperly set. Take this information and classify each department's security needs as high, medium, or low.

You will need to have a clear picture of each department's security requirements. These are to be documented and approved by management. Armed with this documentation, you are ready to continue.

With your plan in place, you can now build and apply the IPSec policies for your network. You can manage your IPSec policies from the IP Security Policies MMC Snap-in, which you can open by following these steps:

1. Click on **Start | Run**, type "MMC" in the Run dialog box, and click on **OK** to open an empty MMC window.

2. Click on **Console | Add/Remove Snap-in** to open the Add/Remove Snap-in dialog box.

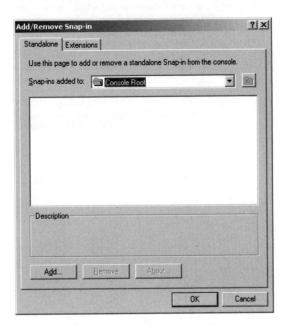

3. Click on **Add** to open the Add Standalone Snap-in dialog box.

4. Select the IP Security Policy Management Snap-in and click on **Add** to add it to the MMC and configure it.

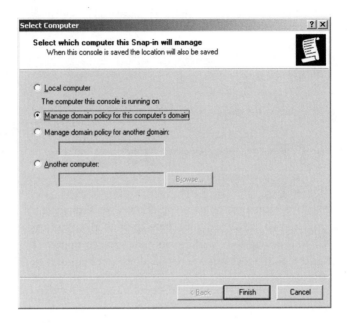

5. Select the appropriate computer or domain that you'll manage with this MMC snap-in. You can choose to set up this snap-in to manage IPSec policies for the computer you're working on, the current domain this computer is in, a different domain on your network, or a different computer on your network. Of course, whichever option you choose, you must have sufficient rights to modify policies on that computer or domain.

6. Click on **Finish** to return to the Add Standalone Snap-in dialog box.

7. Click on **Close** to close the Add Standalone Snap-in dialog box, then click on **OK** to close the Add/Remove Snap-in dialog box, revealing the MMC with the snap-in installed.

Whichever computer or domain you choose, you'll manage the policies in the same way. The policies you define and select here apply to all communications on this computer if you set up this snap-in to manage only the local computer. If this snap-in is set up to manage the domain, changes here will affect all computers in this domain.

When defining policies for your IPSec solution, you have to specify the following five main items:

- The IP filter this policy applies to
- The details of the IPSec transaction, including security method and encryption protocols
- The allowed authentication methods
- The tunneling settings
- The type of connections this rule applies to

The following sections will explore each of these topics in detail.

Creating a New Policy

To create a new IPSec policy for your computer or domain, follow these steps:

1. From the MMC Snap-in console tree, right-click on IP Security Policies. Choose **Create IP Security Policy** from the shortcut menu to start the IP Security Policy Wizard. Read the introductory message, then click on **Next** to continue.

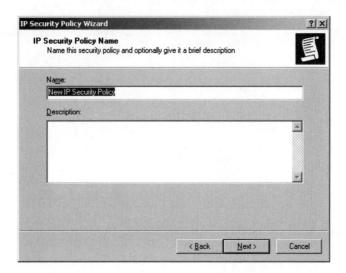

2. Type a name and description for this policy, then click on **Next** to continue.

3. In order to have this computer respond to requests for security when none of the actions defined in this policy apply to the request, enable the **Activate the default response rule** checkbox, then click on **Next**.

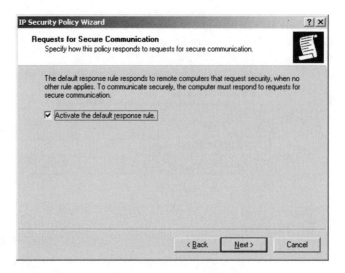

4. Select the authentication method that the default response rule will use, then click on **Next** to continue.

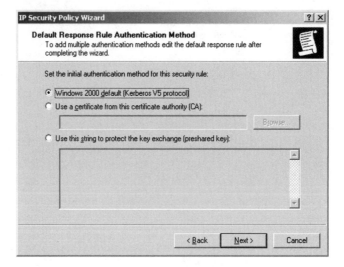

5. Select the **Edit properties** checkbox, then click on **Finish** to complete the wizard and open the Properties dialog box for this policy.

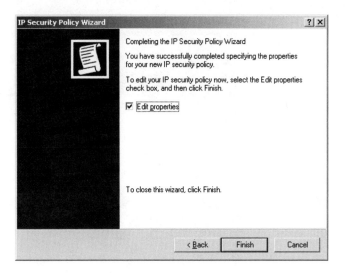

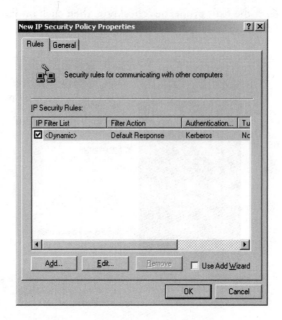

Once you've created a new IPSec policy, you can modify its configuration in its Properties dialog box. If you just completed the IP Security Policy Wizard, the Properties dialog for the new policy opens automatically. To edit other policies, simply right-click on them in the IP Security Policies MMC Snap-in and choose **Properties** from the shortcut menu. The Properties dialog box gives you complete control over the policy in question. The following sections describe how to work with policies from this dialog box.

Defining IP Filters

Each IPSec policy needs to have at least one IP filter defined. IP filters specify a computer or group of computers that the actions of this policy will apply to. In other words, when this computer communicates with computers specified in the IP filter defined in this policy, then the actions defined in this policy will apply to that communication.

To modify the IP filters for a policy, open its Properties dialog box. On the Rules page, disable the **Use Add Wizard** checkbox and click on **Add**. The Rule Properties dialog box opens. By default, this dialog box displays the IP Filter List page when it opens.

To modify the IP filter list, follow these steps:

1. Click on **Add** to open the IP Filter List dialog box.

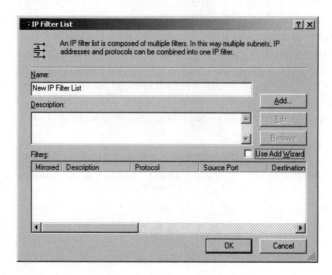

2. Disable the **Use Add Wizard** checkbox, then click on **Add** to open the Filter Properties dialog box.

3. Specify which IP addresses or subnets you want to include in this filter, then click
    on the **Protocol** tab.

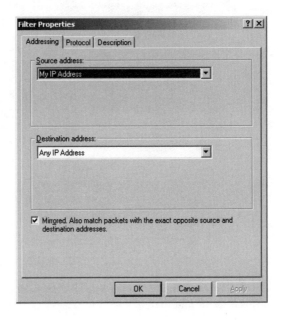

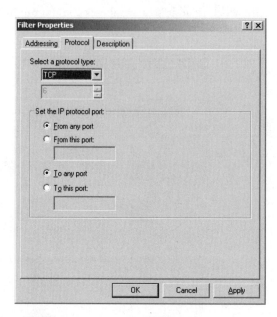

4. Select the protocol that you want this IP filter to apply to, then select the ports that this filter should match.

5. Click on the **Description** tab and enter a description of this IP filter, then click on **OK** to return to the IP Filter List dialog box.

6. Repeat steps 2 through 5 to add as many IP filters as you need to properly describe the group of computers that you want this policy to apply to. Click on **OK** when you are finished.

Defining Filter Actions

The next step is to define filter actions that should occur when this computer is communicating with a computer that matches the IP filter list. To do this, follow these steps:

1. In the Rule Properties dialog box, click on the **Filter Action** tab.

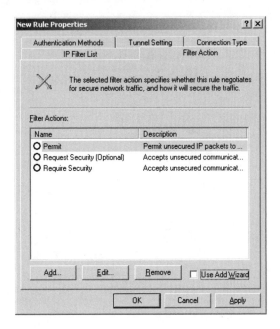

2. Disable the **Use Add Wizard** checkbox, then click on **Add** to open the New Filter Action Properties dialog box.

3.   By selecting the appropriate option, you can either permit communications, block communications, or negotiate security for this connection. If you choose to negotiate security for this connection, click on **Add** to open the New Security Method dialog box, which will allow you to select a security method for this filter action.

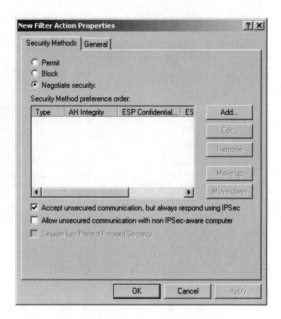

4. You can select either the **High** or **Medium** security option from this dialog box, or you can select the **Custom** option and click on **Settings** to open the Custom Security Method Settings dialog box.

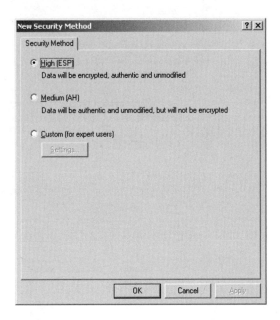

5. This dialog box allows you to set precisely the level of security needed for connections that meet this IP filter. When you've added all of the appropriate actions for this policy, close all of the dialog boxes by clicking on **OK**.

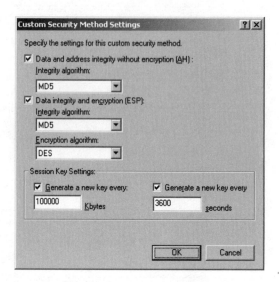

Specifying Authentication Methods

Next, you need to set the authentication methods for this policy. Do this by following these steps:

1. Select the **Authentication Methods** tab from the New Rule Properties dialog box.

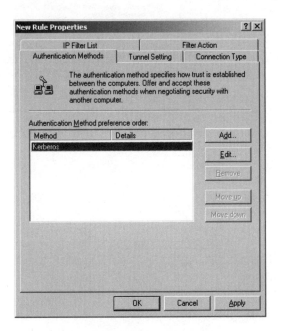

2. Click on **Add** to create a new authentication method in the New Authentication Method Properties dialog box.

3. Select the authentication method you want to use for this policy, then click on OK.

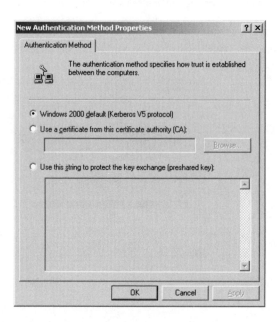

Defining Tunneling Settings

Your next task is to define the tunneling settings for this policy. If this policy is supposed to apply to an IPSec tunnel, click on the **Tunnel Setting** tab, select **The tunnel endpoint is specified by this IP address**, and enter the IP address of the tunnel endpoint.

Specifying Connection Types

Finally, you need to specify the connection type that this policy should apply to. As shown in the following figure, select the appropriate option from the Connection Type page.

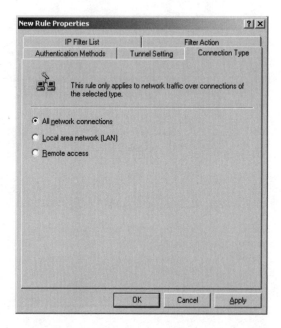

After making your selection, click on **OK** to close the New Rule Properties dialog box.

IPSec Management

There are several tasks that you can perform to assist in the management of your IPSec policies. Each of these features is very easy to perform and can be quite useful in the day-to-day tasks of administration. The basic tasks you can perform toward management of IPSec policies are all available from the shortcut menu either of a particular policy or of the IP Security Policies MMC Snap-in itself. They are as follows:

Check Policy Integrity

> Right-click on IP Security Policies in the Details pane and choose **All Tasks | Check Policy Integrity** from the shortcut menu to verify that the policies you have installed are consistent and do not contradict one another.

Restore Default Policies

Right-click on IP Security Policies and choose **All Tasks |
Restore Default Policies** to restore the default policies to
their default state. This doesn't remove any new policies
you create but it simply restores the default policies to
their original values.

Import Policies

Right-click on IP Security Policies and choose **All Tasks |
Import Policies** to import IPSec policies from a file
exported by the **Export Policies** option. This is useful for
copying policy settings from one computer to others on
your network.

Export Policies

Right-click on IP Security Policies and choose **All Tasks |
Export Policies** to export IPSec policies to a file that can
later be imported by the **Import Policies** option. This is
useful for copying policy settings from one computer to
others on your network.

Rename Policy

Right-click on the IPSec policy you want to rename,
choose **Rename Policy**, type the new name, and press
ENTER.

Delete Policy

Right-click on the IPSec policy you want to delete and
choose **Delete Policy**.

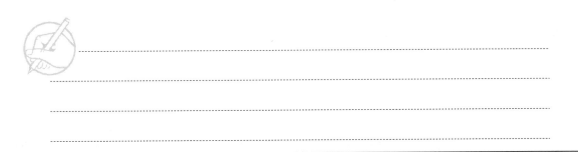

Scenario 8-1: IPSec

This scenario is based on the case studies introduced earlier in the course. You may find it helpful to review the case studies in Appendix C at the end of the manual. Suggested answers are provided in Appendix B at the end of the manual.

Barney's Bank

How should Barney's Bank apply IPSec policies?

....

....

Fairco Manufacturing

How should Fairco Manufacturing apply IPSec policies?

....

....

SUMMARY

During this chapter, you were introduced to the following topics:

- SMB signing
- IPSec
    - IPSec basics
    - Creating an IPSec plan
    - Working with IPSec policies
    - Working with IP filters
    - Working with IPSec properties
    - Managing IPSec policies

Stop now and complete the following NEXTSim exercises on the Interactive Learning CD-ROM:

Windows 2000 Network Security Design
Communication Security
Manage IP Filtering

POST-TEST QUESTIONS

The answers to these questions are in Appendix A at the end of this manual.

1. What are the drawbacks of SMB signing?

....

....

2. What are the three default IPSec policies?

....

....

3. What are the two data integrity algorithms in IPSec and which is more secure?

....

....

4. How does Diffie-Hellman help to increase the efficiency of IPSec?

....

....

Appendix A—Answers to Pre-Test and Post-Test Questions

CHAPTER 1

Pre-Test Answers

1. Any three of authentication, credential management, nonrepudiation, security groups, access control groups, communications encryption, file encryption, and auditing

2. Kerberos v5 authentication

3. An ACL is an Access Control List, which is a list of who can access a particular object and in what manner.

4. They are simply digitally signed statements assuring that the identity of the person who originally obtained the public/private key pair has been verified.

5. IPSec ensures data integrity and confidentiality as it's being passed over the network.

Post-Test Answers

1. Kerberos v5 is a single sign-on network authentication technology that provides mutual authentication between the user and the object being accessed.

2. In a transitive trust, credentials can be passed through from domain to domain; in a nontransitive trust, only the two domains involved in the trust relationship can share credentials.

3. Only users in the Global group's domain can be members of a Global group. You can also nest Global groups.

4. People may feel unable to remember them and write them down, possibly providing intruders with a means of discovering them.

5. Only Windows 2000 NTFS drives support EFS.

CHAPTER 2

Pre-Test Answers

1. A regional organization is relatively small with few locations, possibly only one.

2. Product Division model, Functional Division model, and Matrix model

3. True

4. Calculating the cost of something based on the cost of materials, labor required to deploy it, and support costs over a specific period of time

Post-Test Answers

1. A single domain tree

2. Regional, national, international, subsidiary, and branch office

3. It is organized along product lines, with relatively autonomous company divisions responsible for all stages of a particular product or group of products.

4. Either integrate it as a new tree in your existing domain forest or dismantle its network structure and rebuild it to fit with yours.

5. The final decision ultimately rests on the balance of tolerance for risk versus TCO for the upgrade.

CHAPTER 3

Pre-Test Answers

1. Individual survey, departmental survey, and resource monitoring

2. Centralized and decentralized

3. The upgrade may require features of Active Directory or the security system that are unavailable prior to its implementation.

4. Replication of the Global Catalog could require more bandwidth across a WAN than is currently available, thereby significantly degrading performance of other tasks over that line.

Post-Test Answers

1. Users may not understand the technical issues, may be unaware of how the applications and data interact, or may have become used to accessing data that they don't need for their job assignments

2. Outside contractors in an administrative role on the network may pose a security threat.

3. Online documentation and FAQs, e-mail access to support personnel, phone access to support personnel, and onsite support personnel

4. Direct dial-up, VPN, and leased line

5. They won't integrate with Active Directory, they have proprietary security models, and they require additional administration to keep them working properly

CHAPTER 4

Pre-Test Answers

1. Deters theft, deters physical damage, deters local logon, deters installation of unapproved hardware, deters modification of audit logs

2. Only full administrators

3. Disconnect it from the network and have it loaded only with information prepared for the general public

4. The repetitious and orderly attempting of all possible passwords in an attempt to happen across the correct one

5. The consistent use of the most current Web browser available and diligent application of all issued security patches

Post-Test Answers

1. Schema operations master, domain naming master, infrastructure master, RID operations master, and PDC emulator

2. Only members of a specially trusted applications managers group

3. A passive tap simply collects data that's passed on the network by other users. An active network tap is one that not only listens to data on the network, but also introduces its own network traffic.

4. False. Some users will feel they need to write down extremely complex passwords, which can compromise security.

5. Stateful inspection checks the destination of each inbound data packet to ensure that it matches a previous outbound request.

CHAPTER 5

Pre-Test Answers

1. The recording of a log of significant events that occur on your network

2. True

3. By default, security permissions set on a folder will propagate to all files and subfolders in that folder.

4. To protect files from access by someone who has bypassed the file system and, therefore, goes around the standard ACLs

5. Kerberos v5

6. The System account has full administrative control over the computer, so a service running under this account can do practically anything. To avoid potential problems and spoofing, allow only administrators to install services on computers on your network.

7. Ensuring that the name-to-network address mapping is correct so that users access the computer they expect to

Post-Test Answers

1. If you have too many events audited, finding the important ones will be more difficult.

2. Object access

3. The Delete subfolders and files on the folder the file resides in permission

4. With digest authentication, the authentication client passes a hashed version of the user's credentials to the server, which uses the same algorithm to hash the password stored on the server. If they match, the authentication is successful and access is granted. Digest authentication requires the server to have a reversibly encrypted version of the password.

5. Installation and configuration of client workstations with RIS are not security risks because only the installation defined by a network administrator can be performed. The configuration cannot be modified by the person performing the installation.

CHAPTER 6

Pre-Test Answers

1. An entity created to validate the identity of users and resources, then issue certificates verifying that identity

2. Certificate purpose organization, geographic organization, and political organization

3. By publishing and maintaining a Certificate Revocation List (CRL)

4. In Windows 2000, you can delegate control over specific tasks on specific sets of resources without having to make anyone a full administrator of the domain.

5. Account Policies, Local Policies, Event Log, Restricted Groups, System Services, Registry, File System, Public Key Policies, and IP Security Policies on Active Directory

Post-Test Answers

1. Issuer's identifying information, subject's identifying information, subject's public key, period that the certificate is valid for (start and stop dates), and the issuer's digital signature

2. Each CA has a certificate issued by its parent CA, providing a chain of trust. The root CA issues itself a certificate and that certificate must be stored in the CTL of any resource that will trust certificates issued by any CA in the hierarchy.

3. Adding that CA to the Trusted Root Certification Authorities policy for your domain

4. The OU

5. Domain Controller Security policy, Domain Security policy, and Local Security policy

CHAPTER 7

Pre-Test Answers

1. VPN is the creation of a secure virtual network connection between two computers over an unsecured public network.

2. Brute-force logon attacks, eavesdropping via phone taps, and physical access to the remote computer

3. False. MS-CHAP allows a reversibly encrypted password; CHAP does not.

4. To pass information between two physically separate networks

Post-Test Answers

1. The Disallow all remote access to the network policy

2. By supporting certificate-based authentication, such as smart cards, or by supporting advanced hardware such as biometric scanners

3. A RADIUS server provides centralized authentication services to all dial-up servers on the network.

4. Caller ID checks the number that the remote computer is calling from. The callback number simply specifies the number that the server will call to make the final network connection, so the client must be at that number to complete the connection.

5. Generate a random 14-character password using upper-case and lower-case letters, numbers, and symbols; enter it into both the remote router and the answering router; then destroy all written copies of that password.

CHAPTER 8

Pre-Test Answers

1. SMB signing is a data integrity tool that digitally signs all information transferred over the network.

2. IPSec provides data integrity and encryption to protect your data from corruption, modification, and eavesdropping while it is in transit over the network.

3. IP filters specify a computer or group of computers that the actions of an IPSec policy will apply to.

Post-Test Answers

1. It only provides digital signatures, not encryption; it is limited to 40-bit encryption; and its cipher strength depends on the user's password

2. Client (Respond Only), Server (Request Security), and Secure Server (Require Security)

3. Message Digest 5 (MD5) and Secure Hashing Algorithm (SHA); SHA is slower but more secure.

4. By generating the same secret key on both the sending and receiving computers, shared-secret cryptography can process data much faster than public key cryptography.

Appendix B — Solutions

CHAPTER 2

Scenario 2-1

Barney's Bank

1. Barney's Bank follows the International model.
2. Barney's Bank follows the Functional Division model.

Fairco Manufacturing

1. Fairco Manufacturing follows the Regional model.
2. Fairco Manufacturing follows the Product Division model.

Scenario 2-2

Barney's Bank

1. Barney's Bank currently has dial-up access for a few major customers that they need to manage a modem pool and RAS for. They intend to implement secure online banking over the Internet soon.
2. Barney's Bank tends to grow via acquisitions, then merges each acquired company's network into the domain forest.
3. Barney's Bank, having significant resources to apply to technological situations, strives to maintain a consistently high technological level for its network infrastructure. It also expects a strong technical skill level from its employees.

Fairco Manufacturing

1. Fairco has both dial-up and tunneling connections for their sales force as well as extranet connections for their customers.
2. Fairco relies on slow growth due to sales, preferring to avoid the problems related to acquisitions.
3. Fairco Manufacturing has mixed feelings about its computing resources, attempting to provide cutting-edge connectivity for its sales force and customers but lagging somewhat in its support for its own workforce in areas such as the accounting system. The skill level of the employees at Fairco is a little on the low side, necessitating more basic training for modest upgrades along with a generally strong resistance to change.

CHAPTER 3

Scenario 3-1

Barney's Bank

Management needs far-reaching access to most information but not necessarily full administrative access. IT staff need access to most of the data for typical data-management functions, including a few people at each location who have full administrative permissions. Typical users need access to those specific areas of the network that enable them to do their jobs properly, while the rest of the information can be secured to prevent problems either through accidental misuse or deliberate malicious attack. Bank customers need secured access to their accounts. This access can be partially authenticated through the use of an ATM or debit card, along with the entry of a PIN or password.

Fairco Manufacturing

Management and IT personnel will have far-reaching access to all of the information on the network. The administrative personnel will be able to manage data for each of their own particular areas of functionality. The sales teams need read access to product data for their particular line of specialty as well as limited read access to the other product lines to assist in cross sales. They also need to be able to post sales orders and manage sales histories. The design and production teams will be utilizing CAD software and team management programs.

Scenario 3-2

Barney's Bank

Currently, the bandwidth allocated for Barney's Bank should be sufficient to service its standard traffic. The only exception is the 56K modems that the major customers are using for electronic transactions. When the secure online banking option becomes available, it should alleviate this problem.

Fairco Manufacturing

Fairco Manufacturing has a problem with the connectivity between its warehouses and its main office. Until all of the warehouses are using the VPN connection over the Internet, they will have bandwidth problems.

Scenario 3-3

Barney's Bank

Barney's Bank's practice of upgrading each company it acquires is very helpful to the homogeneous nature of the network, making the security design much more efficient. Also, their practice of diligently applying security updates will significantly increase the security of the network.

Fairco Manufacturing

Fairco's reluctance to upgrade the accounting package could have adverse effects on security there, possibly allowing unapproved people to access sensitive accounting data since that software is not integrated with the Windows 2000 Kerberos v5 single sign-on.

CHAPTER 4

Scenario 4-1

1. Since the bank has few external network connections, the chances of a network attack coming from outside can be minimized by tightly securing each of those connections. The dial-up connections need to be fully authenticated and secured with IPSec, the Web site needs a tight firewall between it and the main network, and the kiosks need clear security features implemented. Physically securing the servers will help prevent a multitude of threats. A password length and complexity policy will assist in keeping out intruders. Diligent virus protection and user training about viruses can help prevent spoofing attacks. Workstations in areas frequented by customers are also at risk and require the attention of users to ensure that they are locked before being left unattended.

2. The dial-up and VPN connections require IPSec encryption to ensure that network taps cannot access the data. Salespeople traveling with laptops must be careful both about theft of the computer and unauthorized access to the data.

Scenario 4-2

1. With properly managed ACLs, secured servers, a highly qualified staff, diligent application of patches and updates, and thorough planning and testing, internal risks are minimized for Barney's Bank. Their greatest risks will likely be from lax user practices, such as users allowing a virus to install itself on a computer where it could be used to spoof an administrative account, accidentally deleting or modifying data, or simply selecting weak passwords that could be easy for an intruder to guess.

2. Probably the biggest internal risk Fairco takes is the possibility of undertrained personnel managing their data. They also have all the standard risks from poor user practices that accompany poor training: virus attacks, accidental data deletions, poor password selections, and even practices such as sharing passwords or writing them down. In addition, without commitment from management to support the upgrading of the software in use, known security holes may go unpatched.

Scenario 4-3

1. With the upcoming implementation of secure online banking, this needs to be one of the principal considerations in the design of an Internet security policy. They need to provide secure access to customer information while still keeping all other access closed off. Requiring users to log on with a long password that includes both upper-case and lower-case letters and numbers will help in that regard. They also need to set up a strong firewall between the Web site and the main corporate network, keeping traffic to a minimum. Internal network users need to be able to access the Internet, but that access could pass through a proxy server to keep unwanted external traffic out.

2. The company's VPN access for traveling salespeople and warehouses is the primary security concern for Fairco's Internet policy. As long as they have IPSec enabled on these connections and the accounts enabled for access to them have reasonably strong passwords, this should be a fairly secure point. Fairco also needs to secure its extranet so that the online ordering process is not compromised. This means thorough testing of the software in use along with secure passwords and sensible user practices.

Scenario 4-4

1. Using Windows 2000 authentication and Kerberos v5 single sign-on capabilities, all employees of the bank will be authenticated each time they access any network resources. The domains provide security boundaries for each of the users, but the automatic trust relationships allow authenticated access to resources in other domains as needed. The servers need to be secured so that only full administrators can log on locally to them, and the ACLs of the various files and resources on them should be set to allow the minimum necessary access for each group of people using those resources.

   Workstations need to have locking screen savers implemented and set to lock the computer within a very short time, perhaps 3 minutes or less, especially on computers on desks frequently visited by customers or other people from outside the company. In addition, the personnel should be trained to manually lock their workstations whenever they leave them unattended.

   The kiosks, which simply provide information about the bank, can be physically disconnected from the network and store only public information on them, thereby providing maximum possible security. However, the ATMs and other public banking terminals need to be able to access account information for the currently logged-on customer, so they will still need to have a network connection. Authentication can involve swiping an ATM card and entry of a PIN, and the data needs to be secured such that only the currently logged-on user can access it. These computers need to be running software that cannot be turned off without shutting down the system, and standard users should not be able to access the power supply. The user interface should provide access only to the standard single-user banking functions.

2. The single-domain model provides a tight security boundary in which all authentication occurs via the Kerberos v5 protocol, except for those computers on the network that are incapable of it, such as the DOS 5 machines. Servers need tight security settings and should allow only full administrators to log on locally. All data needs to be secured via ACLs that permit only the necessary access from each group of users.

   When possible, the workstations need to have a specific account for each person who will be using them. For access to any sensitive information, the user must be authenticated, so the DOS 5 machines cannot be used for such purposes.

Sales people traveling with laptops must have locking screen savers set to lock the computer within 3 minutes or less of inactivity. They also need to be:

- o   Trained to manually lock the computer whenever it's unattended.

- o   Supplied with cables that can physically secure the laptop to deter theft.

- o   Trained on proper methods of handling the laptop while moving through public places like airports.

CHAPTER 5

Scenario 5-1

Barney's Bank

Auditing successful logons will provide a record of who's accessing the network at any particular time. Auditing failed logon attempts exposes brute-force logon attacks. Auditing access to highly sensitive resources provides useful information without overwhelming the security logs.

Fairco Manufacturing

Since Fairco provides external access to the network through their extranet, both successful and failed logon attempts should be logged. Also, logging access to highly sensitive resources provides useful information without overwhelming the security logs.

Scenario 5-2

Barney's Bank

1.   Design security groups based on information the members of each group need access to, then set the ACLs of files and folders to allow access only to those groups. No individual accounts should be specified in network file system ACLs.

2.   In general, IT should encourage network users to use EFS whenever possible to assist in securing files. Each location should have at least one EFS recovery agent designated to restore encrypted files in emergency situations.

Fairco Manufacturing

1. Share only those folders containing documents necessary for the network users, and set the ACLs on those shares to allow only the specific security groups that will be using that information

2. In general, the files in use at Fairco Manufacturing require less security than those of Barney's Bank. Most files do not need to be encrypted with EFS. Management and IT should confer on which files need to be encrypted, such as client lists and accounting information, and keep those files on a separate network drive. At least two EFS recovery agents should be designated to recover encrypted files in emergency situations.

Scenario 5-3

Barney's Bank

Yes, to authenticate their larger customers who have dial-up access to their account information. Each of these clients should be issued a certificate that can be used for authentication purposes.

Fairco Manufacturing

If management does not want to provide resources to implement a certificate authentication system for their clients, they could simply implement a digest authentication system, requesting that each client choose a password complex enough that brute-force logon attacks will be unlikely to succeed.

Scenario 5-4

Barney's Bank

After securing the services as described in the Common Services Security Issues section, they should implement a plan of remote installation to minimize the possibility of unauthorized software being installed on the network workstations, which could compromise security.

Fairco Manufacturing

With a variety of network operating systems, centralized management is impossible, so keeping unnecessary services from running on the network may be difficult.

CHAPTER 6

Scenario 6-1

Barney's Bank

1. Due to the distributed nature of the bank, a reasonable certification hierarchy would place a CA at each location. This would minimize traffic on the WAN links.

2. Yes, since they are in the process of setting up a secure online banking service. In order for their customers to be able to verify transactions with the bank, an external third-party CA must be able to vouch for the bank's identity.

Fairco Manufacturing

1. Since most of the network users are at the same location, a likely scenario for their certification hierarchy would be to assign separate CAs to handle each of the different certification types, if they actually need more than one CA at all.

2. Yes, since they are providing an extranet for their customers, they should have a third-party issue a certificate validating their identity for Internet transactions.

Senario 6-2

Barney's Bank

1. Allow the management of each location to control the resources on that domain. Authority could be further delegated to individual department heads within each location if the manager so desires.

2. Since there are numerous workstations in public places, such as on the desks of loan officers where customers routinely sit, a strict Lockout policy should be enforced, locking out a terminal after as few as three failed logon attempts and keeping the workstation locked for up to 15 minutes after the third failed attempt.

Fairco Manufacturing

1. Since the divisions of the company are fairly autonomous, each division manager should be responsible for managing the users and resources on that portion of the network. The manager can then further delegate tasks on that section of the network to other people in that department.

2. Since users are likely to have less computer training, the complexity requirements for the Password policy should probably be somewhat relaxed to avoid having passwords written down and taped to computer monitors.

CHAPTER 7

Scenario 7-1

Barney's Bank

The only remote access that Barney's Bank currently allows is for a few of their larger clients to dial up for account access. These accounts need to have appropriately complex passwords to prevent brute-force attacks. The computers they are accessed from must not have the passwords stored on them. The remote access server should be set up for client callback to ensure that only the designated clients can connect remotely.

Fairco Manufacturing

Fairco has a couple of remote access situations that it must deal with. Their traveling sales force must properly protect their laptops from theft. Since they are traveling, the server cannot enforce a specific callback number for these accounts. As for the warehouses, those accounts can be assigned callback numbers that cannot be changed by the clients. All connections must have IPSec enabled to protect the information transfers.

Scenario 7-2

Barney's Bank

Probably so since they have so many branch offices and their clients could potentially dial in to any one of them. A RADIUS server could provide centralized authentication services to the entire bank.

Fairco Manufacturing

Probably not since all of their remote users are connecting to the main office network. They would probably find no benefit from the added level of administration introduced by a RADIUS server.

Scenario 7-3

Barney's Bank

They could use VPN router connections for each of their remote offices, especially the European offices, thus saving a good deal of money on connectivity. By applying IPSec and securing the routers, the security of the connection would remain at a reasonably high level.

Fairco Manufacturing

Fairco could provide enhanced connectivity to their warehouses by creating demand-dial routed connections, effectively including the warehouses in the Fairco LAN. By protecting the password as described in the text, they would actually increase security between the two networks by eliminating the chance that a person would somehow reveal the password to an intruder.

CHAPTER 8

Scenario 8-1

Barney's Bank

All transactions on the Barney's Bank network should be authenticated and digitally signed. Any transactions with secure servers need to be encrypted. Also, all remote access connections need to be encrypted.

Fairco Manufacturing

Transactions between workstations don't need to be secured, so workstations can simply respond to IPSec requests from other computers and not instigate security themselves. Most servers on the network should request security, but if the client doesn't support IPSec, the servers could allow unsecured communications. However, critical servers handling accounting details and personnel records should require IPSec, communicating only with compatible clients.

Appendix C — Case Studies

INTRODUCTION TO CASE STUDIES

The following case studies are used in conjunction with scenario-based training activities and are referenced at various times during the course. References appearing with the scenario-based activities are abbreviated, focusing on information relating to that specific scenario only. This appendix includes the full text of each of the case studies.

Barney's Bank

Barney's Bank is a full-service financial institution with branch offices in various locations across the United States. Barney's Bank also has several wholly owned subsidiaries, with five different locations in Europe. The organization has grown traditionally through acquisition and plans to continue to use this as its primary growth model. Each of the remote offices has limited control over day-to-day decisions but all major decisions are made from the main office in Corpus Christi, Texas.

The overall network structure is a forest of Windows 2000 domains. Each of the U.S. locations controls its own domain and these domains are organized into a single tree whose root represents the main office in Corpus Christi. The European subsidiaries each operate their own domains, which have different namespaces, and so are separate trees in the overall forest. The forest root is the Corpus Christi domain.

The bank network exhibits a variety of security issues that the security plan must address. The servers control a great deal of information that must be kept private in order for the bank to remain viable. Various groups of users on the network each have different access needs to that information, from the executive level down to the tellers. The bank has several kiosks that provide simple information about the bank as well as other kiosks and automated tellers customers can access and manipulate account information by.

Barney's Bank management wants to overhaul the security on the network and each of the noted issues must be properly handled by the security infrastructure being designed. The system needs to provide secure access to all users for their appropriate tasks while protecting all the resources from intruders.

Organizational Structure

Barney's Bank offers a variety of features and services to its customers. Those customers range from individuals with simple savings accounts to large companies requiring complex credit lines and investment services.

The company has a layered approach to management. Upper management controls all major decisions but smaller decisions can be made at lower levels of the company tree. The company has at least partially merged the administrative functions of each of its acquisitions to streamline and normalize functionality as well as cut down on overhead. For example, each of the Accounting, Human Resources, and Marketing departments is centrally managed, with basic day-to-day functions being controlled by the personnel at each individual location.

Barney's Bank employs an educated group of people. Almost everyone working at the bank has achieved at least a high school education, while a good portion of them are college graduates.

Technical Analysis

While it's not yet implemented, the bank is currently planning an online banking feature, which would allow all of its customers to access and manipulate account information securely over the Internet. Currently, Barney's Bank offers dial-up access to a few of the larger accounts but these transactions cannot be made over the Internet yet. A couple of the larger accounts have expressed concern about the security of Internet banking, so Barney's Bank is still attempting to develop a detailed security structure prior to implementing this service.

The bank has a commitment to using hardware and software that will provide the greatest benefit to the bank's processes and to its customers. Whenever possible, the newest hardware is brought in to replace any failing systems. As soon as they can be thoroughly tested, new versions of the main software packages are deployed and the employees are trained in their use. However, due to the practice of acquiring other banks, the bank often has several legacy applications that need to be supported while the transitions are made. There typically is also a period following an acquisition when some legacy hardware needs to be supported while technical details and funding are managed in the replacement strategy.

The bank routinely tests and upgrades new software as it becomes available as well as deploys the currently used software at each newly acquired location. Their upgrade and training plan is very aggressive, including keeping up with all the latest security and functionality updates offered by the software makers.

Security

Barney's Bank consists of a variety of groups of people who are considered end users. A few of the more prominent divisions are as follows:

- Management

  Management personnel at Barney's Bank are responsible for overseeing day-to-day activities as well as medium- and long-range planning. Managers of the individual departments will typically create plans for their departments. These plans are expected to fit in with the plans and procedures of the other departments.

  Departmental plans are presented at biweekly management meetings and are then open for discussion with the other departments. Top management expects the departmental managers to present well thought-out plans that fit well with all other departments.

- IT staff

  Data integrity is a primary responsibility of the IT staff. Security planning is performed at the central office in Corpus Christi and implemented by small groups of professionals at the branch locations. All data backup is performed at the remote offices and is consolidated at the central office for archival on a daily basis.

  The IT staff in Corpus Christi expects that when a problem occurs in a remote office, the IT staff in that office will have the access and resources necessary to resolve the problem.

- Direct salespeople, including loan officers, banking representatives, and tellers

  People who have contact with the public have defined tasks and responsibilities. The bank has gone to great lengths to ensure that these representatives have the tools necessary to do their jobs. These representatives, however, do not have more access to the system than is necessary.

- The general public, who may use kiosks and ATMs

  In recent years, the bank has installed ATMs that allow customers access to their own account information by using a bank card and PIN. There is ongoing planning with the goal of providing Web-based banking for customers. The Web site would provide general information relating to bank products and programs. In addition, by using the ATM card number and PIN via the Web, a customer will be able to access personal account information. Several larger customers have expressed concerns about this level of customer access.

Each of these groups has specific needs in relation to network access and security.

Connectivity

Each of the U.S. locations of Barney's Bank is connected by a dedicated T1 line to the home office in Corpus Christi. The European offices, however, are all sharing bandwidth on a single T1 line back to the main office. The dial-up access that the bank provides to its major customers is serviced by a bank of 56K modems. The company intends to utilize a dedicated T1 line for its secure Internet banking service when that becomes available.

Fairco Manufacturing

Fairco Manufacturing designs, manufactures, and distributes a wide variety of items for department stores in the United States. Sales are wholesale only to retail outlets. The organization employs a large number of outside salespeople who travel to the major customers on established routes.

Fairco Manufacturing has a large LAN configured as a single Windows 2000 domain. Access is provided to remote warehouses in strategic locations around the country via dial-in and Virtual Private Network (VPN) across the Internet. Field salespeople can post their orders on a private page on the company's Web site. Also, several of the retail outlets are participating in an early trial of Fairco's extranet, whereby they can directly order stock through automated inventory control software.

The organization wants to refine and revise its security systems. This includes securing the remote access as well as the extranet used by its customers.

Organizational Structure

Fairco has only one location where all their corporate operations take place, including management and manufacturing. The company has a central management that oversees the basic divisions but each division is responsible for its own product and controls the design, production, marketing, and sales of that product from start to end. The divisions tend to share information and ideas with each other but officially, they are separate entities that operate completely autonomously from one another.

Technical Analysis

While they have considered acquiring other companies in the past, Fairco currently believes that a slow, steady growth model based on sales is more appropriate for the company at this time. Management at Fairco doesn't feel comfortable expanding into other facilities, nor do they believe it's necessary right now to add a large group of people or equipment.

Being a manufacturing company, much of Fairco's workforce is educated at the high school level or below. Even many of the team leaders have been promoted from the lines and are not very comfortable using complicated computer software. However, with only a few exceptions, members of the sales force have at least some college-level education with a fair background in standard computer usage.

While management believes in keeping the IT resources running smoothly, information is not really Fairco's main business, so when resources get tight, IT is one of the first areas to feel it. This translates to several workstations running Windows 95 as well as a couple of computers on the shop floor running DOS 5.0. Also, they haven't upgraded the accounting software in several years because the company that produces it hasn't released a version for Windows NT or Windows 2000.

The IT group has been petitioning to buy an accounting package from a different vendor so they can upgrade the systems and shut down the legacy support required for the other package. The Accounting group, however, is resisting the change, and management is reluctant to spend money on something the Accounting group doesn't want. As computers become damaged or no longer fulfill the task they were originally assigned to, they are replaced by newer machines capable of running Windows 2000 Workstation and the standard upgraded software in use by the company, but no regular upgrade schedule is planned.

Security

Management at Fairco Manufacturing is very departmental. Each department is totally responsible for its own area of authority. Decision making is done on a departmental basis. For this reason, each manager expects access to as much information as possible.

The IT staff is centralized and is responsible for system integrity throughout the entire company. Backup of all data is performed centrally by the IT staff.

The end users at Fairco consist of the office personnel, who take care of business processes; the sales staff, who access the latest product information, inventory, and pricing data; and the production and warehouse crews, who utilize product design and team management software.

Connectivity

The company provides a bank of 56K modems for the warehouses and sales force to use. They also have a T1 connection to the Internet where they host their Web site and process orders placed by the traveling sales team. This connection is also being used for the current extranet trial. This T1 connection also provides the connectivity for the tunneling connections used by the VPN clients needing remote access to the network.

Glossary

[ROOT] object

An object in the directory tree that provides the highest point to access different Country and Organization objects and allow trustee assignments granting rights to the entire directory tree. Country, Organization, and Alias objects are created at the [ROOT] object. It is a place holder and contains no information.

16-bit application

An application native to Windows 3.1 or Windows for Workgroups 3.11.

32-bit application

An application native to Windows NT or Windows 95.

2000rkst.msi

Source file for installing Windows 2000 Support Tools. This file is located in the \Support\Tools\ directory of the Windows 2000 Installation CD-ROM.

Accelerated Graphics Port (AGP)

A bus specification that allows 3D graphics to be displayed rapidly and smoothly on personal computers.

Access Control

The method of authenticating user accounts when users log on to a Windows 2000 or NT domain. Users are granted or denied access to network resources through the use of security descriptors.

Access Control Entry (ACE)

An access privilege assigned to a user or group. With Windows NT/2000 Server, the ACE is stored with the object being protected.

Access Control List (ACL)

1. A list of trustees who have been granted rights to an object or rights to the properties of an object. Each object in the NDS contains an Access Control List.

2. Under Windows NT/2000, the Access Control List contains user and group Access Control Entries.

Access Control List and Access Control Entry

When discussing Windows NT Server security, the discretionary Access Control List (ACL) contains an entry for each user or group for which access privileges or restrictions have been defined. The format of each Access Control Entry (ACE) is that of an access mask containing all values appropriate for the type of resource.

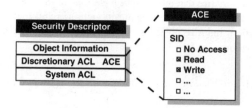

The order in which the entries are listed is significant. SIDs (Security IDs) that have a permission of "No Access" assigned are listed first. This is to ensure that any users or groups specifically restricted from the resource do not accidentally gain access.

Access token

Security token generated during the logon process. The access token includes the user's Security ID (SID), the SIDs of any groups the user belongs to, and explicit user rights assignments.

Accessibility

The level at which the application's user interface supports interaction by users with special needs.

Accessories

Microsoft Windows or Windows NT applets.

Acknowledgment (ACK)

A response by the receiver of a communications message indicating the message was received correctly.

Active Directory

The Windows 2000 directory service. Active Directory treats users, files, directories, applications, and other items as objects. It allows system administratiors to modify the properties of objects. Objects and their properties are described in the Active Directory schema.

Active Directory Installation Wizard

Windows 2000 utility used for promoting a Windows 2000 system to domain controller.

Active Directory Restore Mode Administrative Password

Password required for starting a domain controller in the Active Directory Restore Mode.

Active Directory Services

Microsoft incorporated its automated directory service called Active Directory Services (ADS) into Windows 2000. ADS is a highly integrated set of APIs and protocols that extends its services across multiple servers and name spaces. It also will collect and show resource information that is across LAN and WAN connections.

ADSI allows applications to communicate with Active Directory and provides the means for directory service clients to use one set of interfaces to communicate with any namespace that provides an ADSI implementation. Instead of API calls, ADSI makes it simple to access a namespace's services.

Algorithm   351

Active Directory Services Interface (ADSI)

A COM-based service that allows developers to create Web-based applications that interact with and manage Active Directory from a single interface.

Active Directory-integrated zone

Zone information is stored in the Active Directory database. There is no text file associated with the zone information. The Active Directory replication process performs the replication.

Active Server Pages

A script that can be compiled and run by Internet Information Server. It is written using an ActiveX scripting language, such as VBScript or JScript. Its output is usually plain HTML that can be displayed by any browser.

Address

A unique designation for the location of data, the identity of an intelligent device, or a logical network address. An address allows each device on a single communications line to respond to its own message.

Address resolution

A means for mapping logical addresses to physical addresses.

Address Resolution Protocol (ARP)

A protocol used between routers and nodes to determine the MAC or OSI physical layer address when the Network layer (IP) address is known.

Addressing

The method by which numbers are assigned to identify hardware resources or disk channels. Each controller must have a unique address. The documentation shipped with the controller will list the physical address settings.

Add/Remove Hardware Wizard

Wizard launched by the Control Panel Add/Remove Hardware utility that lets you install, uninstall, and troubleshoot hardware devices.

Adminpak.msi

Source file for installing additional Administrative Tools on a Windows 2000 system. This file is located in the \%systemroot%\system32 folder.

Advanced Configuration and Power Interface (ACPI)

The system interface that enables a motherboard to describe its power management interface, as well as attached devices and their configuration, to the operating system.

Agent

In the client/server model, the part of the system that performs information preparation and exchange on behalf of a client or server application.

Alert

1. Windows 2000 method for monitoring and detecting performance counter limits.

2. An error message sent to the system control point at the host system.

3. A defined response to an event occurring in SQL Server.

Algorithm

The steps that must be performed in order to complete a particular action.

Alias (CNAME) resource record

Resource record used for creating an alias name for a host record already in file, mapping multiple names to a single IP address.

Allocation

Associating a memory address with a block of data and setting aside physical memory to back it.

Analog

The representation of a continuously changing physical variable (sound, for example) by another physical variable (such as electrical current).

Answer file

A text file containing answers to Setup prompts for a Windows NT or Windows 2000 unattended installation. Answer files can be created by using the Windows 2000 Setup Manager Wizard found in the Windows 2000 Resource Kit Deployment Tools.

Applet

A Java program that is embedded in an HTML page and run in a Java-enabled browser.

Application

The use to which an information processing system is put. For example, a payroll application, an airline reservation application, or a network application.

Application layer

OSI Layer 7 providing an interface with user or application programs.

Application Programming Interface (API)

An interface application developers use to invoke the services provided by the operating system or another application. For example, the ODBC API allows developers to use call functions provided by the ODBC library. The WIN32 API allows developers to call functions to interface with 32-bit Windows operating systems.

Application Server Mode

Terminal Services server mode optimized for support of multiuser applications.

Architecture

The specific design and construction of a computer. Architecture usually refers to the hardware makeup of the central processing unit and the size of the byte or set of bytes it processes, such as 8-bit, 16-bit, or 32-bit architecture.

Archive

Storing files on a long-term medium, such as optical disks or magnetic tape.

Area

One part of an autonomous system in OSPF that is used to combine routes to reduce the size of routing tables.

Asynchronous

1. A form of communication where each transmitted character is preceded by a start bit and followed by a stop bit. This eliminates the need for a particular spacing or timing scheme between characters. Personal computers communicate asynchronously via a serial port.

2. An adjective used to describe a method that returns control to the consumer before it completes execution. An asynchronous component cannot return a value.

Asynchronous Transfer Mode (ATM)

 A high-speed (155 to 162 Mbps) communications transport facility capable of carrying voice, data, and video signaling. ATM forms the backbone for broadband ISDN networks.

Attribute

A characteristic that defines an Active Directory (AD) object. Most AD objects are defined by a set of attributes that make the object unique.

Audit policy

Security policy settings that identify security events that will generate Security log entries. Events can be based on the success and/or failure of an action.

Authentication

1. A way to verify that an object sending messages or requests to an NDS is permitted to act on or receive those messages or requests.

2. Login or resource access validation.

Authentication (Connection)

The process by which connection credentials are verified before accepting the connection.

Author mode

Microsoft Management Console (MMC) mode that allows users to modify MMC custom consoles.

Authorization (Connection)

The process by which a connection attempt is verified to ensure that it is allowed.

Automatic Private IP Addressing (APIPA)

An automatic IP configuration process where a client computer that is configured to automatically obtain an IP address can assign itself an IP address when a DHCP server is not available. The APIPA address range is from the 169.254.0.0 network, with a subnet mask of 255.255.0.0.

Autonomous system

The entire OSPF network and routers that are under the control of one corporation.

Autostatic routes

Routes that are learned using a routing protocol like RIP, but the actual process of collecting the routing information only happens when initiated by an administrator.

Backup

Pertaining to a system, device, file, or facility that can be used to recover data in the event of a malfunction or loss of data.

Backup Domain Controller (BDC)

Windows NT domain controller that serves as a backup/failover to the Primary Domain Controller (PDC).

Bandwidth

1. The range of frequencies that can be transmitted through a particular circuit.

2. The speed at which data travels over a particular media. Bandwidth is measured in bits per second.

Bandwidth throttling

Limiting the amount of network or Internet connection bandwidth that will be made available to a Web site or Web server.

Basic disk

> A hard disk configured for industry-standard disk storage. Basic disks are supported by MS-DOS, all Windows versions, all Windows NT versions, and Windows 2000.

Basic Rate ISDN

> ISDN connection using two 64-Kbps channels.

Batch

> A method of computer job processing where input is collected and run through the processing programs all at once and outputs are produced in the form of files and reports. Batch is the opposite of interactive job processing in which an operator at a terminal interacts with the processing program directly during data entry. Most personal computers employ interactive processing. Mainframes use batch processing.

Batch program

> A text file that contains operating system commands. When you run a batch program, the operating system carries out the commands in the file as if you had typed them at the command prompt.

Binary

> Having two components or possible states. Usually represented by a code of zeros and ones.

Binding

> The process by which an object's type library is located.

Binding and unbinding

> Binding assigns a communication protocol to network boards and LAN drivers. Unbinding removes the protocol. Each network board needs at least one communication protocol bound to its LAN driver to process packets. Multiple protocols can be bound to the same LAN driver and board. You can also bind the same protocol stack to more than one LAN driver on the server. Workstations with different protocols can be cabled on the same scheme.

Boot

> To start or restart your computer, loading the operating system from a disk drive.

Boot Information Negotiation Layer (BINL)

> Service that responds to client requests, controls file downloads, and manages other processes during remote installations using RIS.

Border routing

> The practice of splitting a large network into multiple areas with combined IP routes. Usually implemented using OSPF areas.

Break

> An interruption in program execution or data transmission; a loss of communication between sender and receiver. Also a keyboard key that enables the interruption.

Bridge

Bridges are network devices that are more intelligent than repeaters, in that they can read the specific physical address of devices on one network and filter information before passing it on to another network segment.

Bridge Functionality

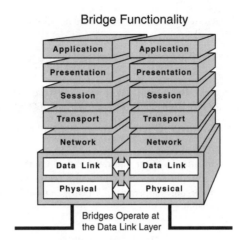

Bridges Operate at
the Data Link Layer

Bridges operate at the Data Link layer of the OSI Model or, more precisely, at the Media Access Control (MAC) sublayer. Bridges go beyond simply amplifying the signal and are able to regenerate the signal. This prevents the duplication and spread of line noise. Only a clean signal is sent. This allows bridges to expand a network beyond that which can be accomplished with only repeaters.

In general, bridges are transparent to higher-level protocols. Segments connected through a bridge remain part of the same logical network. Bridges can filter traffic based on addresses. This allows a bridge to reduce traffic between segments and can also be used to improve security by selecting the packets that can be passed between segments.

Broadcast

1. A transmission of a message intended for general reception rather than for a specific station.

2. In LAN technology, a transmission method used in bus topology networks that sends all messages to all stations even though the messages are addressed to specific stations.

3. A NetWare console command that transmits a message to all network nodes or list of nodes.

Browser

1. This client program (software) is used to look at various Internet resources and retrieve information.

2. Windows service that collects and organizes shared network resources in a hierarchical manner.

3. A NetWare console command that transmits a message to all network nodes or list of nodes.

Browsing

1. Allows you to find objects in the NetWare Directory, which is arranged in hierarchical order.

2. Viewing and retrieving data from the Internet.

3. Viewing available network resources in hierarchical order.

Buffer

A temporary storage place for information. Many times it is a device used to compensate for a difference in either the rate of data flow or the time of occurrence of events in transmission from one device to another.

Built-in Domain users

User accounts created when Active Directory services are installed and the Active Directory is created.

Built-in Local users

User accounts created when Windows 2000 is installed.

Bus

1. A pathway on which data travels. Examples of buses in a typical Macintosh computer include the expansion bus (NuBus or PCI), Apple Desktop Bus (ADB), and SCSI bus.

2. LAN data pathway based on a single cable terminated at both ends.

Bus topology

A bus network topology consists of a linear transmission medium that is terminated at both ends. Nodes attach directly to the bus, making failures difficult to troubleshoot. Any break in the bus causes the entire network to become inoperable. Difficulty in troubleshooting is considered the biggest drawback for a bus topology.

Simple Bus Network

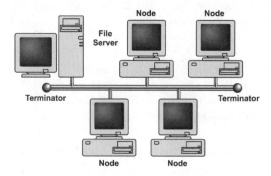

Although a bus normally is drawn as a straight line in pictures and diagrams, most bus networks represent cables that snake, weave, and wrap their way through building's conduits and corridors. This can make the overall length of buses grow rapidly.

Bus topologies commonly use coaxial cable as their transmission medium. Traditionally, Ethernet has used a bus topology.

Byte

Short for "binary digit eight." A unit of information consisting of usually 8 bits. A file's size is measured in bytes or potential storage capacity is measured in bytes, but when dealing with very large numbers, the terms kilobyte, megabyte, or gigabyte are used.

Cache

An area of computer memory set aside for frequently used data to speed operations. Some caches are general purpose, while others are for specific operations. A disk cache is an area of system memory reserved for caching disk reads and writes. A CPU cache is a dedicated, high-speed memory array used to cache pending instructions.

Cell

1. This is a fixed length data element that can be transmitted in asynchronous transfer mode (ATM).

2. Cellular transmission boundary.

Certificate

The document (usually digital) issued by a Certificate Authority that includes the Certificate Authority's digital signature, the user's public and private key, and user information.

Certificate Authority (CA)

A server that issues certificates for the purpose of authenticating users and computers or securing data transmission.

Chart view

System Monitor view displaying real-time performance counter data as a line chart.

Checksum

Used in data communications to monitor the number of bits being transmitted between communication devices by means of a simple mathematical algorithm. The checksum is used to ensure that the full complement of bits is received successfully by the receiving device.

Cipher

A Windows 2000 command used for managing data encryption.

Classless Interdomain Routing (CIDR)

A new way of designing IP address configuration; used on the Internet to aggregate blocks of addresses together in order to make more addresses available and to group routing information to ease the load on Internet routers.

Clean installation

Refers to a new installation of Windows 2000 as opposed to an upgrade.

Cleanup

SQL Server replication process-distributed updates and sync information are removed.

Client

1. A workstation that requests services of another computer (server).

2. The portion of a client/server application providing the end-user interface (front-end).

Client Access License (CAL)

Microsoft software license allowing one client connection for either per-server or per-seat licensing.

Client Installation Wizard (CIW)

Installation wizard downloaded to the remote client during RIS installation. CIW is also known as the OSChooser.

Client software

A software program used to contact and obtain data from a server software program on another computer, often across a great distance. Each client program is designed to work with one or more specific kinds of server programs, and each server requires a specific kind of client.

Clock/Calendar

Used to identify the date and time of computer transactions. Certain software programs utilize the date and time functions more than others.

Cluster

1. A group of data stored together on one or more sectors of a floppy disk or hard disk. (A sector usually contains 512 bytes of data.) When DOS stores data on a disk, it usually breaks the data into smaller sections, which it writes to various places on the disk as appropriate.

2. A group of servers that perform the same service. A cluster of servers can be used to provide load balancing and for fault tolerance.

CMOS RAM

This memory stores system configuration data, for example, the number of drives, types of drives, and amount of memory. It is battery-powered, so it can retain the date, time, and other information that must be stored when the computer is turned off.

Code

A set of rules that specify the way data is represented, such as ASCII or EBCDIC. Code is also used to describe lines of instructions for the computer, as in program code.

Collision

In some networking schemes, any station may transmit when it senses that the carrier is free. A collision occurs when two stations transmit simultaneously. If a collision is detected, each station will wait for a randomly determined interval before retransmitting the data.

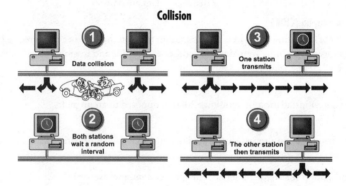

Collision

Most network operating systems track retransmissions, which is a good indication of the number of collisions occurring on the network.

Column

Vertical section of a table that stores one attribute for many entities.

Com

An extension for Internet addresses representing commercial enterprises. For example, galedsl@msen.com.

Command

Any executable statements.

Command prompt

A displayed symbol, such as C:>, that informs the user that a DOS system is idle. It represents that the command-line interface is ready to receive input.

Common Name (CN)

Refers to a leaf object in the NDS tree. This could be a user's login name, a printer object, or a server object.

Any name that points to a leaf object, usually seen as CN=leafobject.

Compact

Windows 2000 command-line command for managing data compression.

Compact Disc Read-Only Memory (CD-ROM)

A read-only optical disc commonly used to distribute applications software or archive data.

Complete Trust Model

In Microsoft Windows NT's complete trust model, each domain can act as both a master domain and a resource domain. In most cases, each domain is managed separately, with access to other domains granted through two-way trust relationships.

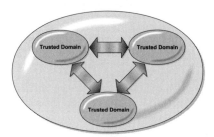

The complete trust model is a mix of independence and interdependence—independent in that each domain has its own users and groups. Each domain sets its own access, rights, and permission policies. Each domain administrator is responsible for his or her domain and must be trusted to manage that domain properly.

The model is interdependent because, unless there is a need to share resources between domains, there would be no reason for setting up a complete trust model. Domain administrators must work together to provide resource access while ensuring that security is not compromised.

This model is most appropriate to organizations that do not have a central MIS department available to manage master domains. It often fits well into organizations made up of somewhat independent departments or divisions. Companies must be ready, however, to accept the potential risks inherent in a noncentralized management structure.

Component

Hardware or software that is part of a functional unit.

Component Load Balancing

Allows middle-tier components to run on a cluster of servers. This provides fault tolerance and scalability.

Component Object Model (COM)

A binary specification that allows unrelated objects to communicate with each other. Also known as COM, the Component Object Model is the foundation of the OLE and ActiveX technologies.

Compulsory tunnel

A tunnel created by an intermediary system or device that a client can communicate through with the target server.

Computer Emergency Response Team (CERT)

This organization was formed by DARPA in November 1988 to work with the Internet community to improve its response to computer security events for Internet hosts, to raise awareness of computer security issues, and to improve the security of existing systems. CERT products and services include 24-hour technical assistance for computer security incidents, product vulnerability assistance, technical documents, and tutorials. In addition, the team has a number of mailing lists (including one for CERT Advisories) and has an anonymous FTP server at cert.org, where security-related documents and tools are archived. The CERT may be reached by e-mail at cert@cert.org and by telephone at +1-412-268-7090 (24-hour hotline).

Computer object

A leaf object representing a computer on the network. Its properties can store data, such as the name of the person the computer is assigned to or the computer's serial number.

CONFIG.NT

The replacement for CONFIG.SYS for DOS programs running under Windows NT.

CONFIG.SYS

The DOS environment is set up and configured by loading device drivers. This is done through two system configuration files: AUTOEXEC.BAT and CONFIG.SYS. When DOS is booted, these two files are executed.

CONFIG.SYS is a text file. It must be located at the root directory of the boot drive. The CONFIG.SYS is called by the IO.SYS file and contains commands to configure hardware and load device drivers.

It is always a good idea to make a backup of this file prior to installing a new application. Many applications will automatically make changes to this file during the installation process. It is wise to make note of these changes in case of system errors. Applications that alter this file typically make a backup copy. Refer to the application's documentation for details.

Changes to the CONFIG.SYS file will not take effect until the system is rebooted.

Mistakes in the CONFIG.SYS file may cause system startup errors. You can bypass the execution of CONFIG.SYS by pressing the *F5* key when you see the "Starting DOS" message. Using *F8* instead of *F5* will allow you to selectively bypass commands in the CONFIG.SYS file. This can help isolate problem lines within the configuration file.

CONFIG.SYS is still supported with Windows 95 to provide backward compatibility.

Configuration partition

Replication partition containing information about Active Directory structure. The configuration partition replicates to all domain controllers in a forest.

Connection object

An object representing a potential source server for Active Directory replication.

Connection-oriented

The model of interconnection in which communication proceeds through three well-defined phases: connection establishment, data transfer, and connection release. Examples include X.25, Internet TCP and OSI TP4, and ordinary telephone calls.

Connectionless

The model of interconnection in which communication takes place without first establishing a connection. Sometimes called datagram. Examples: LANs, Internet IP and OSI CLNP, UDP, ordinary postcards.

Constant

A name used to refer to a value that does not change during application execution.

Consumer

The application or component that uses the services provided by another component. For example, if an application uses the Spell Search functionality exposed by Microsoft Word, that application is a consumer of Microsoft Word.

Container

Special type of object within Windows 2000 Active Directory that is used to hold other objects.

Container object

1. Active Directory object that is able to contain other objects. Container objects are used in organizing the Active Directory's logical structure.

2. The type of object in NetWare's NDS used to organize other objects on the network into groups such as workgroups, departments, or divisions. A container object will contain other objects.

3. A Visual Basic object defining a set of objects as a group.

Context

The context points to where you are located in the NDS tree. This serves as a logical pointer to an object such as a user, printer, or server.

Context switch

The immediate switching from one program to another without first closing the files, allowing users to operate several programs concurrently, such as a graphics program and a word processing program. With context switching, unlike multitasking, when one program is being used, the other halts. Advantages of context switching are rapid switching, exchange of clipboard files, and fast data transfer. In a multiple loading operating system such as Macintosh, the programs are held in random access memory.

Control

Visible Visual Basic object used to generate an event or display on-screen information.

Control Panel

1. On a Macintosh, the Control Panel is a system software utility stored in the Control Panels folder (found in the System Folder). Panels are used to configure various services such as AppleTalk and user preferences such as desktop patterns and wallpaper.

2. Windows-family utility containing management tools.

Controller

An application that can be used to build solutions using ActiveX objects. Visual Basic is a controller.

Counter log

A log used for collecting performance counter data over time.

Crash

A system failure or *bomb*. A system crash requires that the user perform a reboot to restart the computer.

Crop

Cut the edges off an object so that it can fit in a particular area. Typcally used in reference to graphics.

Cscript

Windows Script Host component that hosts a script in a command-line environment.

Cursor

1. An indicator that keeps track of the current position in the result set.

2. Visual cue provided for data input or user interaction.

Cyclic Redundancy Check (CRC)

A mathematically calculated value that is attached to a network packet at the Physical layer, which is used to do low-level error checking on network packets. If any bit of the packet has changed during transmission, the CRC will no longer be valid and the packet will have to be retransmitted.

Data

1. In a database, facts about places, individuals, objects, events, concepts, and so on.

2. Used to refer to any stored information.

Data compression

A process by which a sampling algorithm is used to reduce the size of a data file. Windows 2000 supports data compression on NTFS volumes only.

Data integrity

The data quality that exists as long as accidental or malicious destruction, alteration, or loss of data does not occur.

Data modification

Changing data. Under SQL Server, this is through the SQL Statements INSERT, DELETE, and UPDATE.

Data stream

All data transmitted through a data channel in a single read or write operation. Also, a continuous stream of data elements being transmitted, or intended for transmission, in character or binary-digit form, using a defined format.

Data Transfer Rate

Determines how fast a drive or other peripheral can transfer data with its controller. The data transfer rate is a key measurement in drive performance.

Database

A collection of interrelated data stored together that is fundamental to a system or enterprise. A data structure for accepting, storing, and providing on-demand data for multiple independent users.

Database server

1. A server running database management system software.

2. The Microsoft SQL Server that houses the SMS site database.

Datagram

A message transmitted in a network, requiring no response or acknowledgment.

Dcpromo.exe

Windows 2000 command-line utility that launches the Active Directory Installation Wizard for promoting and demoting domain controllers.

Debugger

An application that allows a programmer to see the statement that is being executed and the contents of variables or registers to facilitate the location of programming errors.

Default

    1. One of a set of operating conditions that is automatically used when a device such as a printer or computer is turned on or reset. Pertaining to an attribute, value, or option when none is explicitly specified.

    2. An access modifier that limits access to a class's variables and methods to other classes in the same package.

Default domain controller policy

    Group Policy Object (GPO) created automatically during Active Directory installation and linked to the domain controller's container.

Default domain policy

    Group Policy Object (GPO) created automatically during Active Directory installation and linked at the domain level.

Default drive

    The drive the workstation is currently using. It is identified by a drive prompt, such as A:> or F:>.

Delegation

    Assignment of administrative permissions and control to selected users and groups.

Demand-dial router

    A router that can open a modem, ISDN, or VPN connection to a remote network when packets need to be routed to the remote network.

Desktop

    Most Graphical User Interfaces (GUIs) refer to the work area on the computer screen as the desktop. All window items appear and are moved around on this desktop area.

Device

    Any computer peripheral or hardware component (such as printer, mouse, monitor, or disk drive) capable of receiving and/or sending data, generally through the use of a device driver.

Device driver

    Hardware-specific software that acts as an interface between the operating system and the hardware attached to a computer. Device drivers allow applications to communicate with hardware in a controlled and orderly fashion. A device driver is installed when the system is initialized, either by the operating system or through an installable device driver. Some examples of installable device drivers are mouse, graphical/video monitor, communications port, printer, and network interface card.

Device Driver Interface (DDI)

    A set of functions a driver provides to allow communication between the device driver and the operating system.

Device Manager Snap-in

    MMC snap-in that lets you view and manage hardware devices.

Dfs link

    Dfs association with an existing network share.

Dfs link replica

    Copy of a Dfs link hosted on a different server. It provides redundancy for failover and load balancing and is only supported under domain Dfs roots.

Dfs root

    Topmost point (root) of a Dfs hierarchy.

Dfs root replica

Copy of a Dfs root hosted on a different server. It provides redundancy for failover and load balancing and is only supported for domain Dfs roots.

DHCP Relay Agent

A special function that can be configured on a Windows 2000 server. It configures the computer to forward DHCP broadcast traffic across the router.

DHCPAck

DHCP server response verifying a DHCP client's acceptance of an IP address and containing a valid lease. The broadcast may include client configuration parameters.

DHCPDiscover

DHCP client broadcast used to locate a DHCP server and request an IP address.

DHCPNAck

DHCP server response for an unsuccessful lease attempt.

DHCPOffer

DHCP server broadcast used to offer an IP address and lease to a DHCP client.

DHCPRequest

DHCP client broadcast used to accept an offered IP address and lease.

Dial-in router

Windows 2000 RRAS configuration that supports IP and IPX WAN connections over dial-up or persistent links.

Dialog box

An on-screen window used to display information. Generally used when user intervention is required, such as clicking on the **OK** or **Cancel** buttons.

Digital

Devices that represent data in the form of digits, based on the binary system where the binary digits (bits) are zero or one. Also, pertaining to data that consists of digits.

Digital, Intel, Xerox (DIX)

A type of Ethernet connector.

Digital signature

1. An arithmetic function that uses a user's private key to create a unique signature that can only be read using the user's public key. The digital signature ensures that the data is coming from the correct user and that it has not been tampered with.

2. Verifies that the sender of a package is who he claims to be. A digital signature is encrypted with the private key and verified using the corresponding public key.

Digital Subscriber Line (DSL)

A digital service that can be run on normal phone lines that provides very fast (up to 10 Mbps) and, in most cases, inexpensive access to the Internet. The two most common forms of DSL are Asymmetric Digital Subscriber Line (ADSL) and Symmetric Digital Subscriber Line (SDSL). DSLs require specialized equipment and are limited by distances to central connection points, so DSL technology is not available everywhere.

Digital to Analog Converter (DAC)

DAC chips are found on analog adapters. Because the PC operates digitally, it sends digitized information to the adapter. If the device accepts analog input only, the DAC on the adapter must convert the digital data into analog instructions for the device.

Digital Video Disc (DVD)

An optical storage device that can store up to 17 GB of data. It is typically used for storing video and other types of multimedia. A DVD player can read standard CD-ROMs.

Direct replication partner

A direct source for Active Directory replication.

Directory

1. Part of a structure for organizing files on a disk. A directory can contain files and subdirectories. The structure of directories and subdirectories on a disk is called a directory tree. The top-level directory in a directory tree is the root directory. In Windows 2000, the Active Directory provides the methods for storing directory data and making this data available to network users and administrators.

2. In NetWare, the highest organizational level is the file server. Each server's main directory is called a VOLUME, and subdirectories are called directories.

Directory and file permissions

These permissions, assigned to users and groups, set user access level.

Directory permissions

Access permissions assigned to users or groups.

Directory services

Services utilized within Active Directory that store information about network resources in one centralized location in order to simplify administrative management of the domain.

Directory structure

Most computers use a tree or filing system to organize volumes, directories, files, and data on their hard disks.

Directory tree

A hierarchical structure of objects, based on a logical or physical organization of objects, in the Directory database.

Directory User Agent (DUA)

The software that accesses the X.500 Directory Service on behalf of the directory user. The directory user may be a person or another software element.

Discretionary ACL (DACL)

The DACL lists the Security IDs (SIDs) for all users and groups granted or denied access to an object.

Disk

A circular object with a magnetic surface used to store files (programs and documents) on a computer. For example, a floppy or hard disk.

Disk Cleanup

Utility that can be used to locate and remove temporary and other unused or unneeded files.

Disk Defragmenter

MMC snap-in used to analyze and defragment disk partitions, logical drives, and volumes.

Disk drive

A magnetic or optical device used to store files and folders. Types of disk drives include fixed (hard) disks, floppy disks, and removable media such as Syquest, Jaz, Zip, and magneto-optical (MO) disks.

Disk Management

MMC snap-in used for managing hard disks, disk partitions, and disk volumes.

Disk mirroring

Disk mirroring is an implementation of Redundant Arrays of Independent Disks (RAID) Level 1. It uses two disk drives configured with equal-sized partitions and connected to the same disk controller. During each data write, the same data is written to both disk partitions.

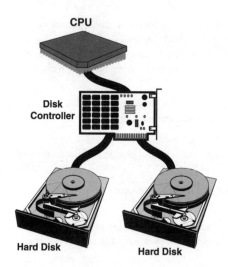

With disk mirroring, disk utilization is 50% of the dedicated storage space. I/O performance generally is better than when using disk striping with parity. A mirrored pair can be split without loss of data.

Disk mirroring is designed to keep the computer operational in spite of disk errors or loss of a hard disk. If a read error occurs, data from the other disk is used. If one drive fails, the server will continue running by using the other drive.

Use disk mirroring when data must be protected against drive failures, and hard disk resources are and will be plentiful as system requirements grow.

Disk mirroring is normally used on peer-to-peer networks and smaller LANs to protect critical data files. Due to the amount of storage lost through redundancy, it is not commonly used on larger LANs.

Disk Operating System (DOS)

The software programs that control the operation of the computer and the movement of information throughout the computer system.

DOS is the medium by which the user communicates with the computer system and manipulates data.

Disk quota

Windows 2000 feature allowing limits to be set on users' available disk space. Disk quotas are set by volume and by user. Disk quotas are only supported on NTFS volumes.

Diskperf

Command-line command that is used to activate and deactivate disk performance counters.

Distance-vector protocol

A routing protocol that uses a routing table that consists of routes that are configured with a distance (hop count) and a vector (the gateway to the destination network).

Distributed database

This collection of information files or databases resides at different sites yet appears to the user to be a single database.

Distributed File System (Dfs)

A hierarchical file display that consists of logical links to shared folders. Dfs displays a logical file system to users, allowing them to see and access all shared available network resources in a way that makes their physical location on the network transparent to the user.

Distribution folder

Shared folder used as the installation source during Windows NT and Windows 2000 over-the-network installations.

Distribution group

Active Directory domain group used for distribution management.

Domain

1. In NetWare, DOMAIN is used as a console command that will create a protected operating system domain for running untested NLMs in Ring 3. This prevents a module from interfering with the core operating system.

2. In the Internet, a domain is a part of the naming hierarchy. The domain name is a sequence of names (separated by periods) that identify host sites. For example: galenp@mail.msen.com.

Domain Controller

Server within a domain and storage point for domainwide security information. This also refers to a partition of the Active Directory the Windows NT Server holds.

Domain controller (Windows 2000)

A Windows 2000 Server that has been promoted into the domain controller role. Each domain controller has a copy of the Active Directory domain database and SYSVOL folder.

Domain Dfs root

Dfs root hosted by a server but stored in Active Directory services. Root and link replicas are supported.

Domain Global group

Active Directory domain group scope. In mixed mode, members can include user accounts from the same domain. In addition, Global groups from the same domain are supported in native mode.

Domain Local group

Active Directory domain group scope. In mixed mode, members can include user accounts from any domain in the forest or Global groups from any domain in the forest. In addition, Domain Local groups from the same domain and Universal groups from any domain in the forest are supported in native mode.

Domain Model

A method of organizing Windows NT Server domains for security and management.

Domain name

A unique domain name designates a location on the Internet. Domain names always have two or more parts separated by periods. The leftmost part is the most specific, and the part on the right is the most general. A given machine may have more than one domain name, but a given domain name points to only one machine.

Domain Name System (DNS)

A hierarchical, distributed method of organizing systems and network names on the Internet. DNS administratively groups hosts (systems) into a hierarchy of authority that allows addressing and other information to be widely distributed and maintained. A big advantage of DNS is that using it eliminates dependence on a centrally maintained file that maps host names to addresses.

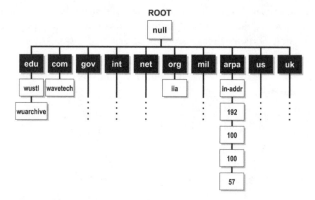

The diagram shows the hierarchical organization of domain names. The bottom level of the tree structure contains the names of companies or even machines within a company. For example, consider wuarchive.wustl.edu. The bottom of the tree is wuarchive. This is the name of a particular piece of equipment within the wustl domain, which is under the edu domain.

The name of a particular domain is read from the bottom of the tree up to the root. The root is unnamed and is represented with just a period. For example, wavetech.com is a particular domain. If we were to give the fully qualified domain name (FQDN), we would include the unnamed root, so it would be written as "wavetech.com." The final period at the end of the name specifies the root of the tree. The root must always be specified for the host equipment. To make it easy, most software will convert a domain name to an FQDN for the user by appending any missing domain names all the way to the root.

The top of the tree lists the top-level domains. These are reserved names. Every domain will have a top-level domain by type or country.

Domain Naming master

Forest-wide operations master role responsible for addition of domains to the forest or removal of domains from the forest.

Domain partition

Replication partition containing domain objects and attributes. The domain partition fully replicates to all domain controllers in a domain.

Domain Universal group

Active Directory domain group scope that is only supported in native mode. Members can include users from any domain in the forest, Global groups from any domain in the forest, and Universal groups from any domain in the forest.

Domain user account

A user account created as an Active Directory object and used for domain logon and resource access verification.

Domainwide master roles

Operations master roles implemented at the forest level. These are Relative ID master, PDC emulator, and Infrastructure master.

Dotted decimal notation

The syntactic representation for a 32-bit integer that consists of four 8-bit numbers written in base 10 with periods (dots) separating them. Used to represent IP addresses in the Internet, as in 192.67.67.20.

Download

A process where a file is transferred from a host computer to a user's computer. Download is the opposite of upload.

Driver

Software used to allow the operating system to communicate with an add-on hardware device such as a disk controller or display adapter.

Drop

Individual connections (sometimes called nodes) on a multipoint (also called multidrop) circuit.

Dynamic

Pertaining to a priority of a process that is varied by the operating system. Contrasts with absolute priority.

Dynamic Data Exchange (DDE)

A process that allows two applications to exchange information.

Dynamic disk

A Windows 2000 disk configuration that supports disk volumes rather than industry-standard disk partitions.

Dynamic DNS (DDNS)

A newer standard of DNS where client hosts can automatically register A (host) and PTR (pointer) resource records. DDNS allows clients with a dynamically assigned address to register directly with the Windows 2000 DNS server and update the DNS table dynamically.

Dynamic Drive

Dynamic attach and release of network drives under Microsoft Mail.

Dynamic Host Configuration Protocol (DHCP)

A TCP/IP application-layer protocol that provides for dynamic address assignment on a network.

Dynamic-Link Library (DLL)

A module that is linked at load time or run time.

Dynamic linking

Using an update command to ensure that all data changed in one program is automatically changed in another program, thereby keeping the data consistent. Dynamic linking is particularly useful in database management.

Dynamic Random Access Memory (DRAM)

The most commonly used memory type for personal computers. Because of its passive componentry design, DRAM requires a periodic refresh signal to maintain valid data.

Echo

The reflection of transmitted data back to its source. Also a phenomenon in voice circuits.

Electronic Frontier Foundation (EFF)

A foundation established to address social and legal issues arising from the increasingly pervasive use of computers as a means of communication and information distribution.

Electronic Mail (e-mail)

The most popular Internet application and the driving force behind the Internet's rapid growth. While controlling another computer remotely or transferring files from one computer to another may be useful, neither is as exciting as being able to communicate with millions of Internet users around the globe. Many users join the Internet just for e-mail access.

Fortunately, it is possible to exchange e-mail with people that are not directly part of the Internet. For example, by using gateways to other public e-mail networks, Internet e-mail can reach users with commercial service provider accounts such as CompuServe, BITNET, America Online, Prodigy, and the Microsoft Network. E-mail can also reach users who work at companies that get their mail access from corporate network providers such as MCImail, Applelink, and uuNet.

E-mail is popular because it works very quickly, while traditional mail can take a day or two to cross town or weeks to reach an international destination. E-mail can travel from sender to receiver within hours (sometimes minutes) despite the distance between them. If the network is extremely busy or if an administrator configures a user's system to send e-mail once a day (as opposed to every few minutes), the e-mail may take a little longer to arrive. In general, however, e-mail moves around the world at a rapid pace. It is possible for a person in the U.S. to send a message to West Africa, receive a response, and send another message, all in the space of an hour.

E-mail is also very flexible. Users can attach different types of files to their e-mail messages. Marketing can embed audio and video clips within text messages, co-workers can transfer spreadsheets or project updates, families can share pictures and birthday messages.

Electronic mail address

Designation given to an individual or domain that directs messages or other information over computers in general to a specific person or destination.

Emulation

The imitation of all or part of one system by another. This can be accomplised either in hardware or software. The imitating system accepts the same data, executes the same programs, and achieves the same results as the imitated system.

Products such as SoftWindows and Virtual PC allow Macintosh computers to emulate the Windows or Windows 95 operating system and an Intel-based PC.

Apple designed the "68K" emulator for the PowerPC processor in order to allow Power Macintosh computers to run older 680x0-specific software.

Encapsulated PostScript File (EPS or EPSF)

A file format used by graphics and publishing applications.

Encapsulation

In object-oriented programming (OOP), encapsulation defines a data structure of attributes and a group of member functions as a single unit called an object. In networking, encapsulation is the process of enclosing packets of one type of protocol by another.

Encrypting File System (EFS)

Windows 2000 data encryption service based on a user's public and private keys. Data encryption is only supported on NTFS volumes.

Encryption

Involves encoding a packet's data prior to transmission to ensure data security. The Data Encryption Standard (DES) is an algorithm used for coding and decoding data for security purposes.

End-to-end

Governs the interaction from the source computer to the destination device and vice versa; i.e., a program in the source machine exchanges messages with a similar program in the destination machine. The transport layer (fourth layer) of the International Standards Organization (ISO) reference model of open systems interconnection (OSI) is an end-to-end process, as are layers five to seven. In contrast, layers one to three of the ISO model specify intermediate, or subnetwork, interactions between a device and its immediate neighbor. Layers one to three are referred to as chained.

Enhanced Graphics Adapter (EGA)

Introduced as an enhancement to the first color display for PCs (CGA). The EGA was equipped with two more wires providing intensity for each of the three primary colors and the ability to produce more color combinations. Also, the horizontal scanning frequency was synchronized for a much clearer output display.

Entity

1. OSI terminology for a layer protocol machine. An entity within a layer performs the functions of the layer within a single computer system, accessing the layer entity below and providing services to the layer entity above at local service access points.

2. A definable object during database definition.

Errors

A term used to refer to errors or messages generated by DB-Library, the OS, or the network software.

Ethernet

A Carrier Sense, Multiple Access with Collision Detection (CSMA/CD) specification.

Ethernet was originally developed by Xerox, Intel, and Digital Equipment Corporation in the late 1970s, with specifications first released in 1980. The standard defines the cabling, connectors, and other characteristics for the transmission of data, voice, and video over local area networks at 10 Mbps. Recent improvements have increased the speed to 100 Mbps.

There are four types of Ethernet frames defined: 802.2, 802.3, Ethernet_SNAP, and Ethernet II. These are similar but incompatible.

The types of Ethernet cables are Thin Ethernet (Thinnet), Thick Ethernet (Thicknet), Twisted Pair, and Fiber Optic.

Event

An action that results in a message being sent or activity in a program. An event can be generated by a user, an application, or the operating system.

Exceptions

An event that indicates that something unexpected occurred. An exception can be generated by hardware, by the operating system, or by an application.

Expanded Memory (EMS)

Created when PC processors were limited to 1 MB of Random Access Memory (RAM). Spreadsheet users needed a way to create extremely large spreadsheets and could not do this in the 640 KB available in PCs of that era. A way to work around this memory limitation was needed.

To answer this need, Lotus, Intel, and Microsoft (LIM) developed the Expanded Memory Specification.

This specification utilized a special EMS adapter board to store additional memory where data could be stored for later use. When needed, data is moved from the EMS board to system memory by *paging* the data through a 64-KB page frame in the Upper Memory Area (UMA). The page frame is made up of four 16-KB pages. An expanded memory manager, such as EMM386.EXE, is used to control the paging of data between the EMS board and system memory.

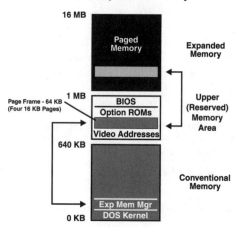

LIM Expanded Memory

Eventually, the special EMS board was entirely emulated in software, making the special hardware requirement obsolete.

EMS is typically only used by older DOS applications.

Extended partition

A basic disk partition. An extended partition can have multiple logical drives. An extended partition is not bootable. A basic disk can have one extended partition.

Extension snap-in

A snap-in designed to add additional administrative features to another snap-in. Also referred to as an extension.

Extranet

Extends the intranet to include other users, such as customers or partner organizations, who will be able to access some part of the intranet. The extranet is configured to give access to only a small part of the information that exists on the intranet, and in most cases, the users must be authenticated before they can get access to the information.

Fault tolerance

Operating-system features designed to accommodate failures, therefore improving disk reliability and application accessibility. Related terms are "Disk Mirroring," "Disk Duplexing," "Disk Striping with Parity," "Clustering," and "Load Balancing."

File

A sequence of bytes stored on a secondary storage medium such as a floppy disk or hard disk. Generally, a computer file contains either a program or data.

Program files contain instructions or commands that are to be executed by the computer. Data files that contain only ASCII characters are text files, while files containing binary data, i.e., data other than ASCII characters, are called binary files. Bytes that comprise a file are not necessarily stored on contiguous disk blocks and may be scattered across a disk due to fragmentation.

Macintosh files generally consist of a Data Fork (the file contents) and a Resource Fork (a pointer to the application that created the file).

File caching

This improves file access time by using the RAM memory to store recently accessed files.

File compression

More data can be stored on server hard disks by compressing files that are not being used. NetWare and Windows NT support identifying files and directories to be compressed. With DOS, Windows, and Windows 95, disk partitions are identified for compression.

File format

The arrangement of information in a file. There are many standard and nonstandard file formats used on various computing platforms. The use of standard formats for information such as vector graphics, bitmapped graphics, audio, word processing, and spreadsheets allows information to be accessed by applications from multiple vendors.

File Format API (FFA PI)

API sets supporting message transfer between Microsoft Mail and foreign mail systems.

File server

A computer that stores files and provides access to them from workstations. File servers generally contain large hard disks and high amounts of memory.

If a computer is used exclusively as a file server, it is a dedicated file server. If a computer is used as a workstation and a file server simultaneously, it is a nondedicated file server.

The NOS (Network Operating System) runs on the file server and controls access to files, printers, and other network resources.

File server protocol

A communications protocol that allows application programs to share files.

File transfer

The process of copying a file from one computer to another over a network. FTP is a popular program used to copy files over the Internet.

File Transfer Protocol (FTP)

A part of the TCP/IP suite that is used to transfer files between any two computers, provided they support FTP. The two computers do not have to be running the same operating system.

In general, people use FTP to move files from one account or machine to another or to perform what is called an "anonymous FTP." For example, if storage space on a particular machine is low, the user can free up storage space by using FTP to move the files to a machine with more space. Another reason to move a file to a different account is to print a file to a particular printer. If the file is on a machine that cannot access the desired printer, it must be moved to a machine that does have access.

Whatever the reason for the transfer, FTP requires the user to know the proper login name and the password for both computers to move files between them.

While an anonymous FTP also moves from one computer to another, it has two main differences. An anonymous FTP session usually involves gathering files that a user does not have. Anonymous FTP does not require the user to know a login name and password to access the remote computer.

The Internet has many anonymous FTP sites. Each site consists of an FTP server, a large number of files, and guest login names such as "anonymous" or "FTP." This allows any user to visit these systems and copy files from the FTP site to their personal computer. With the appropriate authority, users can copy files from their system to an anonymous FTP site.

Despite the variety of FTP servers and clients on the Internet and the different operating systems they use, FTP servers and clients generally support the same basic commands. This standard command set allows users to accomplish tasks such as looking at a list of files in the current directory of the remote system, regardless of the operating system in use. Other common commands allow users to change directories, get specific file information, copy files to a local machine, and change parameters.

Graphical Web browsers transform the traditional character-based, command-line FTP interface into a point-and-click environment. The only way a user may know that they are in the middle of an FTP session is that the Universal Resources Locator (URL) box in the browser will change from an address that begins with "http://..." to "ftp://...".

Filter

A device or program that separates data, signals, or material in accordance with specified criteria.

Filtering (Group Policy Object)

A way of controlling whether a Group Policy Object (GPO) is processed and assigned based on security group membership.

Firewall

Used as a security measure between a company's local area network (LAN) and the Internet. The firewall prevents users from accessing certain address Web sites. A firewall also helps to prevent hackers from accessing internal resources on the network. A combination of hardware and software that separates a LAN into two or more parts for security purposes. Today, firewalls are commonly used to prevent unauthorized access to a network from the Internet.

FireWire

A high-speed serial interface designed by Apple Computer to allow communications between a Macintosh computer and peripherals such as scanners, disk drives, printers, digital cameras, etc.

Flag

A variable indicating that a certain condition holds.

Focus

Term used to refer to the active screen object or control.

Folder

A directory. The Macintosh operating system uses folders as an analogy for directories. Folders may contain files and other folders.

Folder Redirection

A process whereby user profile information is redirected to a network share location.

Foreground category

A classification of processes that consists of those associated with the currently active screen group.

Foreground process

A process that can receive user input.

Forest

A collection of two or more trees. They do not share a common namespace but do share a Global Catalog and a common schema.

Forestwide master roles

Operations master roles implemented at the forest level. These are Schema master and Domain Naming master.

Forward

A feature of electronic mail transmission that enables a message recipient to re-address the mail and send it to a third party.

Forward Lookup query

DNS query used for mapping host names to IP addresses.

Forward Lookup Zone

DNS zone used for host name-to-IP address resolution.

Fragment

Part of an IP message.

Frame

In IEEE (Institute of Electrical and Electronics Engineers) terminology, the unit of data transferred at the OSI (Open Systems Interconnection) data link layer.

Frame type

A data-link level specification describing the packet structure on a network. Different frame types are incompatible with each other.

Frequency

The number of times one complete incident or function occurs. In electronics, frequency usually refers to the number of waveforms that are repeated per second, measured in Hertz.

From

The field in an electronic mail header that contains the return address of the message originator.

Full-text database

A computer file that holds the complete text of original sources, such as newspaper or periodical articles, books, court decisions, and directories.

Full-text search

The SQL Server 7.0 feature that allows you to create a catalog of the text contained in particular fields. A column with full-text search enabled and the catalog populated allows users to search for records based on a field containing certain words.

Full zone transfer

Zone transfer method requiring transfer of the full DNS database from the source name server to the destination name server.

Function Key

"Extra" keys on a computer keyboard. PCs and Macintosh keyboards generally have 12 function keys. Other types of computers have more.

Function keys are used for various purposes by the operating system and applications software.

Gateway

The primary linkage between mixed environments such as PC-based LANs and host environments such as SNA.

Gateways generally operate at all seven layers of the OSI Reference Model. They may provide full content conversion between two environments, such as ASCII to EBCDIC, as well as other application and presentation layer conversions.

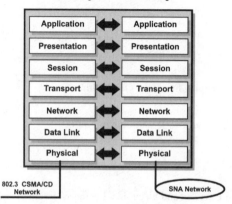

Gateway Functionality

Other types of gateways include fax gateways, which allow users to send and receive faxes from their workstations. These may also be integrated with mail service gateways, which allow communications between users of different mail systems.

Generic Routing Encryption (GRE) protocol

A protocol used by PPTP to encapsulate the encrypted packets that are being transmitted across the Internet.

Global Catalog (GC)

A database containing scaled-down attributes of every Active Directory object from every domain in a tree or forest. The GC replies to queries so that users in one domain can locate resources in another domain.

Global Catalog server

The first domain controller created in a tree that, by default, stores the Global Catalog.

Global group

A group definition allowing permission assignments to local machines or other domains through local group membership of the Global group.

Gov

A governmental organization is identified by this Internet address suffix. For example, whitehouse.gov.

Graphical Identification and Authentication (GINA)

Windows 2000 component that collects logon information that it packages and sends to the Local Security Authority.

Graphical User Interface (GUI)

A program that executes commands given by the user to the computer. A GUI uses graphic representations of commands and/or a menu format to display commands that the user may execute with a mouse or similar device.

The graphical user interface makes using a computer easier, especially for the beginner. Mosaic is a Graphical User Interface for the Internet. Microsoft Windows, OS/2, and the Macintosh operating system are examples of graphical user interfaces for personal computers.

Group

Collection of users used for security management or distrubtion management. Windows 2000 groups can contain other objects such as computers.

Group nesting

A term referring to one group being a member of another group.

Group object

A leaf object that represents several User objects. It provides collective, rather than individual, network administration. Group objects are created based on the use of applications, printers, or print queues. Group objects may also be created based on users who perform similar tasks or need similar information, or to simplify trustee assignments.

Group Policy (GP)

Windows 2000 feature that allows administrators to assign security settings and additional properties to domain members based on their personal accounts or group memberships.

Group Policy Container (GPC)

Active Directory object that stores Group Policy Object (GPO) attributes.

Group Policy Object (GPO)

An Active Directory object that contains configuration information on desktop environments, servers, users, and other objects. GPOs can be applied to domains, sites, or OUs for the purpose of simplifying administrative control over Active Directory objects. Each Windows 2000 computer, regardless of if it is a member of an Active Directory domain, will also have a local GPO.

Group Policy Snap-in

Utility for editing Group Policy Object (GPO) policy settings.

Group Policy Templates (GPT)

Folder created each time a new Group Policy Object (GPO) is created. The GPT contains policy settings for the GPO.

Handle

1. In draw programs and similar object-oriented graphics programs, handles are the small black squares that appear around a selected object so the object can be resized, moved, copied, or scaled by using a mouse or similar pointing device.

2. An operating system object that contains a reference to an object like a window or printer.

Hard disk

A peripheral mass-storage device that uses sealed, rotating, nonflexible, magnetically coated disks to store data and program files. Hard disk types include SCSI, IDE, and EIDE.

Hardware

All electronic components of a computer system, including peripherals, circuit boards, and input and output devices. Hardware is the physical equipment, as opposed to software consisting of programs, data procedures, rules, and associated documentation.

Hardware Abstraction Layer (HAL)

Windows NT module that isolates the operating system kernel from the hardware platform.

Hardware Compatibility List (HCL)

A list of systems and adapters maintained by Microsoft. The HCL is a list of systems tested and verified as compatible with a specific operating system version.

Header

Contains identifying information.

Electronic mail message headers contain the message originator's name and address, receiver, subject, date, etc.

A packet header carries the source and destination addresses along with other information.

Heap

1. A block of memory that is set aside for dynamic allocation.

2. SQL Server term for the collection of all pages containing all rows in a table.

High-Density (HD)

The density refers to how tightly data can be recorded on the media. This is usually used to describe floppy diskettes. Using a magnetic medium that has much finer (smaller) magnetic particles, more data can be recorded on the media. HD diskettes require high-density drives.

Histogram view

System Monitor view displaying average performance counter data as a bar chart.

Hive files

Component files making up the Windows NT Registry.

Home directory

1. The topmost (root) directory for Web sites using IIS. Serves as the default location for a Web site's content pages.

2. On Local Area Networks, a directory that belongs to a single user for storage of data. Normally, the user is the only person with access to this directory. On most networks, the supervisor or administrator can also access any user's home directory.

Home page

A document coded in HTML (HyperText Markup Language) that acts as a top-level document for an Internet site or a topic. A home page contains hypertext links to related documents.

Hop

Describes routing through a network. A hop is a data packet moving through routers from the point of origination to the destination.

Hop count

The number of cable segments a message packet passes through between its source and network or internetwork destination. The destination can be no more than 16 hops from the source.

Host

A computer that is remotely accessible and provides information or services for users on a network. It is quite common to have one host machine provide several services, such as WWW and USENET. A host computer on the Internet can be accessed by using an application program such as electronic mail, telnet, or FTP. A host computer may also be a bulletin board.

Host (A) resource record

Forward zone host name-to-IP address mapping record.

Host Information (HINFO) resource record

Resource record identifying a host's CPU and operating system.

Hostname

The name given to a computer that identifies it as an Internet or other site.

Hub

1. In disk drives, the hub is the central mechanism within the drive that causes the disk to rotate and keeps it centered during the rotation. On floppy diskettes, the hub fits into the hole in the center of the diskette to keep it level and balanced during rotation.

2. In networking, a central connecting point for network wiring.

Hypertext

Allows users to move from one site or place in a document to another. Hypertext links in World Wide Web documents link the user from terms in one document to the site referenced in the original document.

Hypertext Transfer Protocol (HTTP)

A set of directions for Web servers that tells them how to respond to various events initiated by users. HTTP is the most important protocol used in the World Wide Web (WWW).

The simplest example is clicking on a link to another part of the same file. The server receives the information that the link has been activated and sends back the designated part of the file for display.

An HTTP client program is required on one end, and an HTTP server program on the other.

I/O

I/O (Input/Output) refers to the sending and receiving of data from the central processing unit (CPU) to other peripheral devices such as disk drives. The input/output channel carries out all transfer of data so as to free up the CPU. The keyboard is the most common input device, and the monitor is the most common output device.

I/O address

Space used to access I/O hardware such as I/O adapters, buses, and special registers used by I/O devices known as control status registers (CSR). I/O address space is one of two equal parts of primary memory, or addressable memory. The other equal part is memory address space.

I/O privilege mechanism

A facility that allows a process to ask a device driver for direct access to the device's I/O ports and any dedicated or mapped memory locations it has. The I/O privilege mechanism can be used directly by an application or indirectly by a dynamic link package.

Icon

A graphical picture used to represent an application, folder, file, disk drive, or printer.

Identifier

The name of a database or database object.

Incremental Zone server (IXFR)

Zone transfer method where only changes are transferred from the source name server to the destination name server.

Index

A database object that provides efficient access to rows in a table, based on key values.

Infrastructure master

Domainwide operations master role responsible for updating user-to-group references in a multidomain environment.

Inheritance

1. The means by which a child object can get information from its parent.

2. The process by which Access Control Entries are passed from a parent object to a child object.

3. The process by which permissions are passed from a group to its members.

Inheritance chain

The path from a particular class to its superclasses in the class hierarchy.

Inheritance hierarchy

The collection of all subclasses that extend from a common parent class. Each subclass inherits the properties of its parent class.

INI Files in Windows for Workgroups

WIN.INI contains environmental information, while SYSTEM.INI contains system configuration information. The settings for the desktop, color schemes, and multimedia information are located in CONTROL.INI. PROGMAN.INI contains Program Manager appearance and configuration information, and WINFILE.INI contains the settings for File Manager's appearance and operation. The network drivers and protocol information is found in PROTOCOL.INI. MSMAIL.INI contains information for the Mail program. EFAXPUMP.INI is only present if the fax is installed and contains information about fax modems, security, and received faxes. SCHDPLUS.INI contains information about Schedule+'s appearance and behavior. Finally, there is SHARED.INI, which contains settings that allow users in the same workgroup to share custom commands and messages for Mail.

Many Windows applications create their own .INI files during installation. Others will add entries to the WIN.INI file.

The contents of the .INI files are read during Windows for Workgroups startup. After editing the files, restart Windows for Workgroups to activate the changes.

INSTALL

1. Common software installation filename.

2. A NetWare 3.x and 4.x loadable module used to install, modify, or update the NetWare operating system. The module is contained in the INSTALL.NLM file and is loaded with the LOAD console command. NetWare 3.12 and 4.x also have DOS INSTALL programs that are used to initialize the original install process.

Instance

An occurrence of an object in memory.

Institute of Electrical and Electronics Engineers (IEEE)

A professional ANSI-accredited body of scientists and engineers based in the U.S. IEEE promotes standardization and consults to the American National Standards Institute on matters relating to electrical and electronic development. The IEEE 802 Standards Committee is the leading official standard organization for LANs (Local Area Networks).

Integrated Drive Electronics (IDE)

The standard interface for a hard disk drive. Controller electronics are integrated into the drive. The controller connects to a paddleboard that may be external to, or on, the system board. The paddleboard then interfaces with the bus to the CPU. An IDE bus can be identified by its 40-pin connector, as opposed to the 50-pin connector of a SCSI bus.

Integrated Services Digital Network (ISDN)

A special kind of telecommunications network designed to handle more than just data. Digital network operating over PSTN local loop wiring. Multiple services, including video, text, voice, data, facsimile images, and graphics, are supported over 64-Kbps channels. Standard configurations combine multiple channels to provide higher transfer rates.

Integrity

Data consistency and accuracy.

IntelliMirror

The Microsoft technology that stores a mirror image of a client computer on a server. In Microsoft 2000, the umbrella term for a collection of technologies designed to reduce the cost of network ownership.

Interactive

The exchange of information and control between the user and a computer process.

Interactive also refers to time-dependent (real-time) data communications. Typically communications in which a user enters data and then waits for a response message from the destination before continuing.

Interface

1. A shared boundary between two functional units, defined by functional characteristics, signal characteristics, and other characteristics, as appropriate. Also, any of the electrical and logical devices that permit computers and peripherals to be interconnected.

2. A contract between an object and its users.

Interfaces

A set of methods that can be implemented by Java classes.

Interior Gateway Protocol (IGP)

The protocol used to exchange routing information between collaborating routers in the Internet. Router Information Protocol (RIP) and Open Shortest Path First (OSPF) are examples of IGPs.

International Standards Organization (ISO)

Founded in 1946, the ISO promotes the development of international standards for the computer, communications, and other fields. ISO members are the standards organizations of 89 countries. The United States representative is the American National Standards Institute (ANSI).

Internet

An international computer network of networks that connect government, academic, and business institutions. Networks on the Internet include MILNET, NSFnet, and other backbone networks, as well as mid-level networks and stub (local) networks.

Internet networks communicate using TCP/IP (Transmission Control Protocol/Internet Protocol). The Internet connects colleges, universities, military organizations and contractors, corporations, government research laboratories, and individuals.

Although parts of the Internet operate under single administrative domains, the Internet as a whole reaches around the globe, connects computers (from personal computers to supercomputers), and is not administered by any single authority. The Internet in July 1995 roughly connected 60,000 independent networks into a vast global Internet.

Used as a descriptive term, an internet is a collection of interconnected packet-switching networks. Any time you connect two or more networks together, you have an internet—as in *inter*national or *inter*state.

Internet Activities Board (IAB)

The IAB is the technical body that oversees the development of the Internet suite of protocols commonly referred to as "TCP/IP." It has two task forces, the IRTF and the IETF, each charged with investigating a particular area.

Internet address

A 32-bit value written or displayed in numbers that specify a particular network and node on that network.

Internet Connection Server

RRAS configuration within Windows 2000 Server that enables you to share a single Internet connection with other computers on the network.

Internet Connection Sharing (ICS)

A service available in Windows 2000 Professional and Server that allows the sharing of a single connection to the Internet or a remote network with multiple network clients. ICS is very easy to configure but also limited to using a single small network.

Internet Control Message Protocol (ICMP)

Used for error reporting and recovery, and is a required component of any IP implementation.

Internet Engineering Task Force (IETF)

One of the task forces of the IAB, the IETF is responsible for solving short-term engineering needs of the Internet. It has more than 40 Working Groups.

Internet Group Management Protocol (IGMP)

Part of the TCP/IP protocol suite. Provides multicasting broadcasts for communications and passing management information in a multicasting group.

Internet Information Server (IIS)

Microsoft Internet Information Server is a network file and application server that transmits information in Hypertext Markup Language.

Internet Protocol (IP)

The OSI layer 3 routed protocol used to transmit packetized information on a TCP/IP network.

Internet Relay Chat (IRC)

An Internet protocol that supports real-time conversations between Internet users worldwide.

Internet Service Provider (ISP)

Companies that provide an Internet connection for educational institutions, individuals, companies, and organizations.

Internetwork

Two or more networks connected by a router.

Internetwork Packet Exchange (IPX)

Used with SPX as the resident protocol in NetWare. A router with IPX routing can interconnect local area networks (LANs) so that Novell NetWare clients and servers can communicate.

In NetWare 3.x, IPX is the name of the command-line utility used to see the versions and options of IPX.COM. This was used prior to the introduction of ODI drivers.

Internetwork Packet Exchange Open Data-Link Interface (IPXODI)

This is a module that takes the workstation requests determined to be for the network by the NetWare DOS Requester and packages them with transmission information (such as their destination), then transfers them to the Link Support Layer (LSL). IPXODI requires that each packet have an initialized header specifying information targeting network delivery and announcing from where the packet came, where it is going, and what happens after delivery.

InterNIC

The Internet Network Information Center (InterNIC) was developed in 1993 by General Atomics, AT&T, and NSI to provide information services to Internet users. It offers a reference desk that provides networking information, referrals to other resources, and associate users with their local NICs. It also provides coordination to share information and activities with U.S. and international organizations, as well as education services to train mid-level and campus NICs, and to end users to promote Internet use.

Interoperability

The ability to use products from different vendors in the same system. Communication protocols, such as IP or AFP, can be used in ODI to process information from the network. The user does not have to know each protocol's required method of packet transmission. Interoperability also means an application can share files, even when running on different platforms, such as Macintosh or UNIX.

Intersite replication

Replication occurring between Active Directory sites, between direct connections, and across site links.

Intranet

1. A network or series of networks that is private to an organization. In some cases, the definition of an intranet or extranet is limited to using Internet technologies to provide and access resources. This is the most accurate description of intranets and extranets, but the meaning is often extended to include other technologies such as simple file and print sharing.

2. A private internet, usually within a company, for facilitating information sharing. It looks and acts just like the public Internet.

Intrasite replication

Replication occuring within an Active Directory site.

IP address

Each host in the network is assigned a unique IP address for each network connection (installed network adapter). The IP address is used to identify packet source and destination hosts.

An IP address is a 32-bit address, written as 4 octets (bytes) separated by periods. For example, 195.143.67.2.

This way of representing an IP address is also known as dotted decimal notation. Each address will also have an associated subnet mask, dividing the address into its network prefix and host suffix. For example, you might have the following defined as a subnet mask: 255.255.255.0. The subnet mask is used to identify the network and host portions of the address.

The network portion identifies where the host is located, and the host portion identifies the device connected to that network.

When dealing with a network the size of the Internet, address assignments must be carefully coordinated. With millions of hosts operating on thousands of networks, the potential for duplicate addresses is significant. The job of coordinating Internet IP addresses is given to the Network Information Center.

An assigned address is only required if your network is connected to the Internet. If connected to the Internet, your network address will be assigned through the Internetwork Network Information Center, or InterNIC.

To get an Internet address, contact the InterNIC at InterNIC Registration Services, c/o Network Solutions, Inc., 505 Huntmar Park Drive, Herndon, Virginia 22070, (703) 742-4777, or at hostmaster@internic.net.

An organization is assigned a network address. The organization can further divide this into its own subnets and assign the host addresses.

Rather than going to the InterNIC, it is more likely that an organization will work through a local provider for address assignment. The organization will then subdivide the address, if necessary, and assign host addresses.

IP datagram

The fundamental unit of information passed across the Internet. It contains source and destination addresses along with data and a number of fields that define the length of the datagram, the header checksum, and flags to indicate whether the datagram can be (or has been) fragmented.

IP number

Sometimes called a *dotted quad*, it is a unique number consisting of four parts separated by periods. For example, 109.123.251.2. Each value in the dotted quad ranges from 0 to 255, representing the decimal form of an 8-bit binary number.

Every machine that is on the Internet has a unique IP number. If a machine does not have an IP number, it is not really *on* the Internet. Most machines also have one or more Domain Names so that they are easier for people to remember.

IP Security (IPSec)

A part of TCP/IP standards in which all IP traffic between two computers is encrypted so that the packets cannot be captured on the network and read by unauthorized users.

IPSec transport mode

An implementation of IPSec where the data is encrypted for the whole path from one computer to another.

IPSec tunnel mode

An implementation of IPSec where the data on the network is encrypted for only part of the entire path. Usually implemented on routers connected to public networks.

IPX external network number

A network number that uniquely identifies a network cable segment. An IPX external network number is a hexadecimal number, one to eight digits (1 to FFFFFFFE). When the IPX protocol is bound to a network board in the server, the number is assigned. IPX can be bound with multiple frame types or protocols to the same network board. Network number and network address are two terms used to refer to the IPX external network number.

IPX internal network number

A logical network number that identifies an individual NetWare server. During installation, the service is assigned an IPX internal network number. It is a hexadecimal number, 1 to 8 digits (1 to FFFFFFFE), that is unique to each server on a network. The IPX internal network number must also be different from any IPX external network number on the internetwork.

IPX internetwork address

A 12-byte number (represented by 24 hexadecimal characters) divided into three parts: the 4-byte (8-character) IPX external network number, the 6-byte (12-character) node number, and the 2-byte (4-character) socket number.

Iterative query

A query usually made by one DNS server to another asking for the IP address of a specific host name. The responding DNS server either provides the IP address or it refers the first DNS server to another DNS server that might have the information.

Job

Contains instructions for actions that will be performed. This replaces the SQL Server 6.5 term task.

Join

A relational operator that produces a single table from two tables, based on a comparison of particular column values (join columns) in each of the tables. The result is a table containing rows formed by the concatenation of the rows in the two tables. The values of the join columns compare or, if specified, include nonmatching rows.

Kerberos

Default authentication protocol for Windows 2000 clients and services.

Kernel

A set of essential operating routines used by the operating system (usually hidden from the user) to perform important system tasks such as managing the system memory or controlling disk operations.

Kernel mode

Lower-level Windows NT or Windows 95 operating system functions.

Key Distribution Center (KDC)

Kerberos protocol authentication server and ticket-granting service.

Keyboard

The device that allows the user to input data into the computer or to execute commands. Most keyboards resemble a typewriter. The standard is a 101-key keyboard.

Keys

Attribute columns that show a unique value for each entity.

Knowledge Consistency Checker (KCC)

A Windows 2000 service that uses site and subnet information, provided by domain administrators, for the purpose of generating a replication topology. The KCC uses its topology information to calculate the best connections for Active Directory replication.

Landscape

A document orientation that has a vertical dimension greater than its horizontal dimension.

Latency (replication latency)

The delay between when a change is made to an object attribute on one domain controller and when the change is replicated to other domain controllers in the domain.

Layer 2 Tunneling Protocol (L2TP)

A protocol that provides authentication services over public networks. Often used in conjunction with IPSec to create secure VPN connections.

Leaf Object

A type of NetWare object that does not contain other objects. Examples are user, printer, or server objects.

Legacy hardware

Term referring to hardware devices that require continued support in a new operating system environment.

Library

A group of programs or objects in a file.

Lightweight Directory Access Protocol (LDAP)

Modeled from X.500 and Directory Access Protocol (DAP), LDAP is a scaled-down version of its predecessor, DAP, which was unsuccessful because it was too inefficient (heavy) with thin clients, personal computers, and Internet use. Active Directory directly supports the Lightweight Directory Access Protocol.

Lines per inch (lpi)

Lpi dictates how many typewritten lines will be placed in the height of an inch on the paper.

Link

Any part of a Web page that is connected to something else. Clicking on or selecting a link will make that something else appear. (This is one major difference between virtual reality and real reality.) The first part of the URL named in a link denotes the method or kind of link. The methods include file (for local files), ftp, gopher, http, mailto, news, and wais (for some kinds of searches).

Linking

The process of associating a Group Policy Object (GPO) with a site, domain, OU, or container.

Link State Announcement (LSA)

The process used by OSPF routers to announce their routing tables to adjacent routers.

LMHOSTS

The LMHOSTS file lists the IP address and NetBIOS name for each network machine with which the local machine may need to communicate.

Local account

A Windows NT Server user account not authorized for interactive logon but supporting resource access.

Local Area Network (LAN)

A group of computers running specialized communications software and joined through an external data path.

A LAN will cover a small geographic area, usually no larger than a single building. The computers have a direct high-speed connection between all workstations and servers, and share hardware resources and data files. A LAN has centralized management of resources and network security.

PC-based networks can trace their heritage back to what are now often referred to as legacy systems. These systems were mainframe and minicomputer hosts accessed through dumb terminals.

There are a number of similarities between LANs and these legacy systems, such as centralized storage and backup, access security, and central management of resources. There are, however, a number of differences.

Traditional host systems are characterized by centralized processing, dumb terminals, custom applications, and high expansion costs and management overhead. LANs are characterized by distributed processing, intelligent workstations (PCs), and off-the-shelf applications. LANs are modular, are inexpensive to expand, and have more moderate management costs.

Local drive

The common name for a physical drive attached to a workstation.

Local group

1. Group scope supported by Windows 2000 that defines its members as being local to the machine. Local groups are valid only on nondomain/stand-alone servers and workstations.

2. When discussing Windows NT server domains, it is a group definition supporting local domain resource management. When discussing workstations, it is a group definition supporting local management of a Windows NT workstation.

Local Group Policy Object

Group Policy Object used for setting and managing policies for stand-alone and workgroup member Windows 2000 systems. A system will have only one local Group Policy Object.

Local printer

A printer directly connected to one of the ports on the computer. The opposite is one connected through a network, which would be a remote printer.

Local Security Authority (LSA)

Windows 2000 component that maintains information about local system security and the local security policy.

Logical Unit (LU)

The element within a network based on IBM's System Network Architecture (SNA) by which a user (terminal or program) attaches to the network. LUs are described by type to indicate their functional capabilities. LU2, for example, is a 3270-type device.

Local user account

A user account created on a workstation, member server, or stand-alone system and used for local logon authentication.

Logoff script

Executable file that runs when a user logs off.

Logon script

DOS or NT batch file or executable that may run when a user logs on to a computer system. Logon scripts can be used to map drives and search drives to directories, display messages, set environment variables, and execute programs or menus.

Loop

1. A series of program statements running in cyclic repetition.

2. An iterative programming construct. Loops are used to repeatedly execute a block of code.

Low Entry Networking (LEN)

A form of IBM's System Network Architecture (SNA) that permits PCs and minicomputers to communicate when a network does not contain an IBM mainframe.

LPT port

Also known as a parallel port, it is a connection on the computer, usually LPT1, where the cable for a parallel printer is connected. Generally, LPT1 through LPT3 can exist on a personal computer. Special equipment can be added to extend this capability.

Mail Exchanger (MX) resource record

Resource record identifying a mail server for a specific domain.

Mailbox

An area on a computer used to receive and store electronic mail messages.

Mailing list

A list of electronic mail addresses. A mailing list can be maintained by an individual user to send messages to groups of people. The mailing list is also used by listserv and other mail exploder programs to forward electronic mail messages on a specific topic to the listserv subscriber list.

Mailing lists are like newsletters except that any subscriber may contribute. A message sent to the list will automatically be sent to everyone who has subscribed to the list. A series of messages with the same subject line is called a thread.

Mainframe

A legacy computer that is capable of multitasking and other robust operations. It is generally used as a host for a large number of users.

Makeboot.exe

A utility used to create Setup boot disks for Windows 2000. Makeboot.exe runs on MS-DOS and 16-bit Windows-family systems.

Makebt32.exe

A utility used to create Setup boot disks for Windows 2000. Makebt32.exe runs on 32-bit Windows-family operating systems.

Mandatory user profile

Roaming user profile that does not allow the user to save changes made to the profile while logged on.

Manufacturing Automation Protocol (MAP)

A token-passing bus designed for factory environments by General Motors; standard IEEE 802.4 is nearly identical to MAP.

Mapping

1. The transferring of data between a disk and a computer's RAM.

2. Attaching to a server-based directory using the local drive ID.

Master

An instance where the highest privileges reside in a device (usually a computer) where they have control of other devices or servers.

Master Boot Record (MBR)

The physical section of a hard drive closest to the spindle where configuration and partition information is stored.

Master Domain Model

Windows NT Server domain model where one domain provides user and global group management for a set of trusting domains. Resources and local groups are managed individually at the trusting domains.

Master replica

The Directory replica that is used to create a new Directory partition in the Directory database. It also allows users to read and update Directory information. Although many Directory replicas of the same partition can exist, only one can be the master replica.

Media

A generic term for the medium that is used to record data. Media can be a floppy diskette, a hard disk, or other similar recording surface (an audio tape, for instance).

Media Access Control Sublayer (MAC)

The level of the IEEE 802 data station that controls and mediates access to media.

Megabit (Mb)

1,048,576 bits.

Megabits per second (Mbps)

Millions of bits per second (bps).

Megabyte (MB)

1,048,576 bytes.

Megabytes per second (MBps)

Millions of bytes per second (Bps).

Megahertz (MHz)

A million cycles per second. A CPU that operates at 200 Mhz uses a clock oscillator that runs at 200 million cycles per second.

Memory

A hardware component of a computer system that can store information and applications for later retrieval. Types of memory are RAM (Random Access Memory), ROM (Read-Only Memory), conventional, expanded, and extended memory.

Menu

1. A displayed list of items from which a user can make a selection.

2. A NetWare menu utility in 3.x that allows for the use of customized menus created as ASCII text files.

Menu bar

The bar of selections found at the top of a Macintosh application or the Finder.

Message

A notification from one object to another that some event has occurred.

Messages

A term used to refer to errors or messages generated by SQL Server.

Messaging API (MAPI)

One of the primary ways that people use the computer to communicate with each other. This is accomplished by sending messages and documents to each other via an electronic mail system.

Most companies are using at least one type of electronic mail system. Unfortunately, many companies are not using a single unified mail system for all of their employees, and other companies need interconnectivity with users who work for different companies.

Traditionally, corporations have installed gateways to get around this problem. However, gateways are highly specialized and can only be used to connect a particular pair of mail systems. Corporations often need a number of gateways to handle the different combinations of mail systems used by their employees and other contacts.

To resolve this problem, an API was developed that allowed for connectivity between various mail service providers and mail-aware/mail-enabled client applications. The result was the Messaging API, otherwise known as MAPI.

MAPI has a layered architecture that allows various client applications to communicate with multiple messaging systems. The main components are the client application, the MAPI subsystem, the MAP spooler, service providers, and the messaging system.

The client application is a front-end application that makes MAPI calls.

The MAPI subsystem, also known as the messaging subsystem, handles the client application's calls and provides standard user interface objects, such as dialog boxes and forms.

The MAPI spooler is responsible for forwarding the message to the appropriate transport service provider.

Service providers are responsible for translating MAPI methods to a format the messaging system can understand.

The messaging system is a back-end application that is responsible for routing messages over the network or across phone lines. Messaging systems currently available include Microsoft Mail, cc:Mail, IBM PROFS, X.400, and Novell MHS.

Method

A defined behavior for a particular interface. An object that owns an interface must implement its methods.

Metric

The cost assigned to a route in a routing table based on the bandwidth and availability of the network link.

Metropolitan Area Network (MAN)

A complete communications network set up by a local telephone company. This network services customers in regional locations, providing them with microwave and satellite relay stations, fiber optics, and cellular radio services with a 50-kilometer range operating at speeds from 1 megabit per second to 200 megabits per second.

A MAN is larger than a LAN (Local Area Network) but smaller than a WAN (Wide Area Network). A MAN may be made up of several LANs. MANs provide an integrated set of services for real-time voice, data, and image transmission.

Microsoft Management Console (MMC)

A framework that hosts Microsoft and third-party management tools, called snap-ins, that are used to administer computers, services, networks, users, and other components of the Windows system. The MMC does not provide any management functionality itself, but instead hosts the tools (snap-ins) that do.

The MMC provides the user with a simplified, single interface to the snap-ins. An MMC can be customized and the administrative tasks delegated with limited or full functionality of the included snap-ins.

Microsoft Point-to-Point Encryption (MPPE) protocol

Protocol used for data encryption between RAS servers and clients. Encryption is supported for the MS-CHAP and EAP-TLS remote access protocols.

Microsoft Software Installer file

Microsoft Software Installer (MSI) file type used with the Windows Installer Service. This type of file contains installation instructions and is capable of actively tracking and repairing application installation.

Migration

1. Conversion of NetWare servers from NetWare 2, NetWare 3, or from another operating system, to NetWare 4. Operating system migration is different from data migration, which is the moving of files to near-line or offline storage devices.

2. Transfer of users, groups, directories, and files from a NetWare Server to a Windows NT Server.

3. Transfer of users, groups, and application data from one application to another.

Milliseconds (ms)

A thousandth of a second. Access rates are expressed in milliseconds.

Mirror

Copying a hard disk's partition and data and duplicating it on another hard disk at the same time it is written on the original disk. Mirroring is set up during installation.

Mirror set

Basic disk fault-tolerant configuration using two physical hard disks with identical data. This is an implementation of RAID 1.

Mirrored volume

Dynamic disk fault-tolerant configuration using two physical hard disks with identical data. This is an implementation of RAID 1.

Mixed mode

A domain mode that includes a PDC upgraded to Windows 2000 and BDCs that have not been upgraded. Mixed mode also refers to the upgraded PDC and upgraded BDCs but without the native mode switch turned on.

Modem

An abbreviation for modulator/demodulator. A modem is a peripheral device that permits a personal computer, microcomputer, or mainframe to receive and transmit data in digital format across voice-oriented communications links such as telephone lines.

Monitors

Enforce mutually exclusive access to methods, particularly synchronized methods.

Motherboard

The electronic circuit board containing the primary computer components such as CPU, RAM, ROMs, etc.

Mounting point

A folder in one volume that another volume's data may be accessed through. The folder specified as a mounting point must be empty.

MS-DOS

MS-DOS is Microsoft's version of the DOS operating system.

Mud, Object Oriented (MOO)

One of several kinds of multiuser role-playing environments. MOO is a text-based environment.

Multicast

A special form of broadcast where copies of the packet are delivered to only a subset of all possible destinations.

Multicasting

When packets are sent from one server and received by many computers at the same time. Multicasting uses Class D IP addresses.

Multihomed host

A computer connected to more than one physical data link. The data links may or may not be attached to the same network.

Multimedia

In computing, multimedia refers to the presentation of information using sound, graphics, animation, and text.

Multiple Master Domain Model

Windows NT Server domain model when multiple trusted domains provide user and global group administration for a set of trusting domains. Resources and local groups are managed individually at the trusting domains.

Multiple Master Replication Model

Replication model used for Active Directory replication in which no domain controller is authoritative.

Multiprotocol routing

Windows 2000 RRAS configuration supporting any combination of IP routing, IPX routing, and AppleTalk routing.

Multitasking

A mode of operation that provides for the concurrent performance or interleaved execution of two or more tasks.

Multiuser

The ability of a computer that can support several interactive terminals at the same time.

Name server

Server running DNS server services and able to service queries for at least one zone.

Name server (NS) resource record

Resource record identifying a domain's name servers.

Name resolution

The process of mapping a node name into the corresponding network address. The name of a file can be resolved to the file itself through the Windows NT file system forming a namespace.

Namespace

TCP/IP term for a given subnet assigned by an authoritative body and referring to a group of addresses within a given range associated with a name. There can be only one authoritative DNS server for each domain namespace.

Native mode

Domain mode that only has Windows 2000 domain controllers and doesn't contain any PDC or BDCs.

NDS container object types

There are three container object types in the NDS: Country, Organization, and Organizational Unit.

It is important to note that in the [ROOT], you can create only Country, Organization, or Alias objects.

A Country container object identifies the name of the country. This allows multiple countries to be identified for Wide Area Networks (WANs). A Country container object can contain only Organization and Alias objects. The Country object is a two-character field and is identified by "C=."

An Organization container object identifies the name of the company, divisions within a company, or departments. Each [ROOT] of the NDS requires a minimum of one Organization object. An Organization container object can only contain Organizational Units and Leaf objects. The Organization object name can be up to 64 characters and is identified by "O=."

The Organizational Unit container object identifies different divisions or departments within the company. The Organizational Unit is a sublevel of the Organization container object and can only contain Leaf objects or other organizational units. Organizational Unit objects are optional within the directory tree. The Organizational Unit can be up to 64 characters and is identified by "OU=."

Net

An Internet domain designated for networks that include network service centers, network information centers, and others items. Examples are nyser.net or concentric.net.

NetBIOS

Standard programming interface for the development of distributed applications.

NetBIOS Extended User Interface (NetBEUI)

This is a nonroutable transport protocol written to the NetBIOS interface.

NetBIOS name

Microsoft networks, including workgroups and NT Server domains, always use NetBIOS names to identify workstations and servers. Machines recognize each other through unique machine names. Shared resources, files, and printers are accessed using NetBIOS names. For example, resources are identified by their Universal Naming Convention (UNC) name, which uses the format \\server\share_name.

In a UNC name, "server" is the NetBIOS name of the machine where the resource is physically located, and "share_name" is the name uniquely identifying the resource.

Microsoft NetBIOS names may contain up to 15 characters and are used to identify entities to NetBIOS. These entities include computers, domain names, workgroup names, and users.

In an internetwork TCP/IP environment, it is necessary to support resolution between NetBIOS names and IP addresses. Microsoft provides two methods of supporting this name resolution: LMHOSTS and Windows Internet Name Service (WINS).

LMHOSTS name resolution is based on a locally stored ASCII text file.

WINS Name resolution is based on WINS servers.

When designing your network, you will need to select the most appropriate method for your organizational requirements.

NetWare Client for DOS and MS Windows

Software that connects DOS and MS Windows workstations to NetWare networks and allows their users to share network resources.

Network

A group of computers and other devices connected together so they can communicate with each other.

Network adapter

The card that allows a computer to interface with the network. Also known as a Network Interface Card (NIC).

Network address

1. A network number that uniquely identifies a network cable segment. It may be referred to as the IPX external network number.

2. A network address can also be the network portion of an IP address. For a Class A network, the network address is the first byte of the IP address. For a Class B network, the network address is the first two bytes of the IP address. For a Class C network, the network address is the first three bytes of the IP address. In each case, the remainder is the host address.

Network Address Translation (NAT)

1. A component that is included with Windows 2000 Server that allows multiple users to share one connection, such as a modem or DSL connection, to the Internet. NAT is designed for mid-sized networks and offers more configuration flexibility than ICS. NAT operates as a router forwarding all requests to the Internet as well as supporting address translation. This means that the computers inside the network do not have to have Internet-compatible addresses.

2. A service available through RRAS on a Windows 2000 Server that allows the sharing of a single connection to the Internet or a remote network with multiple network clients. NAT is more difficult to configure than ICS but can also operate in more complex environments.

3. Routing protocol available through an Internet Connection Server (ICS) configuration that allows a home network or small office to share a single Internet connection. This protocol requires that your client computers be configured as DHCP clients.

Network application

A computer program housed on a server and designed to run over the network instead of being installed and run locally.

Network drive

The common name for a logical drive.

Network Driver Interface Specification (NDIS)

A specification that is part of the Windows 2000 networking architecture, which provides a boundary layer between the network protocols and the network card drivers. NDIS makes it possible to run multiple protocols and multiple network cards on one computer as long as all of them are designed to work with NDIS.

Network File System (NFS)

Software developed by Sun Microsystems that allows you to use files on another computer or network as if they were on your local computer.

Network Information Center (NIC)

A resource providing network administrative support as well as information services and support to users. The most famous of these on the Internet is the InterNIC, which is where new domain names are registered.

Network Interface Card (NIC)

Workstations communicate with each other and the network server via this circuit board, which is installed in each computer. It can also be referred to as an NIC, LAN card, or network card.

Network Monitor

An SMS utility that functions as a *sniffer* and is used to capture, transmit, and display network packets.

Network printer

A printer shared by multiple computers over a network.

Network server

A network node that provides file management, printing, or other services to other nodes or workstations. A node can function as a file server exclusively or as both a file server and a workstation.

New Technology File System (NTFS)

A fast and reliable file system provided with Windows NT. It is fully recoverable and allows the implementation of local security.

Node

A device at a physical location that performs a control function and influences the flow of data in a network. Node can also refer to the points of connection in the links of a network. Any single computer connected to a network.

Node address

A number that uniquely identifies a network board. It is also referred to as the node number.

Node number

A number that uniquely identifies a network board. It may also be referred to as a station address, physical node address, or node address. Every node must have at least one network board connecting it to the network. Each board must have a unique node number to distinguish it from other network boards on the network.

Non-Domain Local group

Any group created on a Windows 2000 system configured as a stand-alone system, workstation member, or domain member will be created as a Local group.

Nonresident Attribute

An attribute that is not stored in the NTFS directory entry but elsewhere on the hard disk.

Non-Windows application

An application designed to run with DOS but not specifically with Microsoft Windows. The application may not be able to take full advantage of all Windows features, such as memory management.

NT Lan Manager (NTLM) protocol

Authentication protocol used with Windows NT and earlier Windows-family products.

NWLink

The IPX/SPX-compatible protocol provided with Windows 2000. It is used primarily to connect to NetWare servers that support IPX/SPX.

Object

1. In Novell networking, an object contains information about network resources. An object is made up of categories of information, called properties, and the data in those properties. Some objects represent physical entities, like a user or printer. Others represent logical entities, like groups and print queues.

2. In SQL Server, objects are tables, data types, views, stored procedures, indexes, triggers, rules, and constraints.

3. Objects can be compound documents that incorporate data of different formats.

4. An object can also be any program, file, or utility that can be accessed by the user.

5. In some environments, an object is an item that is contained in the site database.

Object attributes

A set of characteristics defining and describing an Active Directory object.

Object Linking and Embedding (OLE)

Microsoft's specification that allows applications to transfer and share data.

Object ownership

The login username of the object's creator becomes the object owner. The owner has full privileges on that object. The system administrator can set up aliases for object creators to ensure that all objects within a database have the same owner's name.

Object permissions

Available permissions (standard permissions and special permissions) for managing Active Directory object access and security.

Object-oriented programming (OOP)

Component-based application development. C++ is a popular object-oriented language, providing classes that combine data and functionality in a single object.

Octet

A set of 8 bits or one byte.

OLE Automation controller

An application that calls the exposed methods of automation servers to perform various tasks.

OLE container

An application that can accept OLE objects and/or controls.

OLE server

An application that provides and manages OLE objects.

One-Way Trust

> A trust relationship where trust exists in one direction only.

Open Network Computing (ONC)

> A distributed applications architecture promoted and controlled by a consortium led by Sun Microsystems.

Open Shortest Path First (OSPF) protocol

> A routing protocol used in larger internetworks. It is more complex to administer than RIP and requires more processing power on the routers, but it is also more efficient for a large internetwork.

Open Systems Interconnection (OSI)

> To support international standardization of network terminology and protocols, the International Standards Organization (ISO) proposed a reference model of open systems interconnection. Currently under development, OSI ensures that any open system will communicate with any other OSI-compliant system.

Operating system

> The software program that controls all system hardware and provides the user interface.

Operations Master

> Active Directory operations that are not permitted to occur at different places in the network at the same time (i.e., single-master).

Operations master roles

> Special roles assigned as single-master roles to domain controllers.

Organizational Unit (OU)

> Windows 2000 Active Directory container object.

OSI Network Address

> The address, consisting of up to 20 octets, used to locate an OSI Transport entity. The address is formatted into an Initial Domain Part, which is standardized for each of several addressing domains, and a Domain Specific Part, which is the responsibility of the addressing authority for that domain.

OSI Presentation Address

> The address used to locate an OSI Application entity. It consists of an OSI Network Address and up to three selectors, one each for use by the Transport, Session, and Presentation entities.

OSI Transport Protocol Class 0 (TP0)

> Also known as Simple Class, this is the simplest OSI Transport Protocol, useful only on top of an X.25 network (or other network that does not lose or damage data).

OSI Transport Protocol Class 4 (TP4)

> Also known as Error Detection and Recovery Class, this is the most powerful OSI Transport Protocol, useful on top of any type of network. TP4 is the OSI equivalent to TCP.

Over-the-network installation

> Windows NT and Windows 2000 installations where a shared network directory is used as the installation source.

Owner

> An object that creates and/or manages some other object. For example, a dialog box is the owner of the controls that appear on it.

Package

1. An object that contains software installation information. Used to distribute software to client computers.

2. Data Transformation Service (DTS) object defining tasks to be executed.

Packet

A unit of data transmitted at the OSI network layer; or any addressed segment of data transmitted on a network.

Packet Assembler/Disassembler (PAD)

Device that accepts dial-in access for a client system over the PSTN and connects the client to the X.25 public data network.

Packet Internet groper (Ping)

A program used to test reachability of destinations by sending them an ICMP echo request and waiting for a reply. The term is used as a verb: "Ping host X to see if it is operational!"

Parallel ports

In a parallel interface, eight data bits of data are sent at the same time, in parallel, on eight separate wires. Therefore, parallel transmissions are faster than serial transmissions.

Parallel ports, also called LPT ports, were originally used to connect line printers and terminals. Most systems have at least one parallel port, which is called LPT1.

There are two parallel standards: Bi-Tronics and Centronics (IEEE 1284). Centronics cables support a higher data rate. The Centronics connector is a 25-pin D-shell connector and is considered the standard.

Printers generally use parallel communications, as do some early notebook PC network adapters. Devices are available that allow the connection of SCSI devices to a parallel port.

Parity bit

A check bit that is added to each byte to signal the computer that the bits in a byte have transmitted correctly.

Parity check

A technique used to quickly check the integrity of data received after a transmission, or from memory. Parity checking can apply to bytes, words, long words, and other units of information.

Partition

1. An area of storage on a fixed disk that contains a particular operating system or a logical drive where data and programs can be stored.

2. The NetWare Directory database is divided into these logical divisions. A partition represents a distinct unit of data in the Directory tree that can store and replicate Directory information. Each Directory partition has a container object. All objects and data about the objects are contained in it. Directory partitions do not include any information about the file system, directories, or files located therein.

Partition management

A method of management that allows users to divide the Directory into partitions and manage various Directory replicas of these Directory partitions.

Password

A word or set of letters and numbers allowing access to a facility, computer, or network. A password may be accompanied by some other unique identifier before the user is allowed to log in.

Path

1. In hierarchical data structures, such as operating system directories, the path is the chain from a root directory (as in MS-DOS) or volume (as in NetWare) to a specific subdirectory or file.

2. In data communications, the path is the transmission route from sending node to receiving node.

Pathname

The pathname is information that uniquely designates an item on a server. Pathnames have the form "volume/folder/.../name," where the volume is the storage device (typically a hard disk) on which the file resides, and "folder/.../" designates the series of nested folders (or, in the DOS and UNIX worlds, directories) containing the file.

Because pathnames use the slash (/) to separate the labels they contain, it is a good idea not to use slashes in the names of HTML files even when, as on Macs, it is legal to do so. A URL will typically include a pathname.

PDC Emulator

Domainwide operations master role that supports client systems that do not have the Windows 2000 client software and Windows NT domain Backup Domain Controllers (BDCs)

Peer

A Windows Socket application that functions as both a server and a client.

Peer-to-peer

Communication in which two communications systems communicate as equal partners sharing the processing and control of the exchange, as opposed to host-terminal communication in which the host does most of the processing and controls the exchange.

Permissions

Authority to run certain actions on certain database objects or to run certain commands. SQL Server permissions are generated using Grant and Revoke commands.

Per-seat licensing

Microsoft software licensing option where license tracking is based on individual client systems with unlimited server connections supported.

Per-server licensing

Microsoft software licensing option where license tracking is based on concurrent server connections.

PICS

A file format used by some animation applications.

Ping

This utility is used to test the presence of other computers on the network. You can use IP addresses or NetBIOS names if you have a WINS server running or have made the appropriate entry in the LMHOSTS file.

Plug and Play

The specification for a hardware and software architecture that allows automatic device identification and configuration.

Point-to-point

Data communications links are divided into two main categories, depending on how the line is structured: either point-to-point or multipoint. Point-to-point describes a channel that is established between two, and only two, stations. The link may be a dedicated or a dial-up line connecting a processor and a terminal, two processors, or two terminals.

Point-to-Point Protocol (PPP)

The successor to the SLIP protocol, PPP allows a computer to use a regular telephone line and a modem to make IP connections. PPP can also carry other routable protocols such as IPX.

Point-to-Point Tunneling Protocol (PPTP)

Network technology that gives clients using TCP/IP, IPX, or NetBEUI the ability to create a secure VPN over a public TCP/IP network, such as the Internet.

Pointer

Represents the memory address of a data variable.

Pointer (PTR) resource record

Resource record used for reverse lookup zone IP address-to-host name mapping.

Policy

A set of rules regarding resources that are applied to individuals or groups.

Port

1. A memory address that identifies the physical circuit used to transfer information between a microprocessor and a peripheral.

2. On the Internet, *port* often refers to a number that is part of a URL, appearing after a colon (:) immediately after the domain name. Every service on an Internet server listens on a particular port number on that server. Most services have standard port numbers. Web servers normally listen on port 80. Services can also listen on nonstandard ports, in which case the port number must be specified in a URL when accessing the server. You might see a URL of the form: gopher://peg.cwis.uci.edu:7000/, which shows a gopher server running on a nonstandard port (the standard gopher port is 70).

3. Port also refers to translating a piece of software from one type of computer system to another, for example, translating a Windows program to run on a Macintosh.

Portrait

The orientation setting in which the vertical dimension is longer than the horizontal dimension.

Post

To send a message to a network newsgroup or electronic bulletin board.

Preboot Execution Environment (PXE)

Extensions to the DHCP protocol that provide support for RIS to enable Windows 2000 Professional deployment through remote installation.

Preferences

A folder contained in the Macintosh System folder. This folder holds application software preferences established by the system's user.

Preferred Bridgehead server

A site's preferred domain controller for receiving replication data through intersite replication.

Presentation layer

OSI Layer 6. It is the OSI layer that determines how application information is represented (i.e., encoded) while in transit between two end systems.

Prestaging clients

The process of creating a computer account object in the Active Directory that contains the account GUID to uniquely identify the computer. Prestaged clients can be assigned to specific RIS servers as a way of enforcing load balancing between the servers.

Primary Domain Controller (PDC)

> The first domain controller created in a Windows NT domain.

Primary partition

> A basic disk partition that will have one logical drive ID. A primary partition marked Active is a bootable partition. A basic disk can have multiple primary partitions, but only one may be marked as Active.

Primary Rate ISDN

> ISDN connection providing one or more of up to 23 64-Kbps channels.

Print device

> Term used to refer to a physical printer, fax, or other device that can be associated with a logical printer.

Print queue

> A network directory that stores print jobs. The print server takes the print job out of the queue and sends it when the printer is ready. It can hold as many print jobs as disk space allows.

Print server

> A network computer, either dedicated or nondedicated, used to handle the printing needs of workstations.

Print server object

> A Leaf object that represents a network print server in the Directory tree.

Print spooler

> A program that allows background printing so that a computer may be used for other processing tasks while a print job is in progress.

Printer

> A peripheral hardware device that produces printed material. In Windows 2000, refers to a logical printer created on a Windows 2000 system. The logical printer will be associated with one or more physical print devices.

Printer driver

> A program that translates the printed file into the language the printer understands. A printer cannot be used unless the correct driver is installed.

Printer object

> A Leaf object that represents a physical printing device on the network.

Printer port

> A communications port located on the rear panel of a computer, designed for the connection of a printer.

Priority

> Sometimes abbreviated as PRI, PRIO, or PRTY; a rank assigned to a task that determines its precedence in receiving system resources.

Private

> An access modifier that specifies class members to be accessible only by other members of the class in which they are defined.

Private key

> The second part of the key pair. The private key is held by only one person or computer.

Procedure

1. A block of program code with or without formal parameters (the execution of which is invoked by means of a procedure call).

2. A set of executable Visual Basic program steps.

Process

1. Once a 32-bit application is launched, it is loaded into memory. It receives a block of memory addresses. A process cannot execute any commands and does not use any processor time.

2. To perform operations on data in a process; or, a course of events defined by its purpose or by its effect, achieved under given conditions. A course of events occurring according to an intended purpose or effect.

Process throttling

Limiting the amount of processor time that will be made available to a Web site's applications.

Processor

In a computer, the processor, or Central Processing Unit (CPU); this is a functional unit that interprets and executes instructions. A processor contains at least an instruction control unit and an arithmetic and logic unit.

Profile

The group of settings that define a user's working environment. These settings are contained in a Registry file and within the Documents and Settings folder on a Windows 2000 computer.

Program Information File (PIF)

A file used by Microsoft Windows, Windows NT, and Windows 2000 to provide parameters necessary for running non-Windows applications.

Properties

Values related to an object.

Property

A variable containing information about a particular object. Properties can be exposed or private.

Protected

An access modifier that specifies class members to be accessible only to methods in that class and in subclasses of that class.

Protocol

1. A set of strict rules (usually developed by a standards committee) that govern the exchange of information between computer devices. Also, a set of semantic and syntactic rules that determine the behavior of hardware and software in achieving communication.

2. PROTOCOL is also a NetWare 3.x console command that displays the protocols registered on a file server along with the names of their frame types and protocol identification numbers as included by the LAN driver when it is installed.

Proxy

1. The mechanism whereby one system *fronts for* another system in responding to protocol requests. Proxy systems are used in network management to avoid implementing full protocol stacks in simple devices, such as modems.

2. A copy of an out-of-process component's interfaces. Its role is to marshal method and property calls across process boundaries.

Proxy server

A server that is positioned between an internal network and the Internet. The proxy server can be configured to limit which users have access to the Internet, which sites users are allowed to connect to, what protocols users are allowed to use, and to cache Internet requests. Some proxy servers also provide some firewall capability.

Public

An access modifier that specifies class variables and methods to be accessible to objects both inside and outside the class. Public class members have global visibility.

Public key

One of the key pair used for PKI. The public key for each certificate is made available to all users and computers who request the key from the correct source.

Public Key Infrastructure (PKI)

1. A system that is used to provide distributed security to the network. PKI services include Internet Security, logon authentication security, private and public key encryption, and Certificate Services.

2. A method of distributed security that uses certificates and public and private keys to authenticate users and computers, and to secure communication between computers.

3. An encryption scheme that uses a shared key for encryption and decryption of files.

Published printer

This is a printer that has been published in the Active Directory. A printer must be shared before it can be published.

Published resource

A resource that has been published in the Active Directory as an Active Directory object.

Queue

A holding area in which items are removed in a first in, first out (FIFO) manner. In contrast, a stack removes items in a last in, first out (LIFO) manner.

Quota entries

Disk quota limits set for individual users.

RAID 5 volume

Dynamic disk fault-tolerant configuration using multiple disks with data and parity striped across multiple disks. This is an implementation of RAID 5.

Random Access Memory (RAM)

The computer's storage area to write, store, and retrieve information and program instructions so they can be used by the central processing unit. The contents of RAM are not permanent.

Rbfg.exe

Utility used to create an RIS client boot diskette.

Reboot

The process of restarting a computer system.

Recovery Console

Windows 2000 administrative tool that can be launched instead of launching Windows 2000 at startup.

Recursive query

A query made by a client to a DNS server asking that a host name be resolved to an IP address. The DNS server can respond with either the IP address that a client is looking for or with the notification that the host name cannot be resolved to an IP address.

Redirector

Another name for the networking client. The redirector is responsible for redirecting file requests to the network when a client computer is accessing a file that is located on another server.

Registry

Windows NT and Windows 95 configuration database.

Relation

The formal term for a table.

Relationship

The *verb* part of a statement describing the association between two different entities. For example, the relationship between an author and a book is that an author writes books. There is a direct relationship between the two entities. This relationship would be described as many-to-many.

Relative ID master

Domainwide operations master role responsible for managing relative IDs for the domain.

Remote access

The ability of a computer to access an offsite or distant computer using telephone lines or a network.

Remote Access Service (RAS)

In most networks, clients are connected directly to the network. In some cases, however, remote connections are needed for your users. Microsoft provides RAS to let you set up and configure client access.

Users connecting to a RAS server, generally through a modem, can be limited to accessing only that server or can be given access to the entire network. Effectively, this is the same as a local connection to the network except that any type of data transfer runs significantly slower. You will need to select connection options appropriate to your access requirements, available support, and budgetary constraints.

Remote Administration Mode

Terminal Services server mode optimized for support of remote server management.

Remote Authentication Dial-In User Service (RADIUS)

Client/server-based authentication and authorization service for remote access. Connection criteria are passed from the remote access server to the RADIUS server, which will inform the remote access server whether access is allowed or declined.

Remote client

Remote Microsoft Mail user.

Remote Desktop Protocol (RDP)

Protocol used for communication between Terminal Services servers and clients.

Remote Installation Services (RIS)

Windows 2000 services that support remote installation. RIS is based on PXE extensions to DHCP.

Remote management

Use of a remote console by a network supervisor or by a remote console operator to perform file server tasks.

Remote Procedure Call (RPC)

A protocol that standardizes initiation and control processes on remote computers.

Replica

A copy of the data defined by a NetWare Directory partition. The Directory database must be stored on many servers to be distributed across a network. Rather than storing a copy of the entire Directory database at each server, replicas of each Directory partition are stored on many servers. An unlimited number of Directory replicas for each Directory partition can be created and stored on any server.

Replication

The process of copying Active Directory object state to all domain controllers.

Replication partitions

Partitions within the Active Directory database. Each replication partition replicates separately.

Reply

An electronic mail program feature that enables a message receiver to automatically respond to a received message without manually addressing the message.

Resolution

In monitors, this refers to the sharpness of the displayed image or text on a monitor and is a direct function of the number of pixels in the display area. Resolution is the number of pixels across one line of the monitor by the number of lines down the screen (for example, 800x480). The greater the pixel count, the higher the resolution and the clearer the screen image.

Resource record

DNS database entry associating host names with network resources.

Resources

Objects an application needs, such as icons, cursors, and regions.

Restore

To bring back computer data or files that have been lost through tampering or other corruption or through hardware malfunction. Files should be backed up frequently to protect against such loss.

Reverse Address Resolution Protocol (RARP)

Used to map the MAC, or hardware address, to a host's IP, or software address.

If the only thing a station knows at initialization is its own MAC address (usually from configuration information supplied by the manufacturer), how can it learn its IP address? The RARP protocol serves this purpose.

RARP allows a station to send out a broadcast request in the form of a datagram that asks, "Who am I?" or "What is my IP address?" Another host (typically a RARP server) must be prepared to do the inverse of ARP, f. For example, taking the MAC address and mapping it into an IP network and node number. This only happens at startup. RARP is not run again until the next time the device is reset or restarted.

A value of 0x8035 in the Ethernet Type field indicates that the datagram is a RARP datagram. There must be a RARP server on each segment because broadcasting is used, and broadcasts are not normally forwarded by IP routers. All machines on the network receive the request, but only those authorized to supply the RARP service will process the request and send a reply. Such machines are known as RARP servers.

Reverse Lookup query

DNS query used for mapping IP addresses to host names.

Reverse Lookup Zone

DNS zone used for IP address-to-host name resolution.

Ring topology

Provides a closed-loop transmission medium. Repeaters at each node connection duplicate the signal. This is done to minimize signal degradation.

Ring Network

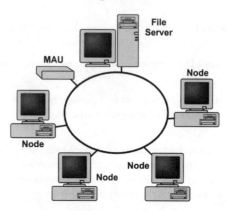

Traditional rings have the same failure risk as a bus topology. Any break brings down the entire network. To prevent this type of failure, most ring implementations (such as Token Ring) are wired in a star topology with an out loop and a return loop from each workstation to the wiring hub.

The Fiber Distributed Data Interface (FDDI) design specification calls for a dual fiber-optic ring. Should a break occur in either ring, it automatically converts to a bus topology.

Riprep.exe

Utility used for creating RIS installation images.

RIPrep image

Installation source image for use with RIS. An RIPrep image is created from an existing Windows 2000 Professional system.

Roaming User Profile (RUP)

User profile that is stored in a network location and made available to the user when logging on to any system in the domain.

Rollback

Cancels a SQL transaction and returns the result set to the state it was in prior to the beginning of the transaction.

Round robin

A DNS configuration option which can be used if multiple computers with different IP addresses have the same host name. The DNS server will provide load balancing by rotating through the IP addresses for successive client requests.

Route

To move data between multiple connected networks.

Router

1. A connection between two networks that specifies message paths and may perform other functions, such as data compression.

2. In early versions of NetWare, the term bridge was sometimes used interchangeably with the term router.

Router configuration

The settings and parameters that configure a NetWare 4 server as a router. They are set through internetwork utilities.

Routing and Remote Access Service (RRAS)

Windows 2000 service that enables a Windows 2000 server to simultaneously support multiprotocol routing, demand-dial routing, and remote access. RRAS supports clients running Windows 2000, Windows NT, Windows 9x, UNIX variants, and Macintosh.

Routing Information Protocol (RIP)

A routing protocol used in small- to medium-sized internetworks. It is easy to configure but not efficient in large internetworks (more than 20 subnets).

Row

The set of data values associated with one instance of the entity that the table describes; one set of columns.

RS-232-C

A low-speed serial interface used to connect data communications equipment (such as modems and terminals) defined as a standard by the Electronic Industries Association. All standards recommended by the EIA have an RS prefix.

Rule

SQL Server referential integrity feature ensuring that a value either falls within a specific range, matches a specified pattern, or matches a value from a specified list.

Scale

Stretch or shrink the contents to fit inside a specific area.

Scheduler

Also known as a dispatcher. The part of the operating system that determines which thread should run and the relative priority of each executing thread.

Schema master

Forestwide operations master role that controls schema updates and modifications.

Schema partition

Replication partition containing the Active Directory schema. The schema partition replicates to all domain controllers in a forest.

Scope

1. A group of IP addresses as well as other TCP/IP configuration information that the DHCP server can provide for DHCP clients.

2. Variable scope refers to where in the application a variable can be seen. Scope can be limited to a procedure, a module, or global (visible throughout the application).

3. Project scope refers to the definition of features, requirements, schedule, and budget for a project.

Screensaver

A system utility used to prevent monitor damage by powering the video monitor down or displaying a moving graphic.

Script

Set of executable statements written in a scripting language supported by Windows Script Host (WSH).

Search engine

A search engine is a computer or group of computers that provides search capabilities for resources on the Internet.

Sector

In disk drives, each track is divided into sectors. Sectors resemble pieces of a pie.

Sector sparing

Disk fault tolerance feature that allows remapping of bad sectors to an alternate sector when disk I/O errors occur.

Secure MIME (S/MIME)

An Internet standard used to digitally sign and encrypt e-mail messages.

Secure Sockets Layer (SSL)

An authentication and encryption standard that uses PKI to authenticate users when connecting to a secure Web site and encrypts all data that flows between the Web server and client.

Security Association (SA)

A security agreement between two computers using IPSec that defines the levels of encryption supported by both computers.

Security Configuration and Analysis

MMC snap-in that can be used to review and analyze local security policy, edit local security policy, and import and apply a security template on a stand-alone or workgroup member Windows 2000 system.

Security descriptor

A structure that contains information about which users can access an object and for what purpose. Only objects created under Windows NT can have security descriptors.

Security Identifier (SID)

Unique identifier value used in Windows NT Workstation and NT Server security management.

Security group

At the time of their creation, the three kinds of groups–Local, Global, and Universal–can be classified within Active Directory as a security group or a distribution group. The security classification allows rights and permissions to be assigned to the group. Distribution groups, on the other hand, are nonsecure groups that are primarily used for e-mail distribution lists or other means of nonsecure communication.

Security Template

File representing a security configuration defined as a group of security settings. Security templates can be applied to domain or local Group Policy Objects.

Segment

1. A self-contained portion of a computer program that may be executed without the entire computer program necessarily being maintained in internal storage at any one time.

2. In computer graphics, a segment is a collection of display elements that can be manipulated as a unit. A segment may consist of several and separate dots, line segments, or other display elements.

3. In TCP/IP, a segment is a message block.

4. Named collection of SQL Server disk storage pieces.

Sender

A component within the SMS Executive service that is used to send data from one site to another.

Serial communication

The transmission of data between devices over a single line, one bit at a time.

Serial interface

A connection point through which information is transferred one digital bit at a time. The term serial interface is sometimes applied to interfaces in which the data is transferred serially via one path, but some control signals can be transferred simultaneously via parallel paths.

Serial Line IP (SLIP)

An Internet protocol used to run IP to connect two systems over serial lines such as telephone circuits or RS-232 cables. SLIP is now being replaced by PPP.

Serial multitasking

The process by which multiple programs execute, but only one at a time.

Serial port

In a serial interface, bits of information are sent in a series, one at a time. Data bits are typically surrounded by starting and ending flags, which provide synchronization.

Serial ports are also called communications (COM) ports and referenced by number; COM1 is serial port 1. Most systems come with two COM ports.

The standard serial port connector is a 9-pin D-shell connector, but some systems still have older 25-pin D-shell connectors. Adapters are available to convert between the two standard connectors. With either connector, only 9 connector pins are soldered to 9 wires inside the cable.

Most serial cables are no longer than 50 feet. Use of longer cables can result in transmission errors.

Modems, serial printers, and serial mice use serial communications.

A new bus type, the Universal Serial Bus (USB), will become more prevalent in the future. The concept behind the USB is to consolidate all desktop peripherals into a single high-speed (12-Mbps) access route.

The USB allows up to 64 devices to be daisy-chained together. The single USB connector type will support many devices, including some that in the past used the serial, parallel, keyboard, mouse, or game ports.

The USB will usher in a new set of hardware peripherals and accessories, including products such as digital cameras and virtual-reality gloves.

More information about USB can be found at the Universal Bus Implementers Forum Home Page: www.usb.org.

Serial transmission

Transmission in which data (binary digits) can be transmitted only one bit at a time using only one communications line. In contrast, parallel transmission sends each byte simultaneously using separate lines. Connections exceeding one meter in distance typically use serial transmission.

Server

A computer or a software package that provides services to client software running on other computers on a network. Possible services include file sharing, printer sharing, or communications services.

Server Manager

In Windows NT Server, the Server Manager lets you manage domain members and provides a quick way of viewing information about your domain. With Server Manager, you can view system properties or view and manage shared directories and services running on Windows NT Workstations and Servers. It will also allow you to add member systems to, or remove member systems from, the domain, promote a backup domain controller into the role of domain controller, and broadcast messages to the domain. You can also view and manage trusting domains.

DOS, Windows 3.x, and Windows for Workgroups stations will be listed while active on the domain but are not registered as domain members.

Server Message Block (SMB)

The protocol used by Microsoft servers to exchange data, such as files and print jobs, across a network connection.

Service provider

A DLL that interfaces with a device or third-party application. A service provider is generally developed by the developer of the device or application it supports.

Service (SRV) resource record

Resource record identifying a server hosting a particular service.

Session

1. That group of processes or tasks associated with an application.

2. A NetWare 3.1x menu utility used to change a user's environment while logged in to the server. It can be used to change file servers, log out, view a list of network groups or users, or send a message to a group or user. It can display, add, delete, or modify drive mappings.

Session key

Encrypts and decrypts the contents of a message. In most PKI implementations, the public key is used to encrypt the session key. Also called a symmetric or bulk encryption key.

Session Layer

OSI Layer 5, which is the OSI layer that provides means for dialogue control between end systems.

Session ticket

Ticket granted in a Kerberos authentication providing access to a network resource.

Sets

Groups of rows to which aggregates apply.

Setup Manager

Utility that can be used to automatically create answer files and distribution folders for unattended Windows 2000 installations.

Setupact.log

File created during Windows 2000 Setup listing all file operations taking place during GUI mode Setup.

Setuperr.log

File created during Windows 2000 Setup listing errors reported by devices or services during Setup.

Setuplog.txt

File created during Windows 2000 Setup listing each driver and service loaded and each DLL registered by Setup.

Share name

The name given to a shared resource. The universal naming convention references machine name and share name.

Share Point

A shared resource identified by a UNC name.

Shared printer

This is a printer that has been shared to the network and can be accessed by its UNC path.

Shell

A portion of a program that responds to user commands, also called user interface. The shell is loaded as a Terminate-and-Stay Resident program (TSR).

Shortcut

A technique that allows a Windows 95 or Windows NT user to create a link to a file or program in an alternative location.

Signed driver

A device driver that has been digitally signed by Microsoft certifying that the driver has passed the WHQL Windows 2000 certification tests. The digital signature is recognized natively by Windows 2000 systems.

Simple Mail Transfer Protocol (SMTP)

The Internet standard protocol for transferring electronic mail messages between computers.

Simple Network Management Protocol (SNMP)

One of the most comprehensive tools available for TCP/IP network management. It operates through conversations between SNMP agents and management systems. Through these conversations, the SNMP management systems can collect statistics from and modify configuration parameters on agents.

The agents are any components running the SNMP agent service and are capable of being managed remotely. Agents can include minicomputers, mainframes, workstations, servers, bridges, routers, gateways, terminal servers, and wiring hubs.

Management stations are typically more powerful workstations. Common implementations are Windows NT or UNIX stations running a product such as HP OpenView, IBM Systemview/6000, or Cabletron Spectrum. The software provides a graphic representation of the network, allowing you to move through the network hierarchy to the individual device level.

There are three basic commands used in SNMP conversations: GET, SET, and TRAP.

The GET command is used by the management station to retrieve a specific parameter value from an SNMP agent. If a combination of parameters is grouped together on an agent, GET-NEXT retrieves the next item in a group. For example, a management system's graphic representation of a hub includes the state of all status lights. This information is gathered through GET and GET-NEXT.

The management system uses SET to change a selected parameter on an SNMP agent. For example, SET would be used by the management system to disable a failing port on a hub.

SNMP agents send TRAP packets to the management system in response to extraordinary events, such as a line failure on a hub. When the hub status light goes red on the management systems representation, it is in response to a TRAP.

An SNMP management station generates GET and SET commands. Agents are able to respond to SET and GET and to generate TRAP commands.

Simple volume

Dynamic disk configuration with all disk space coming from one hard disk. Disk space assigned to the volume does not have to be contiguous.

Single Domain Model

Simplest Windows NT Server domain model where only one domain exists on the network.

Site

1. (Active Directory) A group of domain controllers defined by a set of one or more subnet addresses. Sites are used in managing Active Directory replication, logon, and the Distributed File System (Dfs).

2. Any location of Internet files and services.

3. A group of domains and/or computers. A site can be either a Primary or Secondary site. The Central site is the highest site in the heirarchy and can administer all sites in the system.

Site link

A communication path between two or more servers.

Site link bridge

Object used for bridging site links when the IP transport transitive link feature is turned off.

Site link cost

A relative value used for identifying faster and slower site links. The site link cost is used to determine a preferred path for replication data when multiple paths are available.

SLIP

An Internet protocol used to run IP over serial lines such as telephone circuits or RS-232 cables interconnecting two systems. SLIP is now being replaced by PPP.

Slipstreaming

A process whereby a Windows 2000 service pack is applied to an installation file set. This allows the service pack to be applied automatically to the destination system during installation.

Smart

Containing microprocessor intelligence. A modem or adapter is smart if it has its own computer chip. A dumb device is limited in functions and features and takes processing power from a high-level system.

Smart card

A device used to authenticate users on a network. Within PKI, the smart card contains the user's certificates and private keys.

Snap-in

A management tool designed to run in the Microsoft Management Console (MMC) environment.

Socket

1. Information that is used when two computers are connecting to each other across an IP network. A socket consists of the IP address of the intended computer, a protocol number (TCP or UDP), and a port number.

2. The destination of an IPX packet is represented by this part of an IPX internetwork address in a network node. Some sockets are reserved by Novell for specific applications; all NCP request packets are delivered to socket 451h. By registering those numbers with Novell, third-party developers can reserve socket numbers for specific purposes.

Software

A computer program, or a set of instructions written in a specific language, that commands the computer to perform various operations on data contained in the program or supplied by the user.

Spanned volume

Dynamic disk configuration using disk space from multiple hard disks.

Spooler

System software used to provide background printing.

SRV resource records

A new type of resource record used in Windows 2000 to identify servers on the network that provide network resources, such as domain controllers and LDAP servers.

Stamp

A set of values used for conflict resolution during replication. The stamp includes three values: the USN version number (Version), the time when the change was made (Originating Time), and the originating domain controller (originating DSA).

Stand-alone Dfs root

Dfs root hosted on a server and stored in the server's Registry. Root and link replicas are not supported by a stand-alone Dfs root.

Stand-alone snap-in

A single management utility designed to run in the Microsoft Management Console (MMC) environment.

Standard primary

Zone name server configuration option where the zone database is stored locally as a text file.

Standard secondary

Zone name server with a replica of a standard zone database file.

Start menu

The pop-up menu containing Windows 95 functions that is accessed by pressing the **Start** button on the Taskbar.

Start of Authority (SOA) resource record

Resource record identifying the primary name server or authoritative source for a zone.

Station

A term used as a shortened form of workstation, but it can also refer to a server, router, printer, fax machine, or any computer device connected to a network by a network board and communication medium.

Stream transmission

A connection-oriented transfer of data between two sockets.

Stream-oriented

A type of transport service that allows its client to send data in a continuous stream in the same order as sent and without duplicates.

String

A sequence of characters, whether they make sense or not. For example, "dogcow" is a string, but so is "z@x#tt!." Every word is a string, but relatively few strings are words. A search form will sometimes ask you to enter a search string, meaning a keyword or keywords to search on. Sometimes string means a sequence that does not include space, tab, return, and other blank or nonprinting characters.

Stripe set

Basic disk configuration using multiple disks with data striped across the disks for performance improvement. This is an implementation of RAID 0.

Stripe set with parity

Basic disk fault-tolerant configuration using multiple disks with data and parity striped across multiple disks. This is an implementation of RAID 5.

Striped volume

Dynamic disk configuration using multiple disks with data striped across the disks for performance improvement. This is an implementation of RAID 0.

Structured Query Language (SQL)

An ISO data-definition and data-manipulation language for relational databases. Variations of SQL are offered by most major vendors for their relational database products. SQL is consistent with IBM's Systems Application Architecture and has been standardized by the American National Standards Institute (ANSI).

Subdirectory

This is a directory that lies below another in the file system structure. For example, in SALES/NEW, NEW is a subdirectory of SALES.

Subnet

The primary reason to divide a network into subnets is network performance and available bandwidth. Without separate networks, each transmission would be broadcast across the entire internetwork, waiting for the destination system to respond. As the network grows, this causes increases in traffic until it exceeds the available bandwidth.

Subnets

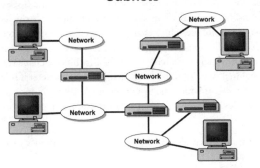

Routers divide, as well as provide, communications between the networks. Packets bound for a destination within the local network are kept local. Only packets bound for other networks are broadcast across the network, moving from router to router. Overall traffic levels are reduced.

Subnet mask

A filter that separates subnetted addresses into network and local entities. Local systems have subnet masks so they can restrict the broadcast to be received on the local network only.

Subnetting

When a complex network is recognized as a single address from outside of the network.

Subnetwork

A collection of OSI end systems and intermediate systems under the control of a single administrative domain and utilizing a single network access protocol. For example, private X.25 networks amid a collection of bridged LANs.

Superscopes

A configuration option in WINS that can be used to combine multiple scopes into one logical scope.

Switch

A statement that selects an action from a number of alternatives. Switch compares the value of an integer test-expression with each of several case labels.

Symmetric Multiprocessing (SMP)

In an SMP operating system such as Windows NT, the operating system can run on any processor or can share tasks between several processors. User and applications threads can also be shared between processors, making best use of processor time and reducing bottlenecks.

Synchronization

1. Replica synchronization is a way to ensure that replicas of a NetWare Directory partition have the same information as other replicas of the same partition. Time synchronization is a way to ensure all servers in a NetWare Directory tree register the same time.

2. Under SQL Server replication, this is the process of copying database schema and data from a publishing server to a subscription server.

3. When discussing the Internet, it is the process of setting the same clock or data rate in the receiving terminal as in the sending terminal. This is a requirement to enable the receiving device to read the incoming bits and to translate them into characters. Synchronization, accomplished by a signal from the sending terminal, enables the receiving band to recognize any single bit and to identify which group of bits belongs in which characters. Once the first bit of a character is recognized, the receiver can count off the required number of bits and identify each character if it learns the number of bits in the character and the speed at which the bits are coming. Two common approaches to synchronized transmission between devices are synchronous transmission and asynchronous transmission.

Synchronous

Pertaining to two or more processes that depend upon the occurrence of a specific event such as a common timing signal.

Sysprep

A Windows 2000 utility that prepares the hard drive of a fully configured master computer for duplication and deployment. Sysprep requires that the master and target computers have identical HALs, ACPI support, and mass storage controllers.

A third-party disk-imaging tool is necessary to both create the actual image of the installation and deploy it to other computers.

Sysprep.inf

Answer file used by the Mini-Setup Wizard as an unattended installation of a Windows 2000 image created using Sysprep.

System ACL (SACL)

The System ACL controls auditing messages to be generated for the object and written to the Security log in the Event Viewer.

System configuration

A process that specifies the devices and programs that form a particular data-processing system.

System Default Profile

A Windows NT profile defining background color, screen saver, and wallpaper settings when no user is logged on.

System Information Snap-in

MMC snap-in that displays system information including, but not limited to, the system configuration summary, resource usage, and resource conflicts.

System Monitor Snap-in

MMC snap-in that is used to view and record activity from performance counters.

System software

The operating system software.

System state data

Critical Windows 2000 local system components such as the Registry and system boot files.

Sysvol folder

Shared folder installed on each Active Directory domain controller. The folder contains scripts and part of the domain's Group Policy Objects.

T1

A leased-line connection capable of carrying data at 1,544,000 bits per second. At maximum theoretical capacity, a T1 line could move a megabyte in less than 10 seconds. That is still not fast enough for full-screen, full-motion video, for which you need at least 10,000,000 bits per second. T1 is the fastest speed commonly used to connect networks to the Internet.

T2

A leased-line connection capable of carrying data at 6,312,000 bits per second.

T3

A leased-line connection capable of carrying data at 45,000,000 bits per second. This is more than enough to do full-screen, full-motion video.

Table

A rectangular display of data values shown as horizontal rows and vertical columns.

Table list

The list of tables, views, or both following the From keyword in a Select statement.

Tape backup device

This internal or external tape drive backs up data from hard disks.

Target

Any server, workstation, or service on the network that has a Target Service Agent loaded. The data can be backed up or restored on a target. When backing up and restoring to the host server, the target and host become the same.

Task

In a multiprogramming or multiprocessing environment, one or more sequences of instructions created by a control program as an element of work to be accomplished by a computer.

Telnet

1. The Telnet protocol is a part of the TCP/IP protocol suite. Many Internet nodes support Telnet, which is similar to UNIX's rlogin program. Telnet lets users log in to any other computer on the Internet, provided that the target computer allows Telnet logins, and the user has a valid login name and password. The computers do not have to be of the same type to Telnet between them.

Some systems expect external access, and a special software package is set up to handle outside calls. This eliminates the need to *log in* once a user reaches the remote host.

The most popular reason to log in to a remote computer is to run software that is available only on the remote computer. Another reason is when a user's computer is incompatible with a particular program, operating system, available memory, or doesn't have the necessary processing power.

People with several Internet accounts can use Telnet to switch from one account to the other without logging out of any of the accounts.

Users can use Telnet as an information-gathering tool by searching databases for information. These databases include LOCIS (the Library of Congress Information System), CARL (Colorado Association of Research Libraries), ERIC (Educational Resources Information Center), and CIJE (Current Index to Journals in Education).

2. An Internet standard user-level protocol that allows a user's remote terminal to log in to computer systems on the Internet. To connect to a computer using Telnet, the user types Telnet and the address of the site or host computer.

Terminal

A device that allows you to send commands to a computer somewhere else. At a minimum, this usually means a keyboard and a display screen and some simple circuitry. Usually you will use terminal software in a personal computer. The software pretends to be ("emulates") a physical terminal and allows you to type commands to a computer somewhere else.

Terminal emulation

The use of hardware and software on a personal computer to duplicate the operation of a terminal device at both the operator and communications interface sides of the connection so that a mainframe computer capable of supporting the emulated terminal will also support the PC.

Terminal emulator

A program that allows a computer to act like a terminal when logged in to a remote host. The VT100 terminal is emulated by many popular communications packages.

Terminal server

A special-purpose computer that has places to plug in many modems on one side and a connection to a LAN or host machine on the other side. Thus, the terminal server does the work of answering the calls and passes the connections on to the appropriate node. Most terminal servers can provide PPP or SLIP services if connected to the Internet.

Terminal Services

Windows 2000 service providing a Windows 2000 desktop environment for clients with Win32 operating systems that are unable to fully support a local installation of Windows 2000.

Text fields

An input box where a user accepts a single line of text.

Thread

The object of a process that is responsible for executing a block of code. A process can have one or multiple threads.

Threads

Each process must have at least one thread. Threads are responsible for executing code.

Ticket-Granting Ticket (TGT)

Ticket granted by a Key Distribution Center (KDC) in Kerberos that is used to request session tickets.

Time out

When two computers are talking and, for whatever reason, one of the computers fails to respond.

Time to Live (TTL)

The amount of time between when a packet of data leaves its point of origin and when it reaches its destination. The TTL is encoded in the IP header and is used as a hop count (to measure the route to the packet's destination).

Title bar

A line displayed at the top of a window or dialog box.

Token

In a LAN (Local Area Network), the symbol of authority that is passed successively from one data station to another to indicate the station temporarily in control of the transmission medium. Each data station has an opportunity to acquire and use the token to control the medium.

Token bus

A form of network, usually a local area network (LAN), in which access to the transmission medium is controlled by a token. The token is passed from station-to-station in a sequence. A station wishing to transmit will do so by removing the token from the bus and replacing it with the data to be transmitted. When transmission is complete, the transmitting station will reinitiate the token-passing process.

Token Ring

IBM originally created Token Ring (IEEE 802.5). Over the last few years, it has steadily gained popularity.

It is a network that runs as a logical ring but is usually wired as a physical star. It has a 4-Mbps or 16-Mbps transfer rate and runs on Unshielded Twisted Pair, Shielded Twisted Pair, or Fiber Optic cabling.

A Token (data frame) passes from system to system. A system can attach data to a token if the token is free (empty). In turn, each system on the ring receives, regenerates, and passes the token.

**Token Passing in a
Token Ring Network**

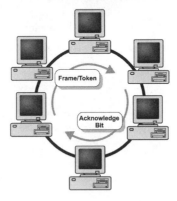

With Token Ring, it is possible to predict the passage of the token. The predictability inherent in Token Ring makes it a popular choice for timing-critical and control applications.

Topology

Refers to the physical layout of network components (such as cables, stations, gateways, and hubs).

Tracks

On a disk, data is organized into concentric circles, or tracks, on the disk medium. One complete circle represents one track. Tracks on disks are analogous to the tracks you might see on a record used in a record player (curving lines on the record surface). Tracks are typically numbered from the outermost track to the innermost, or from the outer edge of the medium to the inner hub area. To figure out the number of tracks on a fixed disk drive, multiply the number of cylinders by the number of heads.

Traffic

The total information flow in a communications system.

Transitive replication partner

An indirect source for Active Directory replication.

Transitive trust

Trust relationships that are propagated to all domains in a Windows 2000 network. Transitive trust rules state, "If A trusts B, and A trusts C, then B trusts C."

Transmission

The electrical transfer of a message signal from one location to another.

Transmission Control Protocol (TCP)

The reliable connection-oriented protocol used by DARPA (Defense Advanced Research Projects Agency) for their internetworking research. TCP uses a three-way handshake with a clock-based sequence number selection to synchronize connecting entities and to minimize the chance of erroneous connections due to delayed messages. TCP is usually used with IP (Internet Protocol), the combination being known as TCP/IP.

Transmission Control Protocol/Internet Protocol (TCP/IP)

1. Originally designed for WANs (Wide Area Networks), TCP/IP was developed in the 1970s to link the research center of the U.S. Government's Defense Advanced Research Projects Agency. TCP/IP is a protocol that enables communication between the same or different types of computers on a network. TCP/IP can be carried over a wide range of communication channels. The Transmission Control Protocol is connection-oriented and monitors the correct transfer of data between computers. The Internet Protocol is stream-oriented and breaks data into packets.

2. The preferred protocol for Windows 2000 networks. In order for Windows 2000 client computers to communicate with Windows 2000 servers, both must have TCP/IP configured correctly.

Transmit

To send data from one place for reception elsewhere. Also, moving an entity from one place to another, as in broadcasting radio waves, dispatching data via a transmission medium, or transferring data from one data station to another via a line.

Transport layer

OSI Layer 4, which is responsible for reliable end-to-end data transfer between end systems.

Tree

A collection of one or more domains that share a common namespace.

Tunneling

A method of encapsulating data for transmission between two authenticated end points.

Unattend.txt

Default name for an answer file used during over-the-network unattended Windows NT and Windows 2000 installations.

Unattended installation

An operating system installation run without end-user interaction. Answers to Setup prompts are supplied by text files called answer files.

Uniform Resource Locator (URL)

A URL is the pathname of a document on the Internet. URLs can be absolute or relative. An absolute URL consists of a prefix denoting a *method* (http for Web sites, gopher for gophers, and so forth). The prefix is followed by a colon, two slashes (://), and an address. The address consists of a domain name followed by a slash and a pathname (or "username@domain name" for mailto). The last part is an optional anchor, which is preceded by a #. The # symbol points to a place within the Web page.

Uniqueness Database File (UDF)

A text file containing unique responses used to override answer file responses during Windows NT and Windows 2000 unattended installations.

Universal group

An Active Directory group available only in native mode that can contain domain users from anywhere within a tree or forest.

Universal Naming Convention (UNC)

A file-naming convention that uses the *machine_name**share_name* format.

Universal Serial Bus (USB)

A standard promoted by Intel for communication between an IBM PC and an external peripheral over an inexpensive cable using biserial transmission.

USB works at 12 Mbps with specific cost consideration for low-cost peripherals. It supports up to 127 devices and both isochronous and asynchronous data transfers. Cables can be up to 5 m long, and it includes built-in power distribution for low power devices. It supports daisy-chaining through a tiered multidrop topology.

Before March 1996, Intel started to integrate the necessary logic into PC chip sets and encourage other manufacturers to do likewise, so currently there is widespread availability and support.

Because of its relatively low speed, USB is intended to replace existing serial ports, parallel ports, keyboard and monitor connectors, and be used with keyboard, mice, monitors, printers, and possibly some low-speed scanners and removable hard drives. For faster devices, existing IDE, SCSI, or emerging FC-AL or FireWire interfaces can be used.

UNIX

A computer operating system originally developed at AT&T's Bell Research Laboratories and later at the University of California Berkeley. It is implemented in a growing number of minicomputer and microcomputer systems.

UNIX is *multi-user* because it is designed to be used by many people at the same time and has TCP/IP built into the operating system. It is the most common operating system for servers on the Internet.

Update Sequence Number (USN)

Value used to track changes made to Active Directory objects.

User

1. An individual permitted to access a computer, network, or other system.

2. SQL Server database access account.

User account

Security object used for logon authentication and resource access verification.

User interface

A program operated by a computer user to interact with the computer. Also known as user agent.

User login script

This login script sets environment specifics for a user. It is optional but most often used for items that cannot be included in a system or profile login script. If used, it will run after container and profile login scripts.

User mode

1. The default Microsoft Management Console (MMC) mode that allows users to use, but not modify, MMC custom consoles. Three modes of varying restrictions are available for setting.

2. Higher-level Windows NT, Windows 95, or Windows 98 operating system functions. The user mode includes the protected subsystems and application sessions.

User object

A leaf object in NDS that represents a person with access to the network and stores information about this person.

User profile

Collection of folders containing information about a user's desktop environment, application settings, and other personal data that is applied when a user logs on.

Username

The name by which a login ID is known within the context of a database.

Utility

The capability of a system, program, or device to perform the functions it was designed for.

Value

A single data element, such as contents of one column-one row intersection.

Variable

In programming, a variable is used for temporary data storage. Each variable will have an identifying name, a data type, and an assigned (or assumed) value.

The term declaration is used to refer to the statement that causes a variable to be created.

The two types of variable declarations in Visual Basic are explicit and implicit.

An explicit declaration is when a variable is defined or created before it is needed. This is normally a better method of defining variables because it forces better planning and control.

With implicit declaration, the variable is defined *on the fly.* You define the variable by referring to it as part of a program statement. Any time Visual Basic encounters a name in your code that is not defined elsewhere, a new variable is created using that name.

Video card

The hardware board that contains the electronic circuitry to drive a video display monitor.

View

A method of creating custom presentation of data stored in database tables.

Virtual directory

Web site directory linked to a different physical directory location that serves as a means to extend the home directory.

Virtual machine

The Windows technique used to execute an application. Virtual machines include a virtual address space, processor registers, and privileges.

Virtual Private Network (VPN)

Remote access configuration where users and remote networks connect to network servers across the Internet. A tunnel is created through the Internet and all of the data that crosses the Internet is encrypted. Windows 2000 supports two protocols for setting up VPNs: Point-to-Point Tunneling Protocol (PPTP) or Layer 2 Tunneling Protocol/IPSec (L2TP/IPSec).

Virus

A program that can destroy data and change itself to escape detection. A virus can move into other computer systems by incorporating itself into programs or files that are shared among computer systems.

Visual Basic

A general purpose programming language for the Microsoft Windows family of products.

Volume set

Multiple basic disk partitions joined as one logical drive.

Voluntary tunnel

A tunnel created by a client computer to a target server.

WebDAV

Protocol that, when used with IIS, supports Web folders. This allows clients to manage remote folders and files through the Internet using an HTTP connection. File and folder maintenance can be performed using Internet Explorer 5, a Microsoft Office 2000 application, or any network connection using Windows 2000. WebDAV is an extention of the HTTP 1.1 standard.

WebDAV Publishing Directory

Special virtual directory that supports client read, write, delete, copy, move, and search operations. The WebDAV Publishing Directory is created by using the IIS Snap-in.

Well-connected sites

Sites that communicate through high-speed connections.

Wide Area Network (WAN)

Expands the basic LAN model by linking Local Area Networks (LANs) and allowing them to communicate with each other. By traditional definition, a LAN becomes a WAN when it crosses a public right-of-way, requiring a public carrier for data transmission. More current usage of the term usually includes any situation where a network expands beyond one location/building. A WAN is characterized by low- to high-speed communication links and usually covers a wide geographic area. The remote links may be operational LANs or only groups of workstations. With the exception of a WAN's wider area of operation, the benefits and features of LANs and WANs are the same.

Win32 Driver Model (WDM)

Specification defining device driver file architecture for Windows 2000 family- and Windows 98-compatible device driver files.

Windows (Microsoft)

A graphical shell operating environment that runs on top of DOS. It contains many accessories and features that access DOS functions, such as file, program, and printer management. Windows is referred to as a GUI (Graphical User Interface).

Windows Hardware Quality Labs (WHQL)

Testing entity for certifying WDM device drivers for digital signing.

Windows NT (NT)

An acronym for New Technology.

Windows Script Host (WSH)

Environment for running scripts without the need of a container application.

Winnt.exe

Windows NT and Windows 2000 Setup program. Winnt.exe runs on MS-DOS and 16-bit Windows-family operating systems.

Winnt.sif

Answer file used when running an unattended installation of Windows 2000 by booting from the Installation CD-ROM.

Winnt32.exe

Windows NT and Windows 2000 Setup program. Winnt32.exe runs on 32-bit Windows-family operating systems.

WINS proxy

A special function that can be assigned to a Windows 2000 server that enables the server to forward registration and name resolution requests from non-WINS clients to a WINS server.

Workgroup

A defined set of Windows for Workgroups, Windows 95, or NT stations that are able to communicate and share file and print resources.

Workstation

A personal computer that is connected to a network. It can perform tasks through application programs or utilities. The term client or station may also be used.

World Wide Web (WWW)

A recent, and the fast-growing, addition to the Internet.

In 1991, Tim Berners-Lee developed the World Wide Web for the European Council for Nuclear Research (CERN). It was designed as a means of communicating research and ideas between members of the high-energy physics community.

Browsers are the client tools that allow users to view the contents of the Web. The Web at that time had no easily accessible viewing capabilities. The browsers were text-only, line-mode tools that offered no graphical capabilities and few navigation links.

Early in 1993, a team at the National Center for Supercomputing Applications (NCSA) at the University of Illinois at Champaign-Urbana developed an Internet browsing program called Mosaic. The NCSA had no way to disseminate or market the program.

Later that year, a former NCSA graduate student (Tim Krauskopf) offered the University of Illinois a business plan and was given the rights to license Mosaic. The company is called Spyglass. Another company, with the help of former NCSA programmers, created its own Internet browser company and wanted to call it Mosaic Communications, but the NCSA would not allow this. The company was renamed Netscape, and their graphical Web browser was named Netscape Navigator. Netscape markets its browsers and servers directly to consumers, while Spyglass markets Mosaic to component suppliers such as AT&T, IBM, and Microsoft.

Because the Mosaic project initiated the graphical browser implementation, the term Mosaic is sometimes still used to describe any graphical Web browser.

The Web unifies many of the existing network tools with hypertext (also called hyperlinks). Hypertext gives users the ability to explore paths of information in nonlinear ways. Instead of reading through files in a preplanned sequential arrangement, users can move from item to item in any order they choose.

Some hyperlinks lead to ftp sites, newsgroups, gopher sites, and other Web sites that house additional graphical Web documents. To navigate these Web sites and find links, search engines are available. While current engines can only identify sites that meet the user's criteria, second-generation search engines will use artificial intelligence to report to users on information that exactly meets their needs.

The graphical interfaces make the Internet much more appealing, powerful, and simple. Besides being more intuitive than text-based tools, graphical browsers offer full hypermedia support. As recently as 1994, few trade journals mentioned the Web.

Today, Web addresses (URLs) are included in television, radio, magazine, and movie advertisements and on billboards. By 1995, Web traffic was doubling every four months and was growing more than twice as fast as general Internet traffic. Entire businesses now reside on the Web, and millions of people use it for communications and educational resources.

Wscript

Windows Script Host component that hosts a script in a Windows GUI environment.

X.25

A data communications interface specification that describes how data passes into and out of packet-switching networks. The protocol suite approved by the CCITT and International Standards Organization (ISO) defines the origination, termination, and use of virtual circuits that connect host computers and terminals across the network.

ZAP file

A file type used with the Windows Installer Service. ZAP files are similar to INI files and provide installation instructions.

Zone

A grouping of logical devices on one or more networks based on DNS domain namespace.

Zone delegation

The process by which an authoritative server is identified for a subdomain, creating a new zone. The procedure will create a new DNS database with initial SOA and NS resource records.

Zone Information Protocol (ZIP)

Responsible for linking users and resources on the network with the appropriate zone.

Zone integration

The process of integrating Active Directory and non-Active Directory domains for interoperability.

Zone List

A list of zones (up to 255).

Zone Root Domain

Topmost zone in a DNS zone hierarchy.

Zone transfer

The process by which standard secondary zone server database copies are updated.

ACRONYMS

—A—

AAL	ATM Adaptation Layer
Abend	Abnormal end
ABR	Automatic Baud Rate Detection
ACDI	Asynchronous Communications Device Interface
ACE	Access Control Entry
ACF/VTAM	Advanced Communications Function/Virtual Telecommunications Access Method
ACK	Acknowledgment
ACL	Access Control List
ACPI	Advanced Configuration and Power Interface
ACSE	Association Control Service Element
AD	Administrative Domain
ADB	Apple Desktop Bus
ADMD	Administration Management Domain
ADO	ActiveX Data Objects
ADSI	Active Directory Services Interface
ADSP	AppleTalk Data Stream Protocol
AEP	AppleTalk Echo Protocol
AFP	AppleTalk Filing Protocol
AGP	Accelerated Graphics Port
AIFF	Audio Interchange File Format
ANI	Automatic Number Identification
ANSI	American National Standards Institute
AOW	Asia and Oceania Workshop
APA	All Points Addressable
API	Application Programming Interface
APM	Advanced Power Management
APPC	Advanced Program-to-Program Communications
ARA	AppleTalk Remote Access
ARP	Address Resolution Protocol
ARPA	Advanced Research Project Agency
ARPANET	Advanced Research Projects Agency Network
ARQ	Automatic Request for Retransmission
ASCII	American Standard Code for Information Interchange
ASD	Automatic Skip Driver Agent
ASMP	Asymmetric Multiprocessing
ASN.1	Abstract Syntax Notation One
ASP	Active Server Pages
ASP	AppleTalk Session Protocol

ATM	Asynchronous Transfer Mode
ATP	AppleTalk Transaction Protocol
AUI	Attachment Unit Interface
AUP	Acceptable Use Policy
AWG	American Wire Gauge

—B—

BBS	Bulletin Board System
bcp	Bulk Copy Program
BDC	Backup Domain Controller
BER	Basic Encoding Rules
BIOS	Basic Input/Output System
BISDN	Broadband ISDN
bit	Binary Digits
BITNET	Because It's Time Network
BNC	British Naval Connector
BOC	Bell Operating Company
Bps	Bytes per second
bps	Bits per second
BRI	Basic Rate Interface
BSC	Binary Synchronous Communications
BSD	Berkeley Software Distribution
BTAM	Basic Telecommunications Access Method

—C—

CAL	Client Access License
CAP	Competitive Access Provider
CATV	Community Antenna Television
CBR	Constant Bit Rate
CBT	Computer-Based Training
CCITT	International Consultative Committee for Telegraphy and Telephony
CCL	Common Command Language
CCR	Commitment, Concurrency, and Recovery
CCTV	Closed-Circuit Television
CD-ROM	Compact Disc Read-only Memory
CDF	Channel Definition Format
CERN	European Laboratory for Particle Physics
CERT	Computer Emergency Response Team
CGA	Color Graphics Adapter
CGI	Common Gateway Interface
CICS	Customer Information Control System
CIR	Committed Information Rate
CISC	Complex Instruction Set Computer
CIX	Commercial Internet Exchange

CLBS	Component Load Balancing Service
CLNP	ConnectionLess Network Protocol
CLTP	ConnectionLess Transport Protocol
CMIP	Common Management Information Protocol
CMOS	Complementary Metal Oxide Semiconductor
CMOT	CMIP Over TCP
CN	Common Name
CO	Central Office
COM	Component Object Model
CONP	Connection Oriented Network Protocol
COS	Corporation for Open Systems
COSINE	Cooperation for Open Systems Interconnection Networking in Europe
CPE	Customer Premise Equipment
CPI	Common Programming Interface
cps	Characters per second
CPU	Central Processing Unit
CRC	Cyclic Redundancy Check
CREN	Corporation for Research and Educational Networking
CRT	Cathode Ray Tube
CSMA	Carrier Sense Multiple Access
CSMA/CA	Carrier Sense Multiple Access with Collision Avoidance
CSMA/CD	Carrier Sense Multiple Access with Collision Detection
CSNET	Computer Science Network
CSP	Cryptographic Service Provider
CSU	Customer Service Unit
CU	Control Unit

—D—

DAC	Digital to Analog Converter
DACS	Digital Access Cross Connects
DARPA	Defense Advanced Research Projects Agency
DAO	Data Access Objects
DAV	Digital Audio Video
DB2	IBM Data Base 2
DBCS	Double Byte Character Set
DBMS	Database Management System
DBO	Database Owner
DBOO	Database Object Owner
DCA	Defense Communications Agency
DCE	Distributed Computing Environment
DCE	Data Communications Equipment
DCOM	Distributed COM
DD	Double Density

DDE	Dynamic Data Exchange
DDI	Device Driver Interface
DDL	Data Definition Language
DDM	Distributed Data Management Architecture
DDN	Defense Data Network
DDNS	Dynamic DNS
DDP	Datagram Delivery Protocol
DES	Data Encryption Standard
DET	Directory Entry Table
Dfs	Distributed File System
DFT	Distributed Function Terminals
DHCP	Dynamic Host Configuration Protocol
DHTML	Dynamic HTML
DID	Direct Inward Dial
DIMM	Dual, In-line Memory Module
DISA	Defense Information Systems Agency
DIX	Digital, Intel, Xerox
DLC	Data Link Control
DLCI	Data Link Connection Identifier
DLL	Dynamic-link library
DMA	Direct Memory Access
DMI	Digital Multiplexed Interface
DML	Data Manipulation Language
DNA	Distributed interNet Application
DNS	Domain Name System
DOS	Disk Operating System
dpi	Dots per inch
DQDB	Distributed Queue Dual Bus
DRAM	Dynamic Random Access Memory
DS	Data Set
DS	Double-Sided
DS1	Digital Signaling Level 1
DS2	Digital Signaling Level 2
DS3	Digital Signaling Level 3
DSA	Directory System Agent
DSDD	Double-Sided, Double-Density
DSE	Data Service Equipment
DSHD	Double-Sided, High-Density
DSP	Digital Signal Processor
DSU	Data Service Unit
DTC	Distributed Transaction Coordinator
DTE	Data Terminal Equipment

DTR	Data Terminal Ready
DTS	Data Transformation Service
DUA	Directory User Agent
DVD	Digital Video Disc or Digital Versatile Disc
DXF	Drawing Exchange Format
DXI	Data Exchange Interface

—E—

E-mail	Electronic mail
EARN	European Academic and Research Network
EBCDIC	Extended Binary-Coded Decimal Interchange Code
ECF	Enhanced Connectivity Facilities
ECP	Extended Capabilities Port
EDI	Electronic Data Interchange
EEHLLAPI	Entry Emulator High-Level Language Application Program Interface
EFF	Electronic Frontier Foundation
EFS	Encrypting File System
EGA	Enhanced Graphics Adapter
EGP	Exterior Gateway Protocol
EIDE	Enhanced IDE
EMF	Enhanced Metafile
EMS	Expanded Memory
EPS or EPSF	Encapsulated PostScript File
ER Model	Entity/Relationship Model
ES-IS	End System-Intermediate System
ESDI	Enhanced Industry Standard Architecture
ESF	Extended Super Frame
EUnet	European UNIX Network
EUUG	European UNIX Users Group
EWOS	European Workshop for Open Systems

—F—

FAQ	Frequently Asked Questions
FARNET	Federation of American Research NETworks
FAT	File Allocation Table
FCB	File Control Block
FCC	Federal Communications Commission
FCS	Frame Check Sequence
FDDI	Fiber Distributed Data Interface
FEP	Front-End Processor
FFAPI	File Format API
FIPS	Federal Information Processing Standard
FM	Frequency Modulation
FNC	Federal Networking Council

	FPU	Floating Point Unit
	FQDN	Fully Qualified Domain Name
	FRICC	Federal Research Internet Coordinating Committee
	FT1	Fractional T1
	FT3	Fractional T3
	FTAM	File Transfer, Access, and Management
	FTP	File Transfer Protocol
	FYI	For Your Information
—G—		
	GDI	Graphics Device Interface
	GIF	Graphics Interchange Format
	GINA	Graphical Identification and Authentication
	GOSIP	Government OSI Profile
	GP	Group Policy
	GPO	Group Policy Object
	GUI	Graphical User Interface
—H—		
	HAL	Hardware Abstraction Layer
	HCL	Hardware Compatibility List
	HCSS	High Capacity Storage System
	HD	High Density
	HDLC	High-level Data Link Control
	HDX	Half-duplex
	HFS	Hierarchical File System
	HID	Human Interface Device
	HLLAPI	High-Level Language Application Program Interface
	HMA	High Memory Area
	HPFS	High Performance File System
	HTML	HyperText Markup Language
	HTTP	HyperText Transfer Protocol
	Hz	Hertz
—I—		
	IAB	Internet Activities Board
	ICM	Image Color Management
	ICMP	Internet Control Message Protocol
	ICS	Internet Connection Server
	IDE	Integrated Drive Electronics
	IEEE	Institute of Electrical and Electronics Engineers
	IESG	Internet Engineering Steering Group
	IETF	Internet Engineering Task Force
	IFS	Installable File System
	IGP	Interior Gateway Protocol

IGRP	Internet Gateway Routing Protocol
IIS	Internet Information Server
IMHO	In My Humble Opinion
INTAP	Interoperability Technology Association for Information Processing
IONL	Internal Organization of the Network Layer
IP	Internet Protocol
IPX	Internetwork Packet Exchange
IPXODI	Internetwork Packet Exchange Open Data link Interface
IRC	Internet Relay Chat
IrDA	Infrared Developers Association
IRF	Inherited Rights Filter
IRQ	Interrupt Request Lines
IRTF	Internet Research Task Force
IS-IS	Intermediate System-Intermediate System
ISAPI	Microsoft Internet Server Application Programming Interface
ISDN	Integrated Services Digital Network
ISO	International Standards Organization
ISODE	ISO Development Environment
ISP	Internet Service Provider
IXC	Inter-exchange Carrier

—J—

JANET	Joint Academic Network
JPEG	Joint Photographic Experts Group
JUNET	Japan UNIX Network

—K—

KB	Kilobyte
Kb	Kilobit
KBps	Kilobytes per second
Kbps	Kilobits per second
KCC	Knowledge Consistency Check
KDC	Key Distribution Center

—L—

L2PDU	Layer Two Protocol Data Unit
L3PDU	Layer Three Protocol Data Unit
LAN	Local Area Network
LAPB	Link Access Protocol Balanced
LAPD	Link Access Protocol Device
LAPS	LAN Adapter and Protocol Support
LATA	Local Access and Transport Area
LCD	Liquid Crystal Diode
LDAP	Lightweight Directory Access Protocol
LDT	Local Descriptor Table

LEC	Local Exchange Carriers
LEN	Low Entry Networking
LLAP	LocalTalk Link Access Protocol
LMI	Local Management Interface
lpi	Lines per inch
LSA	Local Security Authority
LSL	Link Support Layer
LU	Logical Unit

—M—

MAC	Media Access Control Sublayer
MAN	Metropolitan Area Network
MAP	Manufacturing Automation Protocol
MAPI	Messaging API
MAU	Media Access Unit
MB	Megabyte
Mb	Megabit
MBps	Megabytes per second
Mbps	Megabits per second
MBR	Master Boot Record
MCGA	Multi-Color Gate Array
MDI	Multiple Document Interface
MHS	Message Handling System
MHz	Megahertz
MIB	Management Information Base
MIDI	Musical Instrument Digital Interface
MILNET	Military Network
MIME	Multipurpose Internet Mail Extensions
MIPS	Million Instructions Per Second
MLID	Multiple Link Interface Driver
MMC	Microsoft Management Console
MOO	Mud, Object Oriented
MPEG	Moving Pictures Experts Group
MPPE	Microsoft Point-to-Point Encryption
ms	Milliseconds
MSAU	MultiStation Access Unit
MSI	Microsoft Software Installer
MTA	Message Transfer Agent
MTU	Maximum Transmission Unit
MUD	Multi-User Dungeon or Dimension
MVS	Multiple Virtual Storage
MVS-CICS	Multiple Virtual Storage-Customer Information Control System
MVS/TSO	Multiple Virtual Storage/Time-Sharing Option

—N—

NAK	Negative AcKnowledgment
NAT	Network Address Translation
NBP	Name Binding Protocol
NCC	NetWare Control Center
NCP	NetWare Core Protocol
NCP	Network Control Point
NCSA	National Center for Supercomputing Applications
NDS	NetWare Directory Services
NetBEUI	NetBIOS Extended User Interface
NetWare DA	NetWare Desk Accessory
NFS	Network File System
NIC	Network Information Center
NIC	Network Interface Card
NIST	National Institute of Standards and Technology
NLM	NetWare Loadable Module
NLQ	Near Letter Quality
NLSP	NetWare Link Services Protocol
NMS	Network Management Station
NNS	NetWare Name Service
NNTP	Network News Transfer Protocol
NOC	Network Operations Center
NREN	National Research and Education Network
NSAP	Network Service Access Point
NSEPro	Network Support Encyclopedia Professional Volume
NSEPro	Network Support Encyclopedia Professional Edition
NSF	National Science Foundation
NSFnet	National Science Foundation Network
NT	Windows NT
NT1	Network Termination 1
NT2	Network Termination 2
NTAS	Windows NT Advanced Server
NTFS	New Technology File System
NTLM	NT Lan Manager
NTP	Network Time Protocol
NWADMIN	Network Administrator

—O—

OBS	Optical Bypass Switch
ODI	Open Datalink Interface
OHCI	Open Host Controller Interface
OIW	Workshop for Implementors of OSI
OLE	Object Linking and Embedding

ONC	Open Network Computing
OOP	Object-oriented programming
OPAC	Online Public Access Catalog
OpenHCI	Open Host Controller Interface
OSI	Open Systems Interconnection
OSPF	Open Shortest Path First

—P—

PAD	Packet Assembler/Disassembler
PAP	Printer Access Protocol
PBX	Private Branch Exchange
PCI	Peripheral Component Interconnect
PCI	Protocol Control Information
PCL	Printer Control Language
PCM	Pulse Code Modulation
PCMCIA	Personal Computer Memory Card International Association
PDC	Primary Domain Controller
PDF	Printer Definition Files
PDN	Packet Data Network
PDS	Processor-Direct Slot
PDU	Protocol Data Unit
PID	Process Identification Number
PIF	Program Information File
Ping	Packet internet groper
PKI	Public Key Infrastructure
PMMU	Paged Memory Management Unit
POP	Point of Presence
POP	Post Office Protocol
POSI	Promoting Conference for OSI
POST	Power On Self Test
POTS	Plain Old Telephone Service
ppm	pages per minute
PPP	Point-to-Point Protocol
PPTP	Point-to-Point Tunneling Protocol
PRAM	Parameter RAM
PRI	Primary Rate Interface
PRMD	Private Management Domain
PROFS	Professional Office System
PSN	Packet Switch Node
PU	Physical Unit
PUC	Public Utility Commission
PVC	Permanent Virtual Circuit

—Q—

QMF	Query Manager Facility
QoS	Quality of Service

—R—

RADIUS	Remote Authentication Dial-In User Service
RAID	Redundant Array of Independent Disks
RAM	Random Access Memory
RARE	Reseaux Associes pour la Recherche Europeene
RARP	Reverse Address Resolution Protocol
RAS	Remote Access Service
RAS	Remote Access Server
RBOC	Regional Bell Operating Company
RDP	Remote Desktop Protocol
REM	REMARK
RFC	Request For Comments
RFS	Remote File System
RIP	Raster Image Processor
RIP	Router Information Protocol
RIPE	Reseaux IP Europeene
RISC	Reduced Instruction Set Computer
ROM	Read-Only Memory
ROSE	Remote Operations Service Element
RPC	Remote Procedure Call
RRAS	Routing and Remote Access Service
RTF	Rich Text Format
RTMP	Routing Table Maintenance Protocol
RTSE	Reliable Transfer Service Element
RUP	Roaming User Profile

—S—

SAA	Systems Application Architecture
SAP	Service Access Point
SAP	Service Advertising Protocol
SAPI	Service Access Point Identifier
SAPS	Service Access Point Stations
SAR	Segmentation and Reassembly protocol
SCSI	Small Computer Systems Interface
SDH	Synchronous Digital Hierarchy
SDI	Storage Device Interface
SDLC	Synchronous Data Link Control
SDN	Software Defined Network
SDU	SMDS Data Unit
SFT	System Fault Tolerance

SGML	Standard Generalized Markup Language	
SGMP	Simple Gateway Management Protocol	
SID	Security Identifier	
SIMM	Single, In-line Memory Module	
SIP	SMDS Interface Protocol	
SLIP	Serial Line Internet Protocol	
SMDS	Switched Multimegabit Data Service	
SMI	Structure of Management Information	
SMP	Symmetric Multiprocessing	
SMS	Storage Management Services	
SMTP	Simple Mail Transfer Protocol	
SNA	System Network Architecture	
SNMP	Simple Network Management Protocol	
SONET	Synchronous Optical Network	
SPAG	Standards Promotion and Application Group	
SPE	Synchronous Payload Envelope	
SPX	Sequenced Packet Exchange	
SQL	Structured Query Language	
SRAM	Static RAM	
SRPI	Server Requester Programming Interface	
SS7	Signaling System 7	
SSL	Secure Sockets Layer	
STDM	Statistical Time Division Multiplexing	
STI	Still Image Interface	
STM	Synchronous Transport Module	
STS	Synchronous Transport Signal	
SVC	Switched Virtual Circuit	
Sysop	Systems Operator	

—T—

TA	Terminal Adapter	
TAC	Terminal Access Controller	
TCP	Transmission Control Protcol	
TCP/IP	Transmission Control Protocol/Internet Protocol	
TDM	Time-Division Multiplexor	
TE1	Terminal Equipment Type 1	
TE2	Terminal Equipment Type 2	
Telex	Teleprinter Exchange	
TIFF	Tagged Image File Format	
TLI	Transport Layer Interface	
TNX	Teletypewriter Exchange Service	
TP0	OSI Transport Protocol Class 0	
TP4	OSI Transport Protocol Class 4	

	TSA	Target Server Agent
	TSR	Terminate and Stay Resident program
	TTF	TrueType fonts
	TTL	Time to Live
	TTS	Transaction Tracking System
	TWX	Teletypewriter Exchange Service

—U—

	UA	User Agent
	UDP	User Datagram Protocol
	UMA	Upper Memory Area
	UMBs	Upper Memory Blocks
	UNC	Universal Naming Convention
	UPS	Uninterruptible Power Supply
	URL	Uniform Resource Locator
	USB	Universal Serial Bus
	UUCP	UNIX-to-UNIX Copy Program

—V—

	VBR	Variable Bit Rate
	VCI	Virtual Connection Identifier
	VDM	Virtual DOS Machine
	Veronica	Very Easy Rodent-Oriented Netwide Index to Computerized Archives
	VGA	Video Graphics Array
	VLM	Virtual Loadable Module
	VLSI	Very Large-Scale Integration
	VM/CMS	Virtual Machine/Conversational Monitor System
	VMM	Virtual Memory Manager
	VNET	Virtual Network
	VPI	Virtual Path Identifier
	VPN	Virtual Private Network
	VRAM	Video RAM
	VRC	Vertical Redundancy Check
	VRML	Virtual Reality Modeling Language
	VSE/CICS	Virtual Storage Extended/Customer Information Control System
	VT	Virtual Terminal

—W—

	WAIS	Wide Area Information Servers
	WAN	Wide Area Network
	WATS	Wide Area Telephone Service
	WDM	Win32 Driver Model
	WHQL	Windows Hardware Quality Labs
	WWW	World Wide Web
	WYSIWYG	What You See Is What You Get

—X—

XDR	External Data Representation
XMS	Extended Memory
XNS	Xerox Network System

—Z—

ZAW	Zero Administration Initiative for Windows
ZIP	Zone Information Protocol

Index

SPECIAL SUPPLEMENTAL EXERCISES

KEY TERMS

Chapter 1

Access Control List (ACL)

1. A list of trustees who have been granted rights to an object or rights to the properties of an object. Each object in the NDS contains an Access Control List.

2. Under Windows NT/2000, the Access Control List contains user and group Access Control Entries.

Authentication

1. A way to verify that an object sending messages or requests to an NDS is permitted to act on or receive those messages or requests.

2. Login or resource access validation.

Certificate

The document (usually digital) issued by a Certificate Authority that includes the Certificate Authority's digital signature, the user's public and private key, and user information.

Certificate Authority (CA)

A server that issues certificates for the purpose of authenticating users and computers or securing data transmission.

Challenge Response authentication

An authentication method used to verify users through remote access.

Digest Authentication

A digest is a signature for an electronic message. A digest authentication verifies whether the sender of an electronic message is authentic.

Digital signature

1. An arithmetic function that uses a user's private key to create a unique signature that can only be read using the user's public key. The digital signature ensures that the data is coming from the correct user and that it has not been tampered with.

2. Verifies that the sender of a package is who he claims to be. A digital signature is encrypted with the private key and verified using the corresponding public key.

DoD Network Reference Model

The model that the Department of Defense uses to analyze the TCP/IP protocol.

Domain

1. In NetWare, DOMAIN is used as a console command that will create a protected operating system domain for running untested NLMs in Ring 3. This prevents a module from interfering with the core operating system.

2. In the Internet, a domain is a part of the naming hierarchy. The domain name is a sequence of names (separated by periods) that identify host sites. For example: galenp@mail.msen.com.

Domain Local group

Active Directory domain group scope. In mixed mode, members can include user accounts from any domain in the forest or Global groups from any domain in the forest. In addition, Domain Local groups from the same domain and Universal groups from any domain in the forest are supported in native mode.

Encrypting File System (EFS)

Windows 2000 data encryption service based on a user's public and private keys. Data encryption is only supported on NTFS volumes.

Encryption

Involves encoding a packet's data prior to transmission to ensure data security. The Data Encryption Standard (DES) is an algorithm used for coding and decoding data for security purposes.

Encryption key

A key is some data used as a logical key to unlock encrypted information.

Forest

A collection of two or more trees. They do not share a common namespace but do share a Global Catalog and a common schema.

Global Catalog (GC)

A database containing scaled-down attributes of every Active Directory object from every domain in a tree or forest. The GC replies to queries so that users in one domain can locate resources in another domain.

Global group

A group definition allowing permission assignments to local machines or other domains through local group membership of the Global group.

Graphical User Interface (GUI)

A program that executes commands given by the user to the computer. A GUI uses graphic representations of commands and/or a menu format to display commands that the user may execute with a mouse or similar device.

The graphical user interface makes using a computer easier, especially for the beginner. Mosaic is a Graphical User Interface for the Internet. Microsoft Windows, OS/2, and the Macintosh operating system are examples of graphical user interfaces for personal computers.

Group

Collection of users used for security management or distribution management. Windows 2000 groups can contain other objects such as computers.

Inheritance

1. The means by which a child object can get information from its parent.

2. The process by which Access Control Entries are passed from a parent object to a child object.

3. The process by which permissions are passed from a group to its members.

IP Security (IPSec)

A part of TCP/IP standards in which all IP traffic between two computers is encrypted so that the packets cannot be captured on the network and read by unauthorized users.

Kerberos

Default authentication protocol for Windows 2000 clients and services.

Key Distribution Center (KDC)

Kerberos protocol authentication server and ticket-granting service.

Local group

1. Group scope supported by Windows 2000 that defines its members as being local to the machine. Local groups are valid only on nondomain/stand-alone servers and workstations.

2. When discussing Windows NT server domains, it is a group definition supporting local domain resource management. When discussing workstations, it is a group definition supporting local management of a Windows NT workstation.

Microsoft Management Console (MMC)

A framework that hosts Microsoft and third-party management tools, called snap-ins, that are used to administer computers, services, networks, users, and other components of the Windows system. The MMC does not provide any management functionality itself, but instead hosts the tools (snap-ins) that do.

The MMC provides the user with a simplified, single interface to the snap-ins. An MMC can be customized and the administrative tasks delegated with limited or full functionality of the included snap-ins.

Namespace

TCP/IP term for a given subnet assigned by an authoritative body and referring to a group of addresses within a given range associated with a name. There can be only one authoritative DNS server for each domain namespace.

Native mode

Domain mode that only has Windows 2000 domain controllers and doesn't contain any PDC or BDCs.

New Technology File System (NTFS)

A fast and reliable file system provided with Windows NT. It is fully recoverable and allows the implementation of local security.

One-way function

A process that modifies data from its original form in such a way that the process cannot be reversed using the same algorithm.

One-Way Trust

A trust relationship where trust exists in one direction only.

Password

A word or set of letters and numbers allowing access to a facility, computer, or network. A password may be accompanied by some other unique identifier before the user is allowed to log in.

Private key

The second part of the key pair. The private key is held by only one person or computer.

Public key

One of the key pair used for PKI. The public key for each certificate is made available to all users and computers who request the key from the correct source.

Public Key Infrastructure (PKI)

1. A system that is used to provide distributed security to the network. PKI services include Internet Security, logon authentication security, private and public key encryption, and Certificate Services.

2. A method of distributed security that uses certificates and public and private keys to authenticate users and computers, and to secure communication between computers.

3. An encryption scheme that uses a shared key for encryption and decryption of files.

Remote Authentication Dial-In User Service (RADIUS)

Client/server-based authentication and authorization service for remote access. Connection criteria are passed from the remote access server to the RADIUS server, which will inform the remote access server whether access is allowed or declined.

Secure Sockets Layer (SSL)

An authentication and encryption standard that uses PKI to authenticate users when connecting to a secure Web site and encrypts all data that flows between the Web server and client.

Security group

At the time of their creation, the three kinds of groups–Local, Global, and Universal–can be classified within Active Directory as a security group or a distribution group. The security classification allows rights and permissions to be assigned to the group. Distribution groups, on the other hand, are nonsecure groups that are primarily used for e-mail distribution lists or other means of non-secure communication.

Session key

Encrypts and decrypts the contents of a message. In most PKI implementations, the public key is used to encrypt the session key. Also called a symmetric or bulk encryption key.

Smart card

A device used to authenticate users on a network. Within PKI, the smart card contains the user's certificates and private keys.

Snap-in

A management tool designed to run in the Microsoft Management Console (MMC) environment.

Ticket Granting Service (TGS)

A Kerberos v5 service provided by the Key Distribution Center (KDC) that allows users to authenticate to services within the domain.

Ticket-Granting Ticket (TGT)

Ticket granted by a Key Distribution Center (KDC) in Kerberos that is used to request session tickets.

Transitive trust

Trust relationships that are propagated to all domains in a Windows 2000 network. Transitive trust rules state, "If A trusts B, and A trusts C, then B trusts C."

Transport Layer Security (TLS)

A security protocol to allow two systems to safely communicate over a public network.

Tree

A collection of one or more domains that share a common namespace.

Two-Way Trust

A trust relationship where a trust exists in both directions between two domains.

Universal group

An Active Directory group available only in native mode that can contain domain users from anywhere within a tree or forest.

Virtual Private Network (VPN)

Remote access configuration where users and remote networks connect to network servers across the Internet. A tunnel is created through the Internet and all of the data that crosses the Internet is encrypted. Windows 2000 supports two protocols for setting up VPNs: Point-to-Point Tunneling Protocol (PPTP) or Layer 2 Tunneling Protocol/IPSec (L2TP/IPSec).

Wide Area Network (WAN)

Expands the basic LAN model by linking Local Area Networks (LANs) and allowing them to communicate with each other. By traditional definition, a LAN becomes a WAN when it crosses a public right-of-way, requiring a public carrier for data transmission. More current usage of the term usually includes any situation where a network expands beyond one location/building. A WAN is characterized by low- to high-speed communication links and usually covers a wide geographic area.

The remote links may be operational LANs or only groups of workstations. With the exception of a WAN's wider area of operation, the benefits and features of LANs and WANs are the same.

Windows NT 4.0 domain controller

Windows NT 4.0 server configured as either a primary domain controller (PDC) or backup domain controller (BDC).

REVIEW QUESTIONS

1. Which of the following are used in Windows 2000 security?

   a. File Encryption

   b. Authentication

   c. Auditing

   d. Nonrepudiation

   e. Security Groups

   f. All of the above

2. When logging into Windows 2000 which authentication interface is used most often?

   a. Kerberos v5

   b. Smart cards

   c. Secure socket layer (SSL)/transport layer security (TSL)

   d. GUI Logon

   e. NT LAN Manager (NTLM)

3. Which Kerberos v5 component does the client pass a Ticket-Granting Ticket (TGT) to when attempting to obtain access to a particular network service?

   a. Ticket Granting Service (TGS)

   b. Authentication Server (AS)

   c. Kerberos Key Distribution Center (KDC)

   d. One-Way Function

   e. Access Control List (ACL)

4. What type of trust is automatically generated between domains in a forest?

    a. One-way, transitive

    b. Two-way, transitive

    c. One-way, non-transitive

    d. Two-way, non-transitive

5. What type of trust is created between a Windows 2000 domain and a Windows NT based domain or a Windows 2000 domain in another forest?

    a. Automatic, one-way, non-transitive

    b. Automatic, one-way, transitive

    c. Automatic, two-way, transitive

    d. Explicit, one-way, non-transitive

    e. Explicit, one-way, transitive

    f. Explicit, two-way, non-transitive

6. How is an Access Control List used?

    a. Grant access to files

    b. Grant access to folders

    c. Grant access to printers

    d. Deny access to files

    e. All of the above

7. If a user is given full control permissions to a folder, what will that user also have full control permissions to access?

    a. Printers in that folder

    b. Files in that folder

    c. Sub-folders in that folder

    d. Files and Sub-folders in that folder

    e. None of the above

8. What type of group is unavailable for managing user rights and permissions in a mixed mode Windows 2000 domain?

    a. Universal groups

    b. Global groups

    c. Domain Local groups

    d. Local Computer groups

    e. Online Users groups

    f. All of the above

9. You attempt to give 3 users from a trusted domain access to a share in your domain. In which type of group in the trusted domain must the users be placed?

   a. Global group

   b. Domain Local group

   c. Local Computer group

   d. Domain Local or Global group

   e. All of the above

10. Which group includes only users logged in at the console of a particular computer?

    a. Users

    b. Everyone

    c. Interactive

    d. Network

    e. System

11. What type of group's membership is managed automatically by the system rather than through Active Directory Users and Computers?

    a. Universal groups

    b. Global groups

    c. Domain Local groups

    d. Local Computer groups

    e. Online Users groups

    f. All of the above

12. What is the best way to solve user security issues?

    a. Require long passwords

    b. Educate users about security issues

    c. Require complex passwords

    d. Set screen saver passwords on

    e. Use encrypted communication through a VPN for remote users

13. When sending an encrypted e-mail message to a friend, which key will be used to encrypt the message?

    a. Your Public Key

    b. Your Private Key

    c. Your friend's Public Key

    d. Your friend's Private Key

14. Your boss wants a method to send information across the internet in a manner that guarantees that the information has not been modified in transit. Which PKI based system would you describe to him?

  a. Public Key Infrastructure

  b. Public Key Encryption

  c. Digital Signatures 21

  d. Certificates

  e. Certificate Authorities

15. What type of security is best for protecting information on a stolen laptop computer?

  a. Authentication

  b. Access Control Lists

  c. IPSEC

  e. Encrypting File System (EFS)

  f. Digital Signatures

16. Which file system is required for EFS?

  a. FAT

  b. FAT32

  c. NTFS 23

  d. B and C

  e. All of the above

17. Which PKI component hands out digital certificates?

  a. Ticket Granting Service (TGS)

  b. Certificate Authority

  c. Authentication Server (AS)

  d. Domain Controller

  e. Key Distribution Center (KDC)

18. Which of the following are benefits of IPSEC in Windows 2000?

  a. Secures data transmitted across the network

  b. Applications need not be aware IPSEC is being used

  c. Security levels are negotiated

  d. A and C

  e. A and B

  f. All of the above

19. Which security component allows you to track access to resources?

    a. Security Groups

    b. Authentication

    c. Auditing

    d. File Encryption

    e. Credential Management

20. What is the main authentication protocol used in Windows 2000?

    a. NTLM

    b. Certificate-based Authentication

    c. Smart Cards

    d. Kerberos v5

    e. Clear text passwords

21. Which type of security group has its membership stored in the Global Catalog?

    a. Domain Local groups

    b. Universal groups

    c. Local Computer groups

    d. Global groups

    e. All of the above

22. Which Domain Local groups can create new shared printers?

    a. Account Operators

    b. Administrators

    c. Print Operators

    d. Domain Admins

    e. A and C

    f. B and C

    g. B, C and D

23. Which level of IPSec security encrypts transmitted data between two Windows 2000 computers?

    a. Respond

    b. Request Security

    c. Encapsulating Security Payload (ESP)

    d. Authentication Header (AH)

24. Which Windows 2000 security feature allows you to encrypt data transferred on the network for any IP based application?

   a. Kerberos v5

   b. NTLM

   c. EFS

   d. IPSec AH

   e. IPSec ESP

25. Define mutual authentication.

   a. When a client provides identifying information to a server

   b. When a server provides identifying information to a client

   c. When a client and server provide identifying information to each other

26. Why is an encrypted time stamp included in Kerberos requests for access to a network resource?

   a. To protect against a replay attack

   b. To be sure the time is accurately recording in the log file

   c. To synchronize clocks between the client and the server

   d. To decrypt the session key

CASE PROJECTS

Case 1

Southdale Property Management manages apartment buildings for owners. The owners are individuals, groups, and investment companies using the apartment buildings as an investment.

The existing LAN is contained within a single building. There are 50 client workstations and 4 servers. One of the servers is a file and print server. Two servers are used for industry specific accounting applications. The final server is used for hosting a web site and e-mail system. The existing servers are being upgraded from a single domain Windows NT environment to Windows 2000 and the company has decided that, as part of the upgrade, overall security should be evaluated.

For your own reference, make some notes about which Windows 2000 security mechanisms might be used by Southdale Property Management.

Case 2

Prairie Refrigeration is a manufacturing facility with a single location that has recently been purchased by a larger parent company. Sales of refrigeration units are to large accounts such as soft drink manufacturers and grocery chains across the United States.

The existing LAN is a Novell NetWare with 35 client workstations. Some workstations are used to download CAD drawings into metal stamping machines. These workstations must available during manufacturing hours. There are also two traveling sales people that fax in their orders from client sites or hotel rooms.

This network is being redesigned to integrate into the Windows 2000 network of the new parent company.

For your own reference, make some notes about which Windows 2000 security mechanisms might be used by Prairie Refrigeration.

Case 3

Fleetwood Credit Union is a financial services firm that serves the needs of its members in the city of Fleetwood. Its services include mutual fund sales, savings accounts, and loans. There are eight branches of Fleetwood Credit Union, including the head office where the IT staff members are located.

There is a WAN in place to connect all eight branches of Fleetwood Credit Union. Each branch has 20 to 30 workstations and a single server. The main banking application is housed on a server at head office. All workstations connect to this application when doing financial transactions. Some executives require access to the file servers from home or when traveling.

This network is a mix of Windows NT and Windows 2000 servers and management has hired you to do the yearly security analysis.

For your own reference, make some notes about which Windows 2000 security mechanisms might be used by Fleetwood Credit Union.

Key Terms

Chapter 2

Firewall

Used as a security measure between a company's local area network (LAN) and the Internet. The firewall prevents users from accessing certain address Web sites. A firewall also helps to prevent hackers from accessing internal resources on the network. A combination of hardware and software that separates a LAN into two or more parts for security purposes. Today, firewalls are commonly used to prevent unauthorized access to a network from the Internet.

IP Security (IPSec)

A part of TCP/IP standards in which all IP traffic between two computers is encrypted so that the packets cannot be captured on the network and read by unauthorized users.

Kerberos

Default authentication protocol for Windows 2000 clients and services.

Organizational Unit (OU)

Windows 2000 Active Directory container object.

Smart card

A device used to authenticate users on a network. Within PKI, the smart card contains the user's certificates and private keys.

Total Cost of Ownership (TCO)

The figure used to determine how much a product would cost in its entirety. Not just the purchasing of the product but the training, staff, support, maintenance etc. Everything having to do with the purchase of that product.

REVIEW QUESTIONS

1. Which would be the most appropriate domain organization for a regional company?

    a. Single domain

    b. Domain tree

    c. Forest of domain trees

    d. Any of the above

2. Which would be the most appropriate domain organization for an international company?

    a. Single domain

    b. Domain tree

    c. Forest of domain trees

    d. Any of the above

3. Which would be the most appropriate method to implement a branch office of a national company?

    a. Create an OU inside of an existing domain

    b. Create a new domain that is not part of an existing domain tree

    c. Create a new domain inside an existing domain tree

    d. Create a new domain tree inside an existing forest of domain trees

    e. A or B

    f. A or C

4. Which type of organization is most likely to be implemented as a tree within a forest of domain trees?

   a. A regional company

   b. A national company

   c. An international company

   d. A subsidiary of a larger company

   e. A branch office of a national company

5. What acts as a security boundary inside a forest of domain trees?

   a. User object

   b. Organizational unit

   c. Domain

   d. Domain tree

   e. All of the above

6. List four company processes that should be analyzed to understand how security should be applied to an organization.

7. What type of company organizational model is used when the company has independent units responsible for each product?

   a. Product division model

   b. Functional division model

   c. Matrix model

8. What type of company organizational model is used by companies needing to increase the efficiency of decision making by cutting out layers?

   a. Product division model

   b. Functional division model

   c. Matrix model

9. Which of the following describe a functional division model of company organization?

   a. Staff report to multiple managers

   b. The sales division manages sales for all of the firm's products

   c. There is a separate sales organization for each product

   d. Human resources is responsible for hiring staff for all parts of the organization

   e. A and B

   f. B and C

   g. B and D

10. Which of the following are the best ways to allow a business partner secure access to your network?

    a. A secure web site

    b. Create an account for them

    c. Create a trust between your two networks and assign users rights to your resources

    d. A and B

    e. B and C

    f. A, B, and C

11. Which are the best ways to allow customers to buy products from you electronically?

    a. A secure web site

    b. Create an account for them

    c. Create a trust between your two networks and assign users rights to your resources

    d. A and B

    e. B and C

    f. A, B, and C

12. If you know that your company is about to acquire another company you should take this into account when designing domain structure. True or False?

13. When designing network security you should be aware of company strategies to ensure that security policies do not interfere with achieving company goals. True or False?

14. The highest priority goal of all companies is to make a profit. True or False?

15. Which of the following can affect network security?

    a. Company growth

    b. Tolerance for risk

    c. Company priorities

    d. Laws and Regulations

    e. A and C

    f. B and D

    g. A, B, C and D

16. List at least five things that are included in total cost of ownership that needs to be calculated when implementing change.

17. When evaluating the technical environment for your Windows 2000 security system, what needs to be taken into account? Select all that apply.

    a. The hardware that new systems will be running on

    b. Expected company growth

    c. Legacy software support

    d. Company priorities

18. Which of the following best describes the scalability of Windows 2000 security?

    a. Security management is much easier for larger organizations

    b. Security management is much easier for smaller organizations

    c. Security planning for a larger network requires more planning than a smaller network but day to day management is not outrageous

    d. Security planning for a large network is actually easier because of decentralization

19. What is the primary responsibility of a user in the Windows 2000 security framework?

    a. Understanding and implementing file system security

    b. Protecting their files with NTFS permissions

    c. Configuring personal firewalls on their workstations

    d. Understanding local laws and regulations

    e. Remembering their password

20. Which are the benefits of a proper security and network design? Select all that apply.

    a. The network will not be difficult to manage

    b. There will be clearly defined boundaries of responsibility

    c. Administrators will be able to manage all of the resources for which they are responsible

    d. The security system will seem very confusing to administrators from different areas of the company

21. In general, administrators should be responsible for users and resources in close physical proximity. True or False?

CASE PROJECTS

Case 1

Southdale Property Management has only a single location and has no plans to expand to other locations. There are two distinct departments within Southdale Property

Management. One department is responsible for day to day management of the apartment buildings the other is responsible for major repairs such as heating systems and renovations. The two departments are managed independently and the heads of each department report to the owner of the company.

There are 50 client workstations and 4 servers. The client workstations range from Pentium 133 processors to Pentium II 450 processors and all have 64MB of RAM. One of the servers is a file and print server. Two servers are used for industry specific accounting applications. The final server is used for hosting a web site and e-mail system. All four servers have Pentium III 800 and 512MB of RAM.

Which company model does Southdale Property Management use?

Which organizational structure does Southdale Property Management use?

What ramifications will this have for network security and how the domain structure is used?

Write a complete environmental analysis of Southdale Property Management that you can use for future reference.

Case 2

Prairie Refrigeration has only a single location but needs to integrate its network with the Windows 2000 network of its parent company. The company produces many models of freezers but there is a single production department.

The existing LAN is a Novell NetWare with 35 client workstations. Some Pentium 166 workstations running DOS are used to download CAD drawings into metal stamping machines. These workstations must be available during manufacturing hours.

There are two traveling sales people that fax in their orders from client sites or hotel rooms. The parent company would like to see an electronic system implemented for sending in client orders.

Which company model does Prairie Refrigeration use?

Which organizational structure does Prairie Refrigeration use?

What ramifications will this have for network security and how the domain structure is used?

Write a complete environmental analysis of Prairie Refrigeration that you can use for future reference.

Case 3

Fleetwood Credit Union has eight physical locations. All of the locations are within the city of Fleetwood. There are various executives that are experts in different financial products. The customer service reps must sell all of the financial products and are evaluated by each of these experts.

There is a WAN in place to connect all eight branches of Fleetwood Credit Union. Each branch has 20 to 30 workstations and a single server. The main banking application is housed on a server at the head office. All workstations connect to this application when doing financial transactions. Some executives require access to the file servers from home or when traveling. All of the workstations and servers meet the minimum specifications for Windows 2000.

A new application allowing members to access their financial information and pay bills from home is to be implemented over the next few months.

Which company model does Fleetwood Credit Union use?

Which organizational structure does Fleetwood Credit Union use?

What ramifications will this have for network security and how the domain structure is used?

Write a complete environmental analysis of Fleetwood Credit Union that you can use for future reference.

KEY TERMS

Chapter 3

Access Control List (ACL)

1. A list of trustees who have been granted rights to an object or rights to the properties of an object. Each object in the NDS contains an Access Control List.

2. Under Windows NT/2000, the Access Control List contains user and group Access Control Entries.

ActiveX

A set of controls used to provide interoperability with other types of COM components. ActiveX controls provide a number of enhancements specifically designed for distribution of components over slow networks and to provide integration with Web browsers.

Bandwidth

1. The range of frequencies that can be transmitted through a particular circuit.

2. The speed at which data travels over a particular media. Bandwidth is measured in bits per second.

Domain

1. In NetWare, DOMAIN is used as a console command that will create a protected operating system domain for running untested NLMs in Ring 3. This prevents a module from interfering with the core operating system.

2. In the Internet, a domain is a part of the naming hierarchy. The domain name is a sequence of names (separated by periods) that identify host sites. For example: galenp@mail.msen.com.

Global Catalog (GC)

A database containing scaled-down attributes of every Active Directory object from every domain in a tree or forest. The GC replies to queries so that users in one domain can locate resources in another domain.

Hyper–Text Markup Language (HTML)

The language used to program web pages.

Internet

An international computer network of networks that connect government, academic, and business institutions. Networks on the Internet include MILNET, NSFnet, and other backbone networks, as well as mid-level networks and stub (local) networks.

Internet networks communicate using TCP/IP (Transmission Control Protocol/Internet Protocol). The Internet connects colleges, universities, military organizations and contractors, corporations, government research laboratories, and individuals.

Although parts of the Internet operate under single administrative domains, the Internet as a whole reaches around the globe, connects computers (from personal computers to supercomputers), and is not administered by any single authority. The Internet in July 1995 roughly connected 60,000 independent networks into a vast global Internet.

Used as a descriptive term, an internet is a collection of interconnected packet-switching networks. Any time you connect two or more networks together, you have an internet—as in *inter*national or *inter*state.

Internet Information Server (IIS)

Microsoft Internet Information Server is a network file and application server that transmits information in Hypertext Markup Language.

Internet Service Provider (ISP)

Companies that provide an Internet connection for educational institutions, individuals, companies, and organizations.

IP Security (IPSec)

A part of TCP/IP standards in which all IP traffic between two computers is encrypted so that the packets cannot be captured on the network and read by unauthorized users.

Kerberos

Default authentication protocol for Windows 2000 clients and services.

Legacy Application

An application that is considered out of date or older than the current or present set of applications released. Usually an application that was programmed for an older operating system that isn't in current circulation such as DOS based or Windows 3.x based applications.

Multilink

A system to handle simultaneous communications between computers over multiple independent links, increasing the effective communications bandwidth, and therefore speed.

Organizational Unit (OU)

Windows 2000 Active Directory container object.

Replication

The process of copying Active Directory object state to all domain controllers.

Security group

At the time of their creation, the three kinds of groups–Local, Global, and Universal–can be classified within Active Directory as a security group or a distribution group. The security classification allows rights and permissions to be assigned to the group. Distribution groups, on the other hand, are nonsecure groups that are primarily used for e-mail distribution lists or other means of nonsecure communication.

T1

A leased-line connection capable of carrying data at 1,544,000 bits per second. At maximum theoretical capacity, a T1 line could move a megabyte in less than 10 seconds. That is still not fast enough for full-screen, full-motion video, for which you need at least 10,000,000 bits per second. T1 is the fastest speed commonly used to connect networks to the Internet.

Terminal server

A special-purpose computer that has places to plug in many modems on one side and a connection to a LAN or host machine on the other side. Thus, the terminal server does the work of answering the calls and passes the connections on to the appropriate node. Most terminal servers can provide PPP or SLIP services if connected to the Internet.

Virtual Private Network (VPN)

Remote access configuration where users and remote networks connect to network servers across the Internet. A tunnel is created through the Internet and all of the data that crosses the Internet is encrypted. Windows 2000 supports two protocols for setting up VPNs: Point-to-Point Tunneling Protocol (PPTP) or Layer 2 Tunneling Protocol/IPSec (L2TP/IPSec).

XML

An extensible markup language used to define other markup languages. The markup languages defined with XML will allow for the transmission of formatted data across networks.

REVIEW QUESTIONS

1. You have decided to combine analysis methods when doing an analysis of business and security requirements. What is your likely first step?

   a. Individual survey

   b. Departmental survey

    c. Resource monitoring

    d. It does not matter which is done first

2. What are drawbacks to using an individual survey when conducting an analysis of business and security requirements?

    a. Users do not understand how they use resources

    b. Only department managers are surveyed

    c. Logs are required over an extended period of time

    d. The current operating system must be capable of generating the required information

    e. All of the above

3. If different departments within a company fund their own IT projects, which administrative model would they be likely to use?

    a. Centralized

    b. Decentralized

4. Which administrative model allows IT to be most responsive to the needs of different departments or geographic locations?

    a. Centralized

    b. Decentralized

5. Which administrative model would be best for enforcing security standards throughout an entire organization?

    a. Centralized

    b. Decentralized

6. Outsourcing different parts of the IT organization will always increase security on your network because the outsourcer has a higher skill level than internal staff. True or false?

7. What is the name of the process to control and track modifications to your network?

    a. Decision-making

    b. Outsourcing

    c. Change-management

    d. Resource monitoring

8. What is the name of the process by which changes to your system are approved?

    a. Decision-making

    b. Outsourcing

    c. Change-management

    d. Resource monitoring

9. Decisions regarding what should be implemented on a network are based upon which of the following?

   a. The recommendations of the administrators

   b. Needs of the users

   c. Political decisions of upper management

   d. Recommendations of departmental managers

   e. All of the above

10. Which of the following are granted appropriate rights to access and manage resources? Select all that apply.

   a. Administrators

   b. Users

   c. Resource owners

   d. Services

   e. Applications

11. Which of the following are normally mostly concerned with accessing rather than managing resources? Select all that apply.

   a. Administrators

   b. Users

   c. Resource owners

   d. Services

   e. Applications

12. Which of the following access resources on behalf of users? Select all that apply.

   a. Administrators

   b. Resource owners

   c. Services

   d. Applications

13. Managing access to and configuration of resources is the responsibility of which network role?

   a. Administrators

   b. Users

   c. Resource owners

   d. A and B

   e. A and C

   f. All of the above

14. Windows 2000 allows you to decentralize administration within a domain by assigning administrative rights to an organizational unit. True or False?

15. List five things that should be included in the inventory of network resources that is created for planning security.

16. Why is an inventory of network resources taken before implementing a network plan?

    a. To help identify implementation timelines

    b. It is essential to understand the existing situation in order to understand how to implement a new system

    c. So support staff know physically where to find resources

    d. The accounting department will require it

17. Which should be rolled out first: a new security plan or new software?

    a. Security plan

    b. Software

    c. Depends on compatibility and technical issues

18. List four possible technical support resources that will need to be updated as the new security plan is implemented.

19. Which feature makes Windows 2000 administration more flexible to manage in a single domain network than Windows NT?

    a. Delegation of administrative authority

    b. Auditing

    c. Kerberos v5

    d. Automatic trusts between domains in a forest

20. Physical distribution of users and resources refers to the actual location of the users and resources. What does logical distribution of users and resources refer to?

21. Which of the following types of connectivity is the most secure?

    a. Leased lines

    b. Direct dial-up

    c. VPN connectivity over the Internet

22. You do not want the hassle of maintaining you own dial-up modem pool. What type of connectivity would you choose to allow users remote access?

    a. Leased lines

    b. Direct dial-up

    c. VPN connectivity over the Internet

    d. A or C

    e. A, B or C

23. If you require connectivity between to sites to be a minimum of 256Kbps, which connectivity option should you choose?

    a. Leased lines

    b. Direct dial-up

    c. VPN connectivity over the Internet

    d. A or C

    e. A, B or C

24. Which type of application will use the greatest amount of network bandwidth?

    a. Client-based applications

    b. Network-based applications

    c. Web-based applications

    d. Thin-client applications

    e. Legacy applications

25. Which type of application will require the most maintenance on user workstations?

    a. Client-based applications

    b. Network-based applications

    c. Web-based applications

    d. Thin-client applications

    e. Legacy applications

26. Which type of application will allow you to run full-featured Windows-based applications on low-powered clients?

    a. Client-based applications

    b. Network-based applications

    c. Web-based applications

    d. Thin-client applications

    e. Legacy applications

27. Which type of application is most likely to require proprietary solutions to control security?

    a. Client-based applications

    b. Network-based applications

    c. Web-based applications

    d. Thin-client applications

    e. Legacy applications

28. A new security system should be designed to meet the needs of organizations rather than requiring the new security system to mimic what has been done in the past. True or False?

29. Which is the most frequently encountered risk type to network security?

    a. Internal

    b. External

30. A new security system will likely make it more difficult for users to perform their jobs. True or False?

CASE PROJECTS

Case 1

A single administrator is responsible for managing the network and workstations for Southdale Property Management. You are reporting to the administrator but major funding decisions need to be approved by the owner of the company. Users are divided into various groups to help with the administration of the network.

The owner of the company thinks that current staffing levels are adequate for technical support but the administrator believes that he is overworked and would like ideas about how to reduce his workload. Compose an e-mail to the administrator indicating what tasks can be delegated to knowledgeable users and how to do it.

Case 2

There is no full-time administrator at Prairie Refrigeration. An outside consultant does all network management and most workstation management. Some of the workstation management is done by knowledgeable users when the consultant is not available or cannot be there quickly enough. The IT staff of the parent company would like more control over this situation. Your contact in the company is the financial manager.

The new owners would like you to analyze the existing support structure for Prairie Refrigeration and make recommendations about how to make it better if you feel it is necessary. Put your analysis in a report format that show the pros and cons of each option that you considered and the reasoning for your final decision.

In addition, write a small supplemental report with your recommendation for connectivity requirements between the parent company and Prairie Refrigeration.

Case 3

There are three full-time technical support staff members at Fleetwood Credit Union. One person is responsible for overall network management. Two technical support staff members handle calls from users and provide support to the branch locations.

The branch locations are connected to the head office with 128 Kbps ISDN lines. The executives are dialing into small modem pools for connectivity from outside the office. Internet connectivity will be required to allow members to access the new Internet banking system.

The central banking application is a client server application with client components running on Windows workstations and the server component running on a Windows 2000 server. Your users are indicating that the application is very slow compared to the older telnet client that was used several years ago. The developer of the application has indicated that they are willing to work with you to speed up the application in WAN environments.

Management is concerned that the existing support structure is not optimized because they are getting many complaints about slow problem resolution times. The technical support staff members have indicated that they cannot resolve problems any faster because they spend so much time driving between sites. Write a report indicating how you think problem resolution times can be reduced.

Also, write a short report analyzing the options speeding up the central banking application, including your recommendation.

KEY TERMS

Chapter 4

Access Control List (ACL)

1. A list of trustees who have been granted rights to an object or rights to the properties of an object. Each object in the NDS contains an Access Control List.

2. Under Windows NT/2000, the Access Control List contains user and group Access Control Entries.

ActiveX

A set of controls used to provide interoperability with other types of COM components. ActiveX controls provide a number of enhancements specifically designed for distribution of components over slow networks and to provide integration with Web browsers.

Backup Domain Controller (BDC)

Windows NT domain controller that serves as a backup/failover to the Primary Domain Controller (PDC).

Browser

1. This client program (software) is used to look at various Internet resources and retrieve information.

2. Windows service that collects and organizes shared network resources in a hierarchical manner.

3. A NetWare console command that transmits a message to all network nodes or list of nodes.

Denial of Service Attack

An attack used to repeatedly attack a server over and over again and brings the server down by overloading it with requests for data.

Domain

1. In NetWare, DOMAIN is used as a console command that will create a protected operating system domain for running untested NLMs in Ring 3. This prevents a module from interfering with the core operating system.

2. In the Internet, a domain is a part of the naming hierarchy. The domain name is a sequence of names (separated by periods) that identify host sites. For example: galenp@mail.msen.com.

Domain Controller

Server within a domain and storage point for domainwide security information. This also refers to a partition of the Active Directory the Windows NT Server holds.

Domain controller (Windows 2000)

A Windows 2000 Server that has been promoted into the domain controller role. Each domain controller has a copy of the Active Directory domain database and SYSVOL folder.

Encrypting File System (EFS)

Windows 2000 data encryption service based on a user's public and private keys. Data encryption is only supported on NTFS volumes.

File server

A computer that stores files and provides access to them from workstations. File servers generally contain large hard disks and high amounts of memory. If a computer is used exclusively as a file server, it is a dedicated file server. If a computer is used as a workstation and a file server simultaneously, it is a non-dedicated file server. The NOS (Network Operating System) runs on the file server and controls access to files, printers, and other network resources.

File Transfer Protocol (FTP)

A part of the TCP/IP suite that is used to transfer files between any two computers, provided they support FTP. The two computers do not have to be running the same operating system.

In general, people use FTP to move files from one account or machine to another or to perform what is called an "anonymous FTP." For example, if storage space on a particular machine is low, the user can free up storage space by using FTP to move the files to a machine with more space. Another reason to move a file to a different account is to print a file to a particular printer. If the file is on a machine that cannot access the desired printer, it must be moved to a machine that does have access.

Whatever the reason for the transfer, FTP requires the user to know the proper login name and the password for both computers to move files between them.

While an anonymous FTP also moves from one computer to another, it has two main differences. An anonymous FTP session usually involves gathering files that a user does not have. Anonymous FTP does not require the user to know a login name and password to access the remote computer.

The Internet has many anonymous FTP sites. Each site consists of an FTP server, a large number of files, and guest login names such as "anonymous" or "FTP." This allows any user to visit these systems and copy files from the FTP site to their personal computer. With the appropriate authority, users can copy files from their system to an anonymous FTP site.

Despite the variety of FTP servers and clients on the Internet and the different operating systems they use, FTP servers and clients generally support the same basic commands. This standard command set allows users to accomplish tasks such as looking at a list of files in the current directory of the remote system, regardless of the operating system in use. Other common commands allow users to change directories, get specific file information, copy files to a local machine, and change parameters.

Graphical Web browsers transform the traditional character-based, command-line FTP interface into a point-and-click environment. The only way a user may know that they are in the middle of an FTP session is that the Universal Resources Locator (URL) box in the browser will change from an address that begins with "http://..." to "ftp://...".

Firewall

Used as a security measure between a company's local area network (LAN) and the Internet. The firewall prevents users from accessing certain address Web sites. A firewall also helps to prevent hackers from accessing internal resources on the network. A combination of hardware and software that separates a LAN into two or more parts for security purposes. Today, firewalls are commonly used to prevent unauthorized access to a network from the Internet.

Flexible Single Master Operations (FSMO)

A server in charge of background tasks that are comprised of 5 different roles: Schema master, Domain naming master, RID master, PDC master, Infrastructure master.

Internet

An international computer network of networks that connect government, academic, and business institutions. Networks on the Internet include MILNET, NSFnet, and other backbone networks, as well as mid-level networks and stub (local) networks.

Internet networks communicate using TCP/IP (Transmission Control Protocol/Internet Protocol). The Internet connects colleges, universities, military organizations and contractors, corporations, government research laboratories, and individuals.

Although parts of the Internet operate under single administrative domains, the Internet as a whole reaches around the globe, connects computers (from personal computers to supercomputers), and is not administered by any single authority. The Internet in July 1995 roughly connected 60,000 independent networks into a vast global Internet.

Used as a descriptive term, an internet is a collection of interconnected packet-switching networks. Any time you connect two or more networks together, you have an internet—as in *inter*national or *inter*state.

Java

A computer programming language that is platform independent.

Kerberos

Default authentication protocol for Windows 2000 clients and services.

Network Address Translation (NAT)

1. A component that is included with Windows 2000 Server that allows multiple users to share one connection, such as a modem or DSL connection, to the Internet. NAT is designed for mid-sized networks and offers more configuration flexibility than ICS. NAT operates as a router forwarding all requests to the Internet as well as supporting address translation. This means that the computers inside the network do not have to have Internet-compatible addresses.

2. A service available through RRAS on a Windows 2000 Server that allows the sharing of a single connection to the Internet or a remote network with multiple network clients. NAT is more difficult to configure than ICS but can also operate in more complex environments.

3. Routing protocol available through an Internet Connection Server (ICS) configuration that allows a home network or small office to share a single Internet connection. This protocol requires that your client computers be configured as DHCP clients.

New Technology File System (NTFS)

A fast and reliable file system provided with Windows NT. It is fully recoverable and allows the implementation of local security.

Operations Master

Active Directory operations that are not permitted to occur at different places in the network at the same time (i.e., single-master).

Packet Filtering

Controlling access to a network by analyzing the incoming and outgoing packets and letting them pass or halting them based on the IP addresses of the source and destination.

Patches

Software updates to repair or add functionality to existing applications or operating systems without replacing the entire system.

Primary Domain Controller (PDC)

The first domain controller created in a Windows NT domain.

Proxy server

A server that is positioned between an internal network and the Internet. The proxy server can be configured to limit which users have access to the Internet, which sites users are allowed to connect to, what protocols users are allowed to use, and to cache Internet requests. Some proxy servers also provide some firewall capability.

Registry

Windows NT and Windows 95 configuration database.

Remote Access Service (RAS)

In most networks, clients are connected directly to the network. In some cases, however, remote connections are needed for your users. Microsoft provides RAS to let you set up and configure client

Remote Installation Services (RIS)

Windows 2000 services that support remote installation. RIS is based on PXE extensions to DHCP.

Schema

A structured framework or plan used by Active Directory to define the objects and properties allowed in the Domain forest.

Security group

At the time of their creation, the three kinds of groups–Local, Global, and Universal–can be classified within Active Directory as a security group or a distribution group. The security classification allows rights and permissions to be assigned to the group. Distribution groups, on the other hand, are nonsecure groups that are primarily used for e-mail distribution lists or other means of non-secure communication.

Trusts or Trust Relationship

A link between domains in which a trusting domain honors the users of a trusted domain. In two way trusts, each domain trusts each other therefore the users of each domain have access to resources in the other domain.

Virtual Private Network (VPN)

Remote access configuration where users and remote networks connect to network servers across the Internet. A tunnel is created through the Internet and all of the data that crosses the Internet is encrypted. Windows 2000 supports two protocols for setting up VPNs: Point-to-Point Tunneling Protocol (PPTP) or Layer 2 Tunneling Protocol/IPSec (L2TP/IPSec).

Virus

A program that can destroy data and change itself to escape detection. A virus can move into other computer systems by incorporating itself into programs or files that are shared among computer systems.

REVIEW QUESTIONS

1. Which type of computer system should be kept physically secure in a locked room?

   a. Server

   b. Desktop computer

   c. Portable computer

   d. Kiosk

   e. B and C

2. Which type of computer system requires administrators to be highly trained to avoid downtime affecting large numbers of employees?

   a. Server

   b. Desktop computer

   c. Portable computer

   d. Kiosk

   e. B and C

3. In a high security network, which type of computer system should you have unnecessary services disabled?

   a. Server

   b. Desktop computer

   c. Portable computer

   d. Kiosk

   e. All of the above

4. What type of server on your network needs to be kept very secure because it stores Active Directory?

   a. Application server

   b. Domain controller

   c. File and print server

   d. RAS server

   e. Kiosk

5. List the five Flexible Single-Master Operations (FSMO) roles that a domain controller can perform.

6. Which type of server is responsible for running the server side components of client-server applications (e.g. SQL server)?

   a. Application server

   b. Domain controller

   c. File and print server

   d. RAS server

   e. Kiosk

7. Which type of server is the most likely to receive an attack from outside your network?

   a. Application server

   b. Domain controller

   c. File and print server

   d. RAS server

   e. Kiosk

8. On which type of server should users be able to access and run applications but not be able to modify them?

   a. Application server

   b. Domain controller

   c. File and print server

   d. RAS server

   e. Kiosk

9. You have decided not to allow users to share information on their workstations to maintain centralized control of security on the network. Where can users place files to share with other users?

   a. Public shared folder on an application server

   b. Public shared folder on a file and print server

   c. The user's home directory on a file and print server

   d. The user's home directory on a RAS server

10. On what type of computer should average users be able to install their own software programs from home?

   a. Server

   b. Desktop computer

   c. Portable computer

   d. Kiosk

   e. None of the above

11. On which type of computer would a locking screen saver be most useful to prevent unauthorized access when a user leaves a computer while logged in?

    a. Server

    b. Desktop computer

    c. Portable computer

    d. Kiosk

    e. B and C

    f. B, C and D

12. Which type of computer is most likely to use physical restraints to prevent theft?

    a. Server

    b. Desktop computer

    c. Portable computer

    d. Kiosk

    e. C and D

13. Which type of computer needs to be heavily automated so that users cannot close the main program running on the system?

    a. Server

    b. Desktop computer

    c. Portable computer

    d. Kiosk

    e. All of the above

14. Which type of computer needs to be treated as untrusted even though you have installed and configured it?

    a. Server

    b. Desktop computer

    c. Portable computer

    d. Kiosk

    e. All of the above

15. What type of external risk will encrypting file system help to protect against?

    a. Hardware theft and modification

    b. Public network attacks

    c. Network taps

    d. Business partners and trusts

    e. Brute-force logon attacks

    f. Spoofing

16. In order to thwart theft attempts, what should be done with backup tapes?

    a. Test a restore once a month

    b. Store a tape off site once per month

    c. Keep tapes in a physically secure location

    d. All of the above

17. What could be done to help secure a system against a network tap? Select all that apply.

    a. Encrypt network traffic with IPSec

    b. Use shielded twisted-pair cabling instead of unshielded

    c. Secure network cabling so that it cannot be physically accessed

    d. Use Kerberos v5 authentication

18. Which type of external risk can be managed by maintaining careful control over ACLs on your internal resources?

    a. Hardware theft and modification

    b. Public network attacks

    c. Network taps

    d. Business partners and trusts

    e. Brute-force logon attacks

    f. Spoofing

19. Having a password policy that is too complex may actually make your network less secure. True or False?

20. What are three password characteristics that can make it harder to perform a brute force logon attack?

21. Restricting the ability of administrative accounts to run applications can minimize which external risk?

    a. Hardware theft and modification

    b. Public network attacks

    c. Network taps

    d. Business partners and trusts

    e. Brute-force logon attacks

    f. Spoofing

22. What is a possible result of hiring unqualified personnel to manage security on the network?

    a. The company saves money in the long run by paying lower salaries

    b. Simple mistakes may allow hackers into the network

   c. Users will never notice a difference

   d. The network will be more at risk for network taps

23. Which internal risks can be minimized by proper training of end users? Select all that apply.

   a. Hardware security issues

   b. Inappropriate assumption of rights

   c. Accidental data deletion or corruption

   d. User practices

24. The failure to apply patches to known security holes provides an easy way for hackers to access your network. True or false?

25. List two user practices that can negatively affect network security.

26. What type of firewall protection allows users to access the Internet while using IP addresses defined for internal use only?

   a. Packet filtering

   b. Proxy server

   c. Network address translation

   d. Stateful inspection

   e. A and D

   f. B and C

27. What type of firewall protection usually incorporates caching to speed up access to the Internet?

   a. Packet filtering

   b. Proxy server

   c. Network address translation

   d. Stateful inspection

   e. A and D

   f. B and C

28. What type of firewall protection ensures that all incoming packets are in response to a request initiated from inside the firewall?

   a. Packet filtering

   b. Proxy server

   c. Network address translation

   d. Stateful inspection

   e. A and D

   f. B and C

29. List three things you can do to make web browsers more secure.

30. Why should e-mail attachments be of particular concern to administrators?

31. Which Internet-based threat does not normally damage data but stops legitimate users from accessing resources?

   a. Denial of service attacks

   b. Unsigned ActiveX controls

   c. Executable e-mail attachment

   d. E-mail scripting viruses

CASE PROJECTS

Case 1

The owner of Southdale Property Management would like a complete justification for any and all recommendations for security improvements to the existing network. Write a paper that details all of the internal and external risks for their network. Be sure to include any special recommendations you may have for servers that are connected to the Internet or perform special functions.

Case 2

The new owners of Prairie Refrigeration would like a complete analysis of internal and external risks to the security of their network. They consider this an essential tool in evaluating your final security plan for the network. The on-staff security auditor of the new owner will review your work to verify its completeness.

Case 3

As part of any good security plan you have decided to do a compete analysis of internal and external risks to the data of Fleetwood Credit Union. Be sure to pay particular attention to the special needs of a financial institution as compared to an average corporation.

Management has also made a special request that you define an Internet access policy for the staff of Fleetwood Credit Union. This should include what type of access each category of user can have. Management considers all of the staff to fall into four categories: tellers, supervisors, content experts and upper management.

KEY TERMS

Chapter 5

Access Control List (ACL)

1. A list of trustees who have been granted rights to an object or rights to the properties of an object. Each object in the NDS contains an Access Control List.

2. Under Windows NT/2000, the Access Control List contains user and group Access Control Entries.

Audit policy

Security policy settings that identify security events that will generate Security log entries. Events can be based on the success and/or failure of an action.

Certificate

The document (usually digital) issued by a Certificate Authority that includes the Certificate Authority's digital signature, the user's public and private key, and user information.

CHAP

A challenge response authentication protocol that uses Message Digest 5 (MD5) to encrypt the response.

Domain Controller

Server within a domain and storage point for domainwide security information. This also refers to a partition of the Active Directory the Windows NT Server holds.

Domain controller (Windows 2000)

A Windows 2000 Server that has been promoted into the domain controller role. Each domain controller has a copy of the Active Directory domain database and SYSVOL folder.

Domain Name System (DNS)

A hierarchical, distributed method of organizing systems and network names on the Internet. DNS administratively groups hosts (systems) into a hierarchy of authority that allows addressing and other information to be widely distributed and maintained. A big advantage of DNS is that using it eliminates dependence on a centrally maintained file that maps host names to addresses.

The diagram shows the hierarchial organization of domain names. The bottom level of the tree structure contains the names of companies or even machines within a company. For example, consider wuarchive.wustl.edu. The bottom of the tree is wuarchive. This is the name of a particular piece of equipment within the wustl domain, which is under the edu domain.

The name of a particular domain is read from the bottom of the tree up to the root. The root is unnamed and is represented with just a period. For example, coursetech.com is a particular domain. If we were to give the fully qualified domain name (FQDN), we would include the unnamed root, so it would be written as "coursetech.com." The final period at the end of the name specifies the root of the tree. The root must always be specified for the host equipment. To make it easy, most software will convert a domain name to an FQDN for the user by appending any missing domain names all the way to the root.

The top of the tree lists the top-level domains. These are reserved names. Every domain will have a top-level domain by type or country.

Dynamic Host Configuration Protocol (DHCP)

A TCP/IP application-layer protocol that provides for dynamic address assignment on a network.

Dynamic-Link Library (DLL)

A module that is linked at load time or run time.

Encrypting File System (EFS)

Windows 2000 data encryption service based on a user's public and private keys. Data encryption is only supported on NTFS volumes.

File Allocation Table (FAT)

A file system used to organize data on a hard drive with 2 GB of data or less.

File Transfer Protocol (FTP)

A part of the TCP/IP suite that is used to transfer files between any two computers, provided they support FTP. The two computers do not have to be running the same operating system.

In general, people use FTP to move files from one account or machine to another or to perform what is called an "anonymous FTP." For example, if storage space on a particular machine is low, the user can free up storage space by using FTP to move the files to a machine with more space. Another reason to move a file to a different account is to print a file to a particular printer. If the file is on a machine that cannot access the desired printer, it must be moved to a machine that does have access.

Whatever the reason for the transfer, FTP requires the user to know the proper login name and the password for both computers to move files between them.

While an anonymous FTP also moves from one computer to another, it has two main differences. An anonymous FTP session usually involves gathering files that a user does not have. Anonymous FTP does not require the user to know a login name and password to access the remote computer.

The Internet has many anonymous FTP sites. Each site consists of an FTP server, a large number of files, and guest login names such as "anonymous" or "FTP." This allows any user to visit these systems and copy files from the FTP site to their personal computer. With the appropriate authority, users can copy files from their system to an anonymous FTP site.

Despite the variety of FTP servers and clients on the Internet and the different operating systems they use, FTP servers and clients generally support the same basic commands. This standard command set allows users to accomplish tasks such as looking at a list of files in the current directory of the remote system, regardless of the operating system in use. Other common commands allow users to change directories, get specific file information, copy files to a local machine, and change parameters.

Graphical Web browsers transform the traditional character-based, command-line FTP interface into a point-and-click environment. The only way a user may know that they are in the middle of an FTP session is that the Universal Resources Locator (URL) box in the browser will change from an address that begins with "http://..." to "ftp://...".

Internet Authentication Service (IAS)

An authentication method used to verify users through remote access. Equivalent to a RADIUS server.

Internet Engineering Task Force (IETF)

One of the task forces of the IAB, the IETF is responsible for solving short-term engineering needs of the Internet. It has more than 40 Working Groups.

Kerberos

Default authentication protocol for Windows 2000 clients and services.

Key Distribution Center (KDC)

Kerberos protocol authentication server and ticket-granting service.

Microsoft Management Console (MMC)

A framework that hosts Microsoft and third-party management tools, called snap-ins, that are used to administer computers, services, networks, users, and other components of the Windows system. The MMC does not provide any management functionality itself, but instead hosts the tools (snap-ins) that do.

The MMC provides the user with a simplified, single interface to the snap-ins. An MMC can be customized and the administrative tasks delegated with limited or full functionality of the included snap-ins.

Mixed mode

A domain mode that includes a PDC upgraded to Windows 2000 and BDCs that have not been upgraded. Mixed mode also refers to the upgraded PDC and upgraded BDCs but without the native mode switch turned on.

MS-CHAP

Microsoft's version of the CHAP protocol. This version is more secure than CHAP.

Native mode

Domain mode that only has Windows 2000 domain controllers and doesn't contain any PDC or BDCs.

New Technology File System (NTFS)

A fast and reliable file system provided with Windows NT. It is fully recoverable and allows the implementation of local security.

Organizational Unit (OU)

Windows 2000 Active Directory container object.

Policy

A set of rules regarding resources that are applied to individuals or groups.

Registry

Windows NT and Windows 95 configuration database.

Registry keys

Folders in the registry database that contain settings and corresponding data values.

Remote Access Service (RAS)

In most networks, clients are connected directly to the network. In some cases, however, remote connections are needed for your users. Microsoft provides RAS to let you set up and configure client

Remote Authentication Dial-In User Service (RADIUS)

Client/server-based authentication and authorization service for remote access. Connection criteria are passed from the remote access server to the RADIUS server, which will inform the remote access server whether access is allowed or declined.

Remote Installation Services (RIS)

Windows 2000 services that support remote installation. RIS is based on PXE extensions to DHCP.

Request for Comments (RFC)

Documents that detail the standards developed by the Internet Engineering Task Force (IETF).

Reversibly encrypted password

A password that is encrypted with a one-way algorithm that cannot be decrypted.

Secure Sockets Layer (SSL)

An authentication and encryption standard that uses PKI to authenticate users when connecting to a secure Web site and encrypts all data that flows between the Web server and client.

Session ticket

Ticket granted in a Kerberos authentication providing access to a network resource.

Simple Network Management Protocol (SNMP)

One of the most comprehensive tools available for TCP/IP network management. It operates through conversations between SNMP agents and management systems. Through these conversations, the SNMP management systems can collect statistics from and modify configuration parameters on agents.

The agents are any components running the SNMP agent service and are capable of being managed remotely. Agents can include minicomputers, mainframes, workstations, servers, bridges, routers, gateways, terminal servers, and wiring hubs.

Management stations are typically more powerful workstations. Common implementations are Windows NT or UNIX stations running a product such as HP OpenView, IBM Systemview/6000, or Cabletron Spectrum. The software provides a graphic representation of the network, allowing you to move through the network hierarchy to the individual device level.

There are three basic commands used in SNMP conversations: GET, SET, and TRAP.

The GET command is used by the management station to retrieve a specific parameter value from an SNMP agent. If a combination of parameters is grouped together on an agent, GET-NEXT retrieves the next item in a group. For example, a management system's graphic representation of a hub includes the state of all status lights. This information is gathered through GET and GET-NEXT.

The management system uses SET to change a selected parameter on an SNMP agent. For example, SET would be used by the management system to disable a failing port on a hub. SNMP agents send TRAP packets to the management system in response to extraordinary events, such as a line failure on a hub.

When the hub status light goes red on the management systems representation, it is in response to a TRAP.

An SNMP management station generates GET and SET commands. Agents are able to respond to SET and GET and to generate TRAP commands.

Smart card

A device used to authenticate users on a network. Within PKI, the smart card contains the user's certificates and private keys.

Snap-in

A management tool designed to run in the Microsoft Management Console (MMC) environment.

Telnet

1. The Telnet protocol is a part of the TCP/IP protocol suite. Many Internet nodes support Telnet, which is similar to UNIX's rlogin program. Telnet lets users log in to any other computer on the Internet, provided that the target computer allows Telnet logins, and the user has a valid login name and password. The computers do not have to be of the same type to Telnet between them.

Some systems expect external access, and a special software package is set up to handle outside calls. This eliminates the need to *log in* once a user reaches the remote host.

The most popular reason to log in to a remote computer is to run software that is available only on the remote computer. Another reason is when a user's computer is incompatible with a particular program, operating system, available memory, or doesn't have the necessary processing power.

People with several Internet accounts can use Telnet to switch from one account to the other without logging out of any of the accounts.

Users can use Telnet as an information-gathering tool by searching databases for information. These databases include LOCIS (the Library of Congress Information System), CARL (Colorado Association of Research Libraries), ERIC (Educational Resources Information Center), and CIJE (Current Index to Journals in Education).

2. An Internet standard user-level protocol that allows a user's remote terminal to log in to computer systems on the Internet. To connect to a computer using Telnet, the user types Telnet and the address of the site or host computer.

Ticket Granting Service (TGS)

A Kerberos v5 service provided by the Key Distribution Center (KDC) that allows users to authenticate to services within the domain.

Ticket-Granting Ticket (TGT)

Ticket granted by a Key Distribution Center (KDC) in Kerberos that is used to request session tickets.

UNIX

A computer operating system originally developed at AT&T's Bell Research Laboratories and later at the University of California Berkeley. It is implemented in a growing number of minicomputer and microcomputer systems.

UNIX is *multi-user* because it is designed to be used by many people at the same time and has TCP/IP built into the operating system. It is the most common operating system for servers on the Internet.

X.509

A set of standards defined by the ITU-T to describe the syntax and structure of secured communications as part of the X.500 protocol.

REVIEW QUESTIONS

1. Which snap-in is required for MMC to view event logs?

   a. Active Directory Users and Computers

   b. Performance logs and alerts

   c. Computer management

   d. Security templates

   e. System information

2. Which log records auditing events?

   a. Application

   b. DNS

   c. File replication service

   d. Security

   e. System

3. What types of object access does auditing record?

   a. Success

   b. Failure

   c. Both

   d. Depends on what the administrator chooses to audit

4. The most effective auditing generally uses third-party tools to help analyze the audit logs. True or false?

5. List four steps required to implement auditing on your network.

6. For domain controllers, which security policy has the highest priority?

   a. Domain

   b. Domain controllers

   c. Local

7. For a member server, which security policy has the highest priority?

   a. Domain

   b. Domain controllers

   c. Local

8. List five of the nine broad categories of events that can be audited.

9. If you wish to audit how often a particular file is opened, what step must be performed after enabling the auditing of object access?

   a. Add the group Everyone to the audit entries for the file, and audit success of List Folder / Read Data

   b. Add the group Domain Users to the audit entries for the file, and audit success of Read Permissions

   c. Add the group Everyone to the audit entries for the file, and audit success and failure of Read Permissions

   d. Add the group Domain Users to the audit entries for the file, and audit failure of List Folder / Read Data

10. Which criteria are relevant to filtering the security log? Select all that apply.

    a. Error

    b. Success

    c. Failure

    d. User

11. When looking at the properties of the security log what setting can be used to prevent a small hard drive from being filled with auditing information and ensure that the most recent auditing information is always recorded?

    a. Overwrite events as needed

    b. Overwrite events older than X days

    c. Move the log file to a different hard drive

    d. A and C

    e. A, B, and C

12. Which advanced NTFS permission would you grant to allow a group to read a file?

    a. Traverse Folder / Execute File

    b. List Folder / Read Data

    c. Read Attributes

    d. Read Extended Attributes

    e. Read Permissions

13. Which advanced NTFS permission would you grant to allow a group to modify the contents of a file?

    a. Create Files / Write Data

    b. Create Folders / Append Data

    c. Write Attributes

    d. Write Extended Attributes

    e. Change Permissions

14. By default, NTFS permissions are inherited from a folder to files and sub-folders inside that folder. Editing the security settings for which object can prevent this behavior?

    a. The folder where the permissions were originally applied

    b. The folder above the object that the unwanted permissions apply to

    c. The object with the unwanted permissions

15. What permissions exist on a share by default?

    a. Deny Full Control to Domain Users

    b. Allow Full Control to Domain Admins

    c. Allow Full Control to Everyone

    d. No permissions are in place by default

16. In order to adequately protect files shared on volumes formatted as FAT32, share permissions are much more elaborate than NTFS permissions. True or false?

17. What is the default EFS recovery agent for a Windows 2000 Professional computer that is a part of a domain?

    a. Administrator of the local machine

    b. Administrator of the domain

    c. Domain Admins

    d. No user is designated

18. When a file is encrypted using EFS, what is encrypted and stored along with the encrypted data?

    a. The private key of the user

    b. The private key of the recovery agent

    c. The public key of the user

    d. The public key of the recovery agent

    e. The symmetrical encryption key of the file

19. List the two pre-requisites before Certificate-based authentication can be used.

20. What type of authentication is used with smart cards?

    a. Kerberos v5

    b. Certificate-based authentication

    c. Digest authentication

    d. NT LAN Manager (NTLM)

    e. RADIUS

21. During authentication using smart cards the user needs only to swipe the smart card through the reader. True or false?

22. What property of a user object must be set in order to use digest authentication?

    a. Password never expires

    b. Smart card is required for interactive logon

    c. Store password using reversible encryption

    d. Allow remote access

23. Which authentication method is similar to digest authentication and CHAP, but is more secure than CHAP?

24. Which type of authentication is required if your network supports older Windows operating systems such as Windows NT or Windows 95?

    a. Kerberos v5

    b. Certificate-based authentication

    c. Digest authentication

    d. NT LAN Manager (NTLM)

    e. RADIUS

25. Which type of authentication allows users to log into an Internet service provider with the same username and password they use on the Windows 2000 based network at the office?

    a. Kerberos v5

    b. Certificate-based authentication

    c. Digest authentication

    d. NT LAN Manager (NTLM)

    e. RADIUS

26. Which type of authentication can be integrated with UNIX-based networks?

    a. Kerberos v5

    b. Certificate-based authentication

    c. Digest authentication

    d. SSL

    e. RADIUS

27. Why would you not want users to log into a Windows 2000 based FTP server using their regular username and password?

28. Which protocol allows users to securely log on to a web server using their domain username and password regardless of the web browser they are using?

    a. Kerberos v5

    b. Certificate-based authentication

    c. Digest authentication

    d. SSL

    e. RADIUS

29. List five things that can be done to make a service more secure?

30. How do you prevent unauthorized users from changing DNS records?

    a. Adjust the properties of the Domain Users group in Active Directory Users and Computer

    b. Set the security permissions for the server in Active Directory Users and Computers

    c. Set the security permissions for the server in Computer Management | Services and Applications | DNS

    d. Adjust the advanced properties of the server in Active Directory Users and Computers

31. When using RIS to set up workstations, which tasks can be done by a lower-skilled technician if you are concerned about security?

    a. Install Windows 2000 Professional on a workstation including all required applications

b. Run Remote Installation Preparation Wizard to create an image of the workstation

c. Run the client setup wizard to format the drive and install the selected image

d. A and B

e. A, B, and C

32. What component of SNMP controls can read information or change settings?

a. Community name

b. Username

c. Groupname

d. B and C

e. A, B and C

33. Which level of encryption would you choose for terminal server to ensure that traffic from the client to the server is encrypted?

a. Low

b. Medium

c. High

d. B and C

e. A, B, and C

HANDS-ON PROJECTS

Project 5-1

In this hands-on activity, you will enable auditing for the Notepad. Any time a domain user runs NOTEPAD.EXE, access will be logged to the event viewer.

1. Log on as Administrator.

2. Click on **Start**, point to **Programs**, point to **Administrative Tools**, click on **Domain Controller Security Policy**.

3. Expand **Security Settings**.

4. Expand **Local Policies**.

5. Click on **Audit Policy**.

6. Double-click on Audit object access.

7. Click on **Success**.

8. Click on **OK**.

9. Close **MMC** (if prompted save the changes).

10. Right-click on **My Computer** and click on **Explore**.

11. Expand C:.

12. Expand on WINNT.

13. Click on SYSTEM32.

14. Click on Show Files.

15. Right-click on **NOTEPAD.EXE** and click on **Properties**.

16. Click on the **Security** tab.

17. Click on the **Advanced** button.

18. Click on the **Auditing** tab.

19. Click on the **Add** button.

20. Double-click on the **Domain Users** group.

21. Enable the **Successful** checkbox for **Read Permissions**.

22. Click on **OK** twice.

23. Close Explorer.

Project 5-2

In this hand-on activity, you will run Notepad and then view the results of the audit.

1. Click on **Start**, point to **Programs**, point to **Accessories**, and click on **Notepad**.

2. Close **Notepad**.

3. Click on **Start**, point to **Programs**, point to **Administrative Tools**, and click on **Event Viewer**.

4. Click on **Security Log**.

5. Double-click on any event to view the details. What information does the audit provide?

6. Close Event Viewer.

Project 5-3

In this hands-on activity, you will create a shared folder and remove the default permissions for the Everyone group.

1. Right-click on **My Computer** and click on **Explore**.

2. Click on C:.

3. Click on the **File** menu, point to **New**, and click on **Folder**.

4. Type **DATA** as the name of the folder and press **Enter**.

5. Right-click on **DATA** and click on **Sharing**.

6. Click on **Share this folder**.

7. Remove the default permissions.

8. Click on the **Permissions** button.

9. Click on the **everyone** group and click on the **Remove** button.

10. Click on the **Add** button.

11. Double-click on **Domain Admins** group.

12. Click on **OK**.

13. Click on the **Allow for the Full Control permission**.

14. Click on **OK** twice.

15. Close Explorer.

Project 5-4

In this hands-on activity, you will verify that only an EFS recovery agent is able to read the contents of an encrypted file.

1. Create two new user accounts: Bob Jones and Jeff Smith.

2. Log on as Bob Jones.

3. Right-click on **My Computer** and click on **Explore**.

4. Expand C:.

5. Right-click on **DATA** and click on **Properties**.

6. Click on the **Advanced** button.

7. Click on **Encrypt contents to secure data**.

8. Click on **OK** twice.

9. Create a text file named ENCRYPT.TXT in the DATA directory.

10. Log off as Bob.

11. Log on as Jeff Smith.

12. Attempt to view the contents of the file in the DATA directory. Are you able to view the folder contents?

13. Log off as Jeff Smith.

14. Log on as Administrator.

15. Click on **Start**, point to **Programs**, point to **Administrative Tools**, and click on **Domain Security Policy**.

16. Expand Public Key Policies.

17. Click on **Encrypted Data Recovery Agents**. Note that Administrator is the default recovery agent.

18. Close MMC.

19. Attempt to view the contents of the file in the DATA directory. Are you able to see the file ENCYPT.TXT?

20. Close all open windows.

Project 5-5

In this hands-on exercise, you will view service logon information for the Task Schedule to determine how it interacts with the desktop.

1. Click on **Start**, point to **Programs**, point to **Administrative Tools**, and click on **Computer Management**.

2. Expand **Services and Applications**.

3. Click on **Services**.

4. Double click on **Task Scheduler**.

5. Click on the **Log On** tab. Note that Task Scheduler logs on as part of the operating system and is allowed to interact with the desktop.

6. Click on **OK**.

7. Close MMC.

Project 5-6

In this hands-on activity, you will view DNS settings to determine which users and groups by default are allowed to make changes to DNS settings.

1. Click on **Start**, point to **Programs**, point to **Administrative Tools**, and click on **Computer Management**.

2. Expand **Services and Applications**.

3. Expand **DNS**.

4. Right click on **YourServer** and click on **Properties**.

5. Click on the **Security** tab. Note which users and groups are allowed to change DNS settings. Note which group is allowed only read access.

6. Click on the **Cancel** button.

7. Close the MMC.

Project 5-7

In this hands-on activity, you will configure all Configure Terminal Services communication that must be encrypted. This procedure assumes that Terminal Services is not already installed.

1. Click on **Start**, point to **Settings**, click on **Control Panel**.

2. Double-click on **Add/Remove Programs**.

3. Click on **Add/Remove Windows Components**.

4. Enable the checkbox for **Terminal Services**.

5. Click on **Next**.

6. Click on **Next** to keep the default Remote Administration Mode. If required, insert the Windows 2000 CD ROM and click on **OK**.

7. Click on **Finish**.

8. Click on **Yes** to restart your server.

9. Log on as administrator.

10. Close Control Panel.

11. Click on **Start**, point to **Administrative Tools**, click on **Terminal Services Configuration**.

12. Click on the **Connections** folder.

13. Right-click on **RDP-Tcp** and click on **Properties**.

14. Change the Encryption Level drop down list box to **High**.

15. Click on **OK** to save the changes.

16. Close MMC.

CASE PROJECTS

Case 1

Based on everything that you know about Southdale Property Management, document any resources they might want to consider auditing or using encrypting file system to protect. In addition, document any service security issues that you feel need to be dealt with.

Case 2

The new owners of Prairie Refrigeration have a standard guideline for auditing file servers and have no need for an additional analysis. However, they do not have any guidelines for remote users. Document any special concerns that you have related to the laptops of the remote sales staff. Include relevant information about auditing, file system security, authentication types, and service security.

Case 3

The management of Fleetwood Credit Union would like you to do a complete analysis of their system and indicate what type of information should be audited, including guidelines that they can use in the future to decide what should be audited. They would also like documentation regarding when to allow users Full Control NTFS permission instead of Modify permission or Read and Write permissions.

KEY TERMS

Chapter 6

Authentication

1. A way to verify that an object sending messages or requests to an NDS is permitted to act on or receive those messages or requests.

2. Login or resource access validation.

Certificate

The document (usually digital) issued by a Certificate Authority that includes the Certificate Authority's digital signature, the user's public and private key, and user information.

Certificate Revocation List (CRL)

A list of digital security certificates that have been revoked by the certificate authority and are no longer valid.

Digital signature

1. An arithmetic function that uses a user's private key to create a unique signature that can only be read using the user's public key. The digital signature ensures that the data is coming from the correct user and that it has not been tampered with.

2. Verifies that the sender of a package is who he claims to be. A digital signature is encrypted with the private key and verified using the corresponding public key.

Encrypting File System (EFS)

Windows 2000 data encryption service based on a user's public and private keys. Data encryption is only supported on NTFS volumes.

IP Security (IPSec)

A part of TCP/IP standards in which all IP traffic between two computers is encrypted so that the packets cannot be captured on the network and read by unauthorized users.

Private key

The second part of the key pair. The private key is held by only one person or computer.

Public key

One of the key pair used for PKI. The public key for each certificate is made available to all users and computers who request the key from the correct source.

Public Key Infrastructure (PKI)

1. A system that is used to provide distributed security to the network. PKI services include Internet Security, logon authentication security, private and public key encryption, and Certificate Services.

2. A method of distributed security that uses certificates and public and private keys to authenticate users and computers, and to secure communication between computers.

3. An encryption scheme that uses a shared key for encryption and decryption of files.

REVIEW QUESTIONS

1. You have installed an Enterprise Certificate Authority on your network and used a certificate issued by this CA to configure SSL on your web server. When your clients access the web site they are told that the certificate is issued by an untrusted CA. Why?

2. List five things that certificates can be used for.

3. Which key does the receiver of a digitally signed message use to confirm that the message has not been modified in transit?

   a. The receiver's public key

   b. The receiver's private key

   c. The sender's public key

   d. The sender's private key

4. You would like PKI to be integrated with Active Directory. What type of CA must you install first?

   a. Enterprise root CA

   b. Enterprise subordinate CA

   c. Stand-alone root CA

   d. Stand-alone subordinate CA

   e. None of the above

5. If a root CA is compromised, how does this affect certificates that have already been issued? Select all that apply.

   a. Certificates issued by that root CA are revoked

   b. Certificates issued to subordinate CAs are revoked

   c. Certificates issued by subordinate CAs are revoked

6. You are an administrator in a large company that is using PKI. It has been decided that you will have CA within you region and you are responsible for installing it. You have been told your PKI system is not integrated with Active Directory. Which type of CA will you install?

   a. Enterprise root CA

   b. Enterprise subordinate CA

   c. Stand-alone root CA

   d. Stand-alone subordinate CA

   e. None of the above

7. Certificates can be issued through a web page to a user for e-mail encryption. True or False?

8. List two benefits of having subordinate CAs in your PKI hierarchy.

9. Which service must be stopped during the installation of certificate services?

   a. Active Directory

   b. IIS

   c. DNS

   d. DHCP

   e. Kerberos v5

10. When installing a subordinate CA what information is required that is not needed when installing a root CA?

11. What is the purpose of certificate templates?

   a. Make it easier for users to request certificates

   b. Ensures that the proper certificates are issued in the proper situation

   c. Lets users select a template from a list

   d. All of the above

12. List five pieces of information that are included in all standard certificates.

13. Which certificate template would an administrator choose when setting up SSL on a web server for internal use?

   a. Domain Controller

   b. Web Server

   c. Computer

   d. User

   e. Authenticated Session

14. Which certificate template would an administrator choose when setting up the second CA in PKI hierarchy?

   a. Domain Controller

   b. Computer

   c. Subordinate Certification Authority

   d. Enrollment Agent

   e. CEP Encryption

15. If a user certificate is compromised, which server will add the certificate to its own Certificate Revocation List?

    a. The root CA

    b. A CA in the PKI hierarchy

    c. The CA that issued the certificate

    d. All domain controllers

16. Which of the following are reasons that a certificate may be added to a CRL? Select all that apply.

    a. Expired certificate

    b. Key compromise

    c. Superceded certificate

    d. CA compromise

17. Why would a certificate cease working if it has not been added to a CRL?

    a. Expired

    b. Key compromise

    c. Superceded

    d. CA compromise

    e. B and D

    f. A, B and D

    g. A, B, C and D

18. In order to trust a third party CA, what must be done?

    a. Import the public key of the third-party CA

    b. Import the private key of the third-party CA

    c. Import the trusted root certificate of the third-party CA

    d. Export your trusted root certificate and give it to the third-party CA

19. In order for users to log on to the network using smart cards, what task needs to be performed after the smart cards are configured with certificates?

    a. Configure the CA to recognize the user accounts that are mapped to the certificates

    b. Configure the user accounts to be mapped to the certificates in Active Directory Users and Computers

    c. Configure the user accounts to be mapped to the certificate in Active Directory Sites and Services

    d. No configuration is required because the usernames are specified when creating the certificates

20. Users must be granted administrative rights on a per domain basis because domains are security boundaries in Windows 2000. True or false?

21. You have just created a Windows 2000 network with a single domain. It is possible to grant help desk staff the ability to reset user passwords but not allow them to create and delete user accounts. True or false?

22. To set a security policy that would affect all computers in the domain including domain controllers, how would it be done?

    a. Edit the local security policy on each computer

    b. Edit the domain controller's security policy

    c. Edit the domain security policy and confirm that there are no settings in the local security policies that conflict

    d. Edit the domain security policy and confirm that there are no settings in the domain controller's security policy that conflict

HANDS-ON PROJECTS

Project 6-1

In this hands-on activity, you will install and configure Certificate Services to allow users to encrypt e-mail.

1. Click on **Start**, point to **Settings**, click on **Control Panel**.

2. Double click on **Add/Remove Programs**.

3. Click on **Add/Remove Windows Components**.

4. Enable the **Certificate Services** checkbox.

5. Click on **Yes** to continue.

6. Click on **Next** to accept running Terminal Services in Remote Administration Mode.

7. Click on **Enterprise root CA** and click on **Next**.

8. Fill in the Identifying Information and click on **Next**.

9. Click on **Next** to accept the default locations for certificate database and certificate database log.

10. Click on **OK** to stop IIS if it is running. If prompted, insert the Windows 2000 Server CD and click on **OK**.

11. Click on **Finish**.

12. Close Add/Remove Programs.

13. Close Control Panel.

14. Click on **Start**, point to **Programs**, point to **Administrative Tools**, and click on **Certification Authority**.

15. Expand the CA you created.

16. Click on **Policy Settings**. Note the certificate templates that are already installed by default.

17. Add a new certificate template to your CA to allow for the creation of smart cards by right-clicking on Policy Settings.

18. Point to New.

19. Click on **Certificate to Issue**.

20. Click on **Smart card Logon**.

21. Click on **OK**.

22. Close MMC.

Project 6-2

In this hands-on activity, you will create a User Certificate for the administrator to use to encrypt e-mail.

1. Open Internet Explorer.

2. Go to the URL **http://127.0.0.1/certsrv**.

3. Log in as administrator with your domain password.

4. Select **Request a certificate** and click on **Next**.

5. Select **User certificate request** and click on **Next**.

6. Click on **Submit** to process the request.

7. Click on **Install this certificate** to install it in Windows. Note that it has been successfully installed.

8. Close Internet Explorer.

Project 6-3

In this hands-on activity, you will delegate authority to manage users to an administrator in a remote location. This involves creating an OU for the remote location, adding a user account for the remote administrator to the OU, and then delegating authority of the OU to the remote administrator.

1. Click on **Start**, point to **Programs**, point to **Administrative Tools**, click on Active Directory Users and Computers.

2. Right-click on your tree, point to **New**, and click on **Organizational Unit**.

3. Enter **GrandForks** as the name of the OU and click on **OK**.

4. Right-click on the **GrandForks OU**, point to **New**, and click on **User**.

5. Name the new user **Susan Wright**.

6. Enter **Susan** as the logon name.

7. Click on **Next**.

8. Enter a password and click on **Next**.

9. Click on **Finish**.

10. Right-click on the **GrandForks OU**, and click on **Delegate Control**.

11. Click on **Next**.

12. Click on **Add**.

13. Double-click on **Susan Wright** and click on **OK**.

14. Click on **Next**.

15. Click on the checkbox for **Create, delete, and manage user accounts**.

16. Click on **Next**.

17. Click on **Finish**.

18. Test Susan's ability to create new user accounts by logging in as Susan.

19. Click on **Start**, point to **Programs**, point to **Administrative Tools**, and click on **Active Directory Users and Computers**.

20. Right click on **GrandForks**, point to **New**, and click on **User**. Create a new user Jimmy Kent with a logon name of Jimmy.

21. Click on **Next**.

22. Enter a password and click on **Next**.

23. Click on **Finish**.

24. Right-click on **Users**. Note that there is no New option because Susan does not have sufficient rights to create any objects in the Users OU.

25. Close MMC.

26. Log off as Susan.

Project 6-4

In this hands-on activity, you will set the password policy for the domain and view the effect of domain security policy on the local computer.

1. Log on as administrator.

2. Click on **Start**, point to **Programs**, point to **Administrative Tools**, and click on **Domain Security Policy**.

3. Expand **Account Policies**.

4. Click on **Password Policy**.

5. Double click on **Minimum Password Length**.

6. Enter **5** for the minimum number of characters and click on **OK**. Note that even though this policy is available in the Domain Controllers Security Policy and the Local Security Policy they have no effect in a domain environment.

7. Close MMC.

8. Test the new policy by clicking **Start**, point to **Programs**, point to **Administrative Tools**, and click on **Active Directory Users and Computers**.

9. Click on **Grand Forks**.

10. Right-click on **Jimmy Kent** and click on **Reset Password**.

11. Enter **shrt** as the password and click on **OK**. Note the error message you receive when the password is too short and then click on **OK** to clear the error.

12. Right-click on **Jimmy Kent** and click on **Reset Password**.

13. Enter **longer** as the password and click on **OK**. Note that the password has been successfully changed and then click on **OK** to clear the message.

14. Close MMC.

CASE PROJECTS

Case 1

The administrator of Southdale Property Management has recently been reading about how Public Key Infrastructure is used to make services on the Internet more secure. The administrator has e-mailed you asking whether PKI would be useful for their network. Compose a response that you can send back via e-mail.

Case 2

The new owners have not yet decided whether to include Prairie Refrigeration as an OU in their domain or as separate domain in their domain tree. They would like you to write an analysis of both options. This should include how the local consultants would be granted permissions to manage local resources for both situations.

Case 3

Recently one of the branch locations has found an unauthorized person in their back office area trying to log in at one of the workstations. As a result, management would like to have smart cards implemented throughout the company. Write a plan indicating how this could be implemented. The plan should include an analysis of whether to use an internal or external certificate authority and how to setup the user accounts in Active Directory.

KEY TERMS

Chapter 7

CHAP

A challenge response authentication protocol that uses Message Digest 5 (MD5) to encrypt the response.

Demand-dial router

A router that can open a modem, ISDN, or VPN connection to a remote network when packets need to be routed to the remote network.

Digital Subscriber Line (DSL)

A digital service that can be run on normal phone lines that provides very fast (up to 10 Mbps) and, in most cases, inexpensive access to the Internet. The two most common forms of DSL are Asymmetric Digital Subscriber Line (ADSL) and Symmetric Digital Subscriber Line (SDSL). DSLs require specialized equipment and are limited by distances to central connection points, so DSL technology is not available everywhere.

Domain

1. In NetWare, DOMAIN is used as a console command that will create a protected operating system domain for running untested NLMs in Ring 3. This prevents a module from interfering with the core operating system.

2. In the Internet, a domain is a part of the naming hierarchy. The domain name is a sequence of names (separated by periods) that identify host sites. For example: galenp@mail.msen.com.

Dynamic Host Configuration Protocol (DHCP)

A TCP/IP application-layer protocol that provides for dynamic address assignment on a network.

Extensible Authentication Protocol (EAP)

An authentication method used to verify users through remote access.

Firewall

Used as a security measure between a company's local area network (LAN) and the Internet. The firewall prevents users from accessing certain address Web sites. A firewall also helps to prevent hackers from accessing internal resources on the network. A combination of hardware and software that separates a LAN into two or more parts for security purposes. Today, firewalls are commonly used to prevent unauthorized access to a network from the Internet.

Frame Relay

A packet switching based network.

Generic Routing Encryption (GRE) protocol

A protocol used by PPTP to encapsulate the encrypted packets that are being transmitted across the Internet.

Internet

An international computer network of networks that connect government, academic, and business institutions. Networks on the Internet include MILNET, NSFnet, and other backbone networks, as well as mid-level networks and stub (local) networks.

Internet networks communicate using TCP/IP (Transmission Control Protocol/Internet Protocol). The Internet connects colleges, universities, military organizations and contractors, corporations, government research laboratories, and individuals.

Although parts of the Internet operate under single administrative domains, the Internet as a whole reaches around the globe, connects computers (from personal computers to supercomputers), and is not administered by any single authority. The Internet in July 1995 roughly connected 60,000 independent networks into a vast global Internet.

Used as a descriptive term, an internet is a collection of interconnected packet-switching networks. Any time you connect two or more networks, you have an internet—as in *inter*national or *inter*state.

Internet Authentication Service (IAS)

An authentication method used to verify users through remote access. Equivalent to a RADIUS server.

Internet Protocol (IP)

The OSI layer 3 routed protocol used to transmit packetized information on a TCP/IP network.

Internet Service Provider (ISP)

Companies that provide an Internet connection for educational institutions, individuals, companies, and organizations.

IP Security (IPSec)

A part of TCP/IP standards in which all IP traffic between two computers is encrypted so that the packets cannot be captured on the network and read by unauthorized users.

Local Area Network (LAN)

A group of computers running specialized communications software and joined through an external data path.

A LAN will cover a small geographic area, usually no larger than a single building. The computers have a direct high-speed connection between all workstations and servers, and share hardware resources and data files. A LAN has centralized management of resources and network security. PC-based networks can trace their heritage back to what are now often referred to as legacy systems. These systems were mainframe and minicomputer hosts accessed through dumb terminals. There are a number of similarities between LANs and these legacy systems, such as centralized storage and backup, access security, and central management of resources. There are, however, a number of differences.

Traditional host systems are characterized by centralized processing, dumb terminals, custom applications, and high expansion costs and management overhead. LANs are characterized by distributed processing, intelligent workstations (PCs), and off-the-shelf applications. LANs are modular, are inexpensive to expand, and have more moderate management costs.

Modem

An abbreviation for modulator/demodulator. A modem is a peripheral device that permits a personal computer, microcomputer, or mainframe to receive and transmit data in digital format across voice-oriented communications links such as telephone lines.

MS-CHAP

Microsoft's version of the CHAP protocol. This version is more secure than CHAP.

Network Address Translation (NAT)

1. A component that is included with Windows 2000 Server that allows multiple users to share one connection, such as a modem or DSL connection, to the Internet. NAT is designed for mid-sized networks and offers more configuration flexibility than ICS. NAT operates as a router forwarding all requests to the Internet as well as supporting address translation. This means that the computers inside the network do not have to have Internet-compatible addresses.

2. A service available through RRAS on a Windows 2000 Server that allows the sharing of a single connection to the Internet or a remote network with multiple network clients. NAT is more difficult to configure than ICS but can also operate in more complex environments.

3. Routing protocol available through an Internet Connection Server (ICS) configuration that allows a home network or small office to share a single Internet connection. This protocol requires that your client computers be configured as DHCP clients.

Packet Filtering

Controlling access to a network by analyzing the incoming and outgoing packets and letting them pass or halting them based on the IP addresses of the source and destination.

Point-to-Point Protocol (PPP)

The successor to the SLIP protocol, PPP allows a computer to use a regular telephone line and a modem to make IP connections. PPP can also carry other routable protocols such as IPX.

Remote Authentication Dial-In User Service (RADIUS)

Client/server-based authentication and authorization service for remote access. Connection criteria are passed from the remote access server to the RADIUS server, which will inform the remote access server whether access is allowed or declined.

Router

1. A connection between two networks that specifies message paths and may perform other functions, such as data compression.

2. In early versions of NetWare, the term bridge was sometimes used interchangeably with the term router.

Routing and Remote Access Service (RRAS)

Windows 2000 service that enables a Windows 2000 server to simultaneously support multiprotocol routing, demand-dial routing, and remote access. RRAS supports clients running Windows 2000, Windows NT, Windows 9x, UNIX variants, and Macintosh.

Shiva Password Authentication Protocol (SPAP)

A reversible password authentication system used by the Shiva Corporation in some of their remote communication equipment.

T1

A leased-line connection capable of carrying data at 1,544,000 bits per second. At maximum theoretical capacity, a T1 line could move a megabyte in less than 10 seconds. That is still not fast enough for full-screen, full-motion video, for which you need at least 10,000,000 bits per second. T1 is the fastest speed commonly used to connect networks to the Internet.

Tunneling

A method of encapsulating data for transmission between two authenticated end points.

Transmission Control Protocol (TCP)

The reliable connection-oriented protocol used by DARPA (Defense Advanced Research Projects Agency) for their internetworking research. TCP uses a three-way handshake with a clock-based sequence number selection to synchronize connecting entities and to minimize the chance of erroneous connections due to delayed messages. TCP is usually used with IP (Internet Protocol), the combination being known as TCP/IP.

Virtual Private Network (VPN)

Remote access configuration where users and remote networks connect to network servers across the Internet. A tunnel is created through the Internet and all of the data that crosses the Internet is encrypted. Windows 2000 supports two protocols for setting up VPNs: Point-to-Point Tunneling Protocol (PPTP) or Layer 2 Tunneling Protocol/IPSec (L2TP/IPSec).

Wide Area Network (WAN)

Expands the basic LAN model by linking Local Area Networks (LANs) and allowing them to communicate with each other. By traditional definition, a LAN becomes a WAN when it crosses a public right-of-way, requiring a public carrier for data transmission. More current usage of the term usually includes any situation where a network expands beyond one location/building. A WAN is characterized by low- to high-speed communication links and usually covers a wide geographic area.

The remote links may be operational LANs or only groups of workstations. With the exception of a WAN's wider area of operation, the benefits and features of LANs and WANs are the same.

REVIEW QUESTIONS

1. Which type of remote access would a home-based user with a high-speed Internet connection use to connect to the office?

   a. Client to server dial-up

   b. Router to router dial-up

   c. Client to server VPN

   d. Router to router VPN

2. Which type of remote access would you configure for a company with two locations that needed to transfer small amounts of data between offices?

   a. Client to server dial-up

   b. Router to router dial-up

   c. Client to server VPN

   d. Router to router VPN

3. Which type of remote access would you configure for home-based users that need to connect to the office once per day to synchronize files if your server already is modem connected?

   a. Client to server dial-up

   b. Router to router dial-up

   c. Client to server VPN

   d. Router to router VPN

4. If you had a sales force that needed to connect back to the office with minimal hardware maintenance issues, which type of remote access would you configure?

   a. Client to server dial-up

   b. Router to router dial-up

   c. Client to server VPN

   d. Router to router VPN

5. Which security strategy would not be appropriate for a traveling sales force using dial-up remote access?

   a. Set a password policy to require strong passwords

   b. Set laptop screensavers to turn on and lock the workstation after two minutes

   c. Enable remote access only for the sales persons user accounts

   d. Enable callback to a preset phone number

   e. A and D

   f. All options would be appropriate

6. Which security strategy would be appropriate for users accessing company servers over a VPN from their home computers?

   a. Set a password policy to require strong passwords

   b. Set a security policy that forces screensavers to turn on and lock the workstation after two minutes

   c. Enable remote access only for the sales persons user accounts

   d. Enable callback to a preset phone number

   e. A and C

   f. A, B, and C

7. What is the first step in configuring a Windows 2000 server a RAS or VPN server?

8. A Windows 2000 RAS server is capable of querying a single RADIUS server as an authentication provider. True or false?

9. What type of authentication would be required for RAS if all Windows operating systems need to be supported?

   a. EAP

   b. MS-CHAP v2

   c. MS-CHAP

   d. CHAP

   e. SPAP

   f. PAP

10. What type of authentication should be chosen for RAS if all clients are Windows 2000 Professional and smart cards are not used?

   a. EAP

   b. MS-CHAP v2

   c. MS-CHAP

   d. CHAP

   e. SPAP

   f. PAP

11. What type of authentication should be chosen for RAS if all clients are using smart cards with Windows 2000 Professional?

    a. EAP

    b. MS-CHAP v2

    c. MS-CHAP

    d. CHAP

    e. SPAP

    f. PAP

12. What type of authentication should be chosen for RAS if some of the clients are not Windows-based and you require protection from replay attacks?

    a. EAP

    b. MS-CHAP v2

    c. MS-CHAP

    d. CHAP

    e. SPAP

    f. PAP

13. Which MMC snap-in is used to set remote access policies for a server?

    a. Active Directory Users and Computers

    b. Active Directory Sites and Services

    c. Routing and Remote Access

    d. Computer Management

14. By default, which MMC snap-in is used to grant a single user remote access?

    a. Active Directory Users and Computers

    b. Active Directory Sites and Services

    c. Routing and Remote Access

    d. Computer Management

15. You would like to configure your server to be part of RADIUS with your Internet service provider. Which service must be installed on a Windows 2000 server in your office?

    a. RADIUS

    b. IAS

    c. RAS

    d. Routing and Remote Access

16. You have configured RADIUS with your Internet service provider in order that remote users can use the same usernames and passwords when they connect to the ISP as when they are at their desks. Where is the remote access server located?

    a. At their client computer's at home

    b. At their client computer's at the office

    c. At a Windows 2000 server at the office

    d. At the ISP

17. What type of device must be placed between your LAN and the Internet to allow connectivity?

    a. Router

    b. Switch

    c. Gateway

    d. Hub

    e. Server

18. When using demand-dial routing between two physical locations, how many routers are required?

    a. None

    b. One

    c. Two

    d. Depends on whether the dial-up connectivity is ISDN or regular telephone lines

19. List three security goals of VPNs.

20. Running a VPN over the Internet is more expensive than using a leased line because the Internet is extremely reliable. True or false?

21. It is impossible for two NetWare servers to communicate across the Internet because the Internet is TCP/IP only and NetWare servers use IPX/SPX. True or false?

22. What type of encryption is used with L2TP for a Windows 2000 VPN?

    a. MPPE

    b. IPSec AH

    c. IPSec ESP

    d. None; L2TP provides its own encryption

23. Which VPN protocol can travel or be routed through NAT?

    a. PPTP

    b. L2TP

    c. Neither

    d. Both

24. Which VPN protocol can travel or be routed through a firewall?

    a. PPTP

    b. L2TP

    c. Neither

    d. Both

25. How are users granted VPN access?

26. How can you allow VPN access for your clients but still be as secure as possible?

    a. Place the VPN server behind a firewall on a screen subnet

    b. Be sure the VPN server is on a different subnet than client computers and internal servers

    c. Allow only VPN packets to be routed to the server

    d. A and C

    e. A, B and C

27. A VPN can connect two networks using private IP address ranges across the Internet even though the Internet will not route the private IP address ranges. True or false?

HANDS-ON PROJECTS

Project 7-1

In this hands-on activity, you will configure your server as a VPN server in Routing and Remote Access.

1. Click on **Start**, point to **Programs**, point to **Administrative Tools**, and click on **Routing and Remote Access**.

2. Click on your server. Note the red arrow down indicating the RAS is not running.

3. Right click on your server and click on **Configure and Enable Routing and Remote Access**.

4. Click on **Next**.

5. Select **Virtual private network (VPN) server** and click on **Next**.

6. Keep the default selection of all protocols and click on **Next**.

7. Select your network card from the list and click on **Next**.

8. Choose **From a specified range of addresses** and click on **Next**.

9. Click on **New**.

10. Enter a start IP address of **192.168.10.21**.

11. Enter a stop IP address of **192.168.10.30**.

12. Click on **OK**.

13. Click on **Next**.

14. Keep the default selection of not being a RADIUS server and click on **Next**.

15. Click on **Finish**. If you receive a message about relaying DHCP then click on **OK** to clear the message.

16. Click on **Ports** in MMC. Note that there are two types of ports for VPN: PPTP and L2TP.

17. Close MMC.

Project 7-2

In this hands-on activity, you will create a user account with permissions to connect to your server using a VPN connection. The first step is to create a new user account.

1. Click on **Start**, point to **Programs**, point to **Administrative Tools**, click on Active Directory Users and Computers.

2. Right-click on **Users**, point to **New**, and click on **User**.

3. Name the user **VPNuser** with the same logon name.

4. Set a password of **connect** and click on **Next**.

5. Click on **Finish**.

6. Give VPNuser permission to access the network remotely by right clicking on **VPNuser** and clicking on **Properties**.

7. Click on the **Dial-in** tab.

8. Select **Allow Access**.

9. Click on **OK**.

10. Close MMC.

Project 7-3

In this hands-on activity, you will test the VPN by connecting to your partner's server using the user account created in the previous exercise.

1. Click on **Start**, point to **Settings**, click on **Network and Dial-up Connections**.

2. Double-click on **Make New Connection**. Specify location information if prompted then click on **OK** to close the Phone and Modem Options.

3. Click on **Next** to start the **Network Connection Wizard**.

4. Select **Connect to a private network through the Internet** and click on **Next**.

5. Enter in the IP address of your partner and click on **Next**.

6. Select **For all Users** and click on **Next**.

7. Accept the default of not using Internet Connection Sharing and click on **Next**.

8. Click on **Finish**.

9. Enter **VPNuser** as the User name.

10. Enter **connect** as the password.

11. Click on **Connect**.

12. Click on **OK** to close the Connection Complete window.

13. View the status of the VPN connection by right-clicking on **Virtual Private Connection** and click on **Status**. Note the status of connection as well as the amount of traffic that has gone through the connection.

14. Click on **Properties**.

15. Click on the **Security** tab.

16. Select **Advanced**.

17. Click on **Settings**. Note that there are varying levels you can choose for data security as well as logon security (authentication).

18. Click on **Cancel** twice.

19. Disconnect the VPN connection by clicking on **Disconnect**.

Project 7-4

In this hands-on activity, you will configure and test a RAS policy that only allows access between 6 PM and 8 PM Monday to Friday.

1. Click on **Start**, point to **Programs**, point to **Administrative Tools**, and click on **Routing and Remote Access**.

2. Click on **Remote Access Policies**. Note that there is one policy in place by default.

3. Right-click on **Allow access if dial-in permission is enabled** and click on **Delete**.

4. Right-click on **Remote Access Policies** and click on **New Remote Access Policy**.

5. Enter **Evening Only** as the Policy friendly name and click on **Next**.

6. Click on **Add**.

7. Double-click on **Day-And-Time-Restriction**.

8. Allow access from 6pm to 8pm, Monday to Friday and click on **OK**.

9. Click on **Next**.

10. Leave the default selection of denying access and click on **Next**.

11. Click on **Finish**.

12. Double-click on your VPN connection.

13. Enter **VPNuser** as the User name.

14. Enter **connect** as the password.

15. Click on **Connect**. You will get an error indicating that you do not have permission to dial-in.

16. Click on **Cancel**.

17. Close all windows.

CASE PROJECTS

Case 1

Remote access has not been implemented at Southdale Property Management but the owner would like to be able to access e-mail when out of the office. The Administrator is nervous about allowing remote access and is unsure of the best way to do it. Write an analysis that looks at the risks that will be incurred by allowing remote access and the best way to minimize these risks.

Case 2

The parent company of Prairie Refrigeration does not have any users accessing their own servers remotely. They are interested as to what you think is the best way to implement remote access for the two roaming sales people. The sales people travel throughout the United States and need access to e-mail as well as sales and financial files. Create a report that the parent company can use to decide the best way to implement remote access for the sales people.

Case 3

Fleetwood Credit Union Management is concerned that the existing access through dial-up phone lines is not the best way to provide remote access. Given the high security requirements of a financial institution, write a report recommending a remote access solution for executives on the road and at home.

In addition, management is tentatively planning on having members VPN into the Fleetwood Credit Union LAN in order to secure access to the new Web financial application. Management has been told this will keep user passwords secure and prevent hackers from seeing personal information as it is transferred across the Internet. They would like your opinion on the best way to provide members with secure access to this application. Compose a report for management indicating your recommendation. Include a network diagram indicating which protocols are being used.

KEY TERMS

Chapter 8

Certificate

The document (usually digital) issued by a Certificate Authority that includes the Certificate Authority's digital signature, the user's public and private key, and user information.

Data Encryption Standard (DES)

A standard used to encrypt or encode data so the intended recipient can only read it.

Diffie-Hellman

The Diffie-Hellman key agreement protocol (also called exponential key agreement) was developed by Diffie and Hellman in 1976. The protocol allows two users to exchange a secret key over an insecure medium without any prior secrets.

Filter

A device or program that separates data, signals, or material in accordance with specified criteria.

Internet Engineering Task Force (IETF)

One of the task forces of the IAB, the IETF is responsible for solving short-term engineering needs of the Internet. It has more than 40 Working Groups.

Internet Protocol (IP)

The OSI layer 3 routed protocol used to transmit packetized information on a TCP/IP network.

IP Security (IPSec)

A part of TCP/IP standards in which all IP traffic between two computers is encrypted so that the packets cannot be captured on the network and read by unauthorized users.

Kerberos

Default authentication protocol for Windows 2000 clients and services.

Local Area Network (LAN)

A group of computers running specialized communications software and joined through an external data path.

A LAN will cover a small geographic area, usually no larger than a single building. The computers have a direct high-speed connection between all workstations and servers, and share hardware resources and data files. A LAN has centralized management of resources and network security. PC-based networks can trace their heritage back to what are now often referred to as legacy systems. These systems were mainframe and minicomputer hosts accessed through dumb terminals. There are a number of similarities between LANs and these legacy systems, such as centralized storage and backup, access security, and central management of resources. There are, however, a number of differences.

Traditional host systems are characterized by centralized processing, dumb terminals, custom applications, and high expansion costs and management overhead. LANs are characterized by distributed processing, intelligent workstations (PCs), and off-the-shelf applications. LANs are modular, are inexpensive to expand, and have more moderate management costs.

Message Digest 5 (MD5)

A form of creating a digest from a message.

Registry

Windows NT and Windows 95 configuration database.

Secure Hash Algorithm (SHA)

A procedure to create a 160 bit message digest hash function to sign a digital message.

Security Association (SA)

A security agreement between two computers using IPSec that defines the levels of encryption supported by both computers.

Server Message Block (SMB)

The protocol used by Microsoft servers to exchange data, such as files and print jobs, across a network connection.

Tunneling

A method of encapsulating data for transmission between two authenticated end points.

Wide Area Network (WAN)

Expands the basic LAN model by linking Local Area Networks (LANs) and allowing them to communicate with each other. By traditional definition, a LAN becomes a WAN when it crosses a public right-of-way, requiring a public carrier for data transmission. More current usage of the term usually includes any situation where a network expands beyond one location/building. A WAN is characterized by low- to high-speed communication links and usually covers a wide geographic area.

The remote links may be operational LANs or only groups of workstations. With the exception of a WAN's wider area of operation, the benefits and features of LANs and WANs are the same.

REVIEW QUESTIONS

1. Which technology can be used with Windows 2000 and Windows NT to ensure data integrity for all network transactions?

   a. IPSec AH

   b. IPSec ESP

   c. SMB signing

   d. DES

2. To enable SMB signing on a Windows 2000 server, what tool is used?

   a. Routing and Remote Access

   b. Active Directory Users and Computers

   c. Computer Management

   d. Regedit.exe

3. Network response times will be slower if SMB signing is used. True or false?

4. If you wanted to specify the highest level of encryption possible with IPSec ESP, which encryption technology would you chose?

   a. DES

   b. 3DES

   c. 40-bit DES

   d. 128-bit SSL

5. Which part of an IPSec security association is responsible for generating the same secret key on both communicating computers?

   a. Encryption algorithm

   b. Integrity algorithm

   c. Authentication method

   d. Diffie-Hellman group

6. Which IPSec authentication method is the easiest to implement if both computers are part of the same Active Directory tree?

   a. Certificate-based authentication

   b. Preshared key authentication

   c. Kerberos v5 authentication

   d. All are equally easy

7. Which IPSec authentication method is the most secure to implement if both computers are in different Active Directory trees and have access to the Internet?

   a. Certificate-based authentication

   b. Preshared key authentication

    c. Kerberos v5 authentication

    d. All are equally secure

8. Which IPSec authentication method is the fastest?

    a. Certificate-based authentication

    b. Preshared key authentication

    c. Kerberos v5 authentication

    d. All are equally fast

9. If your network has very high security and you would like all of your network traffic encrypted with IPSec, which security policy would you implement on your servers?

    a. Client (Respond Only)

    b. Secure Server (Require Security)

    c. Server (Request Security)

10. After implementing the security policy Server (Request Security) on a Windows 2000 server, which operating systems will be able to communicate with the server? Select all that apply.

    a. Windows 2000 Professional

    b. Windows NT 4.0

    c. Windows 95

11. After implementing the security policy Secure Server (Require Security) on a Windows 2000 server, which operating systems will be able to communicate with the server?

    a. Windows 2000 Professional

    b. Windows NT 4.0

    c. Windows 95

    d. A and B

    e. A, B and C

12. Which MMC snap-in is used to create IPSec policies for the domain?

    a. Routing and Remote Access

    b. Active Directory Users and Computers

    c. Computer Management

    d. IP Security Policy Management

    e. C and D

13. IPSec can be used to set up a secure tunnel for communication across the Internet without using L2TP. True or false?

14. If you wanted to use IPSec to encrypt only communication between domain controllers, what element of an IPSec policy would you configure?

15. Which IPSec task will allow you to verify that no other policies will conflict with a new one?

    a. Check Policy Integrity

    b. Verify Policy Conflicts

    c. Restore Default Policies

    d. Check Filter List

16. What is the relationship between security and communication speed?

    a. Higher security is generally faster

    b. Lower security is generally faster

    c. There is no relationship between security and communication speed

17. Which IPSec integrity algorithm is the fastest?

18. Most Windows 2000 networks use IPSec between all computers because workstation and server processors are so fast it makes little difference to network communication speed. True or false?

19. When setting up an IPSec filter what are four criteria that can be used to define whether traffic will be affected?

20. It is possible to use IPSec to ensure the integrity of data being transferred without encrypting it in transit. True or false?

HANDS-ON PROJECTS

Project 8-1

In this hands-on activity, you will view an IPSec Policy on your server that requires all transmissions to be encrypted.

1. Click on **Start**, click on **Run**.

2. Enter **MMC** and press **Enter**.

3. Add the IPSec Management snap-in by clicking on the **Console** menu.

4. Click on **Add/Remove Snap-in**.

5. Click on **Add**.

6. Double-click on **IP Security Policy Management**.

7. Select **Local Computer**.

8. Click on **Finish**.

9. Click on **Close**.

10. Click on **OK**.

11. View the authentication methods for the Secure Server policy by double-clicking on **Server (Request Security)**. Note the authentication method for all three rules is Kerberos.

Project 8-2

In this project, you will remove Certificate Services and Active Directory from one computer in each pair.

1. Double-click on **Add/Remove Programs**.

2. Click on **Add/Remove Windows Components**.

3. Remove the checkmark beside Certificate Services.

4. Click on **Next**.

5. Click on **Next**.

6. Click on **Finish**.

7. Close all windows.

8. Click on **Start**, click on **Run**.

9. Type **DCPROMO** and press **Enter**.

10. Click on **Next**.

11. Click on **Next** to clear the warning.

12. Click on **This server is the last domain controller in the domain**.

13. Click on **Next**.

14. Enter the credentials for the administrator account and click on **Next**.

15. Enter a new password for the administrator account and click on **Next**.

16. Click on **Next** to confirm.

17. Click on **Finish** and reboot the server.

18. Log on as Administrator.

19. Click on **Start**, point to **Settings**, click on **Network and Dial-up Connections**.

20. Right-click on **Local Area Connection** and click on **Properties**.

21. Double-click on **Internet Protocol (TCP/IP)**.

22. Change the DNS server to be your partner's IP address and click on **OK**.

23. Click on **OK**.

24. Close Network and Dial-up Connections.

25. Right-click on **My Computer**.

26. Click on the **Network Identification** tab.

27. Click on the **Properties** button.

28. Click on **Domain**.

29. Enter the name of your partner's domain and click on **OK**.

30. Enter credentials of your partner's administrator account and click on **OK**.

31. Click on **OK** to clear the welcome message.

32. Click on **OK** to clear the reboot message.

33. Click on **OK**.

34. Click on **Yes** to restart your server.

Project 8-3

In this hands-on activity, you will assign IPSec policies to your servers (completed on the domain controller only).

1. Click on **Start**, point to **Programs**, point to **Administrative Tools**, and click on **Domain Security Policy**.

2. Expand Security Settings.

3. Click on **IP Security Policies**.

4. Right-click on **Server (Request Security)** and click on **Assign**.

5. Reboot both servers to restart the IPSec agent and refresh the machine policy.

6. On the domain controller, log on as Administrator.

7. Click on **Start**, click on **Run**.

8. Type **IPSECMON** and press **Enter**. Note that there is one connection between your computers.

9. Close IP Security Monitor.

CASE PROJECTS

Case 1

A friend in the computer business has told the owner of Southdale Property Management that the absolute best way to secure a network is using IPSec. The administrator of the network has researched IPSec and does not see how it can be used on their network. Write an e-mail to the administrator indicating where IPSec would be useful on their network.

Case 2

The new owners of Prairie Refrigeration are very concerned about security between Prairie Refrigeration and the head office of the parent company. A leased line is being used between the two sites. Write a short report detailing how IPSec would make communication across this link even more secure and how it would be implemented. Include a network diagram that indicates which traffic will be encrypted.

Case 3

Management is concerned about packet level security on their WAN and their LAN. They understand that IPSec can be used to secure communication between Windows 2000 computers but they are concerned about how to secure communication with Windows NT computers. Write a report that explains the best way to secure communication on both the WAN and LAN, including the Windows NT computers. A network diagram indicating which traffic will be encrypted is required for the presentation you will be giving to management.